Fundamentals of Software Engineering

*Designed to provide an insight
into the software engineering concepts*

by

Hitesh Mohapatra
Amiya Kumar Rath

bpb

FIRST EDITION 2020

Copyright © BPB Publications, India

ISBN: 978-93-88511-773

LIMITS OF LIABILITY AND DISCLAIMER OF WARRANTY

Distributors:

BPB PUBLICATIONS
20, Ansari Road, Darya Ganj
New Delhi-110002
Ph: 23254990/23254991

DECCAN AGENCIES
4-3-329, Bank Street,
Hyderabad-500195
Ph: 24756967/24756400

MICRO MEDIA
Shop No. 5, Mahendra Chambers,
150 DN Rd. Next to Capital Cinema,
V.T. (C.S.T.) Station, MUMBAI-400 001
Ph: 22078296/22078297

BPB BOOK CENTRE
376 Old Lajpat Rai Market,
Delhi-110006
Ph: 23861747

Published by Manish Jain for BPB Publications, 20 Ansari Road, Darya Ganj, New Delhi-110002 and Printed by him at Repro India Ltd, Mumbai

Dedicated to Our Students

About the Author

HITESH MOHAPATRA received the B.E. degree in Information Technology from Gandhi Institute of Engineering and Technology, Gunupur, Biju Patnaik University of Technology, Odisha in 2006, the MTech degree in CSE from Govt. College of Engineering and Technology, Bhubaneswar, Biju Patnaik University of Technology, Odisha in 2009. He is currently a full time Ph.D. scholar at Veer Surendra Sai University of Technology, Burla, India since 2017 and expected to complete by August 2020. He has contributed 10+ research level papers (SCI/Scopus), 8 international/national conferences (Scopus) and a book on C Programming. He has 12+ years of teaching experience both in industry and academia. His current research interests include wireless sensor network, smart city, smart grid, smart transportation and smart water.

AMIYA KUMAR RATH received the B.E. degree in computer from Marathwada University, Maharashtra in 1990, the M.B.A. degree in systems management from Shivaji University, Maharashtra in 1993, the MTech. degree in computer science from Utkal University, Odisha in 2001, and the Ph.D. degree in computer science from Utkal University, in 2005, with a focus on embedded systems. He is currently a Professor with the Department of Computer Science and Engineering, Veer Surendra Sai University of Technology, Burla, Odisha, India. He has contributed over 100+ research level papers to many national and international journals and conferences. He has published seven books by reputed publishers. His research interests include embedded systems, ad hoc networks, sensor network, Smart City, evolutionary computation and data mining. Currently, he has been deputed as adviser to National Assessment and Accreditation Council (NAAC), Bangalore, India.

Acknowledgement

We would like to express our gratitude to BPB Publications, who conceived this idea of a concise introductory book and created this opportunity. We would also like to express our thanks to our students as they not only learned from us but also taught us many things.

Preface

As a process of guiding beginners on Software Engineering remains one of the hardest subjects to teach largely because of the wide range of topics the area encompasses. We have believed for some time that we often tend to teach too many concepts and topics in guiding process resulting in shallow knowledge and little insight on the application of these concepts. The Software Engineering is finally about the application of concepts to efficiently engineer good software solutions.

Goals

We believe that guide book on Software Engineering should focus on imparting to students the knowledge and skills that are needed to successfully execute a commercial project of a few person-months efforts while employing proper practices and techniques. It is worth pointing out that a vast majority of the projects executed in the industry today fall in this scope—executed by a small team over a few months. I also believe that by carefully selecting the concepts and topics, we can, in the course of a semester, achieve this. This is the motivation of this book. The goal of this book is to introduce to the students a limited number of concepts and practices which will achieve the following two objectives:

– Teach the student the skills needed to execute a smallish commercial project.

– Provide the students necessary conceptual background for undertaking advanced studies in software engineering, through courses or on their own.

Organization

We have included in this book only those concepts that we believe are foundational and through which the two objectives mentioned above can be met. Advanced topics have been intentionally left out. As executing a software project requires skills in two dimensions—engineering and project management—this book focuses on key tasks in these two dimensions, and discusses concepts and techniques that can be applied to effectively execute these tasks. The book is organized in a simple manner, with one chapter for each of the key tasks in a project. For engineering, these tasks are requirements analysis and specification, design of the module and its architecture, coding and testing. For project management, the key tasks are project planning and project monitoring and control, but both are discussed together in one chapter on project planning as even monitoring has to be planned. In addition, the book contains one chapter that clearly defines the problem domain of Software Engineering and another chapter that discusses the central concept of software process which integrates the different tasks executed in a project. Each chapter opens with some introduction and then clearly lists the chapter goals, or what the reader can expect to learn from the chapter. For the task covered in the chapter, the important concepts are first discussed, followed by a discussion of the output of the task, the desired quality properties of the output, and some practical methods and notations for performing the task. The explanations are supported by examples, and the key learnings are summarized in the end for the reader. The chapter ends with some self-assessment exercises and another chapter which is added on in this is model questions and answers. This chapter will help students to prepare for the examination and for own assessment.

Target Audience
The book is primarily intended for as a beginner's guide for Software Engineering in any undergraduate or postgraduate program. It is targeted for students who know the programme but have not had formal exposure to software engineering. The book can also be used by teachers and trainers who are in a similar state—know some programming but want to be introduced to the systematic approach of software engineering.

Errata

We take immense pride in our work at BPB Publications and follow best practices to ensure the accuracy of our content to provide with an indulging reading experience to our subscribers. Our readers are our mirrors, and we use their inputs to reflect and improve upon human errors if any, occurred during the publishing processes involved. To let us maintain the quality and help us reach out to any readers who might be having difficulties due to any unforeseen errors, please write to us at :

errata@bpbonline.com

Your support, suggestions and feedbacks are highly appreciated by the BPB Publications' Family.

Table of Contents

CHAPTER 1
Introductory Concepts of Software Engineering

Objective

The primary goal of software engineering is to improve the quality of software products, increase the productivity, and job satisfaction of software engineers. Software engineering is a new discipline, distinct from, but based on the foundations of computer science, management science, economics, communication skills, and the engineering approach to problem-solving.

In this chapter, we are going to discuss:

- Users conceptual model and develop a better specification,
- Design languages and reusable code,
- Participatory design and interactive debugging, and
- The specification of interface and mockup to confirm the specifications.
- Software development process during system development.

Introduction

Software Engineering (SE) is a pragmatic discipline that is based on computer science to provide scientific foundations in the same way that traditional engineering disciplines such as electrical engineering and chemical engineering rely on physics and chemistry. Software engineering being a labor-intensive activity requires both technical skill and management control. Management science provides the foundation for software project management. Computing systems must be developed and maintained on time and within cost estimates. Software engineering activities occur within an organizational context, and a high degree of communication is required among the customers, managers, software engineers, hardware engineers, and other technocrats. There are various methodologies for the development of software engineering projects depending on their size. The fundamental principle for managing the complexity is to decompose an extensive system into smaller, more manageable subunits with well-defined interfaces. The approach of divide and conquer is routinely used in the engineering discipline. In software engineering, the units of decomposition are called modules. The modules are not disjointed. The development process begins with a definition of system needs and ends with a product that is supposed to perform specific tasks with a required degree of precision and accuracy within a predefined time length. The success of the system lies with the system development team, the involvement of users from the beginning, commitment and cooperation from both the management groups.

Definition

Software engineering is the application of a systematic, disciplined, and quantifiable approach to the development, operation, and maintenance of software. It encompasses techniques and procedures, often regulated by a software development process, to improve the reliability and maintainability of the software system. The effort is necessitated by the potential complexity of those systems, which may contain millions of lines of code.

According to Boehm, **Software engineering** involves "the practical application of scientific knowledge to the design and construction of computer programs and associated documentation required to develop, operate, and maintain them". The definition covers biological, financial, manufacturing, medical, legal, governments, and many other systems.

The term *software engineering* was popularized by **F. L. Bauer**, during the **NATO Software Engineering Conference** in **1968**. The discipline of software engineering includes knowledge, tools, and methods for software requirements, software design, software construction, software testing, and software maintenance tasks. Software engineering is related to the disciplines of computer science, computer engineering, management, mathematics, project management, quality management, software ergonomics, and system engineering.

Evolution and Impact of SE

During the past few decades, significant advances have occurred in all areas of software engineering. Analysis techniques for determining software requirements have been developed. Methodical approaches to software design have developed and design notations have proliferated. Implementation techniques have been improved and new programming languages have been developed. Software validation techniques have been examined and quality assurance procedures have been instituted. **Computer-aided software engineering (CASE)** tools are developed and deployed during the development process. Formal techniques for verifying software properties have evolved and software maintenance procedures have been interpreted to mean that the problems of **software engineering (SE)** have been solved. The level in **SE** is indicative of the vast number of problems to be solved.

Software Engineering Process

The process, Software engineering, is the structure of the development of a software product. There are different models of software process (software lifecycle) used in different organizations and industries.

Software Engineering

The field, Software engineering, is concerned with the study of complex systems. The complex system is composed of many components with complex relationships. It is essential to make various modules or components and link them together to represent the complex systems. The term **engineering** encompasses to use certain principles and build the software methodically. To apply the principles, the **software engineer** should be equipped with appropriate methods and specific techniques that will help to incorporate the desired properties into process and product. Sometimes, the methods and techniques are packaged to form a **methodology**. The purpose of the **methodology** is to promote a certain approach to solve a problem.

Levels of Software Process

Three levels of software process are identified for its projects.

These levels balance the different needs of different types of projects. Scaling the process to the project is vital to its success; too much process can be as problematic as too little; too much process can slow down a purely R&D exploration, too little process can slow down a large development project with hard deliverables. The levels are briefly identified as follows:

Level 1: R&D
- No software products delivered, pure research
- Minimal software process

Level 2: Research system
- Larger development team, informal software releases
- Moderate software process

Level 3: Delivered system

- The large software development team, formal software releases
- More formal software process

The software process and software engineering practices have become more formalized and more structured as the project proceeded through different levels.

A set of software engineering best practices is implemented in three software process levels. These include source code control, neatly code builds, writing reusable code, using different team models, commitment to deadlines, design and code reviews, risk management, bug tracking, software metrics, software configuration management, and requirements management.

Software configuration management (SCM) is a step up in formality and reproducibility from source code control and includes controlling and versioning of software releases.

Importance of SW Project Construction

At one time, software development and coding were thought to be the same. But, as distinct activities in the software development life cycle have been identified, some of the best minds in the field have spent their time analyzing and debating methods of project management, requirements, design, and testing. The rush to study these newly identified areas has left code construction as the ignorant cousin of software development.

Discussions about construction have also been hobbled by the suggestion that treating construction as a distinct software development activity implies that construction must also be treated as a distinct phase. Software activities and phases don't have to be set up in any relationship to each other, and it's useful to discuss the activity of construction, regardless, of whether other software activities are performed in phases, in iterations, or in some other way.

Typically, construction makes up about 80 percent of the effort on small projects and 50 percent on medium projects. Construction accounts for about 75 percent of the errors on small projects and 50 to 75 percent on medium and large projects. Any activity that accounts for 50 to 75 percent of the errors presents a clear opportunity for improvement.

The irony of the shift in focus away from construction is that construction is the only activity that's guaranteed to be done. Requirements can be assumed rather than developed, architecture can be short changed rather than designed, and testing can be abbreviated or skipped rather than fully planned and executed. But, if there's going to be a program, then there must be construction and that makes construction a uniquely fruitful area in which to improve development practices.

Problems in System Development

Many problems are encountered during a system development process. Before the system is launched, it is abandoned. The reasons for a system failure could be from either side of the development house or the user. An experienced developer having foresightedness can apprehend a problem much earlier and can take remedial action before it is surfaced during development. The developer and the user should work in groups so that they understand each other's problems and solve them amicably. In developing a large and complex software project, many problems are associated as follows:

a. **Time schedule overlap:** Sometimes, a large project becomes very much time-consuming. There may be a drastic change in the system that has been desired at the beginning. The originally designed concepts to solve the scope of the project is no longer valid during development. It causes time delay to deliver the system. The user may lose interest in further developing the project to implement.

b. **User interface:** The man-machine interaction is sometimes not considered initially surfaced in due course of development. This causes further additions of controls and displays. New hardware and software are felt necessary to be included later.

c. **Test and integration:** Often the project find deficiencies during testing and integration of the software project. The inadequate parts are included in the latter part of the development process. This happens due to inadequate thoughts are given at the initial stage.

d. **Maintenance problem:** Many problems are surfaced at this phase after handing over the system to the client. The user intends to include many additions and changes to the system when he operates independently. The developer allows the user to handle the system and takes the modification activity as the user experiences many technological, functional, and performance problems. Therefore, at the time of implementation, a warranty period is considered to set right the teething problems by the developer without any additional cost that is encountered by the user.

Solutions to the Problems

The problems faced at a later stage can be avoided if proper analysis and design are done initially. This may avoid unnecessary cost escalation during the development process. Some of the possible solutions are discussed as follows:

a. **Time schedule overlap:** The problem can be prevented by postponing the technology decisions for as long as possible or reducing the system development cycle time. Since the financial impact is to be ascertained initially, detailed analysis and design are made early in the development process. The detailed cost estimates are made based on the analysis and design. Technology decisions are taken on maturity issues. It is better to use the available software and hardware so that the development time cycle can be reduced. A phased development approach is a better solution. The system is analyzed, designed, developed, tested, and implemented in segments. Any problem encountered in a segment can be settled down immediately referring to the previous phase.

b. **User interface:** Associate the users in the development process who will be finally using the system. Take their views to simplify the system operation. Many interface activities can be simplified and streamlined during the development process.

c. **Test and integration:** Define a comprehensive test program. Assign to a member of the system team having good testing experience. Include a member from the user side during the acceptance test. Obtain agreement from the user step by step after module testing, integration testing, and system testing.

d. **Maintenance problem:** Design the system to accommodate the changes at a later stage. The changes may include additional hardware to increase accuracy and speed, changes in the software to increase the computing power. Have proper documentation of the system so that it can be referred for making a change at a later stage during its life cycle.

Qualities of the Software

Higher the quality of a software product and process, the software produces more serviceability, less problematic and longer life. The user wants the software product to be reliable, efficient and easy to use. At the same time, the software producer wants the product to be verifiable, maintainable, portable and extensible. The external qualities are visible to the users of the system where the internal qualities concern the developers. The qualities of the software product are associated closely. Some of the software qualities are tabulated in *Table 1.1*:

QUALITY	DESCRIPTION
Correctness	The specification of the system meets the desired goal.
Reliability	Least error in software and dependable.
Robustness	Software/hardware sustainability under abnormal conditions.
Usability	Software friendliness during user interface.
Performance	Better usability of the system with optimum utilization of resources.
Productivity	Quality of the software production process with efficiency and performance.

Verifiability	Ability to verify the correctness or performance of the software system.
Maintainability	Ease to modify the system and put it into use without much distress.
Repairability	Correcting the defects of the software with reasonable effort and time.
Evolvability	Modifiable over time to provide new functionality over the existing.
Reusability	Usage of new components along with the existing software.
	Making the software less complex and easy to understand by others.
Portability	The system, adapting to any kind of environment for better usage.
Interoperability	The ability of the system to coexist and cooperative with other systems.
Timeliness	After processing the software, the ability to deliver the product on time.
Visibility	Documenting all the steps and current status available to others.

Table 1.1: Software Qualities

System Analysis and Design

The development of a good system needs proper system analysis and design. The objective of an analysis is to find the customer requirements, to create a base to develop software, and to define various requirements which are to be developed subsequently. A good system analyst can break up the system into various modules for development and integrate them finally into a flawless workable product.

A system engineer or a system analyst performs the following technical tasks:

- Analyze the existing system and make a requirement list by discussing the users.
- Prepare a conceptual (logical) design for the system based on the requirements.
- Establish the boundaries of the system to use the inputs, outputs, and interfaces.
- Define the functions to be performed and the parameters to measure performance.
- Find out the internal structures of the system and their dependencies.
- Prepare mathematical models to support the evaluation of system performance.
- Make alternative solutions and their weighted evaluation to choose the best.
- Decompose the system into various logical sub-systems to be integrated later.
- Participate in system development, testing, integration, and implementation.

- Associate with the users, developers, and management for steering the project.
- Work as a change agent and catalyst for process development.
- Act as a leader in all the phases during the system development.
- Prepare the project plan and schedule for phase-wise project completion.
- Determine the system reliability, availability, and quality.
- Prepare system development a cost estimates and perform cost-benefit analysis.

System Analysis

System analysis is the process of gathering and interpreting the facts, solving the problem and using the information to recommend improvements to the system. System analysis involves the study of an application area to fully understand the problem being posed. This study includes interviews, observations, hands-on experience, consultations, and many other forms of data gathering. Activities are focused on developing a comprehensive knowledge of the existing system, its strengths and weaknesses, and the underlying reasons for the need to restructure, replace, or automate the existing system. The analyst produces a problem statement as a result of this activity.

A **system analyst** is a designated person who is responsible to study and design a system. A system analyst has many roles to play as an investigator, planner, designer, modulator, communicator, implementor, trainer, change agent, architect, psychologist, salesperson, motivator, politician, conflict resolution, persuader, and imposer. An efficient system analyst can take the entire responsibility to take up the software project from initiation to implementation. A successful analyst can dream for a successful software project.

The analyst, during system analysis, has to carry out the following tasks:
- Understand the existing system, its merits and demerits.
- Planning the new application or modification of the existing one.
- Scheduling the activities to be performed during the development.
- Consider alternative candidate solutions.
- Emphasize the re-engineering process and method study.
- Carry out the operations like backup procedure, audit, quality check, and security procedures.
- Lay down the plans and cost reduction activities.
- Give importance to system enhancement and recycling.

System Architecture and Design

The system design involves the development of a structure or architecture of the system. The design is an ongoing process from the stage of inception. The system design begins from "what is to be built" to "how it is to be built". The involvement of the software engineer begins with attending the meetings with the users, reading preliminary documents, and participating in system-level reviews and walkthroughs. This helps the software engineer to gain a deeper understanding of the system. He has to prepare the process modeling that focuses on the design of the software resources, i.e., the programs and procedures needed by the proposed system. It concentrates on developing the detailed specifications for the program modules with specifications and procedures needed to meet user interface and data design specifications. The software engineer should be well versed with the application area. With his knowledge, various software functions and specifications can be designed. The system and sub-system performance requirements can be ascertained by the software engineer. The software engineer can participate in system architecture development.

Summary

Software engineering brings the logical concept of a system into an operational physical system by converting the dreams into a stream. A well experienced and committed software engineer is very much required who works as a driving force in the development team. The system should be implemented well in time and fulfill user requirements. The system should give visible benefits that can be accepted by the user. To have a long life of the software product, it should have proper quality and reliability. The system should be easy to understand and change, so that it can be maintained effectively for sustained use.

Questions and Answers

1. **Define system? What are the characteristics of a system?**

   A system is an ordered set of interdependent components linked together based on some plan, to achieve a specific objective.

2. **Explain briefly the functions of the following business sub-systems. (Production, Finance, Personnel)**

   a. Deployment of manpower and machines, working principle, job allotment, and completion, scheduling, job costing, incentive scheme, raw material requirement planning, work-in-progress, and finished good status.

   b. Accounts payable, accounts receivable, ledger posting, cash section payments and receipts, salary and wages, trial balance, profit and loss accounts, balance sheet, and bank transactions.

  c. Manpower recruitments, training, deployment of manpower, retirements, performance assessment and promotions, employee database, skill database, payrolls, provident fund, leave record, and administrative functions.

Exercises

1. What are the advantages of involving a software engineer or a system analyst in software development?

2. What are the problems encountered during system development?

3. In your view, what is system-level architecture?

4. Do you think a successful system analyst must be an experienced programmer? Give reasons for your answer.

5. What are the qualities necessary to incorporate during the development of software?

6. Describe the tasks of a system analyst during a software development process?

CHAPTER 2

Modelling Software Development Life Cycle

Objectives

Application software, when it becomes large and complex, then there is a need to look into different aspects like readability, reliable, security, repairability or maintainability, and usability. Many analysts, designers, and developers get involved in the process of software development. It becomes essential to breakdown the tasks into clear cut phases of development and assigns to various development groups. There is a dependency among the phases. On completion of specific tasks, the next task can only be taken up. Therefore, a structured development process needs to be adopted.

In this chapter, we are going to discuss:

- Software development models
- Concept of reliability, performance, safety, and security being used in a life cycle model
- Activities that are involved in a software development process

System Analysis and Design

Information is power. An organization having all the information is considered to be more pragmatic. To make the information available, a computerized system is developed which not only provide information but helps the management to take decisions quickly. It is an organizational improvement process. The analysis and design of an information system are based on the objectives, structures, and processes that help to exploit the information technology for the advantage.

Data and Process

An information system consists of data, data flow, and processing logic. *Data* are raw facts that describe an entity (e.g. people, place, or an object). The data form the system produces *information*. The relationships among the data are described using various techniques. *Data flows* are the groups of data that move and flow in a system, including the source and destination. *Processing logic* describes the steps in the transformation of data. The steps are triggered by calling certain events.

Process oriented approach

The importance is given on the process where the emphasis is given on flow, use, and data transformation. How and when the data moves from source to destination, through intermediate steps, is tracked. How the processes use the data and transform the data into information are considered. This approach takes care of the sequence of the processes. The data files are used when they are required by the process. Several data files are created for different applications. It causes duplication of data in various files. The same data element in different files needs to be changed or updated during the process. It becomes more cumbersome to have specialized data files. The same data elements in different files have different names. The standardization of data for the organization is felt necessary since the data plays a vital role in the process.

Data oriented approach

More focus is given on **data** than the **processes**. Many techniques are used to simplify the data and their related problems like data redundancy, data indexing, and establishing their relationships. The data model describes the rules and policies of a business organization. A systematic data organization is becoming more essential. The *process* may change from time to time but the *data* remains the same for the organization. Data files are becoming larger and complex day by day. Therefore, more care is given to data and data normalization rather than the process. In this approach, the process and data are handled separately. Data handling software is available to handle the queries more efficiently. A *database* is used for every software application system. The database can be used by many application systems, simultaneously. Designing a database becomes important that can be used by different applications. A **data repository** can be used for the current and future systems without inviting problems in changing the data. Many organizations maintain a central database for various applications.

Types of Systems and System Developments

The users are many in an organization with their respective usage. With a broad range of people and interests, different types of information systems are required to be developed. The people who are directly or indirectly associated with an information system are system managers, system analysts, programmers, end users, auditors, business managers, heads of the organization, and support technicians. There are different classes of an information system that can be used effectively by different people.

Transaction processing system

A **Transaction Processing System (TPS)** is a set of information that processes the data transaction in a database system that monitors *transaction programs*. The essence of a transaction program is that, it manages data that must be left in a consistent state. For example, if an electronic payment is made, the amount must be either withdrawn from one account with the addition to the other, or none. In case of a failure preventing transaction completion, the partially executed transaction must be '**rolled back**' by the **TPS**. While this type of integrity must be provided also for batch transaction processing, it is particularly important for online processing: e.g., if an airline seat reservation system is accessed by multiple operators, after an empty seat inquiry, the seat reservation data must be locked until the reservation is made, otherwise another user may get the impression a seat is still free while it is actually being booked at the time. Without proper transaction monitoring, double bookings may occur. Other transaction monitor functions include deadlock detection and resolution, and transaction logging (in 'journals') for 'forward recovery' in case of massive failures. The features are:

- **Rapid response:** Fast performance with rapid response time is critical. Businesses cannot afford to have customers waiting for a **TPS** to respond, the turnaround time from the input of the transaction to the production for the output must be a few seconds or less.

- **Reliability:** Many organizations rely heavily on their **TPS**; a breakdown will disrupt operations or even stop the business. For a **TPS** to be effective its failure rate must be very low. If a **TPS** does fail, then quick and accurate recovery must be possible. This makes well–designed backup and recovery procedures essential.

- **Inflexibility:** A **TPS** wants every transaction to be processed in the same way regardless of the user, the customer or the time for the day. If a **TPS** were flexible, there would be too many opportunities for non-standard operations, for example, a commercial airline needs to consistently accept airline reservations from a range of travel agents, accepting different transaction data from different travel agents would be a problem.

- **Controlled processing:** The processing in a **TPS** must support an organization's operations. For an example, if an organization allocates roles and responsibilities to particular employees, then the **TPS** should enforce and maintain this requirement.

Management information system

A **management information system (MIS)** is a subset of the overall internal controls of a business covering the application of people, documents, technologies, and procedures by management accountants to solve business problems such as costing a product, service or a business-wide strategy. Management information systems are distinct from regular information systems in that they are used to analyze other information systems applied in operational activities in the organization. Academically, the term is commonly used to refer to the group of information management methods tied to the automation or support of human decision making, e.g. decision support systems, expert systems, and executive information systems.

MIS combines technology with business to get people the information they need to do their jobs better, faster, and smarter. MIS often requires data from several TPSs. Information is the lifeblood of all organizations. MIS professionals work as systems analysts, project managers, systems administrators, etc., communicating directly with staff and management across the organization."

An 'MIS' is a planned system of collecting, processing, storing and disseminating data in the form of information needed to carry out the functions of management. In a way it is a documented report of the activities those were planned and executed. The terms *MIS* and *information system* are often confused. Information systems include systems that are not intended for decision making. The area of study called MIS is sometimes referred to, in a restrictive sense, as information technology management. That area of study should not be confused with computer science. IT service management is a practitioner-focused discipline. MIS has also some differences with enterprise resource planning (ERP) as ERP incorporates elements that are not necessarily focused on decision support.

Decision support system

Decision Support Systems (DSS) are a specific class of computerized information systems that supports business and organizational decision-making activities. A properly designed **DSS** is an interactive software-based system intended to help decision-makers compile useful information from raw data, documents, personal knowledge, and/or business models to identify and solve problems and make decisions.

Typical information that a decision support application might gather, and present would be:

- An inventory of all of your current information assets (including legacy and relational data sources, cubes, data warehouses, and data marts),
- Comparative sales figures between one week and the next,
- Projected revenue figures based on new product sales assumptions;

Beginning in about 1990, data warehousing and **on-line analytical processing (OLAP)** began broadening the realm of DSS. As the turn of the millennium approached, new Web-based analytical applications were introduced. DSS belongs to an environment with multidisciplinary foundations, including (but not exclusively) database research, artificial intelligence, human-computer interaction, simulation methods, software engineering, and telecommunications.

The advent of better and better reporting technologies has seen **DSS** start to emerge as a critical component of management design. Examples of this can be seen in the intense amount of discussion of **DSS** in the education environment.

A *passive DSS* is a system that aids the process of decision making, but that cannot bring out explicit decision suggestions or solutions. An *active DSS* can bring out such decision suggestions or solutions. A *cooperative DSS* allows the decision-maker (or its advisor) to modify, complete, or refine the decision suggestions provided by the system, before sending them back to the system for validation. The system again improves, completes, and refines the suggestions of the decision-maker and sends them back to her for validation. The whole process then starts again, until a consolidated solution is generated.

Expert system

An *expert system* is software that attempts to reproduce the performance of one or more human experts, most commonly in a specific problem domain, and is a traditional application and/or subfield of artificial intelligence. A wide variety of methods can be used to simulate the performance of the expert however common to most or all are the creation of a so-called "**knowledgebase**" which uses some knowledge representation formalism to capture the **Subject Matter Experts (SME)** knowledge and a process of gathering that knowledge from the SME and codifying it according to the formalism, which is called knowledge engineering. Expert systems may or may not have learning components but a third common element is that once the system is developed it is proven by being placed in the same real-world problem-solving situation as the human **SME**, typically as an aid to human workers or a supplement to some information system. Problem-solving is accomplished by applying specific knowledge rather than a specific technique. This is a key idea in expert systems technology. It reflects the belief that human experts do not process their knowledge differently from others, but they do possess different knowledge. With this philosophy, when one finds that their expert system does not produce the desired results, work begins to expand the knowledge base, not to re-program the procedures.

There are various expert systems in which a rule-base and an inference engine cooperate to simulate the reasoning process that a human expert pursues in analyzing a problem and arriving at a conclusion. In these systems, to simulate the human reasoning process, a vast amount of knowledge needed to be stored in the knowledge base. Generally, the knowledge base of such an expert system consisted of a relatively large number of "if-then" type of statements that were interrelated in a manner that, in theory at least, resembled the sequence of mental steps that were involved in the human reasoning process. Because of the need for large storage capacities and related programs to store the rule-base, most expert systems have, in the past, been run only on large information handling systems. Recently, the storage capacity of personal computers has increased to a point where it is becoming possible to consider running some types of simple expert systems on personal computers.

In some applications of expert systems, the nature of the application and the amount of stored information necessary to simulate the human reasoning process for that application is just too vast to store in the active memory of a computer. In other applications of expert systems, the nature of the application is such that not all of the information is always needed in the reasoning process. An example of this latter type application would be the use of an expert system to diagnose a data processing system comprising many separate components, some of which are optional. When that type of expert system employs a single integrated rule-base to diagnose the minimum system configuration of the data processing system, much of the rule-base is not required since many of the components which are optional units of the system will not be present in the system.

Overview of SDLC

The **Systems Development Life Cycle (SDLC)** is a conceptual model used in project management that describes the stages involved in an information system development project from an initial feasibility study through maintenance of the completed application. Various SDLC methodologies have been developed to guide the processes involved including the **waterfall model** (the original SDLC method), **rapid application development (RAD), joint application development (JAD),** the **fountain model**, and the **spiral model**. Mostly, several models are combined into some sort of hybrid methodology. Documentation is crucial regardless of the type of model chosen or devised for any application and is usually done in parallel with the development process. Some methods work better for specific types of projects, but in the final analysis, the most important factor for the success of a project may be how closely a plan was followed. *Figure 2.1* is the *classic Waterfall model methodology*, which is the first SDLC method and it describes the various phases involved in development.

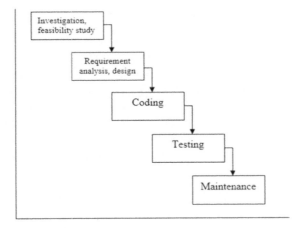

Figure 2.1: *Classic Waterfall model*

Brief Description on Different Phases

Brief descriptions of each phase and their utilities are outlined below. These phases are used for the development of a software system irrespective of the different models discussed in this section.

Feasibility study

The feasibility study is used to determine if the project should get the go-ahead after analyzing the business problems and opportunities. If the project is to proceed, the feasibility study will produce a project plan and budget estimates for the future stages of development. Conduct a study to determine whether a new or improved information system is needed. Develop a project management plan and obtain management approval.

During the feasibility study, the problem/opportunity definition is crystallized. The aspects of the problem are determined to be included in the system. The cost-benefits are estimated accurately, and a formal proposal is made on the nature and scope of problem solution

The feasibility study includes:
- Statement of problem.
- Summary of findings and recommendations.
- Details of finding (methods, procedures, output reports, file structure, cost and benefit analysis).
- Recommendations and conclusions (personal assignment, costs, project schedule, and target dates).

Requirement analysis and design

This stage includes a detailed study of the business needs of the organization. Options for changing the business process may be considered. Analysis gathers the requirements for the system. Analyze in detail the information needs of end-users, the organizational environment, and any system presently used. Develop the logical input, processing, output, storage, and control requirements of a system that can meet the needs of the users. Develop specifications for the hardware (machines and media), software (programs and procedures), people (specialists and end-users), data resources, and information products that will satisfy the information needs of end-users.

The design focuses on a high-level design like, what programs are needed and how are they going to interact, low-level design (how the individual programs are going to work), interface design (what are the interfaces going to look like) and data design (what data will be required). During these phases, the software's overall structure is defined. Analysis and Design are very crucial in the whole development cycle. Any glitch in the design phase could be very expensive to solve in the later stage of software development. Much care is taken during this phase. The logical system of the product is developed in this phase.

Coding

In this phase, the designs are translated into code. Computer programs are written using a conventional programming language or an application generator. Programming tools like Compilers, Interpreters, and Debuggers are used to generate the code. Different high-level programming languages like C, C++, Pascal, and Java are used for coding. Concerning the type of application, the right programming language is chosen.

Testing

In this phase, the system is tested along with the coding. Normally programs are written as a series of individual modules, these subjects to a separate and detailed test. The system is then tested as a whole. The separate modules are brought together and tested as a complete system. The system is tested to ensure that interfaces between modules work (integration testing), the system works on the intended platform and with the expected volume of data (volume testing) and that the system does what the user requires (acceptance/beta testing).

Maintenance

Use a post-implementation review process to monitor, evaluate, and modify the system as needed. Before handing over the software to the user, the necessary training and documentation are provided. Inevitably the system will need maintenance. The software will change once it is delivered to the customer. There are many reasons for the change. The change could happen because of some unexpected input values into the system. Also, the changes in the system could directly affect the software operations. The software should be developed to accommodate changes that could happen during the post-implementation period.

Types of Models

As a product development life cycle, from its inception to maturity, the software product also passes through different phases. The phases are from the investigation stage to the maintenance phase through which the sequence of operations is carried out by proving different resources. As per the size of the system, its complexity and the user requirement various development models are used.

Developing computer software can be a complicated process, and in the last 25 years, researchers have identified numerous distinct activities that go into software development. They include

- Problem definition
- Requirements development
- Construction planning
- Software architecture or high-level design
- Detailed design
- Coding and debugging
- Unit testing
- Integration testing
- Integration
- System testing
- Corrective maintenance

All these activities are not very specifically shown while discussing various models. However, all these are considered more or less while developing the software using different models.

The Iterative Waterfall Model

This is the "classical" model of system development. An alternative name for this model is a *one-shot* approach. As can be seen from *figure 2.2*, there is a sequence of activities working from top to bottom. The diagram shows some arrows pointing upwards and backward. This indicates that a later stage might reveal the need for some extra work at an earlier stage, but this should be the exception rather than the rule. After all, the flow of a waterfall should be downwards with the possibility of just a little splashing back. The limited scope for iteration is, in fact, one of the strengths of this process model. With a large project, you want to avoid having to go back and rework tasks that you thought had been completed.

For a start, having to reopen what was previously thought to be a completed activity plays havoc with a promised completion date.

Feasibility study: It the initial study before the system analysis and design is started. Many feasibility studies are disillusioning for both users and analysts. The feasibility study is to serve as a decision document to answer three key questions. Is there a new and better way to do the job that will benefit the user? What are the costs and benefits of the alternatives? What is recommended? Three key considerations are involved in the feasibility analysis: economic, technical and behavioral. The feasibility report is generally prepared by a senior person who has got a sound knowledge of the system and organization. Depending on the results of the initial investigation, the survey is expanded to a detailed feasibility study. The study summarizes what is known and what is going to be done. It consists of:

a.   Statement of the problem
b.   Summary of findings and recommendations
c.   Details of findings
d.   Recommendations and conclusions.

Requirement analysis and definition: The system's services, constraints and goals are established by consultation with system users. They are then defined in detail and serve as a system specification. The analysis is a detailed study of the various operations performed by a system and their relationships within and outside of the system. The solution to this phase is *what must be done to solve the problem*. In this phase the system boundaries are determined. Data flow diagrams, entity-relationship diagrams, interviews, on-site observations, and questionnaires are used. Once the analysis is complete, the system analyst has a firm understanding of what is to be done in the next phase.

System and software design: The systems design process partitions the requirements to either hardware or software systems. It established overall system architecture. Software design involves identifying and describing the fundamental software system abstractions and their relationships. This phase is the most creative and challenging phase of the system life cycle. Interface for input and output of data, data processing are designed and tested to meet the system objective along with documentation. Information on personnel, money, hardware, and software, facilities, and their estimated cost must be available.

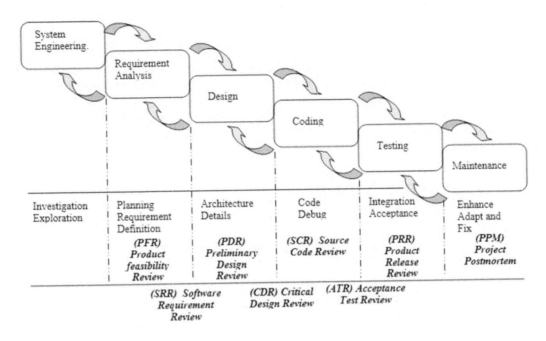

Investigation Exploration	Planning Requirement Definition	Architecture Details	Code Debug	Integration Acceptance	Enhance Adapt and Fix
	(PFR) Product feasibility Review	*(PDR) Preliminary Design Review*	*(SCR) Source Code Review*	*(PRR) Product Release Review*	*(PPM) Project Postmortem*

(SRR) Software Requirement Review *(CDR) Critical Design Review* *(ATR) Acceptance Test Review*

Figure 2.2: *Waterfall Model- A Traditional Approach*

Coding: In many organizations, separate groups of programmers do the programming. Each programmer is assigned with one or more modules for coding. The analyst or the designer will integrate the program modules and integrate them at a later stage.

Implementation and unit testing: During this stage, the software design is realized as a set of programs or program units. Unit testing involves verifying that each unit meets its specifications. It is primarily concerned with user training, site preparation, and file conversion. Linking to remote sites and terminals, establishing telecommunication network and testing are included. All the manuals are handed over to the users at the time of system implementation.

Integration and system testing: The individual program units or programs are integrated and tested as a complete system to ensure that the software requirements have been met. System testing checks the readiness and accuracy of the system. After testing, the software system is delivered to the customer.

Operation and maintenance: Normally, this is the longest life-cycle phase. The system is installed and put into practical use. The user staff is adjusted to the changes created by the candidate system. Maintenance involves correcting errors that were not discovered in earlier stages of the life cycle, improving the implementation of system units and enhancing the system's services as new requirements are discovered. The importance of maintenance is to continue to bring the new system to standards.

We contend that there is nothing intrinsically wrong with the waterfall approach, even though more recent writers have suggested different models. Ideally, the project manager strives for. The waterfall approach allows project completion times to be forecasted with more confidence than is the case with some more iterative approaches and this allows projects to be controlled effectively. When there is uncertainty on the system implementation this flexible and iterative method is very much desired.

The V-process Model

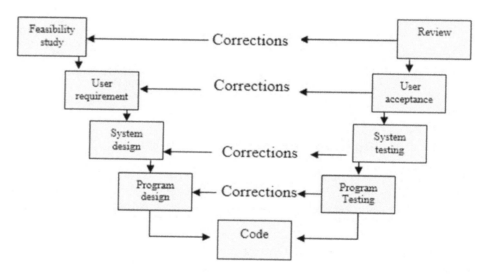

Figure 2.3: *V-process Model*

Figure 2.3 gives a diagrammatic representation of this model. This is an elaboration of the waterfall model and stresses the necessity for validation activities that match the activities which create the products of the project.

The V-process model can be seen as expanding the testing activity in the waterfall model. Each step has a matching validation process that can, where defects are found causes a loop back to the corresponding development stage and a reworking of the succeeding steps. Ideally, this feedback should only occur where a discrepancy has been found between what was specified by a particular activity and what implemented in the next lower activity on the descent of the V loop. For example, the system designer might have written that a calculation is carried out in a certain way. The person who structured the software that fulfilled this design might have misunderstood what was required. At the system testing stage, the system designer would carry out checks that ensure that the software is doing what was specified in the design document and would discover the program designer's misreading of that document. Only corrections should be fed back, not the system designer's second thought, otherwise, the project would be slipping into an *evolutionary prototyping* approach.

The Spiral Model

This is another way of looking at the basic waterfall model shown in *figure 2.4*. In the waterfall model, there is a possible escape at the end of any of the activities in the sequence. A feasibility study might decide that the implementation of a proposed system would be beneficial. The management, therefore, authorizes work on the detailed collection and analysis of user requirements. Some analysis, for instance, the interviewing of users, might already have taken place at the feasibility stage, but a more thorough investigation is now launched. This might reveal that the costs of implementing the system would be higher than originally estimated and lead managers to decide to abandon the project.

A greater level of detail is considered at each stage of the project and a greater degree of confidence about the probability of success for the project should be justified. This can be portrayed as a loop or a spiral where the system to be implemented is considered in more and more detail in each sweep and an evaluation process is undertaken before the next iteration is embarked upon. The figure above illustrates how SSADM can be interpreted in such away.

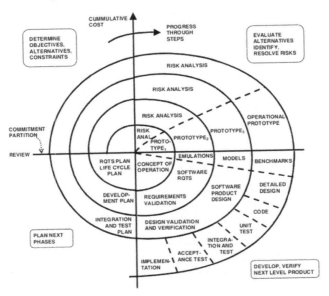

Figure 2.4: A Spiral Model

Software Prototyping

Before starting the actual development, a working prototype of the system should first be built as in *figure 2.5*. This is a working model that is functionally equivalent to a subset of the product. The prototype is a toy implementation of a system having limited functional capabilities, low reliability and inefficient performance. The model is illustrated to the customers along with input data formats, messages, reports, and interactive dialogs. The technical issues associated with the product are critically examined. The issues like response time of a hardware controller, efficiency of sorting algorithms, etc. are discussed. Since it is not possible to get the right one for the first time, we must be ready to throw away the first product to develop a good product.

The next step is to start with an approximate requirement and carry out a quick design. The model is built using several short-cuts which may involve inefficient, inaccurate or dummy functions. The dummy function may be using a table look-up rather than performing the actual computations. Then the developed prototype is submitted to the customer for its further evaluation. Based on the user feedback, requirements are refined. This cycle continues until the user approves the prototype. The actual system is developed using the classical waterfall approach.

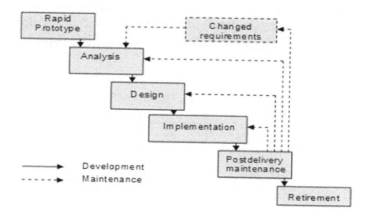

Figure 2.5: A Prototype Model

In this model, the requirement analysis and specification phase is becoming redundant. The final working prototype after incorporating the user feedback serves as an animated requirement specification. Even though the construction of a working prototype model involves additional cost, the overall development cost will be lower for the systems with unclear user requirements and unresolved technical issues. Using the prototype approach many user requirements get properly defined and technical issues are resolved through these would appear as change requests and resulting in incurring massive redesign costs.

Prototypes can be classified as a throw-away, evolutionary or incremental. *Throw-away prototypes* are used only to test out some ideas and are then discarded when the development of an operational system is commenced. The prototype could be developed using a different software environment where the machine efficiency is important or even on a different hardware platform.

Evolutionary prototypes are developed and modified until it is finally in a state where it can become an operational system. In this case, the standards that are used to develop the software have to be carefully considered.

Incremental prototypes, strictly speaking, is not prototyping. The operational system is developed and implemented in small stages so that the feedback from the earlier stages can influence the development of the later stages. This can be termed as *learning by doing*. When we have just done something for the first time we can usually look back and see where we have made mistakes. This will improve communication, user involvement, consistency and completeness of a specification. This will reduce the need for documentation and maintenance costs.

Incremental Approach

The approach involves (advocated by Tom Gilb – published by Addition-Wesley in 1988) breaking the system down into small components that are then implemented and delivered in sequence. Each component that is delivered must give some benefit to the user. *Figure 2.6* gives a general idea of the approach.

The feedback from early increments can influence the later stages. The possibility of changes in requirements is not very much as with the large monolithic projects because of the shorter period between the design of a component and its delivery. Users get benefits earlier than with a conventional approach. Early delivery of some useful components improves cash flow because you get some return on investments early. Smaller sub-projects are easier to control and manage. "Gold plating', the requesting of features that are unnecessary and not used, should be less as users will know that they get more than one opportunity to make their requirements known if a feature is not in the current increment then it can be included in the next.

On the other hand, the disadvantages are 'software breakage' that is later increments might require the earlier increments to be modified. Developers might be more productive working on one large system than on a series of smaller ones.

```
┌─────────────────────────────┐
│   Incremental delivery plan  │
│  ┌───────────────────────┐  │
│  │ Identify system objective │  │
│  └───────────────────────┘  │
│  ┌───────────────────────┐  │
│  │    Plan increments      │  │
│  └───────────────────────┘  │
│  ┌───────────────────────┐  │
│  │ Create open technology plan │  │
│  └───────────────────────┘  │
└─────────────────────────────┘

        ┌───────────────────────┐
        │    Design increment     │
        └───────────────────────┘
        ┌───────────────────────┐
        │    Build the increment   │
        └───────────────────────┘
Repeat for   ┌───────────────────────┐   Feed back
each increment │ Implement the increment │
        └───────────────────────┘
        ┌───────────────────────┐
        │    Evaluate the result   │
        └───────────────────────┘
```

Figure 2.6: Incremental Model

Evolutionary Model

An evolutionary model, see *figure 2.7*, is developed with successive versions. The system is broken down into several modules which can be incrementally implemented and delivered to the customers. First, develop the core modules of the system. The initial product skeleton is refined into increasing levels of capability by adding new functionalities in successive versions which can perform some useful work. This becomes a new version being enhanced over the old one. Many organizations use a combination of iterative and incremental developments. A new release may include new functionality which may be a modified one on the current version. Initially, the first version was developed as A. More functionality was added to A. The new version became a larger one consisting of both A and B. Similarly, C was added to the previous one making a new version having more capabilities to its predecessors.

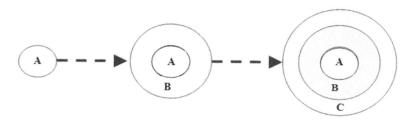

Figure 2.7: Evolutionary Models

Advantages: In this model development process the users get a chance to experiment with a partially developed system much before the full working version is released. This helps in finding the exact user requirements before the full working system is developed. The core modules get tested in this model that reduces the chance of errors in the final product. The advantages of an *evolutionary model with iteration* are the possibility of starting training on an earlier release taking the customer feedback into account. The frequent releases allow developers to fix unanticipated problems quickly.

Disadvantages: The model is often difficult to subdivide problems into functional units which can be incrementally implemented and delivered. The evolutionary model is useful for very large problems where it is easier to find modules for incremental implementation.

The Importance of Metaphors

The history of science is full of discoveries based on exploiting the power of metaphors. Metaphors contribute to a greater understanding of software-development issues in the same way that they contribute to a greater understanding of scientific questions. In his 1973 Turing Award lecture, Charles Bachman described the change from the prevailing earth-centered view of the universe to a sun-centered view. Ptolemy's earth-centered model had lasted without serious challenge for 1400 years. Then in 1543, Copernicus introduced a heliocentric theory, the idea that the sun rather than the earth was the center of the universe. This change in mental models led ultimately to the discovery of new planets, the reclassification of the moon as a satellite rather than a planet, and a different understanding of humankind's place in the universe.

Bachman compared the Ptolemaic-to-Copernican change in astronomy to the change in computer programming in the early 1970s. When Bachman made the comparison in 1973, data processing was changing from a computer-centered view of information systems to a database-centered view. Bachman pointed out that the ancients of data processing wanted to view all data as a sequential stream of cards flowing through a computer (the computer-centered view). The change was to focus on a pool of data on which the computer happened to act (a database-oriented view).

Today it's difficult to imagine anyone's thinking that the sun moves around the earth. Similarly, it's difficult to imagine anyone's thinking that all data could be viewed as a sequential stream of cards. In both cases, once the old theory has been discarded, it seems incredible that anyone ever believed it at all. More fantastically, people who believed the old theory thought the new theory was just as ridiculous then as you think the old theory is now. A software metaphor is more like a searchlight than a roadmap.

Summary

In this chapter, we have discussed various models for software development and introduced you to information systems analysis and design to be adopted for a complex system in an organization. The difference between process-oriented design and data-oriented design have been discussed. Process orientation focuses on what the system is supposed to do. The data orientation focuses on the data the system needs to operate. Process orientation provides a less stable design than data orientation as the business processes change faster than the data change. In process orientation, data files are designed for a specific application but in data orientation, the data files are designed for the whole organization with control of data redundancy. The various people in the organization who are involved in system development are system analysts, programmers, information system managers, important end-users, software testing, and quality control personnel, telecommunication engineers, software experts, and system auditors. The different kinds of systems are developed like transaction processing, management information system, decision support systems, and expert system. Various system development models are discussed with their respective phases in a life cycle. The merits and demerits of each type model are also discussed.

Questions and Answers

1. **Multiple choices and Answers**

    1.1   The next major step before system design and after the feasibility study.
      a. Analysis activity
      b. Equipment selection
      c. Implementation activity
      d. None of these

    1.2   The first step in SDLC is
      a. Preliminary investigation and analysis
      b. System design
      c. Database design
      d. None of these

    1.3   In a passenger seat reservation system, which of the following is most critical?
      a. Ease of program
      b. Response time
      c. GUI
      d. None of these

    1.4   The detailed study/investigation of the present system is frequently referred to as:
      a. System planning
      b. Feasibility study
      c. System analysis
      d. None of these

1.5   The present trend in the data processing system is

   a. Distributed processing   *b.* Remote processing

   c. Real-time processing   *d.* None of these

1.6   The system development phase associated with the creation of test data is

   a. System analysis   *b.* Physical system

   c. System acceptance   *d.* Logical design

1.7   Prototype is a

   a. Mini model of the existing system

   b. Mini model of the proposed system

   c. Working model of the existing system

   d. None of the above

2.   **State whether the following statements are true or false.**

   a. Hardware selection is an implementation activity.

   b. The results of the feasibility study are forwarded to corporate management along with a recommendation to continue or discontinue the project.

   c. Maintenance is the process of incorporating changes in the existing system.

   d. The detailed study / investigation of the present system is frequently referred to as system planning.

   e. CASE is not used in SDLC.

   f. An information system is a closed system.

   g. The output of each phase of the SDLC must be verified and validated before starting with the next phase.

   h. Information means the same as data.

   i. Once a new system is implemented, no subsequent evaluation of its performance is necessary.

   j. User interaction is required only during the system study and the analysis phases of SDLC.

   k. The next major step before system design and after the feasibility study is the analysis of the system.

   l. Documentation means putting it in the written form about how a system is designed or functioning.

   m. The process of converting a new system design into operation is known as evaluation.

n. The documentation of a program is a continuous process.

o. User interaction is required only during the system study and analysis phases of SDLC.

3. **Use the right word**

a. Flexibility   *b.* Budget   *c.* Detailed

d. Real-time   *e.* Closed system   *f.* Debugging

g. Menu-driven   *h.* Enhancement   *i.* Distributed

j. Analysis activity   *k.* Testing   *l.* Prototyping

3.1. .... is the process of making sure that the programs perform the intended tasks.

3.2. .... implies adding new functions or additional capabilities to the system.

3.3. .... refers to the capability of the system to adapt to changing environmental factors.

3.4. The next major step before system design and after the feasibility study is ....

3.5. .... allocation is a management decision.

3.6. An information system is ....

3.7. .... implies correcting the bugs in the existing software.

3.8. The .... investigation of the present system is referred to as system analysis.

3.9. .... is creating, developing and refining a working model of the final operational system.

3.10. .... processing shares resources between computer users.

4. **How does a phased life cycle model assist software management?**

The phased life cycle improves the visibility of the project. The project can be managed by using the phases as milestones. More detailed phases will allow closer monitoring of progress.

5. **What are the two required characteristics of a milestone?**

Characteristics of milestone are:

a. Must be related to progress in software development and

b. It must be obvious when it has been accomplished.

6. For each of the following documents, indicate in which phase(s) of the software life cycle it is produced: final user manual, architectural design, SQA plan, module specification, source code, statement of work, test plan, preliminary user manual, detailed design, cost estimate, project plan, test report, documentation.

- Final user manual in the Implementation phase
- Architectural design in the Design phase
- SQA plan Project in the planning phase
- Module specification in the Design phase
- Source code in the Implementation phase
- Statement of work in the Feasibility phase
- Test plan in Requirements phase
- Preliminary user manual in the Requirements phase
- Detailed design in the Design phase
- Cost estimate in Project planning phase
- Project plan in Project planning phase
- Test report in Testing phase
- Documentation in the Implementation phase

7. Order the following tasks in terms of the waterfall model: acceptance testing, project planning, unit testing, requirements review, cost estimating, high-level design, market analysis, low-level design, systems testing, design review, implementation, requirement specification.

- Market analysis
- Project planning, cost estimating, requirement specification (may be done concurrently)
- Requirements review
- High-level design
- Low-level design
- Design review
- Implementation
- Unit testing
- Systems testing
- Acceptance testing

Answer:

1. a, a, b, b, a, c, b
2. T, T, T, F, F, F, T, F, F, F, T, T, F, T, F
3. k, h, a, j, b, e, f, c, l, i

Exercises

1. **Mention the proportion of time taken by different phases of the software development life cycle (SDLC).**

Requirement:	1%	Unit testing:	7%
Design:	2%	Acceptance testing:	17%
Coding:	3%	Maintenance:	70%

2. **Match the following terms to the appropriate definitions.**

   Maintenance

   a. phase of SDLC in which the information system is coded, tested, and installed.

   Analysis

   b. phase of the SDLC in which an organization's information system needs are analyzed and arranged.

   Design

   c. phase of the SDLC in which the current system is studied and alternative other systems are proposed.

   Project initiation and planning

   d. process of the SDLC in which the system was chosen development is described in detail with a particular physical form in mind.

   Project identification and selection

   e. phase of SDLC in which an information system is systematically improved.

   Implementation

   f. phase of the SDLC in which a potential project is identified and an argument for the project is presented.

3. Contrast process-oriented and data-oriented approaches to system analysis and design. How these are complimentary but not competing for system development?

4. Why it is important to use system analysis and design methodologies while building a system? Why not just build the system in whatever way seems to be quick and easy? What value is added by using a system engineering approach?

5. List and explain the different phases in the system development life cycle.

6. What is prototyping? Explain.

7. What is the system development life cycle? Explain the first three phases of SDLC.

CHAPTER 3

Software Requirement Analysis and Specification

Objectives

In this chapter, we are going to discuss:

- Need for high-quality specifications and the important role played by the requirement specifications at all levels of the software system development process.

- The main and all-important interfaces to all system elements

- The information flow and the structure definitions, the basic diagrams, the major functions

- The realistic design constraints, the technological risks of system development, the alternative software requirements

- The existence of inconsistencies, module redundancy is considered, and validation of the system is performed.

- Various tools and techniques for determining the system requirement

- How Joint Application Design and prototyping is used to ascertain the system requirement

Introduction To Software Requirement

A system analyst must understand the information domain, before building a software product. He should know the required functions, behavior, performance and interfacing to be used in the software. The requirement for the system and software are documented and reviewed with the customer for further analysis.

Conceptually, requirement analysis includes three types of activity:

a. **Eliciting requirements:** The task of communicating with customers and users to determine what their requirements are. This is sometimes also called requirements gathering.

b. **Analyzing requirements:** Determining whether the stated requirements are unclear, incomplete, ambiguous, or contradictory, and then resolving these issues.

c. **Recording requirements:** Requirements might be documented in various forms, such as natural-language documents, use cases, user stories, or process specifications.

Requirements analysis can be a long process during which many delicate psychological skills are involved. New systems change the environment and relationships between concerned people, take into account all their needs and ensure they understand the implications of the new systems. Analysts can employ several techniques to elicit the requirements from the customer. This includes holding interviews, or holding focus groups and creating requirements lists. More modern techniques include prototyping, and use cases. Where necessary, the analyst will employ a combination of these methods to establish the exact requirements of the stakeholders, so that a system that meets the business needs is produced.

The success of a software development directly related to the following:

- Level of detail in which the team activities are recorded
- Quality of the software specification
- Integrity of the software specification
- Accuracy of the software specification
- Established development processes
- Rigor with which the established process is followed
- Quality and number of reviews and audits
- Accuracy of the models used to estimate software attributes
- Effectiveness of the test and integration plan, specification, and test data
- Level of preparation for system maintenance

Seven of the ten items are directly related to specification.

Requirement Engineering

Systematic requirements analysis is also known as **requirements engineering**. It is sometimes referred to loosely by names such as *requirements gathering, requirements capture,* or *requirements specification*. The term **requirements analysis** can also be applied specifically to the analysis, as opposed to elicitation or documentation of the requirements.

Requirement engineering is a sub-discipline of systems engineering and software engineering that is concerned with determining the goals, functions, and constraints of hardware and software systems. In some life cycle models, the requirement engineering process begins with a feasibility study activity, which leads to a feasibility report. If the feasibility study suggests that the product should be developed, then requirement analysis can begin. If requirement analysis precedes feasibility studies, which may foster outside the box thinking, then feasibility should be determined before requirements are finalized.

Software Requirement Specification

A **software requirement specification (SRS)** is a complete description of the behavior of the system to be developed. It includes a set of use cases that describe all of the interactions that the users will have with the software. **Use cases** are also known as functional requirements. Besides, to use cases, the **SRS** also contains non-functional (or supplementary) requirements. Non-functional requirements are requirements that impose constraints on the design or implementation (such as performance requirements, quality standards, or design constraints). The requirements in software development are shown in *figure 3.1* below.

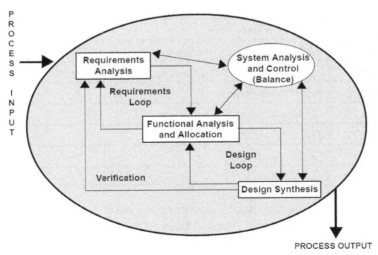

Figure 3.1: Requirements in software development

Software Requirement Definition

There are two phases in the analysis phase. They are *planning* and *software requirement definition*. The outcome of planning is system definition, the project plan, and the preliminary user's manual. The outcome of the software requirements definition activity is recorded in the software specification. The technical requirements for the software product are specified completely and concisely in an unambiguous manner. Depending on the size and complexity of the problem the size of the document varies.

Software Requirement Specification

A Software Requirement Specification (SRS) is a complete description of the behavior of the system to be developed. It includes a set of use cases that describe all of the interactions that the users will have with the software. Use cases are also known as functional requirements. In addition, to use cases, the SRS also contains nonfunctional (or supplementary) requirements. Non-functional requirements are requirements that impose constraints on the design or implementation (such as performance requirements, quality standards, or design constraints).

The format of a requirement specification is presented in *Table 3.1.*

Section 1	Product overview and summary
Section 2	Development. Operating and maintenance environment
Section 3	External interfaces and data flow
Section 4	Functional requirements
Section 5	Performance requirements
Section 6	Exception handling
Section 7	Early subsets and implementation priorities
Section 8	Foreseeable modifications and enhancements
Section 9	Acceptable criteria
Section 10	Design hints and guidelines
Section 11	Cross-reference index
Section 12	Glossary of items

Table 3.1: *Format of a software requirement specification*

Sections 1 and 2 of the requirements documents present an overview of product features and summarize the processing environments for the development operation and maintenance of the product. This information is an elaboration in the software product characteristics contained in the system definition and the preliminary users manual.

External interfaces such as user displays and report formats, a summary of user commands and report options, data flow diagrams, and data dictionary are included in section 3. High-level data flow diagrams and data dictionary are derived. Data flow diagrams specify data sources and data sinks, data store transformations.

Software Requirement Collection

Gathering system requirements is like conducting any investigation. A good system analyst should have the following characteristics for the required determination. These characteristics include

- *a.* **Impertinence:** You should question everything. You need to ask such questions as: Are all transactions processed the same way?

- *b.* **Impartiality:** Your role is to find the best solution to a business problem or opportunity. For example, to find a way to justify the purchase of new hardware.

- *c.* **Relaxed constraints:** Assume anything is possible and eliminate the infeasible. For example, do not accept this statement: "We have always done it that way, so we have to continue the practice".

- *d.* **Attention to details:** Every fact must fit with every other fact. One element out of place means that the ultimate system will fail at some time.

- *e.* **Reframing:** Analysis is a creative process. You must look at the organization in new ways and find a better way of the work process.

The **deliverables** for requirement determination are:

- *a.* Information collected from conversations with or observations of users: interview transcripts, questionnaire responses, notes from observation, meeting minutes.

- *b.* In existing written information, the business mission and strategy statements, sample business forms and reports and computer display, procedure manuals, job descriptions, training manuals, flowcharts and documentation of existing systems, consultant reports.

- *c.* In computer-based information the results from Joint Application Design sessions, transcripts or files from group support system sessions, CASE repository contents and report of existing systems, and display and reports from system prototypes.

Traditional Methods for System Requirements

The basic requirement in system analysis is to collect information on the existing procedure and to propose an improved system. The best practice is to talk to the people who have been involved in the existing system in various capacities and seek their suggestions on constraints being faced and opportunities that can be availed.

Interviewing and listening

This is one of the primary ways of gathering information. Spend a lot of time interviewing people about their work, the information they use, the type of information processing and their suggestions for overcoming the constraints. The stakeholders may be interviewed to understand the organizational direction, vision, mission, policies, and expectations. Gather facts and opinions. Observe body language, emotions, and other signs what people want and how they assess the present situation. You need to decide what mix and sequence of *open-ended* and close-ended questions you will ask. Open-ended questions are used for which there are no precise answers. It helps in surfacing the unknown information. *Close-ended* questions are yes or no, true or false, and multiple-choice type.

Questionnaires

Since interviews are time-consuming and expensive, a limited number of questions need to be framed. It helps in gathering information from many people in a short time. Choose a representative sample of people who will be your questionnaire respondent. The difficult part is to design the questionnaire which can cover your total requirements. This includes only close-ended questions.

There are other methods of information gathering like group discussion, brainstorming, and directly observing people at the site. All the facts and findings need to be documented properly and analyzed which need to be placed before the management before proceeding further.

Modern Methods for System Requirements

There are more other techniques through which the information on the current system and the new system can be gathered. **Joint Application Development (JAD), Group Support Systems (GSS), Computer-Aided Software Engineering (CASE)** tools, and prototyping are some of the modern methods used for information gathering.

Joint application development

This is a structured process in which the users, managers, and analysts work together in the design and development of a software application through succession collaborative workshops called the **JAD session**. The objective of **JAD** is to bring the key users, managers, and system analysts involved in the current system to gather information and discuss the business needs. The group defines the new system requirements, design a solution and monitor the project till completion.

The typical participants in a **JAD** are:

- **JAD session leader** organizes and runs the JAD. He has sound knowledge in group management, facilitation of session, and system analysis. The JAD leader sets the agenda and sees it is met. He remains neutral on issues and does not contribute ideas and opinions. He keeps the group on the agenda and resolves the conflicts and disagreements.

- The **key users** of the system are vital participants in a JAD. They have a clear understanding of what it means to use the system daily.

- **Managers** of the workgroups who use the system provide insight into the new organizational directions, motivations in the impact of the system, and support for requirements determined in the JAD.

- A JAD must be sponsored by someone at a relatively high level who can meet the expenses. The **sponsor** usually attends the meeting at the beginning or at the end.

- Members of the system analysis team attend the JAD although their actual participation may be limited. **System analysts** are there to learn from the users and managers.

- A **scribe** takes notes during the JAD sessions. This is done on a computer using a word processor and CASE tools for diagrams.

- **IS staff** such as programmers, database analysts, IS planners, and data center personnel may attend to learn from the discussion and possibly to contribute their ideas on the technical issues on the proposed system and on technical limitations of the current system.

The advantages of JAD are:
- It brings people together working in business organizations and IT professionals in a highly focused workshop.

- JAD eliminates many of the problems associated with the traditional meeting. JAD turns a meeting into a workshop.

- They are less frequent, more structured and more productive.

- JAD approach leads to faster development and greater client satisfaction due to client involvement.

- It improves the quality of the final product by focusing on the development life-cycle by reducing the errors that are expensive to correct at a later stage.

- JAD may be costly but highly effective.

CASE tools in JAD

The CASE tools most useful to analysis during a JAD are those referred to as upper CASE, as they are applied to the early phases of the system development life cycle. These include planning tools, diagramming tools, and prototyping tools such as computer display and report generation. Running a CASE tool during a JAD allows analysts to enter system models directly into a CASE tool, providing consistency and reliability in the joint model-building process. The CASE tool captures system requirements in a more flexible and useful way than a scribe or analyst takes the note.

GSS with JAD

Since **JAD** is a structured group process, it can benefit from the same computer-based support that can be applied to any group process. **Group Support Systems (GSS)** can be used to support group meetings. In **JAD**, meeting there is not enough time for each member to contribute or some people dominate the meeting when others do not get a chance to speak. Some people are afraid to speak before a group meeting where they might be criticized, or some are not willing to challenge what their bosses have told. **JAD** suffers from these types of problems in the meeting. **GSSs** have been designed specifically to help alleviate some of the problems with group meetings. To provide the same chance to everybody in the meeting, group members type their comments into the computer rather than speak them. No one knows who typed what. It provides a chance to criticize your boss. The whole process also takes less time instead of waiting for anyone to complete first.

Prototyping for system requirement

Prototypes are required in the analysis phase because users may not be sure what functions the computer could perform, or how one would use computers. Prototyping is an iterative process. A rudimentary version of an information system is built with the help of analysts and users. This is again rebuilt with the users' feedback. The prototyping can augment the requirement determination process. To gather an initial basic set of requirements there is a need to interview users and collect information. Prototyping will allow converting quickly the basic requirements into a working, though a limited, version of the desired information system. The prototype will then be viewed and tested by the user. If necessary, redesign the prototype to incorporate the suggested changes. Prototyping is possible with several 4GLs and with CASE tools.

Development of prototype is quite useful especially in the following situations:
  a. Where the user is unable to specify the requirements in advance.
  b. Users can not visualize the desired system he wants. The new users who do not have any idea of what a system would look like.
  c. When the environment is new and not fully understood by the user or the analyst.

Radical Methods for System Requirement

In some organizations, management is looking for new ways to perform the current task other than the above two methods. These new ways may be radically different from how things are done now expecting better payoffs. The new method that has replaced the current ones is referred to as **Business Process Reengineering (BPR).** **BPR** occurs in a top-down manner beginning with the identification of major business objectives and goals and culminating with a much more detailed specification of tasks that define a specific business process.

Business process reengineering is an iterative process. A changing business environment is adopted to achieve the goals and processes. This model defines six activities.

- **Business definition:** The business goals are defined with the following guidelines: cost reduction, time reduction, quality improvement, and manpower development and empowerment. Goals may be defined for a specific component of the business.

- **Process identification:** To achieve the goals, the critical processes are identified and prioritized by importance and need for change.

- **Process evaluation:** The existing process is analyzed in detail and measured. The tasks of the process are identified. The costs and time consumed by individual process tasks are considered.

- **Process specification and design:** Use cases are prepared for each process with outcomes to a customer. With the specification of the process, a set of tasks is designed.

- **Prototyping:** A redesigned business process is prototyped before it is fully integrated into the business. The activity tests the process to allow further refinement.

- **Refinement and instantiation:** Based on the feedback of the prototype, the business process is refined and then instantiated within a business system.

BPR can be effective if the people are motivated and trained who understand that this process is a *continuous* activity. When the information system is integrated with the business process, the result of BPR is expected.

Principles of Re-engineering

There are seven principles of reengineering suggested by *Michael Hammer and James Champy* to streamline the work process and achieve significant levels of improvement in quality, time management, and cost.

- a. Organize around outcomes and costs.

- b. Identify all the processes in an organization and prioritize them in order of redesign urgency.

- c. Integrate information processing work into the real work that produces the information.

d. Treat geographically dispersed resources as though they were centralized.

e. Link parallel activities in workflow instead of just integrating their results.

f. Put the decision point where the work is performed and build control into the process.

g. Capture information once and at the source.

Software Requirement Classification

Requirements are categorized in several ways. The following are common categorizations of requirements that relate to technical management.

Customer Requirements: Statements of fact and assumptions that define the expectations of the system in terms of mission objectives, environment, constraints, and **measures of effectiveness and suitability (MOE/MOS)**. The customers are those that perform the eight primary functions of systems engineering, with special emphasis on the operator as the key customer. Operational requirements will define the basic need and, at a minimum, answer the questions posed in the following listing:

- **Operational distribution or deployment:** Where will the system be used?
- **Mission profile or scenario:** How will the system accomplish its mission objective?
- **Performance and related parameters:** What are the critical system parameters to accomplish the mission?
- **Utilization environments:** How are the various system components to be used?
- **Effectiveness requirements:** How effective or efficient must the system be in performing its mission?
- **Operational life cycle:** How long will the system be in use by the user?
- **Environment:** What environments will the system be expected to operate effectively?

Functional Requirements

Functional requirements explain what has to be done by identifying the necessary task, action or activity that must be accomplished. Functional requirements analysis will be used as the top-level functions for functional analysis.

Performance Requirements

The extent to which a mission or function must be executed; generally measured in terms of quantity, quality, coverage, timeliness, or readiness. During requirements analysis, performance (how well does it have to be done) requirements will be interactively developed across all identified functions based on system life cycle factors; and characterized in terms of the degree of certainty in their estimate, the degree of criticality to system success, and their relationship to other requirements.

Design Requirements

The "build to," "code to," and "buy to" requirements for products and "how to execute" requirements for processes expressed in technical data packages and technical manuals.

Derived Requirements

The requirements are implied or transformed from the higher-level requirement. For example, a requirement for long-range or high speed may result in a design requirement for low weight.

Allocated Requirements

This is a requirement that is established by dividing or otherwise allocating a high-level requirement into multiple lower-level requirements. Example: A 100-Kg item that consists of two subsystems might result in weight requirements of 70 Kg and 30 Kg for the two lower-level items.

Software Requirement Analysis

Systematic requirements analysis is also known as **requirements engineering**. It is sometimes referred to loosely by names such as requirements gathering, requirements capture, or requirements specification. The term requirements analysis can also be applied specifically to the analysis proper, as opposed to elicitation or documentation of the requirements, for instance.

Requirement engineering is a sub-discipline of systems engineering and software engineering, that is, concerned with determining the goals, functions, and constraints of hardware and software systems. In some life cycle models, the requirement engineering process begins with a feasibility study activity, which leads to a feasibility report. If the feasibility study suggests that the product should be developed, then requirement analysis can begin. If requirement analysis precedes feasibility studies, which may foster outside the box thinking, then feasibility should be determined before requirements are finalized.

Requirements analysis in systems engineering and software engineering encompasses those tasks that go into determining the needs or conditions to meet for a new or altered product, taking account of the possibly conflicting requirements of the various stakeholders, such as *beneficiaries or users*.

Requirements analysis is critical to the success of a development project. Requirements must be actionable, measurable, testable, related to identified business needs or opportunities, and defined to a level of detail enough for system design.

Software Requirement Documentation

Requirements documentation is the description of what a software does or shall do. It is used throughout development to communicate what the software does or shall do. It is also used as an agreement or as the foundation for agreement on what the software shall do. Requirements are produced and consumed by everyone involved in the production of software: end-users, customers, product managers, project managers, sales, marketing, software architects, usability experts, interaction designers, developers, and testers, to name a few. Thus, requirements documentation has many different purposes.

The variation and complexity of requirements documentation make it a proven challenge. Requirements may be implicit and hard to uncover. It is difficult to know exactly how much documentation is needed and how much can be left to the architecture and design documentation, and it is difficult to know how to document requirements considering the variety of people that shall read and use the documentation. Thus, requirements documentation is often incomplete (or non-existent). Without proper requirements documentation, software changes become more difficult - and, therefore, more error-prone (decreased software quality) and time-consuming (expensive).

The need for requirements documentation is typically related to the complexity of the product, the impact of the product, and the life expectancy of the software. If the software is very complex or developed by many people (*e.g.,* mobile phone software), requirements can help to better communicate what to achieve. If the software is safety-critical and can harm human life (*e.g.,* nuclear power systems, medical equipment), more formal requirements documentation is often required. If the software is expected to live for only a month or two (*e.g.,* very small mobile phone applications developed specifically for a certain campaign) very little requirements documentation may be needed. If the software is a first release that is later built upon, requirements documentation is very helpful when managing the change of the software and verifying that nothing has been broken in the software when it is modified.

Traditionally, requirements are specified in requirements documents (*e.g.* using word processing applications and spreadsheet applications). To manage the increased complexity and changing nature of requirements documentation (and software documentation in general), database-centric systems and special-purpose requirements management tools are advocated.

Architecture/Design Documentation

Architecture documentation is a special breed of the design document. In a way, architecture documents are the third derivative from the code (design document being the second derivative, and code documents being first). Very little in the architecture documents are specific to the code itself. These documents do not describe how to program a routine, or even why that routine exists in the form that it does, but instead merely lays out the general requirements that would motivate the existence of such a routine. A **good architecture document** is short on details but thick on explanation. It may suggest approaches for lower-level design, but leave the actual exploration trade studies to other documents.

Another breed of design docs is the comparison document or trade study. This would often take the form of a **white paper**. It focuses on one specific aspect of the system and suggests alternate approaches. It could be at the user interface, code, design, or even architectural level. It will outline what the situation is, describe one or more alternatives, and enumerate the pros and cons of each. A good trade study document is heavy on research, expresses its idea clearly and most importantly is impartial. It should honestly and clearly explain the costs of whatever solution it offers as best. The objective of a trade study is to devise the best solution, rather than to push a particular point of view. It is perfectly acceptable to state no conclusion or to conclude that none of the alternatives are sufficiently better than the baseline to warrant a change. It should be approached as a scientific endeavor, not as a marketing technique.

A very important part of the design document in enterprise software development is the **Database Design Document (DDD)**. It contains Conceptual, Logical, and Physical Design Elements. **Database Design Document** includes the formal information that the people who interact with the database needs. The purpose of preparing the **DDD** is to create a common source to be used by all players within the scene. The potential users are:

- Database Designer
- Database Developer
- Database Administrator
- Application Designer
- Application Developer

When talking about Relational Database Systems, the document should include following parts:

- **Entity-Relationship Schema**, including the following information and their clear definitions:
  - o Entity Sets and their attributes

      o   Relationships and their attributes

      o   Candidate keys for each entity set

      o   Attribute and Tuple based constraints

- **Relational Schema**, including the following information:
  - o   Tables, Attributes, and their properties
  - o   Views
  - o   Constraints such as primary keys, foreign keys
  - o   The cardinality of referential constraints
  - o   Cascading Policy for referential constraints
  - o   Primary keys

It is very important to include all the information that is to be used by all actors in the scene. It is also very important to update the documents as any change occurs in the database as well.

Technical Documentation

This is what most programmers mean when using the term *software documentation*. When creating software, code alone is insufficient. There must be some text along with it to describe various aspects of its intended operation. The code documents need to be thorough, but not so verbose that it becomes difficult to maintain them. Several How-to and overview documentations are found specific to the software application or software product being documented by API (Application Programming Interface) writers. This documentation may be used by developers, testers and also the end customers or clients using this software application. Today, we see a lot of high-end applications in the field of power, energy, transportation, networks, aerospace, safety, security, industrial automation and a variety of other domains. Technical documentation has become important within such organizations as the basic and advanced level of information may change over sometime with architecture changes. Hence, technical documentation has gained a lot of importance in recent times, especially in the software field.

Often, tools such as *Doxygen, NDoc, Javadoc, Eiffel Studio, Sandcastle, ROBODoc, POD, TwinText, or Universal Report* can be used to auto-generate the code documents, that is, they extract the comments and software contracts, where available, from the source code and create reference manuals in such forms as text or **HTML (Hyper Text Markup Language)** files. Code documents are often organized into a reference guide style, allowing a programmer to quickly lookup an arbitrary function or class.

Many programmers like the idea of auto-generating documentation for various reasons. For example, because it is extracted from the source code itself the programmer can write it while referring to his code and can use the same tools, he used to create the source code, to make the documentation. This makes it much easier to keep the documentation up to date.

Elucidative Programming is the result of practical applications of Literate Programming in real programming contexts. The *Elucidative* paradigm proposes that source code and documentation be stored separately. Often, software developers need to be able to create and access information that is not going to be part of the source file itself. Such annotations are usually part of many software development activities, such as code walks and porting, where third party source code is analyzed functionally.

User Documentation

Unlike code documents, user documents are usually far more diverse concerning the source code of the program, and instead, simply describe how it is used.

In the case of a software library, the code documents and user documents could be effectively equivalent and are worth conjoining, but for a general application this is not often true. On the other hand, the Lisp machine grew out of a tradition in which every piece of code had an attached documentation string. In combination with strong search capabilities (based on a Unix-like *apropos* command) and online sources, Lisp users could look up documentation prepared by these API Writers and paste the associated function directly into their code. This level of ease of use is unheard of in putatively more modern systems.

Typically, the user documentation describes each feature of the program and assists the user in realizing these features. A good user document can also go so far as to provide thorough troubleshooting assistance. It is very important for user documents not to be confusing, and for them to be up to date. User documents need not be organized in any particular way, but they need to have a thorough index. Consistency and simplicity are also very valuable. User documentation is considered to constitute a contract specifying what the software will do. API Writers are very well accomplished towards writing good user documents as they would be well aware of the software architecture and programming techniques used.

There are three broad ways in which user documentation can be organized.

a. **Tutorial:** A tutorial approach is considered the most useful for a new user, in which they are guided through each step of accomplishing particular tasks.

b. **Thematic:** A thematic approach, where chapters or sections concentrate on one particular area of interest, is of more general use to an intermediate user. Some authors prefer to convey their ideas through a knowledge-based article to facilitating the needs. This approach is usually practiced by a dynamic industry, such as this information technology, where the user population is largely correlated with the troubleshooting demands.

c. **List of Reference:** The final type of organizing principle is one in which commands or tasks are simply listed alphabetically or logically grouped, often via cross-referenced indexes. This latter approach is of greater use to advanced users who know exactly what sort of information they are looking for.

A common complaint among users regarding software documentation is that only one of these three approaches was taken to the near exclusion of the other two. It is common to limit provided software documentation for personal computers to online help that gives only reference information on commands or menu items. The job of tutoring new users or helping more experienced users get the most out of a program is left to private publishers, who are often given significant assistance by the software developer.

Summary

There are three sub-phases in the system analysis phase of the system development life cycle. They are *requirement determination, requirement structuring,* and *alternative generation of choice.* In requirement, determination covers the gathering of information on the existing system and then the need to replace the system is analyzed. The traditional sources of information are gathered through interviews, questionnaires, observation, and group discussions. Formulating questions in questionnaires, preparing agenda in a group discussion, preparing relevant questions in an interview must be very precise to avoid ambiguity so that a proper response is obtained. The results of all methods should be compared and normalized. **JAD** begins with an idea of a group interview and adds structure. The **JAD** group includes session leader, a scribe, key users, managers, a sponsor, and the system analyst. The **JAD** session is held off-site and may last for a week or so. It has been discussed how the information system can support the requirement analysis using **CASE** tools and prototyping. In prototyping, the user and the analyst work together to determine the requirements. This continues by revising the model till it meets the user requirement. **BPR** is an approach used to change the process radically using the new information requirements by changing traditional business rules. This would help to form a base guideline for further analysis and design.

Questions and Answers

1. **What are the attributes of a good SRS document?**

   An SRS document must be:

Correct	Precise	Unambiguous	Complete
Complete	Verifiable	Consistent	Understandable
Modifiable	Traceable	Describe the system	Encompass the entire system

2. **What is requirement engineering?**

   Requirement engineering is the systematic use of verifiable principles, methods, languages and tools in the analysis and description of the behavioral and non-behavioral features of a software system specifying user needs. A principal by-product of requirement engineering is Software Requirement Specification (SRS).

3. What are the activities of the specification phase of clean room technology?
    Requirement analysis, function specification process, usage specification process, architecture specifications, incremental planning process.

4. **What is requirement management?**
    Require management establishes an understanding between the client and the software development team concerning the client's requirement.

5. **Name different components of requirement analysis.**
    Interface requirements, functional requirements, performance requirements, design constraints, software system attributes etc.

6. **What are the objectives of system analysis?**
    *   Identifying customer needs.
    *   Evaluating the system concept for feasibility.
    *   Performing economic and technical analysis.
    *   Allocating functions to hardware, software, people, database and other system elements.
    *   Establishing cost and schedule constraints.
    *   Creating a system definition.

7. **Name some interface requirements.**
    User interface, hardware interface, software interface, and communication interface.

8. **Name some functional requirements.**
    Information flow, process description, data construct specification, and data dictionary.

9. **What is requirement analysis? Name five areas of requirement analysis.**
    Requirement analysis is a software engineering task that bridges the gap between system level software allocation and software design. The five areas are:
    *   Problem recognition
    *   Evaluation and synthesis
    *   Modeling
    *   Specification
    *   Review

10. **Name three types of requirement.**

Normal requirement, Expected requirement, and Exciting requirement.

Exercises

1. **What are the attributes of a good SRS document?**

   A SRS document must be:

Correct.	Precise.	Unambiguous.
Complete.	Verifiable.	Consistent.
Understandable.	Modifiable.	Traceable.
Localized.	Describe the system.	Encompass the entire system.

2. **Define the following terms.**

Joint Application Design	Requirement structuring
Prototyping	Business Process Reengineering
Requirement determination	Formal and informal system

3. Describe four traditional techniques for collecting information during analysis. When might one be better than another?

4. What is **JAD**? How is it better than traditional information-gathering technique? What are its weaknesses?

5. How can CASE tools be used to support requirement determination? Which types of CASE tools are appropriate for use during requirement determination?

6. Describe how prototyping can be used during requirements determination. How it is better or worse than traditional methods?

7. What do you mean by **Business Process Reengineering**? What are the principles of reengineering?

8. Explain any three fact gathering techniques in detail.

CHAPTER 4

Software Project Management Framework

Objectives

Project management is the discipline of planning, organizing and managing resources to bring about the successful completion of specific project goals and objectives. It is often closely related to and sometimes conflated with program management.

A **project** is a temporary endeavor, having a defined beginning and end (usually constrained by date, but can be by funding or deliverables), undertaken to meet particular goals and objectives, usually to bring about beneficial change or added value. The temporary nature of projects stands in contrast to business as usual, which are repetitive, permanent or semi-permanent functional work to produce products or services. In practice, the management of these two systems is often found to be quite different, and as such requires the development of distinct technical skills and the adoption of separate management.

In this chapter, we are going to discuss:
- Techniques for activity scheduling and cost optimization

Project Definition

A **project** is a multitask job with due consideration of performance, cost, time, and scope requirements and is done only one time. It has a definite starting and ending time with budgets and costs having clearly defined scope or magnitude of work to be done.

There is a need to optimize the project resources considering the complexity of the business, time, and resources at least cost.

Project Management

Project management is the application of knowledge, skills, tools, and techniques to project activities to meet project requirements. **Project management** is accomplished through the application and integration of the project management processes of initiating, planning, executing, monitoring and controlling, and closing. The *project manager* is the person responsible for accomplishing the project objectives.

This does not mean that the knowledge, skills, and processes described should always be applied uniformly on all projects. The *project manager*, in collaboration with the project team, is always responsible for determining what processes are appropriate, and the appropriate degree of rigor for each process, for any given project.

Managing a project includes:

- Identifying requirements
- Establishing clear and achievable objectives
- Balancing the competing demands for quality, scope, time and cost
- Adapting the specifications, plans, and approach to the different concerns and expectations of the various stakeholders

Project managers often talk of a "triple constraint", i.e., project scope, time, and cost in managing competing project requirements. Project quality is affected by balancing these three factors. High-quality projects deliver the required product, service or result within scope, on time, and within budget. The relationship among these factors is such that if anyone of the three factors changes, at least one other factor is likely to be affected. *Project managers* also manage projects in response to uncertainty.

Scope Management

Project Scope Management describes the processes involved in ascertaining that the project includes all the work required, and only the work required, to complete the project successfully. It consists of the Scope Planning, Scope Definition, Create WBS, Scope Verification, and scope Control project management processes.

Control - Controlling changes to the project scope.

These processes interact with each other and with processes in the other knowledge areas as well. Each process can involve effort from one or more persons or groups of persons, based on the needs of the project. Each process occurs, at least once, in every project and occurs in one or more project phases if the project is divided into phases.

In the project context, the term scope can refer to:

- **Product scope:** The features and functions that characterize a product, service, or result.
- **Project scope:** The work that needs to be accomplished to deliver a product, service, or result with the specified features and functions.

Scope planning

Defining and managing the project scope influences the project's overall success. Each project requires a careful balance of tools, data sources, methodologies, processes, and procedures, and other factors to ensure that the effort expanded on scoping activities is commensurate with the project's size, complexity, and importance. The prerequisites of project can be represented as:

Inputs:	Tools and Techniques:
1. Enterprise environmental factors	1. Expert judgment
2. Organizational project assets	2. Templates, forms, standards
3. Project charter	
4. Preliminary project scope statement	**Outputs:**
5. Project management plan	1. Project scope management plan

Scope definition

The preparation of a detailed project scope statement is critical to project success and builds upon the major deliverables, assumptions, and constraints that are documented during project initiation in the preliminary project scope statement. During planning, the project scope is defined and described with greater specificity because more information about the project is known. Stakeholder needs, wants, and expectations are analyzed and converted into requirements. The points given below are the details of the scope definition.

Inputs:	Tools and Techniques:
1. Organizational process assets	1. Project identification
2. Project charter	2. Alternatives identification
3. Preliminary project scope statement	3. Expert judgment
4. Project management plan	4. Stakeholder analysis
5. Approved change requests	

	Outputs:
	1. Project scope statement
	2. Requested changes
	3. Project scope management plan (updates)

Create work breakdown structure (WBS)

The **WBS** is a deliverable-oriented hierarchical decomposition of the work to be executed by the project team, to accomplish the project objectives and create the required deliverables. The **WBS** organizes and defines the total scope of the project. The **WBS** subdivides the project work into smaller, more manageable pieces of work, with each descending level of the **WBS** representing an increasingly detailed definition of the project work. The planned work contained within the lowest-level **WBS** components, which are called **work packages**, can be scheduled, cost estimated, monitored, and controlled. Points below describe the details of the scope of work breakdown structure.

Inputs:	Outputs:
1. Organizational process assets	1. Project scope statement (updates)
2. Project scope statement	2. Work breakdown
3. Project scope management plan	3. WBS dictionary
4. Approved change requests	4. Scope baseline
	5. Project scope management plan
Tools and Techniques:	6. Requested changes
1. Work breakdown structures templates	
2. Decomposition	

Scope verification

Scope verification is the process of obtaining the stakeholders' formal acceptance of the completed project scope and associated deliverables. Verifying the project scope includes reviewing deliverables to ensure that each is completed satisfactorily. If the project is terminated early, the project scope verification process should establish and document the level and extent of completion. Scope verification differs from quality control in that scope verification is primarily concerned with acceptance of the deliverables, while quality control is primarily concerned with meeting the quality requirements specified for the deliverables. **Quality control** is generally performed before scope verification, but these two processes can be performed in parallel. Points below describe the details of the scope verification.

Inputs:	Tools and Techniques:
1. Project scope statement	1. Inspection
2. WBS dictionary	
3. Project scope management plan	**Outputs:**
4. Deliverables	1. Accepted deliverable
2. Requested changes	
3. Recommended corrective actions	

Scope control

Project scope control is concerned with influencing the factors that create project scope changes and controlling the impact of those changes. Scope control assures all requested changes and recommended corrective actions are processed through the project Integrated Change Control process. *Project scope control* is also used to manage the actual changes when they occur and is integrated with the other control processes. Uncontrolled changes are often referred to as project scope creep. The details of the scope control are given below.

Inputs:	Outputs:
1. Project scope statement	1. Project scope statement
2. WBS	2. WBS
3. WBS dictionary	3. WBS dictionary
4. Project scope management plan	4. Scope baseline
5. Performance report	5. Requested changes
6. Approved project requests	6. Recommended corrective action
7. Work performance	7. Organizational project asset
	8. Project management
Tools and Techniques:	
1. Change control system	
2. Variance analysis	
3. Re-planning	
4. Configuration management system	

Time Management

Project Time Management describes the processes concerning the timely completion of the project. It consists of the Activity Definition, Activity Sequencing, Activity Resource Estimating, Activity Duration Estimating, Schedule Development, and Schedule Control project management processes.

Project Time Management includes the processes required to accomplish timely completion of the project. The *Project Time Management processes* include the following:

- **Activity Definition:** Identifying the specific schedule activities that need to be performed to produce the various project deliverables.
- **Activity Sequencing:** Identifying and documenting dependencies among schedule activities.
- **Activity Resource Estimating:** Estimating the type and quantities of resources required to perform each schedule activity.
- **Activity Duration Estimating:** Estimating the number of work periods that will be needed to complete individual schedule activities
- **Schedule Development:** Analyzing activity sequences, durations, resource requirements, and schedule constraints to create the project schedule.
- **Schedule Control:** Controlling changes to the project schedule.

These processes interact with each other and with processes in the other Knowledge Areas as well. Each process can involve effort from one or more persons or groups of persons, based on the needs of the project. Each process occurs at least once in every project and occurs in one or more project phases, if the project is divided into phases. Although the processes are presented here as discrete components with well-defined interfaces, in practice they can overlap and interact.

Activity definition

Defining the schedule activities involves identifying and documenting the work that is planned to be performed. The Activity Definition process will identify the deliverables at the lowest level in the *Work Breakdown Structure (WBS),* which is called the work package. Project work packages are planned (decomposed) into smaller components called *schedule activities* to provide a basis for estimating, scheduling, executing, and monitoring and controlling the project work. Points below give detail.

Inputs:	Tools and Techniques:
1. Enterprise environmental factors	1. Decomposition
2. Organizational project asset	2. Templates
3. Project scope statement	3. Rolling wave planning
4. Work breakdown structure	4. Expert judgment
5. WBS dictionary	5. Planning component
6. Project management plan	
	Outputs:
	1. Activity list

	2. Activity attributes
	3. Milestone list
	4. Requested changes

Activity sequencing

Activity sequencing involves identifying and documenting the logical relationships among schedule activities. Schedule activities can be logically sequenced with proper precedence relationships, as well as leads and lags to support later development of a realistic and achievable project schedule. *Sequencing* can be performed by using project management software or by using manual techniques. Manual and automated techniques can also be used in combination. The details of input, tools and techniques and output are shown below.

Inputs:	Tools and Techniques:
1. Project scope statement	1. Project diagramming method (PDM)
2. Activity list	2. Arrow diagramming method (ADM)
3. Activity attributes	3. Schedule network templates
4. Milestone list	4. Dependency determination
5. Approved change request	5. Applying leads and lags
Outputs:	
1. Project schedule network diagrams	
2. Activity list (updates)	
3. Activity attributes (updates)	
4. Requested changes	

Activity resource estimation

Estimating schedule resources involves determining what resources (persons, equipment, or material) and what quantities of each resource will be used, and when each resource will be available to perform project activities. The Activity Resource Estimating process is closely coordinated with the Cost Estimating process. For example:

- A construction project team will need to be familiar with local building codes.
- An automotive design team will need to be familiar with the latest in automated assembly techniques.

Inputs:	Tools and Techniques:
1. Enterprising environmental factors	1. Expert judgment
2. Organizing process assets	2. Alternatives analysis
3. Activity list	3. Published estimating data
4. Activity attributes	4. Project management software
5. Resource availability	5. Bottom-up estimating
6. Project management plan	
Outputs:	
1. Activity resource requirements	
2. Activity attributes (updates)	
3. Resource breakdown structure	
4. Resource calendar (updates)	
5. Requested changes	

Precedence Diagramming Method (PDM)

PDM is a method of constructing a project schedule network diagram that uses boxes or rectangles, referred to as nodes, to represent activities, and connects them with arrows that show the dependencies. *Figure 4.1* shows, a simple project schedule network diagram drawn using **PDM**. This technique is also called **activity-on-node (AON)** and is the method used by most project management software packages.

PDM includes four types of *dependencies or precedence* relationships:

- **Finish-to-Start (FS).** The initiation of the successor activity depends upon the completion of the predecessor activity.

- **Finish-to-Finish (FF).** The completion of the successor activity depends upon the completion of the predecessor activity.

- **Start-to-Start (SS).** The initiation of the successor activity depends upon the initiation of the predecessor activity.

- **Start-to-Finish (SF).** The completion of the successor activity depends upon the initiation of the predecessor activity.

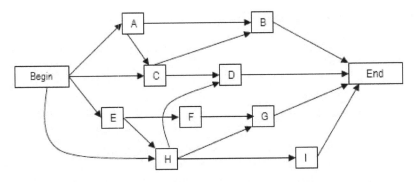

9 Activities, 18 Logic dependencies

Figure 4.1: *Precedence Diagram Method*

In **PDM**, finish-to-start is the most commonly used type of precedence relationship. *Start-to-finish* relationships are rarely used

Arrow Diagram Method

ADM is a method of constructing a project schedule network diagram that uses arrows to represent activities and connects them at nodes to show their dependencies. *Figure 4.2* shows a *simple network logic diagram drawn using* **ADM**. This technique is also called **activity-on-arrow (AOA)** and, although less prevalent than **PDM**, it is still used in teaching schedule network theory and in some application areas.

ADM uses only finish-to-start dependencies and can require the use of "dummy" relationships called *dummy activities*, which are shown as dashed lines, to define all logical relationships correctly. Since, dummy activities are not actual schedule activities (they have no work content), they are given a zero-value duration for schedule network analysis purposes. For example, in *figure 4.2*, schedule activity "H" is dependent upon the completion of schedule activities "A" and "F", in addition to the completion of schedule activity "G".

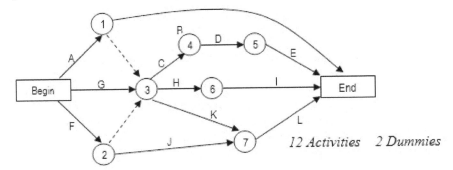

Figure 4.2: *Arrow Diagram Method*

Activity duration estimating

The process of estimating schedule activity durations uses the information on schedule activity scope of work, required resource types, estimated resource quantities, and resource calendars with resource availabilities. The inputs for the estimates of schedule activity duration originate from the person or group on the project team who is most familiar with the nature of the work content in the specific schedule activity. The duration estimate is progressively elaborated, and the process considers the quality and availability of the input data. For example, as the project engineering and design work evolve, more detailed and precise data is available, and the accuracy of the duration estimates improves. Thus, the duration estimate can be assumed to be progressively more accurate and of better quality.

Cost Management

Project Cost Management describes the processes involved in planning, estimating, budgeting, and controlling costs so that the project is completed within the approved budget. It consists of the Cost Estimating, Cost Budgeting, and Cost Control project management processes.

The cost of the project depends upon the size of code in terms of a number of source instructions or the number of function points. The process through which the development takes place also adds to cost. It takes care of avoiding non-value adding activities such as rework, delays, and communication overhead. The capabilities and productivity of the persons engaged in the project give an impact on the cost of the project. The required quality for the product features, performance, reliability, and adaptability are necessary to be decided for controlling the cost.

It provides a process flow view of these processes and their inputs, outputs, and other related Knowledge Area processes:

- **Cost Estimating -** Developing an approximation of the costs of the resources needed to complete project activities.

- **Cost Budgeting -** Aggregating the estimated costs of individual activities or work packages to establish a cost baseline.

- **Cost Control-** Influencing the factors that create cost variances and controlling changes to the project budget.

Project Cost Management is primarily concerned with the cost of the resources needed to complete scheduled activities. However, Project Cost Management should also consider the effect of project decisions on the cost of using, maintaining, and supporting the product, service, or result of the project. The broader view of Project Cost Management is often called *life-cycle costing*. Life-cycle costing, together with value engineering techniques, can improve decision-making and is used to reduce cost and execution time and to improve the quality and performance of the project deliverable.

Software Measurement

Measurement is a standard practice in engineering and in management, too. We believe that measurement increases the depth of our understanding, and we express a normal impulse to try to measure what we do or seek to do [Stan Rifkin]. How to measure the business value of the software to be constructed is a concern typically found in the business data processing. Since, we do not know how to measure the value of what we are producing, a number of surrogates are created such as **Lines of Code (LoC),** functional size, and functional points, etc.

Empirical Cost Estimation

Expert judgment, a qualitative approach is adopted for cost estimation of a project. A group of experts is responsible to give their individual views through their past experience on a similar project and predicting the cost estimation of the target project. Any variation of the target project in comparison to the previous one is adjusted by increasing or decreasing the cost. Experts give different cost estimates on the same project. The final figure has to be reconciled and the experts have to arrive at a consensus without having a group meeting in order to avoid undesirable side effects. A technique called the *Delphi technique* adopted here. In this technique, all the experts work separately. Each one will produce their estimates and rationale for the estimate. These estimates and rationales are distributed to all experts, who now produce a second estimate. The process of estimation and distribution continues until the experts agree within an acceptable tolerance.

Heuristic Cost Estimation

COCOMO (COnstructive COst estimation MOdel) was first developed by **Barry W. Boehm** in **1981** as a model for cost estimating effort, cost, the requirement of manpower, and schedule for software projects. It was established on a study of 63 projects each having 2,000 to 10,000 **lines of code (LOC)** and programming language from Assembly to PL/1. This was called **COCOMO 81**, the *basic* model. It is good for quick, early, rough order magnitude estimates of software cost but its accuracy is limited due to its lack of factors to account for the difference in project attributes (cost drivers). In 1997, **COCOMO II** was developed and finally came into force in 2001. This *intermediate* model is better suited for estimating modern software development projects. It provides more support for the modern software development process and an updated project database. The *detailed* **COCOMO** additionally accounts for the influence of individual project phases. The three types of **COCOMO** models consisting of a hierarchy with detailed and accurate forms are in use.

It is a static, single-valued model that computes software development effort and cost as a function of program size expresses in estimated lines of code. **COCOMO** applies to three classes of software projects:

The equation of the basic model is:

$$E = a.Sb.M(x)$$

Where, M(x): adjustment multiplier

E: Person-months of effort

S: Thousands of lines of delivered instructions (KSDI)

a and b: adjustment factors

The schedule time of development is given by:

$$T = c.E^d$$

Where, E: Development effort in person months

T: Time for development in months

a, b, c, and d: Parameters are determined by model and development mode

Three classes of software products are considered in COCOMO

- **Organic:** Used for relatively small groups with a familiar environment and well-understood application programs.
- **Semidetached:** Used when there is a mix of experience in the project team and a less familiar environment. It is more convenient for the new text editor or statistical software development.
- **Embedded:** Used when the project is strongly coupled with complex hardware and stringent regulations in operating procedures for example development of new operating system software.

A COCOMO Problem:

Two software managers separately estimated a given project to be of 10,000 and 15,000 lines of codes respectively. Bring out the Effort and Schedule time implications of their estimation using COCOMO. For the effort estimation, use a coefficient value of 3.2 and an exponent value of 1.05. For the schedule time estimation, the similar values are 2.5 and 0.38 respectively. Assume all adjustment multipliers to be equal to unity.

Answer:

All adjustment multipliers are equal to unity.

Effort estimation: $E = 3.2 * S^{1.06}$ (E in person months, S in KDSI)

The schedule time of development estimation: $T = 2.5 * E^{0.38}$

T is time for development in months.

Line of Codes estimations are below 50 KSDI. We can assume the given project to be an organic one.

Now, for 10,000 lines of code: S = 10 KSDI

Effort E = 3.2 * $10^{1.06}$ = 35.90 person months

Schedule time T = 2.5 * $35.90^{0.38}$ = 9.75 months

For 15,000 lines of code: S = 15 KSDI

Effort E = 3.2 * $15^{1.06}$ = 54.96 person months

Schedule time T = 2.5 * $54.96^{0.38}$ = 11.46 months

Basic COCOMO

The basic **COCOMO** model computes software development effort as a function of program size expressed in estimated lines of code. **Effort (E)** is in person-months and **Time (T)** is the development time in chronological months. **KLOC** is the estimated number of delivered thousand lines of code for the project. The *coefficients* of a and c and the *exponents* of b and d are given, in *table 4.1.*

Effort E = $a*(KLOC)^b$

Time T = $c*(E)^d$

Software Project	a	b	c	d
Organic	2.40	1.05	2.50	0.38
Semi-detached	3.00	1.12	2.50	0.35
Embedded	3.60	1.20	2.50	0.32

Table 4.1: Basic model parameters

A Basic COCOMO Problem

For a project, the LOC estimate is 33,200 lines to be developed. Use table 4.1 where the project is assumed to be organic. Calculate the effort and schedule time required for the project.

Answer:

Effort E = 2.4 $(KLOC)^{1.05}$

= 2.4 $(33.2)^{1.05}$

= 95 person months

Project duration T = 2.5 E0.35

= 2.5 (95) 0.35

= 12.3 months

The project duration time will help the analyst to determine the recommended number of software professionals, N to be deployed.

$$N = E/T = 95/12.3 \approx 8 \text{ people}$$

Intermediate COCOMO

The basic model is extended to consider a set of *cost driver attributes* that can be grouped into four major categories: product attributes, hardware attributes, personnel attributes, and project attributes. Each of the 15 attributes in these categories is rated on a six-point scale ranging from *very low* to *extra high* (in importance or value). Based on the rating, an effort multiplier is determined. The product of all effort multiplier results in an **effort adjustment factor (EAF)**. The typical values for **EAF** range from 0.9 to 1.4. The effort, in this case, will vary but the time will not vary.

$$E = a*(KLOC)^b * EAF$$
$$\text{and, } T = c*(E)^d$$

The value of a and b will change, as shown in *table 4.2*. The value of c and d will remain the same.

Software project	A	B
Organic	3.2	1.05
Semi-detached	3.0	1.12
Embedded	2.8	1.20

Table 4.2: Intermediate model

Effort Adjustment Factors

The **effort adjustment factor (EAF)** is calculated using 15 cost drivers. The cost drivers are grouped into four categories. Each cost driver is rated on a six-point scale ranging from low to high importance. Based on the rating, an effort multiplier is determined using *table 4.3*. The product of all effort multiplier is the **EAF**.

Code	Description	RATING					
		Very low	**Low**	**Nominal**	**High**	**Very high**	**Extra high**
Product							
RELY	Required software reliability	0.75	0.88	1.00	1.15	1.40	-
DATA	Size of application database	-	0.94	1.00	1.08	1.16	-
CPLX	Complexity of product	0.70	0.85	1.00	1.15	1.30	1.65
Hardware							
TIME	Execution time constraint	-	-	1.00	1.11	1.30	1.66
STOR	Main storage constraint	-	-	1.00	1.06	1.21	1.56
VIRT	Virtual machine volatility	-	0.87	1.00	1.15	1.30	-
TURN	Computer turn-around time	-	0.87	1.00	1.07	1.15	-
Personal							
ACAP	Analyst capability	1.46	1.19	1.00	0.86	0.71	-
AEXP	Applications experience	1.29	1.13	1.00	0.91	0.82	-
PCAP	Programmer capability	1.42	1.17	1.00	0.86	0.70	-
VEXP	Virtual machine experience	1.21	1.10	1.00	0.90	-	-
LEXP	Language experience	1.14	1.07	1.00	0.95	-	-
Project							
MODP	Modern programming practice	1.24	1.10	1.00	0.91	0.82	-
TOOL	Software tools	1.24	1.10	1.00	0.91	0.83	-
SCED	Development schedule	1.23	1.08	1.00	1.04	1.10	-

Table 4.3: Software Development Effort Multipliers

Advanced COCOMO

The **advanced COCOMO model** computes effort as a function of program size and a set of cost drivers, weighted according to each phase of the software life cycle. The advanced model applies the intermediate model at the component level, and then a phase-based approach is used to consolidate the estimate. It is usually complex to carry out the cost estimation.

The four phases used in the detailed **COCOMO** model are: **requirement planning and product design (RPD), detailed design (DD), code and unit test (CUT),** and **integration and testing (IT).** Each cost driver is broken down by phase as in the example shown in table 4.4 below.

Cost Driver Rating	RPD	DD	CUT	IT
ACAP Very Low	1.80	1.35	1.35	1.50
Low	0.85	0.85	0.85	1.20
Nominal	1.00	1.00	1.00	1.00
High	0.75	0.90	0.90	0.85
Very High	0.55	0.75	0.75	0.70

Table 4.4: Analyst capability effort multiplier for detailed COCOMO

The overall project estimates made for each module by combining all the subsystems. Using the detailed cost drivers, an estimate is determined for each phase of the lifecycle.

Analytical Cost Estimation

In the last three decades, many quantitative software cost estimation models have been developed. They range from empirical models such as **Boehm's COCOMO models** to analytical models. An *empirical model* uses data from previous projects to evaluate the current project and derives the basic formulae from analysis of the particular database available. An *analytical model,* on the other hand, uses formulae based on global assumptions, such as the rate at which developer solve problems and the number of problems available.

Halstead Software science method

Halstead proposed the *code length* and *volume* metrics. *Code length* is used to measure the source code program length and is defined as:

$$N = N1 + N2$$

where, N1 is the total number of operator occurrences, and

N2 is the total number of operand occurrences.

Volume corresponds to the amount of required storage space and is defined as:

$$V = N \log(n1 + n2)$$

where, n1 is the number of distinct operators, and n2 is the number of distinct operands that appear in a program. There have been some disagreements over the underlying theory that supports the software science approach. This measurement has received decreasing support in recent years.

Resource and Schedule Estimates

SLIM

Putnam developed a constrained model called **SLIM** to be applied to projects exceeding 70,000 lines of code. **Putnam's model** assumes that effort for software projects is distributed similarly to a collection of *Rayleigh* curves. *Putnam* suggests that staffing rises smoothly during the project and then drops sharply during acceptance testing. The *SLIM model* is expressed as two equations describing the relation between the development effort and the schedule. The first equation, called the *software equation*, states that development effort is proportional to the fourth power of the development time. The second equation, the *manpower-buildup equation*, states that the effort is proportional to the cube of the development time.

(*a*) **The Norden-Rayleigh Curve**

The Norden-Rayleigh curve represents manpower as a function of time. SLIM uses separate Rayleigh curves for design and code, test and validation, maintenance and management. A Rayleigh curve is shown in *figure 4.3*.

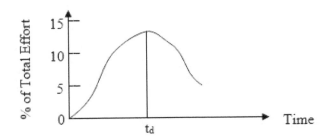

Figure 4.3: *Rayleigh Curve*

(b) The Software Equation

Putnam used some empirical observations about productivity levels to derive the software equation from the basic Rayleigh curve formula. The software equation is expressed as:

Size $L = C.K^{1/3}.td^{4/3}$

Where L = Delivered lines of code

K = Effort in person-years

td = Development time in years

C = Software development environment

$C = 2000$ (poor), $C = 8000$ (good), $C = 11000$ (excellent)

From the above equation $L^3 = C^3.K.t_d^4$

Hence, $K.t_d^4 = (L/C)^3$

= Constant for a given software project

Thus, Effort in person-years, $K \alpha (1/td4)$

i.e. $K1/K2 = t_{d2}^4/t_d^4$

Effect of Schedule Change

(1) Putnam Model

Effort in person-years, $K \alpha (1/t_d^4)$

where, t_d = Development time in years

(2) Jensen Model

Effort in person-years, $K \alpha (1/t_d^2)$

where, t_d = Development time in years

Putnam's model is more pessimistic while the Jensen model returns a more optimistic schedule. Although $K.t_d^4$ = constant, it does not mean that we can vary td as much as we like. In reality, td can only be varied between 80 percent and 120 percent of its original value. Thus, for the 10-month project, the schedule can only become between 8 and 12 months but neither below 8 months nor above 10 months.

Example 4.1:

Schedule Change

Original effort = 36.9 person-month

Development time = 9.85 months

New effort for project completion in 8 months:

According to Putnam model:

New effort = $36.9 * (9.85/8)^4 = 84.8$ person-months

= 2.3 times more!

According to Jensen model:

New effort = $36.9 * (9.85/8)^2 = 55.9$ person-months

= 1.5 times more!

(c) The Manpower-Buildup Equation

To allow effort estimation, Putnam introduced the manpower-buildup equation:

$D = E/t^3$

where D is a constant called manpower acceleration.

E is the total project effort in years, and

T is the elapsed time to delivery in years

Human Resource Management

Project Human Resource Management describes the processes that organize and manage the project team. It consists of the Human Resource Planning, Acquire Project Team, Develop Project Team, and Manage Project Team project management processes.

Communication Management

Project Communications Management describes the processes concerning the timely and appropriate generation, collection, dissemination, storage and ultimate disposition of project information. It consists of the Communications Planning, Information Distribution, Performance Reporting, and Manage Stakeholders project management processes.

Risk Management

Project Risk Management describes the processes concerned with conducting risk management on a project. It consists of the Risk Management Planning, Risk Identification, Qualitative Risk Analysis, Quantitative Risk Analysis, Risk Response Planning, and Risk Monitoring and Control project management processes. In general, software engineers do nothing about risks until something goes wrong. They get into action to correct the problem rapidly.

Project risks cause problems to project plan like schedule slip and increase in cost. Risk identification is essential to avoid and control. There are some predictable risks in the following generic categories.

- **Product size:** Risks associated with the size of the software.
- **Business impact:** Risks associated with constraints imposed by management.
- **Customer characteristics:** Risks associated with the customer and the developer's ability to communicate promptly.
- **Process identification:** Risks associated with the degree to which the software process has been defined and followed.
- **Development environment:** Risks associated with the availability and quality of tools to be used to build the product.
- **Technology to be built:** Risks associated with the complexity of the system to be built and the newness of the technology to be used in the system.
- **Staff size and experience:** Risks associated with the overall technical and project experience of the software engineers.

An effective strategy should be made for risk avoidance, risk monitoring, and contingency planning. This is achieved by developing a plan for risk mitigation, monitoring the activities by the project manager. A **risk mitigation, monitoring, and management plan (RMMM plan)** can be organized.

Project Planning

Project Planning is an aspect of Project Management that focuses a lot on Project Integration. The project plan reflects the current status of all project activities and is used to *monitor* and *control* the project. The Project Planning tasks ensure that various elements of the Project are coordinated and therefore guide the project execution.

Project Planning helps in
- Facilitating communication
- Monitoring/measuring the project progress, and
- Provides overall documentation of assumptions/planning decisions

The Project Planning Phases can be broadly classified as follows:
- Development of the Project Plan
- Execution of the Project Plan
- Change Control and Corrective Actions

Project Planning is an ongoing effort throughout the *Project Lifecycle*.

"If you fail to plan, you plan to fail."

Project planning is crucial to the success of the Project. Careful planning right from the beginning of the project can help to avoid costly mistakes. It assures that the project execution will accomplish its goals on schedule and within budget.

Steps in Project Planning

Project Planning spans across the various aspects of the Project. Generally, Project Planning is a process of estimating, scheduling and assigning the project's resources to deliver an end product of suitable quality. However, it is much more as it can assume a very strategic role, which can determine the very success of the project. A *Project Plan* is one of the crucial steps in Project Planning in General!

Typically, Project Planning can include the following types of planning:
- **Project Scope Definition and Scope Planning:** In this step, we document the project work that would help us achieve the project goal. We document the assumptions, constraints, user expectations, business requirements, technical requirements, project deliverables, project objectives, and everything that defines the final product requirements. This is the foundation for successful project completion.

- **Quality Planning:** The relevant quality standards are determined for the project. This is an important aspect of project planning. Based on the inputs captured in the previous steps such as the project scope, requirements, deliverables, etc. various factors influencing the quality of the final product are determined. The processes required to deliver the product as promised and as per the standards are defined.

- **Project Activity Definition and Activity Sequencing:** In this step, we define all the specific activities that must be performed to deliver the product by producing various product deliverables. The project activity sequencing identifies the interdependence of all the activities defined.

- **Time, Effort, and Resource Estimation:** Once the Scope, Activities and Activity interdependence is clearly defined and documented, the next crucial step is to determine the effort required to complete each of the activities. The *Effort* can be calculated using one of the many techniques available such as Function Points, Lines of Code, Complexity of Code, Benchmarks, etc. This step estimates and documents the time, effort, and resources required for each activity.

- **Risk Factors Identification:** "Expecting the unexpected and facing it". It is important to identify and document the risk factors associated with the project based on the assumptions, constraints, user expectations, specific circumstances, etc.

- **Schedule Development:** The schedule for the project can be arrived at based on the activities, interdependence, and effort required for each of them. The schedule may influence the cost estimates, the cost-benefit analysis and so on.

- **Project Scheduling** is one of the most important tasks of Project Planning and the most difficult tasks. In very large projects, several teams may work on developing the project. They may work on it in parallel. However, their work may be interdependent. Again, various factors may impact successfully scheduling a project. Popular Tools can be used for creating and reporting schedules such as Gantt Charts.

- **Cost Estimation and Budgeting:** Based on the information collected in all the previous steps it is possible to estimate the cost involved in executing and implementing the project. A Cost-Benefit Analysis can be arrived at for the project. Based on the Cost Estimates, the Budget allocation is done for the project.

- **Organizational and Resource Planning:** Based on the activities identified, schedule and budget allocation resource types and resources are identified. One of the primary goals of resource planning is to ensure that the project should run efficiently. This can only be achieved by keeping all the project resources fully utilized as possible. The success depends on the accuracy in predicting the resource demands that will be placed on the project. Resource planning is an iterative process and necessary to optimize the use of resources throughout the project life cycle thus making the project execution more efficient. There are various types of resources like Equipment, Personnel, Facilities, Money, etc.

- **Risk Management Planning:** Risk Management is a process of identifying, analyzing and responding to risk. Based on the Risk factors Identified a Risk resolution Plan is created. The plan analyses each of the risk factors and their impact on the project. The possible responses for each of them can be planned. Throughout the lifetime of the project, these risk factors are monitored and acted upon as necessary.

- **Project Plan Development and Execution:** Project Plan Development uses the inputs gathered from all the other planning processes such as Scope definition, Activity identification, Activity sequencing, Quality Management Planning, etc. A detailed Work Break down structure comprising of all the activities identified is used. The tasks are scheduled based on the inputs captured in the steps previously described. The Project Plan documents all the assumptions, activities, schedules, timelines, and drives the project.

  Each of the Project tasks and activities are periodically monitored. The team and the stakeholders are informed of the progress. This serves as an excellent communication mechanism. Any delays are analyzed, and the project plan may be adjusted accordingly

- **Performance Reporting:** As described above the progress of each of the tasks/activities described in the Project plan is monitored. The progress is compared with the schedule and timelines documented in the Project Plan. Various techniques are used to measure and report the project performance such as **EVM (Earned Value Management)**. A wide variety of tools can be used to report the performance of the project such as *PERT Charts, GANTT charts, Logical Bar Charts, Histograms, Pie Charts, etc.*

- **Planning Change Management:** Analysis of project performance can necessitate that certain aspects of the project be changed. The Requests for Changes need to be analyzed carefully and its impact on the project should be studied. Considering all these aspects the Project Plan may be modified to accommodate this request for Change. Change Management is also necessary to accommodate the implementation of the project currently under development in the production environment. When the new product is implemented in the production environment it should not negatively impact the environment or the performance of other applications sharing the same hosting environment.

- **Project Rollout Planning:** In Enterprise environments, the success of the Project depends a great deal on the success of its rollout and implementations. Whenever a project is rolled out it may affect the technical systems, business systems, and sometimes even the way business is run. For an application to be successfully implemented, not only the technical environment should be ready, but the users should accept it and use it effectively. For this to happen, the users may need to be trained on the new system. All this requires planning.

Project size estimates

Accurately estimating the project size, cost, effort, and time for development are the biggest challenges for the software industry nowadays. It is important to accurately estimate the project size for the further estimation of project cost and schedule.

The initial project size estimates are made from the system requirements and, further, estimation can be carried out through various techniques. Those are:

- Loc/Kloc
- Function Point Analysis
- Feature Point Analysis

LOC/KLOC

Each source line acts as one loc irrespective of the number of instructions used in that source line. For N number of source lines, it becomes NLOC.

When, N = 1,000 it becomes KLOC.

Function Point Analysis

The *empirical estimation* is done based on countable measures of the software information domain. Some adjustments are done depending on the complexity of the software. The functionality cannot be measured directly. This is derived indirectly using other direct measures called function points. The function points are collected by the core team on the discussion at the client site. The function points are categorized into:

- **External Inputs (EI)** to the application given by the users (data).
- **External Outputs (EO)** from the application (reports, screen, message, etc.).
- Number of **External enQueries (EQ)** by the users of the software as a combination of input requests and output retrievals.
- The number of master **Internal Logical Files (ILF)** would be maintained and updated by the application.
- Number of **External Interface Files (EIF)** of other applications

Function points are computed by *using table 4.5* where counts are provided.

Function Point (FP) = Count-total * [0.65 + (0.01 * sum (Fj))]

The Fj (j = 1 to 14) are complexity adjustment values based on the questions. Each one is expressed on a scale from 0 to 5 depending on their influence on the development process.

0 – No influence	1 – Incidental	2 – Moderate
3 – Average	4 – Significant	3 – Essential

Computable Measure	Multipliers		
	Simple	Average	Complex
External Inputs (EI)	3	4	6
External Outputs (EO)	4	5	7
No. of External enQuiries (EQ)	3	4	6
No. of master Internal Logical Files (ILF)	7	10	15
No. of External Interface Files (EIF)	5	7	10

Table 4.5: Function Point Computation

Complexity Adjustment Values:

- Does the system require reliable backup and recovery?
- Are data communications required?
- Are there distributed processing functions?
- Is performance critical?
- Will the system run in an existing heavily utilized operational environment?
- Does the system require on-line data entry?
- Does the on-line data entry require the input transaction to be built over multiple screens/operations?
- Are the master files updated on-line?
- Are the inputs, outputs, files, or inquiries complex?
- Is the internal processing complex?
- Is the code designed to be reusable?
- Are conversions and installation included in the design?
- Is the system designed for multiple installations in different organizations?
- Is the application designed to facilitate change and ease of use by the users?

Example 4.2:

Compute the Function Point value for a software project with the following details: **User inputs** = 12, **number of files** = 6, **user outputs** = 25, **external interfaces** = 4, **inquiries** = 10, and **number of algorithms** = 8. Assume the multipliers at average and all the complexity adjustment factors at their moderate to average values. **Multiplier** = 1.

Computable Measure	Countable measure values	Multipliers at average	Count = measure * multiplier
External Inputs (EI)	12	4	48
External Outputs (EO)	25	5	125
No. of External enQuiries (EQ)	10	4	40
No. of master Internal Logical Files (ILF)	6	10	60
No. of External Interface Files (EIF)	4	7	28
Count-Total	301		

Function Point (FP) = Count-total * [0.65 + (0.01 * sum (Fj))]

14 Fj – each assumes a value of 2.5 in case the influence is moderate to average.

Hence, sum (Fj) = 14 * 2.5 = 35

Thus, FP = 301 * (0.65 + (0.01 * 35)) = 301

Number of algorithms is not relevant here!

Equivalent LOC of FP

Depending on the programming language there is a relationship between LOC and Function Points. This is used to implement the software and the quality of design. *Table 4.6* provides a rough estimate of the average number of LOC required to build one FP in different programming languages.

Language	Equivalent LOC of FP
C	130
COBOL	110
JAVA	55
C++/Turbo PASCAL	50
Visual BASIC	30
Access/Excel	10-40

Table 4.6: Equivalent LOC of FP

Example 4.3:

The FP of a software product is 270.

Assuming C++ environment, LOC = 270 * 50 = 13500 = 13.5 KLOC

Using COCOMO (Basic, Organic)

Effort E = 2.4 * (13.5) * 1.05 = 36.9 person-months (P-M)

Development Time D = 2.5 * (36.9) * 0.38 = 9.85 months (M)

Compare this with EFP = 270/7 = 38.6 person-month (assuming 7 FP/P-M)

Development Time D = 9.85 M ≈ 10 M

Hence, software engineers required = 36.9/10 ≈ 4

If one engineer costs Rs. 50,000 per month

Project cost = Rs. 50,000 * 10 * 4 = Rs. 20,00,000

The estimates give a constant number of software engineers, meaning a uniform distribution of effort throughout the project period. However, in reality, software development effort is not uniform. Rather, it follows a Rayleigh distribution in *figure 4.3.*

Projects as Proxies

An alternative proxy is the *Object line of Code*. The idea, here, is that there is a relationship between the size of the code when written as messages to objects and the final code size. The link between the two is made by estimating the size of the objects. Humphrey shows, in his book, a good regression line between **OLC (object lines of code)** and **LOC**.

The size of an object can be estimated in terms of the number of methods that are required to implement the object and an estimate of the category of the object. The following *table 4.7*, taken from Humphrey's book shows a collection of estimates of object size in LOC per method. Your lineage may be different!

Category	Very Small	Small	Medium	Large	Very Large
Calculation	2.34	5.13	11.25	24.66	54.04
Data	2.60	4.79	8.84	16.31	30.09
I/O	9.01	12.06	16.15	21.62	30.09
Logic	7.55	10.98	15.98	23.25	33.83
Set-Up	3.88	5.04	6.56	8.53	11.09
Text	3.75	8.00	17.07	36.41	77.66

Table 4.7: C++ Object Size in LOC per method

It highlights the process requires that we design the system before you estimate its size. The process can be considerably improved by using statistical methods to track the accuracy of your estimates.

Feature Point Analysis

A superset of Function Points called Feature Points was introduced in **1986** by Jones in an attempt to improve the accuracy of estimates for real-time, operating systems, embedded, communications, and process control software systems **(Garmus 1996)**. Feature Points introduce a new parameter (algorithms) to the five standard function point parameters. Algorithms are assigned a default weight of three and Logical Files are reduced to seven (from ten), which has the effect of reducing the significance of data storage and grouping more prevalent in **MIS** applications.

Jones (1995) found that when Feature Points are used in classical MIS applications, the results are often similar, except in the case where MIS applications are severely dominated by files. For a telephone-switching project, the Feature Point estimate was notably higher due to the high algorithmic complexity.

Feature Points must be counted like the Function Points they are a superset of the later. This prompted Jones to introduce ten rules specifically identifying exactly under what conditions an algorithm exists. Further research is underway to develop a more rigorous taxonomy and weighing scale for algorithms.

Mythical Man-Month

Cost varies as the product of men and months. Therefore, man-month as a unit for measuring the size of the job is a dangerous and deceptive myth (Fred Brooks). Why software project disaster so common? The answer is estimation techniques are poor and assume things will go well. The estimation techniques fallaciously confuse effort with progress, hiding the assumption that men and months are interchangeable. When the schedule slippage is recognized, the natural response is to add manpower which is like dousing a fire with gasoline.

Mostly all the programmers are optimistic. The first false assumption is *all will go well* or *each task takes only as long as it ought to take*. The programmer should consider the larger probabilities without using fuzzy milestones (get true status). In many cases, the process is sequential in nature which will take the basic minimum time. Don't try to reduce it further. The bearing of a child takes nine months, no matter how many women are assigned. Testing is the most unpredictable and unscheduled part of the process. Therefore, allocate more test times and understand the task dependencies.

It is a misconception that adding more people will complete the job early. To calculate, how long does a 12-month project take? One person will take 12 months. Suppose, two persons take 7 months which adds two man-months extra. If three persons take 5 months that adds 3 man-months extra. There is no linear relationship between man and time. The myth of additional manpower relies on hunches and guesses which invites gutless estimation. Brooks law states that *"adding manpower to a late project makes it later"*.

Project Scheduling through PERT/CPM

Many times, a big project consists of a large number of activities that pose complex problems in planning, scheduling, and control, especially when the project activities have to be performed in a specified technological sequence. With the help of PERT (Program Evaluation and Review Technique), and CPM (Critical Path Method), the project manager can

- Plan the project ahead of time and foresee possible sources of troubles and delays in completion.

- Schedule the project activities, at the appropriate times, to confirm with proper job sequence, so that the project is completed as soon as possible.

- Coordinate and control the project activities so as to stay on schedule in completing the project.

Thus, both **PERT** and **CPM** are aided in efficient project management. They differ in their approach to the problem and solution techniques. The nature of the project generally dictates the proper technique to be used.

Origin and Use of PERT

PERT was developed in the *U.S. Navy* during the late **1950s** to accelerate the development of the Polaris Fleet Ballistic Missile. The development of the weapon involved the coordination of the work of thousands of private contractors and other government agencies. The coordination by **PERT** was so successful that the entire project was completed two years ahead of the schedule. This has resulted in further application of **PERT** in other weapon development programs in the navy, air-force, and army. Nowadays, it is extensively used in industries and other service organizations as well.

PERT incorporates uncertainties in activity times in its analysis. It determines the probability of completing various stages of the project by specified deadlines. It also calculates the expected time to complete the project. The **PERT analysis** identifies various bottlenecks in a project. It identifies the activities that have a high potential for causing delays in completing the project on schedule. It helps to take necessary preventive measures to reduce possible delays. Because of its ability to handle uncertainty in job times, **PERT** is mostly used in research and development projects.

Origin and Use of CPM

Critical Path Method closely resembles **PERT** in many aspects but was developed independently by **E.I. du Pont de Nemours Company**. Both **PERT** and **CPM** techniques were developed simultaneously. The major difference is that **CPM** does not incorporate uncertainties in job times. Instead, it assumes that activity times are proportional to the number of resources allocated to them, and by changing the level of resources the activity times and the project completion time can be varied. Thus, **CPM** assumes prior experience with similar projects from which the relationships between resources and job times are available. **CPM** then evaluates the trade-off between project costs and project completion time. CPM is mostly used in construction projects where there is prior experience in handling similar projects.

Application of PERT and CPM

A partial list of applications of **PERT** and **CPM** techniques in project management as follows:

- Development of large integrated software projects.
- Installation of computer hardware, networking, and hardware procurement.
- Construction projects (e.g. buildings, highways, bridges, and houses).
- Preparation of bids and proposals for large projects.
- Maintenance planning of oil refineries, ship repairs, and other large operations.
- Manufacture and assembly of large items such as airplanes, ships, and computers.
- Development of new weapons systems, space missions, and new manufactured products.
- Simple projects such as home remodeling, moving into a new house, home cleaning, and painting.

Project network

Analysis by **PERT/CPM** techniques uses the network formulation to represent the project activities and their ordering relations. The explanation was given, in section 4.3.2. Construction of a project network is done as follows:

- a. Arcs in the network represent individual jobs in the project.
- b. Nodes represent specific points in time which mark the completion of one or more jobs in the project.
- c. Direction on the arc is used to represent the job sequence. It is assumed that any job directed toward a node must be completed before any job directed away from that node can begin.

Mathematical Programming Method

Given that the project must be completed by time T, we want to determine how the project activities are to be expedited such that the total cost of crashing is minimized. The problem can be formulated as a LP problem as follows:

Model-I

$$Min \; Z = \sum_{(i,j)} C_{ij}(k_{ij} - t_{ij})$$

Subject to
$$t_j - t_1 \geq t_{ij}$$
$$t_u - t_1 \leq k_{ij}$$
$$t_n - t_1 \leq T$$
$$t_i > 0 \text{ for all } i=1, 2, \ldots \ldots n$$

Where,

k_{ij} = the normal completion time of the job(i,j) if no additional resources are assigned.

ℓ_{ij} = crash completion time with the maximum amount of resources

C_{ij} = unit cost of shortening the duration of the job(i,j)

t_{ij} = the completion time of the job (i,j) which is an unknown variable between ℓ_{ij} and k_{ij}

$C_{ij}(k_{ij}-t_{ij})$ = Cost of crashing.

Model-II

Suppose, an additional budget of B(money) is available for crashing the project activities. We want to determine how these additional resources may be allocated in the best possible manner so as to minimize the project completion time.

$$\text{Min.} \quad Z = t_n - t_1$$
$$\text{S.t.} \quad t_j - t_i \geq t_{ij} \text{ for all jobs(i,j)}$$
$$\ell_{ij} \leq t_{ij} \leq k_{ij} \text{ for all jobs(i,j)}$$
$$\sum_{i,j} C_{ij}(k_{ij} - t_{ij}) \leq B$$
$$t_{i,j} \geq 0 \text{ for all } i=1,2,\ldots \ldots n$$

The solution gives the least project duration that can be achieved by additional budget B, the activities to be crashed and their durations.

Model-III

Let T^* = optimal length of the project

$$F = \frac{\text{Indirect } cost(OH)}{\text{Per unit time}} \alpha \text{ project duration}$$

$F(t_n - t_1)$ = Indirect cost,

$t_n - t_1$ = unknown length of project.

$$F = \frac{\text{Indirect } cost(OH)}{\text{Per unit time}} \alpha \text{ project duration}$$

t_{ij} = unknown length of job (i,j) i.e., the completion time of job(i,j)

Minimize the total cost.

$$Min Z = F(t_n - t_1) + \sum_{(i,j)}^{n} C_{ij}(k_{ij} - t_{ij})$$

Subject to $t_j - t_i \geq t_{ij}$ for all jobs (i,j)

                     $\ell_{ij} \leq t_{ij} \leq k_{ij}$ for all jobs (i,j)

                     $t_i \geq 0$ for all i=1,2,......n

Diagram representation

Example 4.4:

Consider seven jobs A, B, C, D, E, F, and G with the following job sequence:

Job A precedes B and C

Job C and D precede E

Job B precedes D

Job E and F precede G

The project network is shown in *figure 4.4:*

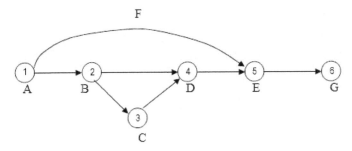

Figure 4.4: Network Diagram

In the network, every arc (i, j) represents a specific job in the project. Node 1 represents the start and node 6 denotes the completion of project. The intermediate nodes represent the completion of various stages of the project. The nodes of the project network are called *events*.

An *event* is a specific point in time that marks the completion of one or more activities, well recognizable in the project.

Example 4.5:

Consider a project with five jobs A, B, C, D, and E with the following job sequence:

Job A precedes C and D

Job B precedes D

Job C and D precede E

The completion times for A, B, C, D, and E are 3, 1, 4, 2, and 5 days respectively.

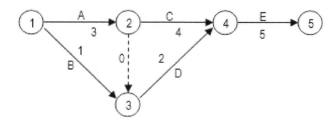

Figure 4.5: Network Diagram with Times

Arc (2, 3) represents a **dummy** job that does not exist in reality in the project. It is necessary so as to avoid ambiguity in the job sequence. The completion time of the dummy job is always 0, and it is added in the project network whenever we want to avoid an arc (i, j) representing more than one job in the project. Event 3 represents the completion of job B and the dummy job. Since, the dummy job is completed as soon as A is completed, event 3, in essence marks the completion of job A and B.

Critical path

A path in the project network connecting the starting event (node) and the ending event such that it passes through the critical jobs is called a **Critical Path**. It is shown in *figure 4.6*.

Figure 4.6: The critical Path

It can be shown that finding a critical path in a project network is equivalent to finding the **longest path** in the network.

Solution by Network Analysis

The earliest time of node j, denoted by U_j, is the earliest time at which event j can occur. We know that event j can occur as soon as all the jobs (arcs) directed towards node j are completed. In the following *figure 4.7, 4.8 and 4.9* event j occurs as soon as jobs A, B, and C are completed.

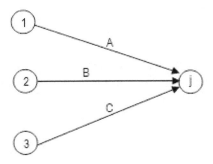

Figure 4.7: Activities joining into a Node

The earliest time of node j is then given by

$$U_j = \max (U_1 + t_{1j}, U_2 + t_{2j}, U_3 + t_{3j})$$

Where, t_{1j}, t_{2j} and t_{3j} are completion times of A, B, and C.

The general formula for calculating U_j is

$$\mathbf{U_j = maxi\ (U_i + t_{ij})}$$

Where, the index I range over all nodes for which arc (i, j) exists and t_{ij} is the completion time of the job represented by an arc (i, j).

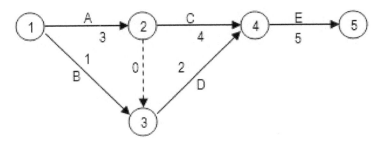

Figure 4.8: Project Network – An Example

For the above network, the U_j are calculated as follows:

Set $U_1 = 0$

Then, $U_2 = U_1 + t_{12} = 3$

$U_3 = \max [(U_2 + t_{23}), (U_1 + t_{13})]$

$= \max (3, 1) = 3$

$U_4 = \max [(U_2 + t_{24}), (U_3 + t_{34})]$

$$= \max (7, 5) = 7$$

$$U_5 = U_4 + t_4 5 = 12$$

Hence, the minimum duration of the project is 12 days from the start. We need to calculate the *latest time* of an event. The *latest time* of node i, denoted by V_i, is the latest time at which event i can occur without delaying the completion of the project beyond its earliest time.

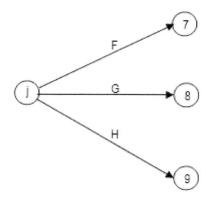

Figure 4.9: *Activities Emerging from a Node*

The project will not be delayed if the three jobs F, G, and H are completed by V_7, V_8, and V_9 respectively.

$$V_i = \min [(V_7 - t_{i7}), (V_8 - t_{i8}), V_9 - t_{i9})]$$

Hence, the general formula to calculate V_i becomes

$$V_i = m_{inj} (V_j - t_{ij})$$

Set the latest time of the last event equal to its earliest time and work backward.

Thus,

$$V_5 - t_{45} = 12$$
$$V_4 = V_5 - t_{45} = 7$$
$$V_3 = V_4 - t_{34} = 5$$
$$V_2 = \min [(V_4 - t_{24}), (V_3 - t_{23})]$$
$$= \min (3, 5) = 3$$
$$V_1 = \min [(V_2 - t1_2), (V_3 - t_{13})]$$
$$= \min (0, 4) = 0$$

The difference between the latest time and the earliest time of an event is called **slack time** of that event. The slack time denotes how much delay can be tolerated in reaching that event without delaying the project completion date (is called **float**).

For the project network shown in *table 4.8*, the slack times of events 1, 2, 3, 4, and 5 are given by 0, 0, 2, 0, and 0 respectively. Those events that have zero slack times are the **critical events**, where every care must be taken to stay on schedule if the project is to be completed on time. The *critical jobs* are the arcs (jobs) in the critical path having zero slack time.

The critical path is $1 \rightarrow 2 \rightarrow 3 \rightarrow 4$

The jobs are   A, C, and E

Events	Earliest Time	Latest Time	Slack Time	Remarks
1	0	0	0	Critical
2	3	3	0	Critical
3	3	5	2	Non-Critical
4	7	7	0	Critical
5	12	12	0	Critical

Table 4.8: Results of Network Analysis

To prepare a *project schedule* in terms of the activities, it is essential to have the starting time and the ending time of all jobs. From the event times it is possible to get the following information on each one of the activities in the project:

1. The earliest starting time
2. The latest starting time
3. The earliest finishing time
4. The latest finishing time
5. The slack time (float)

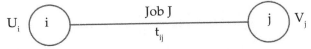

U_i – the earliest occurrence time of event i

V_j – the latest occurrence time of event j

T_{ij} – the completion time of job J

$V_j - t_{ij}$ – latest starting time of job J

$U_i + t_{ij}$ – earliest completion time of job J

$V_j - U_i$ – maximum time available for job J

$V_j - U_i - t_{ij}$ – the slack time of job J (maximum delay in completion)

$V_j - U_i = t_{ij}$ – if job J is critical

Job	Expected Duration (days)	Earliest Start	Latest Start	Earliest Finish	Latest Finish	Slack Time (Max. delay)	Remarks
A	3	0	0	3	3	0	Critical
B	1	0	4	1	5	4	Non-critical
C	4	3	3	7	7	0	Critical
D	2	3	5	5	7	2	Non-critical
E	5	7	7	12	12	0	Critical

Table 4.9: *Schedule of Network*

Critical Path Method (CPM)

The basic assumption in **CPM** is that the activity times are proportional to the level of resources allocated to them. By assigning additional resources (capital, people, materials, and machines) to an activity, its duration can be reduced to a certain extent. Shortening the duration of an activity is known as **crashing** in the CPM technology. The additional cost incurred in reducing the activity time is called **crashing cost**.

For critical path analysis, it is assumed that every job has a *normal completion time* (maximum time) if no additional resources were assigned, and a *crash completion time* (minimum time) with the maximum amount of resources. The project management problem is to be crashed that will minimize the total cost of the project.

Example 4.6:

(Enumerative Method)

Consider a software project of 8 jobs Analysis-module-1 and system requirement study (SRS)-1, Analysis-module-2, System requirement Study (SRS)-2, GUI Design, GUI Coding and Unit Testing-1, Database (DB) Design, DB Coding and Unit Testing, and Integration and System Testing. Two groups of professionals are deployed to develop the system. The required time of each activity and precedence of activities are given in *table 4.10*.

Job	Job Description	Predecessor	Normal Time (days)	Crash Time (days)	Cost of Crashing (100 Rs)
A	Analysis-1 and SRS-1	-	10	7	4
B	Analysis-2	-	5	4	2
C	SRS-2	B	3	2	2
D	GUI Design	A, C	4	3	3

E	DB Design	A, C	5	3	3
F	GUI Coding and Unit Testing	D	6	3	5
G	DB Coding and Unit Testing	E	5	2	1
H	Integration and System Testing	F, G	5	4	4

Table 4.10: *Activity and Precedence of the Project Work with Crashing*

Given overhead (OH) cost as Rs. 500 per day, we want to determine the optimal duration of the project in terms of both the crashing and overhead costs and to develop an optimal project schedule.

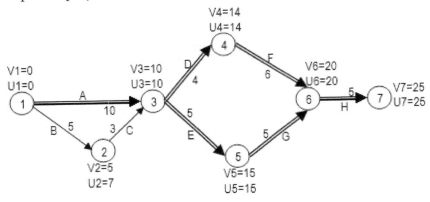

Figure 4.10: *The Network of Software Project with Activities*

Job	Expected Duration	Earliest Start	Latest Start	Earliest Finish	Latest Finish	Slack Time (Max. delay)	Remarks
A	10	0	0	10	10	0	Critical
B	5	0	2	5	7	2	Non-critical
C	3	5	7	8	10	3	Non-critical
D	4	10	10	14	14	0	Critical
E	5	10	10	15	15	0	Critical
F	6	14	14	20	20	0	Critical
G	5	15	15	20	20	0	Critical
H	5	20	20	25	25	0	Critical

Table 4.11: *The Computation of Software Project*

If all the jobs are done at their normal times, the project duration (length of the longest path) is 25 days. Hence, under a *no crashing schedule*:

$$A \rightarrow D \rightarrow F \rightarrow H = 25 \text{ days}$$

$$\text{Or,} \quad A \rightarrow E \rightarrow G \rightarrow H = 25 \text{ days}$$

$$\text{Total cost} = \text{Overhead costs} + \text{Crashing costs}$$

$$= \text{Rs. } 500 (25) + 0 = \text{Rs. } 12,500$$

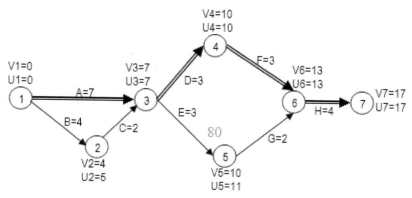

Figure 4.11: *The Network of Software Project with Crashed Activities*

If all jobs are crashed as per *figure 4.11,* the new critical duration is 17 days.

$$(A=7) + (D=3) + (F=3) + (H=4) = 17 \text{ days} \qquad \text{critical duration}$$

Total cost		
= ₹ 500 (17) +	→	cost of the critical path length
+ ₹ 400 (10-7)	→	cost of activity A/day
+ ₹ 200 (5-4)	→	cost of activity B/day
+ ₹ 200 (3-2)	→	cost of activity C/day
+ ₹ 300 (4-3)	→	cost of activity D/day
+ ₹ 300 (5-3)	→	cost of activity E/day
+ ₹ 500 (6-3)	→	cost of activity F/day
+ ₹ 100 (5-2)	→	cost of activity G/day
+ ₹ 400 (5-4)	→	cost of activity H/day

$$₹ \mathbf{13,200}$$

This is not advisable to crash all the activities at random paying such a big cost. Moreover, the critical path is changed. An economic consideration has to be given which will not further increase the cost. We have to explore the critical activities, the duration of which can further be reduced without increasing the total cost. Therefore, the objective is to determine the optimal duration of jobs that will minimize the total cost. Let us consider the two critical paths of 25 days each for finding the scope of cost reduction.

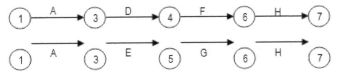

Figure 4.12: Scope of cost reduction

The total cost of the project under normal time = Rs. 12,500

Consider the critical path to reduce the duration.

Activity H can be crashed by 1 day at cost	Rs. 400
Due to the reduction in OH cost	Rs. 500
Saving	**Rs. 100**

The total project cost reduced from Rs. 12,500 to (500 X 24 days) Rs. 12,200

Activity A can be crashed by 2 days (originally 10 days). More than this both B and C will be critical since the sum of both activities will be 5+3 = 8 days.

$$\text{Crashing cost} = 200 \text{ X } 4 = \text{Rs. } 800$$
$$\text{Reduction of OH cost} = 200 \text{ X } 5 = \text{Rs. } 1000$$
$$\text{Total savings} = \text{Rs. } 200$$

The total project cost further will come down from Rs. 12,500 to Rs.12,200.

To reduce the project duration by one more day, we must crash job A by 1 day and either B or C by 1 day. The total cost of crashing A and B is Rs. 600, which is more than the savings on OH costs. Similarly, crashing A and C activities is not economical.

Now, consider the critical jobs D, E, F, and G. Since, we have parallel critical paths between nodes 3 and 6, we have to crash one job in path between 3 and 6 as shown in *figure 4.13(a)* and one job in path as shown in *figure 4.13(b)* to reduce the project length. We must try four different combinations as given in *table 4.12*.

Figure 4.13(a)   Figure 4.13(b)

Jobs	Increase in Crashing cost	Decrease in OH cost	Net change in Total cost
D and E	300 + 300 = ₹ 600	₹ 500	Increase by ₹ 100
D and G	300 + 100 = ₹ 400	₹ 500	Decrease by ₹ 100
F and E	500 + 300 = ₹ 800	₹ 500	Increase by ₹ 100
F and G	500 + 100 = ₹ 600	₹ 500	Increase by ₹ 100

Table 4.12: Alternative Combinations of Activities

Only combination D and G is economical when we crash both jobs D and G by one day. The total project cost is reduced from Rs. 12,200 to Rs. 12,100. No further crashing is economical. Hence, the optimal schedule is:

Crash job A to 8 days

Crash job D to 3 days

Crash job G to 4 days

Crash job H to 4 days

Jobs B, C, E, and F are completed in normal time. The optimal length of the project is 21 days. The activity-wise schedule is shown in figure 4.14. The minimum project cost is Rs. 12,100.

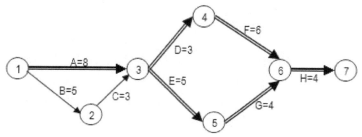

Figure 4.14: *The optimal network after crashing of events*

Time-Cost Curve

CPM places equal emphasis on time and cost. This is done by constructing a *time-cost curve* for each activity as shown in *figure 4.15*. This curve plots the relationship between the budgeted *direct cost* for the activity and its resulting *duration time*. The plot normally based on two points, the manual and crash. The normal point gives the cost and time involved when the activity is performed in the normal way without any extra cost.

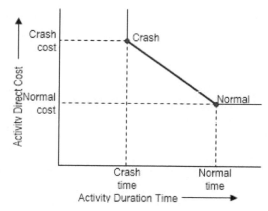

Figure 4.15: *Budgeted cost with time duration*

The crash point gives the time and cost when the activity is performed on a crash basis, i.e., it is fully expedited with no cost spared to reduce the duration time as much as possible. As an approximation, it is then assumed that all intermediate time-cost tradeoffs also are possible and that they lie on the line segment between these two points.

The basic objective of CPM is to determine just which time-cost trade-off should be used for each activity to meet the scheduled project completion time at minimum cost.

Figure 4.16 gives a typical plot of the direct (activity) costs against the project duration.

T_{max} = The project duration with all jobs in their normal time.

T_{min} = The project duration with all jobs reduced to their crash time.

The cost function is called a piecewise linear function.

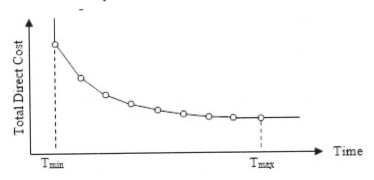

Figure 4.16: *Time cost curve*

The *figure 4.16* shows the direct cost of completing the project activities increases when the project duration is reduced. But the indirect costs discussed earlier reduced with a reduction in project duration. Hence, it will be of interest to study how the total cost (direct + indirect cost) varies with the project duration. For various project lengths, the indirect cost is added to the direct cost, and a plot of points is obtained to get a relationship between the project length and the total project cost. The figure below is a U-shaped curve is called a *project cost figure 4.17*.

With the help of this curve, a project manager can select the optimal project duration (T*) that will minimize the total costs. Corresponding to the optimal value of T, project manager can determine the optimal durations of all the jobs, the cost of crashing, and the critical path.

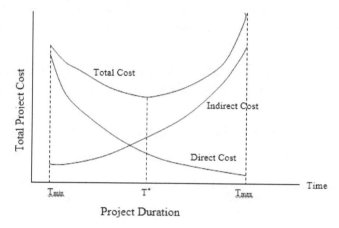

Figure 4.17: Optimal Project Duration with Costs

From this information the optimal project schedule can be prepared.

PERT (Program Evaluation and Review Technique)

PERT is a variation on Critical Path Analysis that takes a slightly more skeptical view of time estimates made for each project stage. This technique is used to find the probability of completion of a project before it is taken up where the individual task completion time is not clearly known. Therefore, three types of time estimates are considered. To use it, estimate the shortest possible time each activity will take (pessimistic time), the most likely length of time for completion of the task, and the longest time (optimistic time) that might be taken if the activity takes longer than expected. The characteristic of this type of project is considered as a Beta distribution which is having unimodal asymmetric distribution and finite non-negative end point *figure 4.18*.

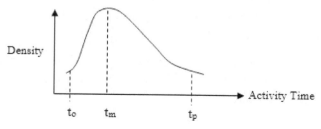

Figure 4.18: Beta Distribution

Use the formula below to calculate the time to use for each project stage:

Expected Time $= T_e = (t_o + 4 t_m + t_p)/6$

Variance $\quad = V_e = \{(t_p - t_o)/6\}2$

Where, $\quad t_o$ = Optimistic time

$\qquad t_m$ = Most likely time

$\qquad t_p$ = Pessimistic time

This helps to bias time estimates away from the unrealistically short time-scales normally assumed.

Example 4.7: Consider a project consisting of 9 jobs (A, B, ...I) with the following relations and time estimates.

Job	Predecessor	Optimistic Time(a)	Most probable Time(n)	Pessimistic Time (b)
A	--	2	5	8
B	A	6	9	12
C	A	6	7	8
D	B,C	1	4	7
E	A	8	8	8
F	D,E	5	14	17
G	C	3	12	21
H	F, G	3	6	9
I	H	5	8	11

Table 4.13: Activity wise Times in the Network

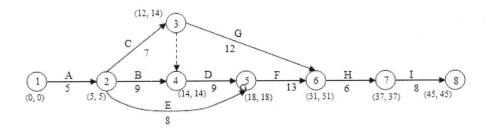

Figure 4.19: Network Events with Earliest and Latest Time

Job	Average time	Standard deviation	Variance
A	5	1	1
B	9	1	1
C	7	1/3	1/9
D	4	1	1
E	8	0	0
F	13	2	4
G	12	3	9
H	6	1	1
I	8	1	1

Table 4.14: *Time Computation of each Activity*

First we compute the average time from the three times given in *table 4.13* and the variance for each one of the jobs. They are tabulated in *table 4.14*. *Figure 4.19* gives the project network, where the numbers on the arcs indicate the average job times. Using the average job times, the earliest and latest times of each event are calculated.

The critical path is found as $1 \rightarrow 2 \rightarrow 4 \rightarrow 5 \rightarrow 6 \rightarrow 7 \rightarrow 8$.

Let T denotes the project duration. Then the expected length of the project is

E(T) = sum of the expected times of jobs A,B,D,F,H and I

= 5 + 9 + 4 + 13 + 6 + 8 = 45 days.

The variance of the project duration is

V(T)=Sum of the variance of jobs A,B,D,F, H and I

= 1 + 1 + 1 + 1 + 1 + 1 + 1 + 1 + 1 = 9

The standard deviation of the project duration is

$$\sigma(T) = \sqrt{V(T)} = 3$$

Example 4.8: (on optimum duration and minimum duration cost). *Table 4.15* shows, jobs, their normal time and cost, and crash time and cost for a project.

Job	Normal Time(days)	Cost (Rs.)	Crash Time (days)	Crash Cost (Rs.)
(1-2)	6	1400	4	1900
(1-3)	8	2000	5	2800
(2-3)	4	1100	2	1500
(2-4)	3	800	2	1400

(3-4)	Dummy	-	-	
(3-5)	6	900	3	1600
(4-6)	10	2500	6	3500
(5-6)	3	500	2	800

Table 4.16: Activity wise Values of the Network

Indirect cost for the project is Rs. 300 per day.

(i)   Draw the network of the project

(ii) What is the normal duration cost of the project?

(iii) If all activities are crashed, what will be the project duration and their costs?

(iv) Find the optimum duration and minimum project cost.

(i) Network is shown in the *figure 4.20.*

(ii) Assuming that all activities occur at normal times, the critical path calculations are shown in the figure under normal conditions. The critical path is 1→ 2→3 →4 →6. The duration of the project is 20 days and its associated (normal) cost is Rs. 9200.

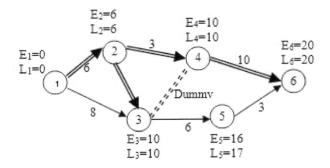

Figure 4.20

(iii) Now compute the different minimum cost schedule that can occur between normal and crash times mainly depending on the cost time slopes for the different activities. To calculate these, use the formula

$$Cost\ Slope = \frac{Crash\ cost - Normal\ cost}{Normal\ time - Crash\ time}$$

These slopes are summarized in the following tabular form :

Activity :	(1-2)	(1-3)	(1-3)	(2-4)	(3-5)	(4-6)	(5-6)
Slope :	250	267	200	600	233	250	300

Step 1. Because the present schedule involves more time, the schedule is reduced by crashing some of the activities. As the activities lying on the critical path control the duration of the project, therefore the duration of some activities lying on the critical path is reduced.

Start reducing the duration of that activity which involves minimum cost slope. As the activity (2-3) has the minimum cost slope, the duration of this activity is reduced from 4 to 2 days resulting additional cost of Rs. 2 x 200 = Rs. 400. But this activity should be shortened only by one day, since path 1→2 →4→6 becomes a parallel critical path. So, the revised schedule corresponds to 19 days with a cost of Rs. (9200 + 200) = Rs. 9400.

Step 2. Now it is evident that the activities (1-2) and (4-6) among the remaining activities lying on the critical paths have the least slope. Therefore, either (1-2) or (4-6) can be compressed only for days. This is due to the fact that 1 → 3 →5 →6, 1→2 →3 →4→6, and 1 →2 →4 →6, becomes three parallel critical paths. So three alterative choices are given below:

  (*i*)   Compress (1-2) by 2-days at a cost of Rs. 250.

  (*ii*)   Compress (4-<)) by 2-days at a cost of Rs. 250.

  (*iii*)   Compress (1-2) and (4-6) by 1 -day at a cost of Rs. 250 each.

   The additional cost thus will be Rs. 2 x 250 = Rs.500. Thus a 17 days least cost schedule is obtained with a cost of Rs. (9400 + 500) = Rs.9900.

  (*iv*)   To determine the optimum schedule, compute the total cost by adding, the indirect corresponding to each schedule to the cost of crashing (slope) optimum schedule (duration) is then obtained for which the total cost is least. Required calculations are put in the following tabular *figure 4.16*:

Normal Project Length (days)	Crashing time and cost (days/Rs)	Indirect cost @Rs.300	Total cost (Rs.)
20		20x300	600
19	1 x200 = 200	19x 300	5900
18	1x250 = 250	18x300	5650
17	1x250 = 250	17x300	5350
16	1x200 + 1x600 + 1x233 =1033	16x300	5833

Table 4.16: Cost Computation

Example 4.9: For the project. Find the earliest and latest expected times to each event and also critical path in the network. *(figure 4.21, 4.22) Table (4.17, 4.18, 4.19)*

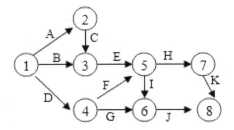

Figure 4.21

Task	A	B	C	D	E	F	G	H	I	J	K
Last Time	4	5	8	2	4	6	8	5	3	5	6
Greatest Time	8	10	12	7	10	15	16	9	7	11	13
Most likely time	5	7	11	3	7	9	12	6	5	8	9

Table 4.17: Activity wise Times

Task	Last time a	Greatest time B	Most likely time m	Expected time (a+b+4m)/6
A	4	8	5	5.33
B	5	10	7	7.17
C	8	12	11	10.66
D	2	7	3	3.50
E	4	10	7	7.00
F	6	15	9	9.50
G	8	16	12	12.00
H	5	9	6	6.33
I	3	7	5	5.00
J	5	11	8	8.00
K	6	13	9	9.17

Table 4.18: Expected Time Computations

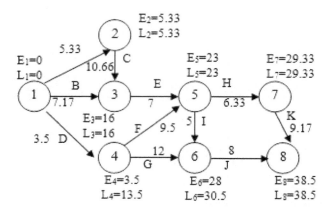

Figure 4.22

Task	Expected Time(t_a)	Start		Finish		Total Float
		Earliest	Latest	Earliest	Latest	
A	5.33	0.00	0.00	5.33	5.33	0.00
B	7.17	0.00	8.81	7.17	16.00	8.81
C	10.70	5.33	5.33	16.00	16.00	0.00
D	3.50	0.00	10.00	3.50	13.50	10.00
E	7.00	16.00	16.00	23.00	23.00	0.00
F	9.50	3.50	13.50	13.00	23.00	10.00
G	12.00	3.50	18.50	15.50	30.50	15.00
H	6.33	23.00	23.00	29.33	29.33	0.00
I	5.00	23.00	25.50	28.00	30.50	2.50
J	8.00	28.00	30.50	36.00	38.50	2.50
K	9.17	29.33	29.33	31.50	38.50	0.00

Critical path is A→ C→ E→ H→K.

Table 4.19: Computation of Float Time for each Activity

Example 4.10: A project is represented by the network shown in *figure 4.23* and *table 4.20* has the following data:

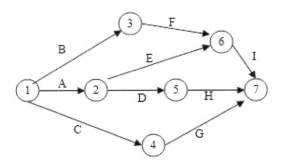

Figure 4.23

Task	A	B	C	D	E	F	G	H	I
Leal time	5	18	26	16	15	6	7	7	3
Greatest time	10	22	40	20	25	12	12	9	5
Most likely time	8	20	33	18	20	9	10	8	4

Table 4.20: Activity wise Times

Determine the following:

(i) expected task time and their variance,

(ii) the earliest and latest expected times to reach each node.

(iii) the critical path, and

(iv) the probability of node occurring at the proposed completion date if the original contract time of completing the project is 41.5 weeks

(i) Proceeding as in above example we obtain the *table 4.21*.

t_o - Optimistic time $\qquad$ t_m – Most likely time

t_p - Pessimistic time $\qquad$ t_e - Expected time

E_i – Early start time of ith node $\qquad$ L_i – Late finish time of ith node

Activity	to	tp	tm	te	σ2
(1-2)	5	10	8	7.8	0.69
(1-3)	18	22	20	20.0	0.44
(1-4)	26	40	33	33.0	5.43
(2-5)	16	20	18	18.0	0.44

(2-6)	15	25	20	20.0	2.78
(3-6)	6	12	9	9.0	1.00
(4-7)	7	12	10	9.8	0.69
(5-7)	7	9	8	8.0	0.11
(6-7)	3	5	4	4.0	0.11

Table 4.21: Variance Computation

(ii) Proceeding exactly as in above example, find earliest times in usual notations.

$E_1 = 0$, $E_2 = 0 + 7.8$, $E_3 = 0 + 20 = 20$, $E_4 = 0 + 33 = 33$, $E_5 = 7.8 + 18 = 25.8$,

E_6 = max $[7.8 + 20, 20 + 9] = 29$, E_7 = max $[33 + 9.8, 25.8 + 8, 29 + 4] = 42.8$.

Moving backwards, calculate the latest times as before,

$L_7 = 42.8$, $L6 = 42.8 - 4 = 38.8$, $L5 = 42.8 - 8 = 34.3$, $L4 = 42.8 - 9.8 = 33$,

$L_3 = 38.8 - 9 = 29.8$

L_2 = min$[34.8-18, 38.8-20] = 16.8$, L_1=min $(16.8 -7.8. 29.8-20, 33-33] = 0$.

(iii) To find the critical path, calculate slack time by taking difference between the earliest expected times and latest allowable times. Calculations are given in the *table 4.22* and critical path is shown by double line in the *figure 4.24*.

Node (i)	t_e	E_i	L_i	Slack	$\sigma 2i$
2	7.80	7.8	16.8	9.0	0.69
3	20.0	20.0	29.8	9.8	0.44
4	33.0	33.0	33.0	0.0	5.42
5	18.0	25.8	34.8	9.0	1.13
6	9.0	29.0	38.8	9.6	1.44
7	9.8	42.8	42.8	0.0	6.12

Table 4.22: Computation of Slack Time

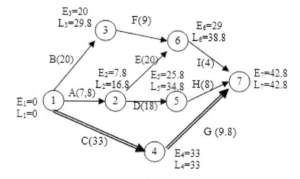

Figure 4.24: Critical Path of the Network

(iv) The scheduled time of completing the project is 41.5 weeks. Therefore, the distance in standard it deviations, that schedule time from earliest expected times E_t is given by:

$$D_i = \frac{ST_i - E_i}{\sqrt{(Var\,(i))}} = \frac{41.5 - 42.8}{\sqrt{(6.12)}} = -0.52 \quad \text{where, ST denotes the schedule time}$$

Therefore, $P(Z \geq -0.52) = 1 - P(Z \to 0.52] = 1 - 0.70 = 0.30$ (from *Normal Table*) which is the area under the standard normal curve bounded by ordinates at $x = 0$, and $x = 0.52$.

From this, it is concluded that if the project is performed 100 times under the same conditions, there will be 30 chances when this job would take 41.5 weeks or less to complete it.

Mathematical Programming Method

Given that the project must be completed by time T, we want to determine how the project activities are to be expedited such that the total cost of crashing is minimized. The problem can be formulated as a LP problem as follows:

Model-I

$$Min\ Z = \sum_{(i,j)} C_{ij}(K_{ij} - t_{ij})$$

Subject to

$$t_j - t_i \geq t_{ij}$$

$$\ell_j - t_i \leq k_{ij}$$

$$t_n - t_1 \leq T$$

$$t_i \geq 0 \qquad \text{for all i=1,2,.......n}$$

K_{ij}—the normal completion time of job(i,j) if no additional resources are assigned.

ℓ_{ij}—Crash completion time with the maximum amount of resources.

C_{ij}—Unit cost of shortening the duration of job(i,j).

$T_{i,j}(K_{ij}-t_{ij})$—Cost of crashing.

Model-II

Suppose, an additional budget of B(money) is available for crashing the project activities. We want to determine how these additional resources may be allocated in the best possible manner to minimize the project completion time.

$$Min \qquad Z = t_n - t_1$$

$$S.t. \qquad t_j - t_i \geq t_{ij} \text{ for all jobs (i, j)}$$

$$\ell_{ij} \le t_{ij} \le k_{ij} \qquad \text{for all jobs (i, j)}$$

$$T_{ij} \ge 0 \quad \text{for all } i = 1,2,\ldots\ldots n$$

The solution gives the least project duration that can be achieved by additional budget B, the activities to be crashed and their durations.

Model-III

Let $\quad$ T* --optimal length of the project

$$F = \frac{Indirect\ cos\,t(off)}{Per\,unit\,time}\,\alpha\ project\ duration$$

$F\,(t_n\text{-}t_1) = \text{Indirect cost},\qquad t_n\text{-}t_1 = \text{unknown length of project.}$

$$\sum_{(i,j)}^{n} C_{ij}(K_{ij} - t_{ij}) = Direct\ cos\,t$$

t_{ij}—unknown length of job(i,j) i.e., the completion time of job(i,j)

Minimize the total cost.

$$Min\,Z = f\,(t_n - t_1) + \sum_{(i,j)}^{n} C_{ij}(K_{ij} - t_{ij})$$

s.t. $\qquad t_j\text{-}t_i \ge t_{ij}$ for all jobs (i,j)

$\qquad\qquad \ell i_j \le t_{ij} \le kij$ for all jobs (i,j)

$\qquad\qquad t_i \ge 0$ for all $i=1,2,\ldots\ldots n$

In the previous **example** (section 4.5.5):

$\qquad\qquad$ Duration of project $= t_7\text{-}t_1$

$\qquad\qquad$ Overhead cost $\qquad =5(t_7\text{-}t_1)$

$\qquad\qquad$ Cost of crashing A $= 4(10\text{-}t_{1,3})$

$\qquad\qquad\qquad$ B $= 2(5\text{-}t_{1,2})$

LP formulation:

Min Z= $5(t_7\text{-}t_1)+ 4(10\text{-}t_{13})+ 2(5\text{-}t_{12})+ 2(3\text{-}t_{23})+ 3(4\text{-}t_{34})+ 3(5\text{-}t_{35})+ 5(6\text{-}t_{46})+ 1(5\text{-}t_{56})+ 4(5\text{-}t_{67})$

S.t. $\qquad t_3\text{-}t_1 \ge t_{13} \qquad\qquad 7 \le t_{13} \le 10$

$\qquad\qquad t_2\text{-}t_1 \ge t_{12} \qquad\qquad 4 \le t_{12} \le 5$

$\qquad\qquad t_3\text{-}t_2 \ge t_{23} \qquad\qquad 2 \le t_{23} \le 3$

$\qquad\qquad t_4\text{-}t_3 \ge t_{34}\,. \qquad\qquad 3 \le t_{34} \le 4$

$\qquad\qquad t_5\text{-}t_3 \ge t_{35} \qquad\qquad 3 \le t_{35} \le 5$

$$t_6 - t_4 \geq t_{46} \qquad 3 \leq t_{46} \leq 6$$
$$t_6 - t_5 \geq t_{56} \qquad 2 \leq t_{56} \leq 5$$
$$t_7 - t_6 \geq t_{67} \qquad 4 \leq t_{67} \leq 5 \qquad\qquad t_1, t_2, \ldots \ldots \ldots t_7 \geq 0$$

The above LP has 15 decision variables. Setting t=0, an optimal solution is found by the simplex method as

$t_2=5$, $t_3=8$, $t_4=11$, $t_5=13$, $t_6=17$, $t_7=21$, $t_{13}=8$, $t_{12}=5$, $t_{23}=3$, $t_{34}=3$, $t_{35}=5$, $t_{46}=6$, $t_{56}=4$, $t_{67}=4$.

The optimal project length=21 days minimum cost of project = \$121. Job A is crashed by 2 days jobs D, G and H each crashed by 1 day.

Gantt Chart

This technique of using a special type of bars representing activities has been developed by Henry Gantt and named as *Gantt chart*. The Gantt chart is also known as the *Timeline chart*. It is useful, used to allocate resources to various activities. The resources are manpower, computer hardware, workspace etc. Each bar, an activity, is drawn against a timeline. The shaded part of the bar is the estimated time and the white part of the bar is called the *slack time* by which the activity has to finish. Therefore, the shaded part can be shifted, if necessary, to any part to the extent of the white bar limitation. This allows the project manager to allocate resources suitably by shifting the activity on the timeline without affecting other activities. Many activities can start concurrently. *Figure 4.25* shows the activities to be carried out on a timeline.

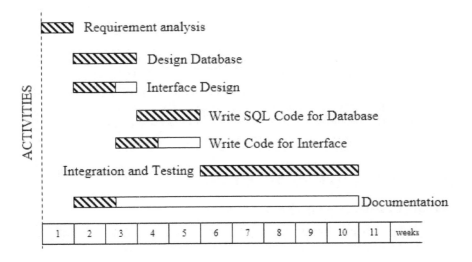

Figure 4.25: *Gantt Chart for Software Development*

Points to be Remembered

Critical Path Analysis is an effective and powerful method of assessing:

- What tasks must be carried out
- Where parallel activity can be performed
- The shortest time in which you can complete a project
- Resources needed to execute a project
- The sequence of activities, scheduling and timings involved
- Task priorities
- The most efficient way of shortening time on urgent projects.

An effective Critical Path Analysis can make the difference between success and failure on complex projects. It can be very useful for assessing the importance of problems faced during the implementation of the plan.

PERT is a variant of Critical Path Analysis that takes a more skeptical view of the time needed to complete each project stage.

Summary

To improve the software process, the managers and the practitioners need to do proper planning, tracking and control the software project. The software project, the process, and the software product to be judiciously measured which will help the management to determine the requirement of resources. A function point is required to measure the problem complexity. The size of the problem is assessed through a line of code to measure the man month/effort requirement. The planner plays a great role in estimating project duration, effort, and resource requirements. Scheduling of a project, on combining with estimation and risk analysis becomes a road map for the project manager. In scheduling, the process is decomposed into various tasks along with their precedence. The tasks are critically examined after obtaining the project critical path. The necessary resource allocation is done to further reduce the individual task completion times which helps in reducing the project cost.

Questions and Answers

1. **What is software project planning?**

   It sets up a time based plan for a software project and software process management. It includes time, cost, manpower and precedence of activities.

2. **What is software project tracking (PT)?**

   Project tracking is the visibility of software process activities to facilitate identifying deviation from software project planning.

3. **What is intergroup coordination (IC)?**

   Intergroup coordination establishes collaboration between teams of different project.

4. **Name three generic project team organizations.**

   Democratic decentralized (DD)

   Controlled decentralized (CD)

   Controlled centralized (CC)

5. **Define a DD type team organization.**

   This software engineering team does not have a permanent leader. Task coordinators are appointed leaders for short duration. Communication among team members is horizontal.

6. **Define a CD type team organization.**

   This has a defined leader who coordinates specific tasks while secondary leaders have responsibility of sub-tasks. Communication among sub-groups and individuals is horizontal.

7. **Define a CC type team organization.**

   Top-level problem solving and internal team coordination are managed by a team leader. Communication between the leader and the team member is vertical.

8. **What are the characteristics of a DD team structure?**

High level difficulty is expected.	Size of team is small.
The team has a long lifetime.	Team reliability is high.
Delivery date of the project is lax.	Team sociability is high.

9. **What are the characteristics of a CD team structure?**

Low difficulty.	Team size is large.
Lifetime of the team is short.	Reliability is high.
Delivery date of project is lax.	Low sociability among team members.

10. **What are the characteristics of a CC team structure?**

Low difficulty.	Team size is large.
Lifetime of the team is short.	Reliability is high.
Delivery date of the project is strictly fixed.	Team sociability is low.

11. Name a few project coordination techniques.

Formal and impersonal approach.

Formal and interpersonal procedure.

Informal and interpersonal procedure.

Electronic communication.

Interpersonal network.

12. What is the objective of project planning?

The objective of software project planning is to provide a framework that enables managers to make reasonable estimates of resources, cost and schedules. The first activity in software project planning is determining software scope.

13. What resources are needed for software development?

Human resources.

Usable software resources.

Environmental resources.

14. Name the different types of projects.

- **Concept development projects.** These are initiated to explore some new business concept or application of some new technology.
- **New application development projects.** These are undertaken as a consequence of a specific customer request.
- **Application enhancement projects.** These occur when existing software undergoes major modifications. Its function, performance or interface are observable by the end user.
- **Application maintenance projects.** These correct, adapt or extend existing software in ways that may not be immediately obvious to the end user.
- **Re-engineering projects.** That are undertaken with the intent of rebuilding an existing legacy system in part or in whole.

15. Name two project scheduling tools.

Program evaluation and review techniques (PERT).

Critical path method (CPM).

16. Which activities are involved in project planning?

Estimation of effort.

Breaking down the product function.

Selective the appropriate process model.

Selecting the project type and task set.

17. What are the different ways of tracking the schedule of the project?

Conducting periodic project status meeting.

Evaluating results of all reviews conducted throughout the software engineering process.

Determining whether formal project milestones have been accomplished.

Comparing the actual starting date to the planned date for each project task.

18. List the main components of a software project plan.

Purpose of the plan.

Project scope and objectives.

Project estimate.

Risk management strategy.

Schedule.

Project resources.

Staff organization.

Tracking and control mechanism.

19. What specific questions should a project plan consider?

What is to be produced for delivery?

What tasks must be accomplished?

When must these tasks be started and completed?

What is the order in which these tasks must be accomplished?

What are the activities needed for the task?

What are the criteria for accepting the end product?

How is the task to be performed and who will do it?

20. Name some important reviews.

Acceptance test readiness review.

Build design review.

Critical design review.

Operational readiness review.

Preliminary design review.

System concept review.

System specification review.

System test readiness review.

21. What is the role of a project manager?

A project manager plans, monitors and controls a team of software engineers.

22. What is the role of a software engineer?

A software engineer manages day-to-day activities, and plans, monitors, and controls the technical tasks.

23. What the role of a senior manager?

A senior manager coordinates the interface between the market and the software professionals. He also defines the business issues that have a significant impact on the project.

24. List the activities those are carried out during software project management.

a. Project definition

b. Evaluation of project

c. Cost estimation

d. Project plan development

e. Managing for change

f. Measuring and tracking

g. Scheduling

h. Enhancing professionalism

i. Usage of data

j. Incorporating communication mechanism

k. Causal analysis

l. Managing tools and environments

m. Software reliability measures

n. Management practices

o. Identification of human issues involved

25. Name three points that a project planner must estimate before a project begins.

How long it will take.

How much effort is required?

How many people will be involved?

26. What is a timeline chart?

A timeline chart, also called a Gantt chart, enables one to determine what tasks will be performed at a given point of time.

27. What is risk management?

Risk management includes the processes, methods and tools to manage risks in a project. It provides a disciplined environment for proactive decision making to:

Access continuously what could go wrong i.e. risks.

Determine which risks are important.

Implement strategies to deal with them.

28. Why is there pressure to do risk management more systematically?

The pressure to improve project performance, time-to-market, reduce costs, and improve management practices is driving organizations to avoid expensive problems. Hence the need is to manage risk more effectively.

29. What will risk management do for my business?

There will be a behavioral and cultural shift from fire-fighting and crisis management to proactive decision-making so that problems are avoided before they arise. Anticipating what might go wrong will become a part of everyday business, and managing risks will be as integral to program management as problem or configuration management.

30. What are the consequences of not doing risk management?

Management will not have an insight into what could go wrong; consequently, more resources will be spent on correcting problems that could have been avoided. Besides, catastrophic problems (surprises) may occur without warning (and with no recovery possible), decisions will be made without complete information or adequate knowledge of future consequences, the probability of successfully completing the program is reduced, and your program will always be in crisis.

31. What are the categories of a project estimation technique?

Expert judgment is made individually or in teams. For example, Wideband Delphi techniques.

Theoretical models for formulae or algorithms. e.g. Halstead's software science.

Analogy with other similar projects. e.g. Function point analysis.

32. What are the steps involved in structured project management?

Visualize the goal.

Make a list of the jobs that need to be done.

Ensure there is one leader.

Assign people to jobs or tasks.

Manage expectations, allow a margin of error and have a fallback position.

Use an appropriate leadership style.

Know what is going on.

Tell people what is going on.

Repeat the above steps until the last step can be achieved.

Realize the project goal.

33. List the main applications of function points.

The main applications of function points are:

a. Sizing for the purpose of effort/cost estimations.

b. Sizing for the purpose of normalization by using function points to compute quality, density, productivity etc.

34. Compare function points with the measure of lines of code.

a. Unlike LOC, FPs can be extracted early in the software life cycle and so can be used in simple cost estimation models where size is the key parameter.

b. Being a measure of functionality FPs are more closely related to utility than LOC.

c. FPs are language independent.

d. FPs can be used as a basis for contracts in the requirement phase.

However:

e. FPs are difficult to compute, and different people may count FPs differently.

f. Unlike LOC, FPs cannot be automatically extracted.

g. There is some empirical evidence to suggest that FPs are not very good for predicting effort. Empirical evidence also suggests that FPs are unnecessarily complex.

35. What do function points measure?

Function points are supposed to measure the amount of functionality in a software product, where product can mean any document from which the functional specification can be extracted such as the code itself, the detailed design, or the specification. Function points are defined in a language independent manner, so the number of function points should not depend on the particular product representation. Function points are commonly interpreted as a measure of size.

36. What are the drawbacks of function points?

   a. The main drawback of function points is the difficulty in computing them. You must have at least a very detailed specification. This task is not easily automated or even repeatable. Different people will generally arrive at a different FP count for the same specification, although the existence of standards helps minimize the variance.

   b. The definition of function points was heavily influenced by the assumption that the number should be a good predictor of effort. Here the function point measure is trying to recapture more than just functionality. Thus, FPs are not very well defined from the measurement theory prospective.

   c. FPs have been shown to be unnecessarily complicated. It does not measure the functionality and does not help to improve the predictive accuracy when FPs are used for effort prediction.

37. State the productivity equation.

$$\Pr oductivity = \frac{size}{effort}$$

Size is usually measured in lines of code, and effort is measured in person months. Thus software developers calculate productivity as:

$$\Pr oductivity = \frac{lines\_of\_code}{person\_months}$$

38. Is the software quality measure 'number of faults per thousand lines of code' a useful one?

The measure is quite useful for developers but is almost useless for users or potential purchasers. For developers, who measure both LOC and faults in a code in a consistent manner, the measure will indicate:

- Broad differences in quality among different modules, systems and teams.
- Trends that can aid quality control efforts.
- Potential trouble parts in the system.
- When the developers have reached the diminishing point in testing.

Exercise

1. Discuss the benefits of network technique in project planning and control.

2. The basic cost-time data for jobs in a project are as given belowj in table 4.23:

Job	Normal time		Crash time		Cost of Crashing per day
	Days	Cost (Rs)	Days	Cost (Rs)	
A	3	140	2	210	70
B	6	215	5	275	60
C	2	160	1	240	80
D	4	130	3	180	50
E	2	170	1	250	80
F	7	165	4	285	40
G	4	210	3	290	80
H	3	110	2	160	50
Total		1,500		1,890	

Table 4.23: Data Table

The activity (Job) dependencies are as given:

(i) A, B, C are starting activities.

(ii) Activities D, E, and F can start once A is completed.

(iii) Activity G can start after B and D are completed.

(iv) Activity H can start after C and E are completed.

(v) Activities G, F and H are the final activities.

(a) Draw the network and indicate the critical path.

(b) What is the total time required to complete the project? (based on normal time)

(c) If the project is to be completed in 8 days, what is the minimum cost to be incurred? Indicate the cheapest cost schedule.

3. A small software project is composed of seven activities whose time estimates are listed in the listed in the Table 4.24. Activities identified by their beginning (i) and ending (j) node members.

Activity		Estimateed Duration (weeks)		
i	j	Optimistic	Most Likely	Pessimistic
1	2	1	1	7
1	3	1	4	7
1	4	2	2	8
2	5	1	1	1
3	5	2	5	14
4	6	2	5	8
5	6	3	6	15

Table 4.24: Data Table

a. Draw the project network and identify all paths through it.

b. Find the expected duration and variance for each activity.

c. Calculate early and late occurrence times for each node. What is the expected project length?

d. Calculate the total slack for each activity.

3. The following table lists the jobs of a network along with their time estimates:

Activity		Duration (days)		
i	j	Optimistic	Most Likely	Pessimistic
1	2	3	6	15
1	6	2	5	14
2	3	6	12	30
2	4	2	5	8
3	5	5	11	17
4	5	3	6	15
6	7	3	9	27
5	8	1	4	7
7	8	4	19	28

Table 4.25: Data Table

    a. Draw the project network.

    b. Calculate the length and variance of the critical path.

    c. What is the approximate probability that jobs on the critical path will be completed by the due date of 41 days?

    d. What is the approximate probability that jobs on the next most critical path will be completed by the same due date?

    e. What is your estimate of the probability that the entire project will be completed by the due date? Explain.

4. To develop a software project, what are different types of COCOMO estimation models are used? Give suitable examples of software product development projects belonging to each of the types.

5. What do you mean by a project? How do you manage a project?

6. What is project scope? Why is it necessary while developing a project?

7. What is the importance of activity sequencing? What are the tools and techniques are used?

8. For the cost drivers to be multiplied together the underlying assumption is that they must be independent of each other, does this sound reasonable?

9. If all cost drivers were at minimum value, what would be the product of the cost drivers?

10. If all cost drivers were at maximum value, what would be the product of the cost drivers?

11. Based on the results to the two questions above, what is the ratio between maximum and minimum possible predicted effort?

12. Does the possible range from maximum to minimum effort seem reasonable?

13. COCOMO starts from estimate of size, subjective assessment of 15 (independent?) cost drivers (with values - on potentially a 6-point scale - based on 60+ datasets), to estimate effort. How much confidence should you have in the final estimate?

14. Discuss Putnam's model in contrast to Jensen model to estimate effort requirement in software project development.

15. While developing a software product what are risk factors one has to consider?

16. Explain what is a project plan?

17. What do you mean by size of a project? Discuss on size estimation.

18. As the manager of a software project to develop a product for business application, if you estimate the effort required for completion of the project to be 100 man-months, can you complete the project by deploying 100 software professionals for a period of one month? Justify your answer.

   (Hint: A women takes 9 months to produce a baby. Can 9 women produce the baby in one month time?)

19. You are developing a software product in the organic mode. You have estimated the size of the product to be about 2,00,000 lines of code. Compute the nominal effort and the development time of the product.

20. A small maintenance project consists of the jobs in the following table. With each job is listed its normal time and a minimum, or crash, time (in days). The cost in dollar per day of crashing each job is also given in *table 4.26*.

Job		Normal duration (days)	Minimum (crash) duration (days)	Cost of crashing ($/day)
i	j			
1	2	9	6	20
1	3	8	5	25
1	4	15	10	30
2	4	5	3	10
3	4	10	6	15
4	5	2	1	40

Table 4.26: Data Table

   a. What are the normal project length and its minimum project length?

   b. Determine the minimum crashing cost of schedules ranging from normal length down to, and including, the minimum length schedule. That is, if L = length of normal schedule, find the cost of schedules which are L, L-1, L-2, and so on, days long.

   c. Overhead costs total $60 per day. What is the optimum length schedule in terms of both crashing and overhead costs? List the scheduled duration of each job for your solution.

a.   20 days; 12 days

b.

Length (days)	Crashing cost ($)	Total cost ($)
20	0	1200
19	15	1155
18	30	1110
17	45	1065
16	85	1045
15	130	1030
14	195	1035
13	260	1040
12	335	1055

Table 4.27: Data Table

c.   Optimum length = 15 days (see part b.)

job   (1, 2)   :   9 days

(1, 3)   :   8 days

(1, 4)   :   14 days

(2, 4)   :   5 days

(3, 4)   :   6 days

(4, 5)   :   1 day

CHAPTER 5
Software Project Analysis and Design

Objectives

During the analysis and design of a project, the designer must know (a) what the software product will do and (b) how the software accomplishes the task. These are laid down in the **Software Specification Requirement (SRS)** in the form of design-to-specification, and software function and performance specification. At this stage, the software documentation and requirement specification must be complete. The *objective* is to meet the need for a good specification and meticulously usage of the specification requirement at each level of software development. The *objective* of this chapter is to describe the analysis and design requirements, identify and classify the design levels, describe the need to design a database and coordinate and correlate all the steps of the design process.

Introduction

The analysis and design concepts provide the software developer with a foundation from which more sophisticated methods can be applied. A set of fundamental concepts has evolved.

1. **Abstraction -** Abstraction is the process or result of generalization by reducing the information content of a concept or an observable phenomenon, typically to retain only information which is relevant for a particular purpose.

2. **Refinement -** It is the process of elaboration. A hierarchy is developed by decomposing a macroscopic statement of function in a stepwise fashion until programming language statements are reached. In each step, one or several instructions of a given program are decomposed into more detailed instructions. Abstraction and Refinement are complementary concepts.

3. **Modularity -** Software architecture is divided into components called modules.

4. **Software Architecture -** It refers to the overall structure of the software and how that structure provides conceptual integrity for a system. Software architecture is the development work product that gives the highest return on investment concerning quality, schedule, and cost.

5. **Control Hierarchy -** A program structure that represents the organization of program components and implies a hierarchy of control.

6. **Structural Partitioning -** The program structure can be divided both horizontally and vertically. Horizontal partitions define separate branches of modular hierarchy for each major program function. Vertical partitioning suggests that control and work should be distributed top-down in the program structure.

7. **Data Structure -** It is a representation of the logical relationship among individual elements of data.

8. **Software Procedure -** It focuses on the processing of each module individually.

9. **Information Hiding -** Modules should be specified and designed so that information contained within a module is inaccessible to other modules that do not need such information.

Design Considerations

There are many aspects to consider in the design of a piece of software. The importance of each should reflect the goals the software is trying to achieve. Some of these aspects are:

- **Compatibility -** The software can operate with other products that are designed for interoperability with another product. For example, a piece of software may be backward-compatible with an older version of itself.

- **Extensibility -** New capabilities can be added to the software without major changes to the underlying architecture.

- **Testability –** In a good design, every requirement is testable. A design that can not be tested against its requirements is not an acceptable design.

- **Fault-tolerance -** The software is resistant to and able to recover from component failure.

- **Maintainability -** The software can be restored to a specified condition within a specified period. For example, antivirus software may include the ability to periodically receive virus definition updates to maintain the software's effectiveness.

- **Structure –** A good design presents a hierarchical structure that makes logical use of control policies among components.

- **Modularity -** The resulting software comprises well defined, independent components. That leads to better maintainability. The components could be then implemented and tested in isolation before being integrated to form a desired software system. This allows the division of work in a software development project.

- **Discreteness –** A good design separates data, procedures (functions), and timing considerations to the extent possible. Although separated, these three design considerations cannot be completely isolated.

- **Packaging -** Printed material such as the box and manuals should match the style designated for the target market and should enhance usability. All compatibility information should be visible on the outside of the package. All components required for use should be included in the package or specified as a requirement on the outside of the package.

- **Reliability -** The software can perform a required function under stated conditions for a specified period.

- **Reusability -** The modular components designed should capture the essence of the functionality expected out of them and no more or less. This single-minded purpose renders the components reusable wherever there are similar needs in other designs.

- **Robustness -** The software can operate under stress or tolerate unpredictable or invalid input. For example, it can be designed with resilience to low memory conditions.

- **Security -** The software can withstand hostile acts and influences.

- **Usability -** The software user interface must be intuitive (and often aesthetically pleasing) to its target user/audience. Default values for the parameters must be chosen so that they are a good choice for the majority of the users. In many cases, online help should be included and also carefully designed.

- **Documentation –** A good design always comes with a set of well-written documents. An excellent design without good quality documentation becomes a poor design.

Levels of Design

A design process proceeds through a series of discrete levels. Each design level begins with a set of requirements as input and produces some form of realization as its output. The output or realization for one design level is the input or set requirements for the next design level as in *figure 5.1*. Realization means the development of a solution to the problem taken in the requirements at each design level.

The first design level, after analysis of input requirements, is a partition or decomposition of stated requirements. Further, it continues to the next levels until it produces results in the form of a specific physical realization in hardware or software. This process leads to an architecture for that design level. The design progresses top to down. The top-level architecture is system architecture. The software architecture is a detailed extension of the system architecture. The system architecture can provide guidance in developing a software structure.

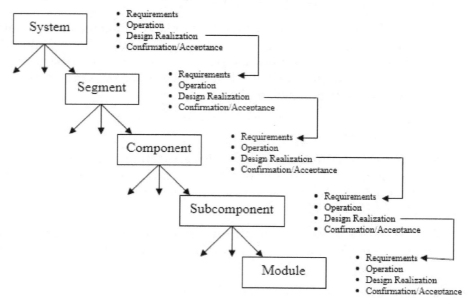

Figure 5.1: *Design Levels*

Level 1: Software System

The first level is the entire system. Some programmers jump right from the system level into designing classes, but it's usually beneficial to think through higher-level combinations of classes, such as subsystems or packages.

Level 2: Division into Subsystems or Packages

The main product of design at this level is the identification of all major subsystems. The subsystems can be a big-database, user interface, business logic, command interpreter, report engine, and so on. The major design activity at this level is deciding how to partition the program into major subsystems and defining how each subsystem is allowed to use each other subsystems.

Level 3: Division into Classes

Design at this level includes identifying all classes or components in the system. For example, a database-interface subsystem might be further partitioned into data access classes and persistence framework classes as well as database metadata. A subsystem might be divided into classes, and it implies that the other subsystems are also decomposed into classes.

Level 4: Division into Routines

Design at this level includes dividing each class into routines. The class interface defined at Level 3 will define some of the routines. Design at Level 4 will detail the class's private routines. When you examine the details of the routines inside a class, you can see that many routines are simple boxes, but a few are composed of hierarchically organized routines, which require still more design. This level of decomposition and design is often left up to the individual programmer, and it is needed on any project that takes more than a few hours. It doesn't need to be done formally, but it at least needs to be done mentally.

Level 5: Internal Routine Design

Design at the routine level consists of laying out the detailed functionality of the individual routines, i.e., modules. Internal routine design is typically left to the individual programmer working on an individual routine. The design consists of activities such as writing pseudo-code, looking up algorithms in reference books, deciding how to organize the paragraphs of code in a routine, and writing programming-language code. This level of design is always done, though sometimes it's done unconsciously and poorly rather than consciously and well.

Low Level Design versus High Level Design

In defensive programming, the use of iterative design writing in pseudo-code is a low-level design that helps in preventing defects. One can review detailed design without examining the source code. The low-level design helps in reviewing the system easier, faster, and at a reduced cost. Making changes at the low-level design stage is easy and further refinement at high-level design is less time-consuming. Successive refinement at small steps allows checking the design as we drive it to lower levels of detail. The top-down incremental integration allows beginning coding before the low-level designs are complete. Hence, the top-down approach usually involves disadvantages, in-spite of advantages, to handle buggy interfaces or performance problems before the end of the project.

The software architecture is the high-level part of software design that holds the most detailed parts of the design. The architecture is described in a single document referred to as the top-level design. A high-level design refers to design constraints that apply at sub-system or multiple class levels. In high-level design, one needs to be careful to handle invalid parameters inconsistent ways throughout the program. It causes robustness and correctness. The high-level design should indicate the inputs to and outputs from the routine. The pre-condition and the post-condition are guaranteed while passing through the routines. The system performance goal is achieved through high-level design. It avoids waste time scrapping in incremental improvements. Big optimization comes from high-level design.

The Software needs to be validated rather than proven, which means it is tested and developed iteratively until it answers the question correctly. Software is a heuristic process that needs iterative revisions and improvements. Both high-level and low-level design attempts should be repeated. A first attempt might produce a solution that works, but it might not be the best solution. Taking several repeated and different approaches it produces insight into the software problem.

Software Design Methodologies

Design is the initial step in the development of an engineering product. This is initiated only after the clear exposition of the expected product function. The design of a software system and its components should follow an orderly sequence of steps. A creative process is generally not structured and predictable. In a thought-provoking creative design process, the ideas and concepts are always continually challenged the current design baseline. The designer aims are to develop a model or abstraction of the product based on experience, heuristics, formal synthesis and realization of techniques or by following some fundamental design principles. Some design elements are intrinsic to any of the methodologies available today. The idea of top-down design and a step-wise refinement makes the design implicit. Nowadays, there is a phase shift from the function-oriented approach towards the object-oriented approach. The SRS is made using functions and performance formats. What functions the software must perform and to what performance level are analyzed.

Function-Oriented Design

The function-oriented design emerged from a popular structure paradigm. The theory of modularity or functionality underwent steady progress during the 1970s and the 1980s. When the software product became larger it was extremely difficult to handle a single monolithic block of code for debugging and maintenance. It was virtually difficult to understand the program written by another programmer. The solution was to break the product into smaller pieces called functions, procedures, or modules. Every functionality of the product is given with a name that is easy to develop or modify. These are a set of contiguous program statements having a name so that other parts of the system can invoke it. Each function can have its user interface and database. The principle of divide and conquer holds well during the design phase by having smaller independent blocks of code to suit a specific function. Testing and integrating functions is also easy.

Object-Oriented Design

Object-oriented design is different than conventional. There are many benefits available in object-oriented design. These are simplification of requirements, ease in design, and faster in implementation. The benefits are achieved by modeling the problem domain with objects that represent the important entities, by encapsulating the functions with data, by reusing the objects within a project and between projects, and by having a solution that is much closer ideally to the problem. In object-oriented design, there is only one kind of module, i.e., abstract data type module. Using object-oriented design terminology, we call such modules as classes. A class exports the operations that may be used to manipulate its instances. Such operations are defined by procedures, usually called methods in object-oriented terminology.

Coupling and Cohesion
Cohesion

The extent to which all instructions in a module related to a single function is called *cohesion*. In a cohesive module, all of the instructions in the module pertain to performing a single, unified task. Try to maximize cohesion in modules. Maximally cohesive modules also tend to be the most loosely coupled. Achieve high levels of cohesion in system design helping in minimizing coupling. If a module is designed to perform one and only one function, then it does not need to know about the interior working of other modules. The cohesive module only needs to take the data it is passed, act on them, and pass its output on to its super-ordinate module. The seven types of cohesion are as follows:

Functional cohesion

It is the most desirable type in that all instructions contained in the module pertain to a single function or task. Many times, the name of a module will indicate that it is *functionally cohesive, e.g.,* maintain the proper temperature for steel furnace, calculate interest rate, or select supplier.

Sequential cohesion

The instructions inside the sequential cohesive modules are related to each other through the data that are input rather than through the task being performed. The first instruction acts on the data that are passed in, and the second instruction uses the output of first instruction then becomes input for the third instruction, and so on. Sequence or the ordering of events is very important.

Example: 5.1   CUT DOWN TREE

CUT TREE INTO PLANKS

PLANE PLANKS

SAND PLANKS

SAW PLANKS TO SPECIFICATIONS

PUT PLANKS TOGETHER TO MAKE DOOR

Communicational cohesion

The activities are also related to each other by the data the module uses but the sequence is not important. Each instruction in this module acts on the same input data or is concerned with the same output data.

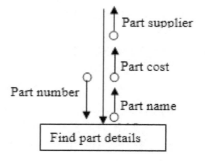

Figure 5.2: *Example of communicational cohesion*

Using Part number

find part_name

find part_name

find part_cost

find part_supplier

Figure 5.3: *Part details on input*

The module *find part detail* shown in *figure 5.2* is so vague that it tips you off to the module as not being functionally cohesive. The module is designed to use part number as input to find a *part's name, cost, and supplier (figure 5.3)*. The sequence is not important as it does not matter whether name, cost, or supplier are found first or last.

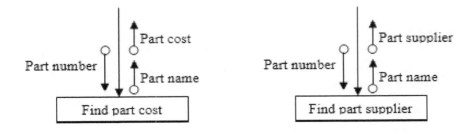

Figure 5.4: Splitting into two functional modules

A communicational cohesive module is easier to understand and maintain if it is split into two functionally cohesive modules shown in *figure 5.4*.

Procedural cohesion

Modules exhibiting these kinds of cohesion become more and more difficult to maintain. Here the instructions in a module are related to each other through the flow of control. Instructions in a procedurally cohesive module are generally related to sequence activities.

Example: 5.2 PICK UP THE NEWSPAPER

CHECK MAILBOX FOR YESTERDAY'S MAIL

PUT NEWSPAPER AND MAIL IN BOX

WATER PLANTS

CHECK ON WATER AND FOOD FOR DOGS

MAKE SURE DOORS ARE LOCKED BEFORE LEAVING

You might leave a set of instructions like this for someone who is watching your house while you are away on vacation. Although it might seem that the order of some of the instructions can be interchanged, there is logic to the order as presented. The instructions are written in the order they would be followed.

Temporal cohesion

The instructions are related to each other through the flow of control, but the sequence does not matter. The only reasons the instructions are in the module occur at about the same point of time, hence the name *temporal*. The classic example is one that contains instructions for initializing a whole host of variables, counters, switches, and so on, throughout the system. Such a module is related to several other modules, making it very difficult to change the timing of a particular initialization step without affecting other modules that rely on the other instructions in the initialization module.

Logical cohesion

The instructions are hardly related to each other. This consists of several sets of instructions, but the particular set being executed is determined from outside the module. Typically, a flag that specifies what is to be done is passed in from the outside. A non-system example is:

Example: 5.3   EAT AT RESTAURANT

                EAT AT YOUR DESK

                EAT AT HOME

                SKIP LUNCH

People write logically cohesive modules to develop parts of functions that have some lines of code or the same buffers. Maintenance is very difficult.

Coincidental cohesion

It is the worst type because the instructions have no relationship to each other at all. These are the result of haphazard factoring, attempts to save time in design. Modules that suffer from this are rare. A *decision tree* that helps to distinguish the types of cohesion given in *figure 5.5*.

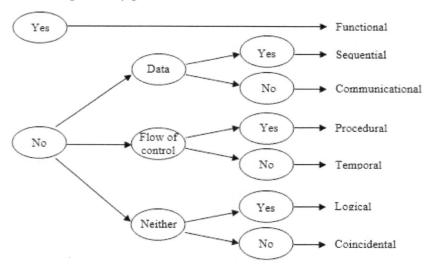

Figure 5.5: Cohesion in the form of a decision tree

Coupling

The extent to which modules are inter-dependent is called *Coupling*. Ideally, you want to minimize interdependence among modules. More dependency among modules causes more errors. Programmer, while modifies the IS has more difficulty if the code inside one module is dependent on the code in other modules. Changing the code in one module may then cause unwanted/unexpected changes in other modules that are dependent. The more the modules are independent more the life easier for the programmer and make a better IS.

Data coupling

Neither module has any idea about what goes on inside the other module. The super-ordinate module has no idea to know what goes on inside to calculate the new balance. Similarly, the sub-ordinate module does not need to know what all goes on inside the super-ordinate module. It only needs to know what data it requires and what data it returns. The data coupling is shown in *figure 5.6*.

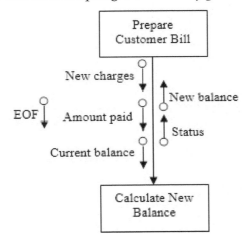

Figure 5.6: Data Coupling

Stamp coupling

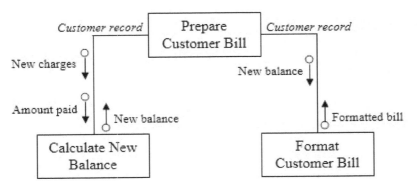

Figure 5.7: Passing Records through Stamp Coupling

Data are passed in the form of *data structure* or *entire records*. It is not quite good as data coupling because using data record instead of data element makes the system more complicated. Changes in data structure will affect all modules that use it. This stamp coupling in *figure 5.7* makes the module more dependent on each other to avoid errors. This coupling exposes modules to more data than they need.

Control coupling

When one module passes control information to another module, the two are said to be *control-coupled*. The sending module must know a great deal about the inner working of the receiving module. This is shown in *figure 5.8*.

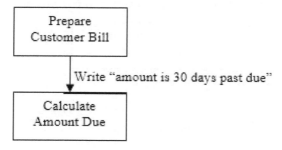

Figure 5.8: Control coupling

Common coupling

When two modules refer to the same global data area, they are commonly coupled. Global data areas are possible in many computer languages like **FORTRAN** (common block) and **COBOL** (data division). This coupling is undesirable because of the tremendous opportunity for errors to spread throughout the system. An error in any module using the global data area can show up in any other module using the same area. The level of module interdependence becomes quite high.

Content coupling

By so far it is the worst type of coupling. It involves one module directly referring to the inner working of another module. For example, one module may alter data in a second module or change a statement coded into another module. Modules are tightly intertwined. There is no semblance of independence. Higher-level languages, fortunately, have no provisions for creating content coupling.

Software Design Approach
Top-Down Design

It is the most widely used approach. It attempts to gain a broad understanding of the information needs of the entire organization. It begins by conducting an extensive analysis of the organization's mission, objectives, and strategy and then determining the information requirements needed to meet each objective. The problem is broken down into the major tasks. Each of the tasks is further broken down into sub-tasks, and so on until each task is sufficiently simple to be a self-contained module. The program then consists of a series of simple modules.

Initially, describe the problem at the highest and most general level. The description of the problem should be *what must be done* but not how it must be done. The initial description is at a higher level is very much complex. All the operations are taken at this level and individually break them down into simpler steps that will describe how to do the tasks. When the steps are represented as acceptable algorithmic steps, no further refinement is required. If not a second step refinement is initiated. The stepwise refinement continues till the highest-level operation is described in terms of acceptable shortest statements.

This method is used throughout the system analysis and design phases. It is started from a general level to gain an understanding of the system and gradually moving down to levels of greater detail. In moving from top to downward, each component is exploded into finer detail.

To summarize, the problem is broken down into major components and then further broken into smaller steps until they are simple to write the code. Therefore, the process involves working from the most general to most specific.

Advantages:

a. **Broader prospective:** If not viewed from the top, the information system (IS) may be implemented without first understanding the business from the general management viewpoint.

b. **Improved integration:** If not viewed from the top, the new management information system may be implemented rather than planning and designing how to evolve the existing system.

c. **Improved management support:** If not viewed from the top, planners may lack sufficient management acceptance of the role of IS in helping them to achieve business objectives.

d. **Better understanding:** If not viewed from the top, planners and designers may lack the understanding necessary to implement IS across the entire business rather than simply to individual operating units.

In the stepwise refinement, we expand and define each of these separate sub-tasks until the problem is solved. Each sub-task is tested and verified before it is expanded further. It helps in:

- Increased intellectual manageability and comprehension.
- Abstraction of unnecessary lower-level details.
- Delayed decisions on algorithms and data structures until they are needed.
- Reduced debugging time.

Bottom-Up Design

It requires the identification of business problems and opportunities which are used to define projects. When the problem is too large and complex it may be very difficult to decompose. It may be easier to attack parts of the problem individually, taking the easier aspects first and thereby gaining the insight and experience to tackle the more difficult tasks, and finally bolt them all together to form the complete solution. Using a bottom-up approach for creating IS plans can be faster and less costly to develop than using a top-down approach and can also have the advantage of identifying pressing organizational problems. Yet the bottom-up approach often fails to view the informational needs of the entire organization. This can result in the creation of disparate IS and databases that are redundant or not easily integrated without substantial network.

Disadvantages:

a. It suffers from the disadvantage that the parts of the program may not fit together very easily.

b. There may be a lack of consistency between modules, and considerable reprogramming may have to be done.

Software Specification Tools

There are a variety of tools and techniques used in developing and representing software specifications. Practitioners use them with great success. The tools are used in developing software requirements specification, and other related specifications. Though the tools are enough to completely develop a successful product they affect a successful software product.

Decision Support Tools

A decision tool is required when one alternative has been chosen from several possible alternatives. The software engineer can make an objective decision based on all the information and wisdom available at the time of decision required. A decision has to be taken when required. A decision process should say why one alternative is better than others. It helps in eliminating the subjectivity and solve the problem in a quantitative approach. There are some tools used in software design are discussed in detail in subsequent sections.

Decision table

A *decision table* is appropriate when a large number of conditions are to be checked in arriving at a set of actions. Decision tables have many other advantages for computer processing. The decision table is not a programming language-oriented. It is oriented towards the specifications of what is to be done in a process. The specification is non-procedural, used for communicating and documenting complex decision procedures. Consider an example: Give a discount of 5% if the customer pays advance or if the purchase is for   Rs 10,000 or more and the customer is a regular one. (*Table 5.1*).

		Rule-1	Rule-2	Rule-3	Rule-4
	Advance payment made?	Y	N	N	N
Conditions	Purchase amount > 10,000?	-	Y	Y	N
	Regular Customer?	-	Y	N	-
Actions	Give 5% discount	X	X	-	-
	No discount	-	-	X	X

Table 5.1: Decision Table of Discount Decision

Rule-1:   If advance payment made

          Then give 5% discount

Rule-2:   If no advance payment is made and if the purchase amount > 10,000 and regular customer

          Then give 5% discount

Rule-3:   If no advance payment is made and if purchase amount > 10,000 and the customer not regular

          Then give no discount

Rule-4:   If no advance payment is made and if purchase amount is not > 10,000

          Then give no discount

Example:5.4 A university has the following rules for a student to qualify for a degree with physics as the main subject and mathematics as the subsidiary. (a) Marks should be 50% or more in physics and 40% or more in mathematics, (b) If marks in physics are less than 50% then marks in mathematics must be 50% or more. However, physics marks must be at least 40%, (c) If marks in mathematics are less than 40%

but those in physics are 60% or more then only examination in mathematics has to be repeated, and (d) In all other cases the student fails. *(Table 5.2)*.

		Rule-1	Rule-2	Rule-3	Rule-4
Conditions	Physics marks	>50%	>40%	>60%	Else
	Mathematics marks	>40%	>50%	<40%	
Actions	Pass candidate	X	X	-	-
	Repeat mathematics	-	-	X	-
	Fail candidates	-	-	-	X

Table 5.2 Decision Table for University Problem

Table 5.3 is interpreted as:

Rule-1:   If physics marks >50% and mathematics marks >40%
            Then pass candidate

Rule-2:   If physics marks >40% and mathematics marks > 50%
            Then pass candidate

Rule-3:   If physics marks >60% and mathematics marks <40%
            Then repeat mathematics examination

Rule-4:   In all other cases fail the candidate (i.e. if none of the rules 1, 2, 3 is true) then the rule marked else holds.

Decision tree

Let us consider an example. Book stores get a trade discount of 25% for orders, from libraries and individuals, 5% allowed on orders of 6 to 19 copies per book title; 10% on orders for 20 to 49 copies per book title; 15% on orders for copies or more on book title.

A policy statement like this can be time-consuming to describe and confusing to implement. The analyst needs to use tools to portray the logic of the policy. The first such tool is the *decision tree*. As shown in *figure 5.9*, a decision tree has many branches as there are logical alternatives. It simply sketches the logical structure based on the stated policy. In this respect, it is an excellent tool. It is easy to construct, easy to read, and easy to update. It shows only the skeletal aspects of the policy, however in the sense that it does not lend itself to calculations or show logic as a set of instructions for action.

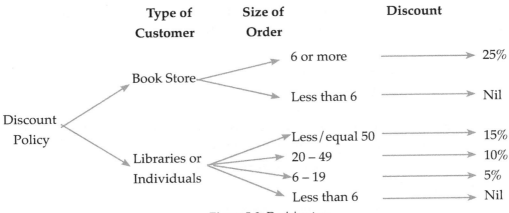

Figure 5.9: Decision tree

Structured english

It borrows heavily from structured programming; it uses logical construction and imperative sentences designed to carry out instructions for action. Decisions are made through IF, THEN, ELSE, and SO statements. The structured English for our publisher's discount policy, discussed in section 5.8.1.2, is shown in the following example. Note the correlation between the decision tree and structured English.

Example:5.5

    COMPUTE_DISCOUNT
            Add up the number of copies per book title
    IF order is from bookstore
            And-IF order is for 6 copies or more per book title
                    THEN: discount is 25%
            ELSE (order is for less than 6 copies per book title)
                    SO: no discount is allowed
    ELSE (order is from libraries or individual customers)
            SO-IF order is for 50 copies or more per book title
                    Discount is 15%
            ELSE IF order is for 20 to 49 copies per book title
                    Discount is 10%
            ELSE IF order is for 6 to 19 copies per book title
                    Discount is 5%
            ELSE (order is for less than 6 copies per book title)
                    SO: no discount is allowed

The process ORDER may have the data elements ORDER_SIZE, which defines four values: MINIMUM: 5 or fewer copies per book title

SMALL: 6 to 19 copies

MEDIUM: 20 to 49 copies

LARGE: 50 or more copies.

Using the values, the structured English example as above would read as shown in the following example with data dictionary values.

Example: Structured English using Data Dictionary values.

COMPUTE_DISCOUNT

Add up the number of copies per book title

IF order is from bookstore

and-IF ORDER_SIZE is SMALL

THEN: discount is 25%

ELSE (ORDER_SIZE is MINIMUM)

SO: no discount is allowed

ELSE (order is from libraries or individuals)

SO-IF ORDER_SIZE is LARGE

discount is 5%

ELSE IF ORDER_SIZE is MEDIUM

discount is 10%

ELSE IF ORDER_SIZE is SMALL

discount is 5%

ELSE (ORDER_SIZE is MINIMUM)

SO: no discount is allowed

From these examples, we see that when logic is written out in English sentences using capitalization and multilevel indentation, it is structured English. Structures are indented to reflect the logical hierarchy. Sentences should also be clear in wording and meaning.

In structured English, the syntax rules are not very strict. The aim is to allow easy readability which aids documentation and maintenance and at the same time ensures some discipline in process description which will help the programmer. Some guidelines for using structured English given below.

(i) **Imperative sentences:** It consists of an imperative verb followed by operations to be performed on variables. It is important to use precise verbs.

Examples are:

    Multiply gross price by the discount rate.

    Store results in rebate.

    Subtract rebate from gross price and obtain net price

(ii) **Arithmetic and relational operations:** Common symbols used in mathematics are used in structured English descriptions. The symbols are:

+ add, - subtract, * multiply, / divide, and = equal

Relations like >, <, <, >, not equal

Logical operations and, or, not

Symbols used as key words *if, then, else, repeat, until, while, do, case, for, of, end*

Example: {Receive 'store issue note'.

    Select item issued record from 'store issue note'.

    Cost of issued item = quantity * price of item.

    Balance in account = balance in account – cost of issued item}

(iii) **Decision structures:** Branch in and branch out conditions are considered here.

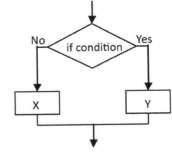

If-then-else

if condition

    then

        (group Y statements)

    else

        (group X statements)

Endif

Case

case (variable)

(variable = P): statement for alt

(variable = Q): statement for alt

...

...

none of the above:

    statement for default case

endcase

Example:5.6 A company makes 3 products which are codified as class A, class B, and class C. On class A, items for purchase above Rs 5,000, 10% discount is given. On class B, for purchase above Rs 8,000, a discount of 5% is given. On class C, for a purchase of Rs 10,000 and above, 4% discount is given. Covert to structured English.

```
case (Prduct class)
(Product class = A)
            {if purchase > 5,000
            then
                    Discount = 10%}
(Product class = B)
            {if purchase > 8,000
            then
                    Discount = 5%}
(Product class = C)
            {if purchase > 10,000
            then
                    Discount = 4%}
None of the above
                    Discount = 0
endcase
```

(iv) **Repetition:** A sequence of operations are carried out many times. The number of repetitions to take place is governed by the type of structure used in the description. If the repetition is fixed use for structure.

Example: Total marks = 0

        for subject = 1 to subject = 5   *do*

                total marks = total marks + marks(subject);

                write students, roll number, total marks

        endfor

Example: *while* there more student records *do*

        read student record

        total marks = 0

      for subject = 1 to subject = 5 *do*

              total marks = total marks + marks(subject);

              write students, roll number, total marks

      endfor

    endfor

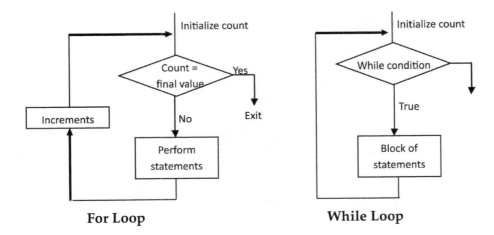

| | For Loop | | While Loop |

Data Structure

This is to specify the name of each data structure and the elements it represents, provided they are defined else wherein the data dictionary. Some elements are mandatory, whereas others are optional. The data element of the data structure is as shown in *table 5.3.*

		Mandatory	Optional
Data structure	BOOK_DETAILS		
	AUTHOR_NAME	X	
	BOOK_TITLE	X	
	EDITION	X	
Data elements	ISBN (International Standard Book No.)		X
	LOCN (Library of Congress Number)		X
	PUBLISHER_NAME	X	
	QUANTITY_ORDERED	X	

Table 5.3: Data Structure of a Book

	Comments
BOOK_DETAIL	rom Prentice Hall of India
AUTHOR_NAME	
BOOK_TITLE	
EDITION	Recent edition
QUANTITY_ORDERED	Minimum 40 copies

Data Dictionary

It is an important tool in the software development process. It is a comprehensive definition of all of the data elements in a given software system. In a data dictionary, one will find a clear and complete definition of each data item. The data dictionary often becomes a source document for the specification and design of input processing, files, and data structures, processing algorithms, and output processing. The information required to design a module to process inputs must include a description of protocols, scaling, encryption, maximum/minimum/average values, timings, etc. The design of files and records requires detailed knowledge of both static and dynamic data elements. Production of structure charts, data flow diagrams, and process specifications are also depending heavily on the data dictionary. Data dictionary features within a CASE repository are especially valuable for the system analyst when cross-referencing data items. Cross-referencing enables us to describe the data item to be stored and accessed by all individuals so that a single definition for a data item is established and used.

Format of a data dictionary

A data dictionary is organized into five sections:
- (*a*) Data Elements
- (*b*) Data Flows
- (*c*) Data Stores
- (*d*) Processes
- (*e*) External Entities

Data dictionary lists all the data elements, data flow, data stores and processes of the system under consideration. It gives the details about each item listed in a prescribed format. The format may contain the followings:

- (*a*) **Data Type:** Data Element, Data Flow, Data Store.
- (*b*) **Data Name:** Name of the Data Element, Data Flow, Data Store.
- (*c*) **Data Aliases:** Alternative names used for the convenience of multiple users.
- (*d*) **Data Description:** A short example of data.
- (*e*) **Data Characteristics:** Frequency of use, Data length, Range of data values, etc.
- (*f*) **Data Composition:** Various data elements contained in a data store or data flow.
- (*g*) **Data Control Information:** Source of data, the user or access authorization, etc. In the case of data flow, the process from which data flow is coming and the process to which data flow is going should be indicated. In the case of data stores, incoming and outgoing data flow needs to be indicated.

(h) **Physical Location of Data:** This is indicated in terms of record, file or database.

Sample Data Dictionary for Data Element: *Emp_code*

DATA ELEMENT	:	Emp_code
DESCRIPTION	:	A unique permanent code assigned to each employee.
TYPE	:	char
LENGTH	:	4
ALIASES	:	EC, E_code
RANGE	:	0001 to 9999
DATA STORES	:	Employee table, Current Payroll table.

Sample Data Dictionary for Data Structure: Pay Slip

It is a data flow as well as a data structure.

DATA STRUCTURE	: Payslip
DESCRIPTION	: Gives the pay details of the employee for the month.
CONTENT	: Emp_code, Name, Grade, Basic_Pay, Deductions
VOLUME	: 200 per month
USED IN PROCESS	: 2.2
DATA FLOW	: Print Pay_Register and Pay_Slip
DATA STORES	: Current Payroll table.

Data Flow Diagram

Data flow diagrams provide a logical model of the system and show the low of data and the flow of logic involved. A **Data Flow Diagram (DFD)** has the following characteristics:

(a) They show the movement of data through the system.

(b) They emphasize the processes that transform incoming data flows (input) into outgoing data flows (outputs).

(c) The processes that perform the transformation of new data and use of data.

(d) The entities send and receive data flows in the system.

(e) DFD supports a top-down approach for analysis by breaking a higher level to many lower-level diagrams to cover the details of the system.

(f) It is also called as *bubble-chart*.

Symbols used in DFDs

DFDs consists of 4 symbols which are joined with lines. There may be a single DFD for the system or it may be exploded into several levels named Level 1, Level 2, and Level 3, etc. The top-level diagram is often called a *context diagram* consisting of a single process that shows the overall view of the system. The symbols used in drawing the dataflow diagram (*figure 5.10*) are:

1. **Entities:** Sometimes these are called source or sink (destinations) of the diagram. This is a noun represented by a rectangle. An entity may be people, place, customer, program or organization. Other entities can interact with the system.

2. **Data Flow:** This shows the movement of data from one point to another in the diagram. The flow is shown with an arrow headline to give the direction of flow. The data flow is given a simple and meaningful name such as a library book deposit or booking a ticket. The data flows from entity to process or process to process.

3. **Processes:** Processes show the transformation of input data flows to output data flows. It is also known as bubbles or transform. A circle denotes a process. All the processes are numbered from left to right for identification. The name of the process describes what happens to data as it flows into the system. The name should consist of a single strong verb or a singular object like calculate_net_pay, compute_balance, etc.

4. **Data Store:** A data store is basically a database or repository. This may be a database file or transaction file. Processes may store or retrieve data from a data store. An arrow pointing to a data store indicates writing and from a data, store indicates to read the data. A double-headed arrow indicates both the operations of reading and writing data in the data store. The examples are master_file, pending_documents, etc.

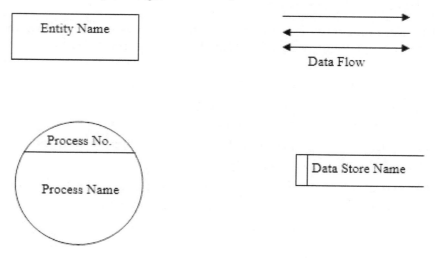

Figure 5.10: Symbols used in DFDs

Construction of DFD

The following steps may be followed to construct a DFD.

(*a*) Processes should be named and numbered for easy identification.

(*b*) The direction of flow is from top to bottom and left to right.

(*c*) Data flow from the upper left corner source to the lower right corner destination.

(*d*) The names of data stores, sources and destinations are written with the first letter being capital.

To start with, a context diagram is made. A context diagram should have a single process. It is to understand the current system with boundaries shown in *figure 5.11.*

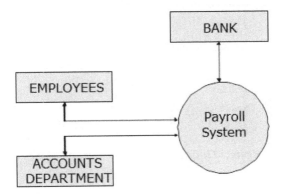

Figure 5.11: *Context Diagram*

The main process given in the context diagram is exploded into sub-processes which covers the total process. The sub-processes are one level lower than the parent process.

Developing zero level data flow diagram

The description of the payroll system in the context diagram is very brief. Hence the next step is to describe the system at level zero linking to sub-processes like Prepare

Attendance and Leave Record, Prepare Payroll Register, Prepare Bank Statements and deduction Reports, etc. in *figure 5.12*.

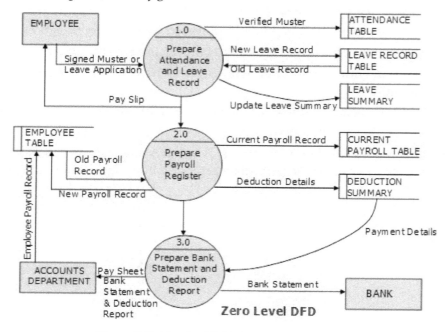

Figure 5.12: Zero level DFD for a Payroll System

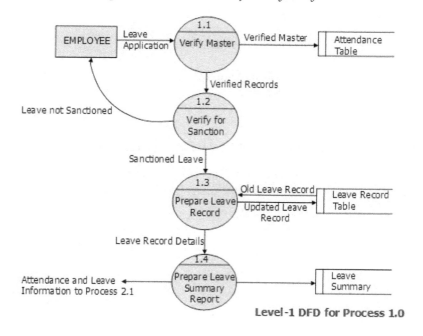

Figure 5.13: Level 1 DFD for Process 1.0

Now, the question is how far the explosions be carried out and how many levels of diagrams are needed depending upon the nature and complexity of the particular system under consideration. Generally, we should go as far as necessary to understand the details of the system and the way it functions. However, DFD must be drawn only after adequate interactions with the users of the system. Normally, the explosion is done when the process has multiple tasks of each requiring data flow.

Explanation of 1st level DFD for payroll system

The process *Prepare Attendance and Leave Statement* shown in *figure 5.12* can be broken into the following parts shown in *figure 5.13*.

    1.1 Verify Muster

    1.2 Verify and Sanction Leave

    1.3 Prepare Leave Record

    1.4 Prepare Leave Summary Report

Similarly, the process *Prepare Payroll Register* in *figure 5.12* can be broken into the following parts in figure 5.14.

    2.1 Calculate Current Pay

    2.2 Print Pay Register and Payslip

    2.3 Prepare Salary Summary Book

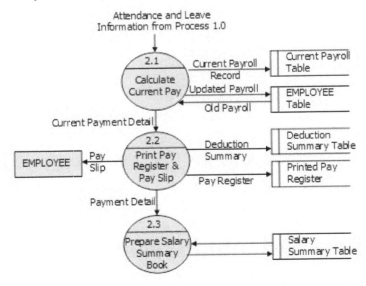

Level-1 DFD for Process 2.0

Figure 5.14: Level 1 DFD for process 2.0

Similarly, the third process *Prepare Bank Statement and Deduction Report* can be further broken into (*figure 5.15*):

3.1 Print Payment Sheet and Deduction Report

3.2 Prepare Arrears Payment Sheet

The sub-Process 2.1 cannot be initiated unless the leave record is available. This is necessary because the employee concerned might have gone on Medical Leave, Long Leave, Maternity Leave, etc. Pay has to be adjusted accordingly. Hence, the input for 2.1 is the attendance and leave information record. The old payroll record from employee Master is needed to know the Basic Pay, Dearness Allowance, House Rent Allowance, City Compensatory Allowance, and Deductions. This has to be worked out with the current payroll record to prepare an updated payroll record. The current payment details flow from 2.1 to 2.2 for printing the payroll register and pay-slips.

A deduction summary file is prepared to consolidate and send the accrued amounts to various agencies like Provident Fund Office, LIC, Income Tax departments, and so on. In sub-process 2.3, a salary summary book is prepared to account for the Government grants utilized.

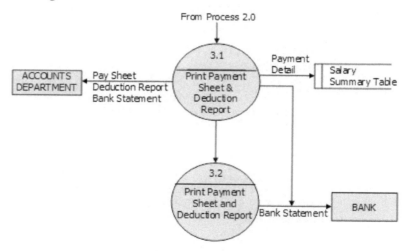

Level-1 DFD for Process 3.0

Figure 5.15: *Level 1 DFD for process 3.0*

Data Flow Oriented Design
Transaction Centered Design

In a *transaction-centered* system, the system's primary function is to send data to their proper destinations within a more general system. Data come into the central module of the system, the transaction center, and they are dispatched to their proper locations based on their data type. An example of a transaction-centered system is a system designed to process banking transactions: check deposit, savings deposit, check withdrawal, withdrawal from savings, car loan payment, and so on. Within the transaction center, the data are evaluated and dispatched, depending on their type. Deposits to checking would take one path, withdrawals from checking another path, car loan payments yet another path. Each path leads to modules designed for processing that particular type of transaction. For on-line systems, each path is a menu choice leading to the part of the system handling that type of transaction. Processes along a transaction path often have user interactions. *(Figure 5.16)*

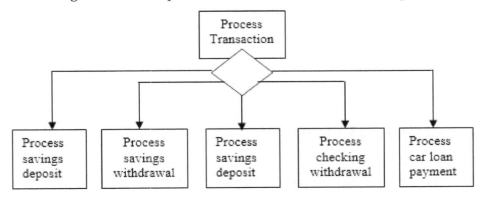

Figure 5.16: *Transaction diagram*

Transform centered design

Information systems (or a part of the information system) are typically either transaction-centered or transform-centered.

A *transform-centered system* has its central function the derivation of new data values from existing data values. The example is converting students' grades and class hours to grade point average. The other example is calculating the loan payment from an interest rate, loan period, and principal amount. The transform-centered systems, the derivation of new data, or the transformation, tends to be the core of the system. The transformation of data is often transparent to the users. The modules that represent the core, in this case, calculate interest is called the central transform. The modules that perform the task of bringing data into the system are called afferent modules. Afferent modules are arranged in groups referred to as afferent branches.

The modules that perform tasks associated with the output of the transformed data are called afferent modules, which are arranged in efferent branches. *(Figure 5.17)*

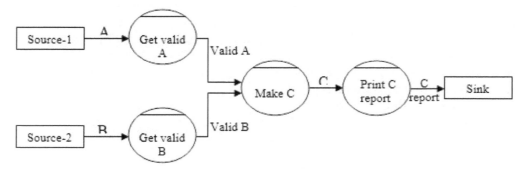

Figure 5.17 *Transform centered system*

Case Studies
Reservation System

Example:

A railway reservation system functions as follows: The passengers fill in a reservation form giving his/her particulars like starting point, destination, number of berths, sex, date of journey, train code, etc. The counter clerk checks the availability of berth from the reservation database. If the required berths are available the clerk prints the ticket, compute the charges for the ticket and a booking statement is composed. If the required berths are not available, the form is returned to the passenger. One copy of the booking statement for the day is retained as office copy, one copy is pasted on the compartment and the last copy is given to the train conductor. A cash statement is prepared at the end of each shift. Prepare a data flow diagram for the above system. *(Figure 5.18, 5.19, 5.20, 5.21)*

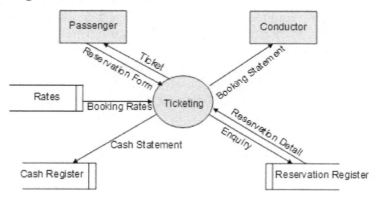

Figure 5.18: *Context Diagram*

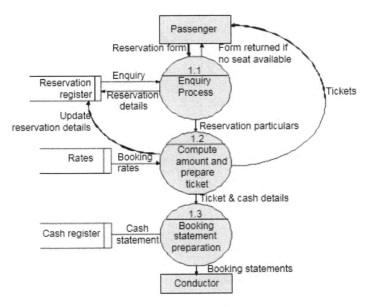

Figure 5.19: *First Level DFD*

Inventory Control

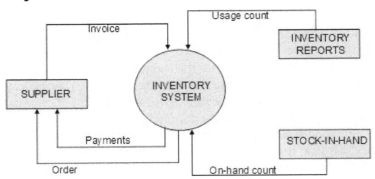

CONTEXT DIAGRAM

Figure 5.20: *Context Diagram*

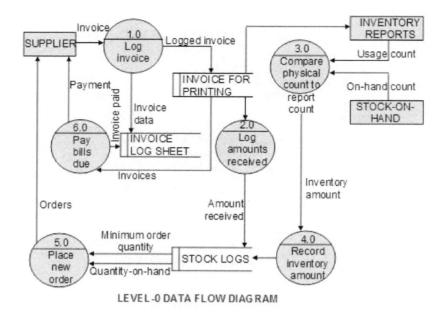

LEVEL-0 DATA FLOW DIAGRAM

Figure 5.21: Level-0 Data Flow Diagram

Summary

Preparing the right specification is the most important activity in software development. After planning, a set of well-defined specification documents will drive to successful completion of a software product. The SRS is the most critical one that plays the role of blueprint for the system. Categorization of the project requirement will be helpful during the development process, especially when there is a strong correlation between a specific requirement and development cost or schedule. Categorizing the requirements may help clients to prioritize requirements in light of cost and schedule implications. In a large software system keeping track of changes, documenting the changes, and tracing the requirements to its origin are very much difficult. These may be easy when the SRS is well written.

Questions and Answers

1. **What is cohesion? Name different types of cohesion.**

   Cohesion is a measure of the relative functional strength of a model. The types are:

   - Coincidental cohesion
   - Logical cohesion
   - Procedural cohesion

- Communicational cohesion
- Sequential cohesion
- Functional cohesion

2. **Define coupling. Name the different types of coupling.**

Coupling is a measure of relative interdependence among modules.

The types are:
- Non-direct coupling
- Data coupling
- Stamp coupling
- Control coupling
- External coupling
- Common coupling
- Content coupling

3. **What are the steps in the design process?**
- Partitioning the software development product.
- Define all the interfaces.
- Develop the operational procedures.
- Develop the data structure and the access methods.
- Using the components with real-time requirements.
- Functioning and representing the design.
- Testing the design components.

4. **What are the advantages of Modular Programming?**
   - *a.* It is easier and less costly to change features, add features or correct errors.
   - *b.* It is easier to write and debug the program.
   - *c.* It is easier to mange the system.
   - *d.* One can divide a large and complex problem into a number of modules with manageable complexity.
   - *e.* The modular concepts fit well with top-down design.
   - *f.* Formal module interface, definition may be helpful in organizing a bottom-up design.

5. **Differentiate between system analysis and system design.**

System Analysis	System Design
a. System analysis is the examination of the problem.	System design is the creation of the Information system which is the solution to the problem.
b. It is connected with identifying all the constraints and influences.	It is concerned with coordination of the activities, job procedures and equipment utilization in order to achieve system goals.
c. It deals with data collection and a detailed evaluation of present system.	It deals with general design specification, detailed design Specifications,
d. It portrays logical model of the system through data flow diagrams and data dictionaries.	It provides technical specifications and reports with which the problem Can be tackled.

6. **Define design. Name some characteristics of a good design.**

Design is the process of applying various techniques and principles for the purpose of designing a device, a process or a system with sufficient details to permit its physical realization. Software design is an iterative process through which requirements are translated into a blueprint for constructing the software.

The characteristics are:

- The design must implement all the explicit requirements contained in the analysis model.
- It must accommodate all the implicit requirements desired by the customer.
- The design must be a readable, understandable guide for those who generate code and for those who test and maintain the software.
- The design should provide a complete picture of the software, addressing the data, functional and behavioral domain from an implementation prospective.
- Software is both a process and a model.

7. **List some design principles.**

- The design process should not suffer from tunnel vision.
- The design should be traceable to analysis model.

- It should not reinvent the wheel.
- It should minimize intellectual distance.
- It should exhibit uniformity and integration.
- It should be structural to accommodate change.
- Design is not coding; coding is not design.
- It should be reviewed to minimize conceptual layout.

8. When a system design is complete?

A system design is complete when:

- A system architecture is in place.
- All system functions are defined.
- Performance parameters are established.
- Function and performance are allocated to hardware, software and computer operator personnel.

9. What are advantages of DFD?

A DFD diagram is one the best SRS techniques because, it has data flowing through a network of processes, each of which operates on a data item to produce transformation in its form. It has storage elements, which may be viewed as simply time delayed data.

10. What factors contribute to good design?

a. Documentation	*b.* Testability structure
c. Modularity	*d.* Discreteness
e. Representation	*f.* Reusability

11. What is data design?

Data design translates the data objects, defines the analysis model in the data structure within the software.

12. What guidelines need to be considered during the analysis phase?

a. Analysis must be independent of the implementation environment.

b. The analysis model must be application oriented.

c. The analysis model should describe the element of the application in application related concepts.

d. The analysis model should not be too elaborate.

13. **Define system development.**

System development is a gradual transformation of a sequence of models. The first module describes the customer requirements and the last step is the fully tested program.

14. **What is software construction?**

It is a foundation of concept and techniques selected from a universe of potential foundations that define the characteristic structure of all buildings designed.

15. Construct a decision table for the following problem. Application for admission to an extension course are screened using the rules as stated. For admission, a candidate should be sponsored by his employer and he should possess prescribed minimum academic qualification. If his fee is also paid, then he is sent a letter of admission. If the fee is not paid, then a letter of provisional admission is sent. In all other cases a letter of regret is sent.

To arrive at a decision table, we first isolate the conditions and actions.

Condition-1: Is the applicant sponsored by employer?

Condition-2: Does the applicant possess the prescribed minimum academic qualification?

Condition-3: Is the fee paid?

Action-1: Send a letter of admission.

Action-2: Send a letter of provisional admission.

Action-3: Send a regret letter.

	Rule-1	Rule-2	ELSE
C1: Is the application sponsored?	Y	Y	
C2: Does he possess prescribed minimum qualification?	Y	Y	
C3: Is the fee paid?	Y	N	
A1: Send a letter of admission.	X	-	-
A2: Send a letter of provisional admission.	-	X	-
A3: Send a regret letter.	-	-	X

16. **A policy to be followed in a stores inventory system is stated as follows:**

(*a*) If the quantity of an item ordered by a customer is available in the store, then it is shipped. The quantity of the specified item remaining in the store is checked against the order level. If it is below the reorder level then a reorder procedure is initiated.

(b)   If the quantity ordered by the customer is greater than the stock, he is asked whether he would be willing to accept partial shipment. If he is willing, then the available quantity is shipped, reorder is initiated, and quantity in stock is set to zero. The quantity to be shipped later is entered in a back-order file. If the customer does not accept partial shipment, then nothing is shipped and the entire order is entered in the back-order file and reorder is initiated. Draw a decision table.

The relevant clauses in this example are:

Conditions:

	R1	R2	R3	R4
C1: Quantity ordered < quantity in stock?	Y	Y	N	N
C2: (Quantity in stock – quantity ordered) < reorder level?	N	Y	-	-
C3: Is partial shipment acceptable?	-	-	Y	N
A1: Set quantity shipped = quantity ordered	X	X	-	-
A2: Set quantity shipped = quantity in stock	-	-	X	-
A3: Set the quantity shipped = 0	-	-	-	X
A4: Set the quantity in stock = 0	-	-	X	-
A5: Enter (quantity ordered – quantity shipped) in the back order file	-	-	X	X
A6: Initiate order procedure	-	X	X	X
A7: Quantity in stock – quantity shipped = quantity in stock	X	X	-	-

17. Extended Entry Decision Tables

There are a number of problems in which a question can have multiple answers and it is clearly and concisely expressed with the questions being extended into the concerned entry part of the decision table.

A manufacturer markets two products to three types of customers. He has the following decision policy:

The products are bulbs and fans and the customers are classified as retailers, distributors and government agencies. If the order is from a retailer for amount up to Rs 500, he allows 5% discount. If it is from a distributor, 7.5% discount is given. On retail orders exceeding Rs 500, 7.5% discount is allowed. For the same order from a distributor, 10% discount is given. In all the above cases a flat discount of 6% is given to government agencies. The above policies apply for bulbs. A flat discount of 5% is given on orders for fans regardless of the amount of purchase or the customer classification.

The action (% discount) to be allowed is dependent on three conditions.

    a.   The type of products: 1-bulbs, 2-fans

    b.   The type of customers: A-retailer, B-distributor, C-government agencies

    c.   The amount of order

	R1	**R2**	**R3**	**R4**	**R5**	**R6**
C1: Product code	1	1	1	1	1	2
C2: Customer code	A	B	A	B	C	-
C3: Order amount						
	<500	<500	>700	>500	-	-
Discount	5%	7.5%	7.5%	10%	6%	5%

It should be observed that each question is formulated combining the statement in the condition stub with that in the condition entry of the decision table. Such a table is called an extended entry decision table. This may be contrasted with the tables where questions are written in the condition stub and there answers in the action entry part of the decision table. Such tables are called limited entry decision tables.

18. In the previous example it should be noted that in an extended entry decision table more than one question is asked in a condition row of the table. This enables the table to be expressed in a condensed form. The same word statement can also be expressed as a limited entry decision table 5.8 as below:

C1: Product code = 1?	Y	Y	Y	Y	Y	N
C2: Customer code = A?	Y	-	Y	-	-	-
C3: Customer code = B?	-	Y	-	Y	-	-
C4: Customer code = C?	-	-	-	-	Y	-
C5: Order amount < 500?	Y	Y	N	N	-	-
A1: Discount 5%	X	-	-	-	-	X
A2: Discount 6%	-	-	-	-	X	-
A3: Discount 7.5%	-	X	X	-	-	-
A4: Discount 10%	-	-	-	X	-	-

Above given table could also be shown in another form, with same questions extending to the entry part and others limited to the stub. Table shown below illustrated is called mixed entry decision table corresponding to Table.

C1: Product code = 1?	Y	Y	Y	Y	Y	N
C2: Customer code	A	B	A	B	C	-
C3: Order amount < 500?	Y	Y	N	N	-	-
Discount	5%	7.5%	7.5%	10%	6%	5%

The choice of the form in which a decision table is formulated depends on the problem, available software system, need to standardize, debugging, ease of communication with lay persons etc.

19. What are the disadvantages of Modular Programming?

a. It is difficult to learn, though the principles are clear.

b. Modular programming requires more design effort.

c. Reluctance in procuring new software with modular design.

d. Needs more memory space and run time.

e. More difficult documentation.

20. What is software scope?

Software scope describes the data and control to be processed, function performance, constraints, interfaces and reliability.

21. How do you develop a design model?

a. Identify the implementation environment.

b. Incorporate conclusions to develop the design model.

c. Describe how the modules interact in specific cases.

22. What is software construction?

It is a foundation of concept and techniques selected from potential foundations that define the characteristic structure of all buildings designed.

23. What guidelines need to be considered during the analysis phase?

a. Analysis must be independent of implementation environment.

b. The analysis model must be application-oriented.

c. The analysis model should describe the element of the application.

24. What are the advantages and disadvantages of a flow chart?

Advantages: It is universally known, it is a pictorial presentation, and most easily understood by people who do not know much programming.

Disadvantages: It requires more memory space, it is clumsy for representing subroutines and interrupts, and difficult to make structural changes.

25. What are the advantages and disadvantages of Pseudo Code?

It is easy to learn, flexible, more compact, easily stored in a computer and easy to update. Some times it is difficult to understand since it not a pictorial presentation and not standardized.

Exercises

1. A bank has the following policy on deposits: On deposits of Rs 5.000 and above and for 3 years and above the interest is 12%. On the same deposit for a period less than 3 years it is 10%. On deposits below Rs 5,000 the interest rate id 8% regardless of the period of deposit. Write the above process using (*i*) structured English, (*ii*) a decision table.

2. An organization maintains an employee file in which each record has the following data: (Employee_Number, Employee_Name, Employee_Gross_Pay). It has been decided to increase the pay as per the following formula:

   For   Pay of Rs 1,000 or less increase 15%

   Pay more than Rs 1,000 but up to Rs 2,500 increase 10%

   Pay over Rs 2,500 increase 5%

   (*i*) Write a structured English processing for the above policy.

   (*ii*) Express the policy as a decision table.

3. **An offshore gas company bills its customers according to the following rate schedule:**

   First up to 500 liters Rs 10 (flat)

   Next 300 liters Rs 1.25 per 100 liters

   Next 30,000 liters Rs 1.20 per 100 liters

   Next 1,00,000 liters Rs 1.10 per 100 liters

   Above this Re 1.00 per 100 liters

   The input record has customer identification, name and address, meter reading past and present. Write a structured English procedure to obtain a bill for the customer.

4. Explain why accuracy is an important attribute for a data dictionary.

5. Use a DFD to characterize a complete credit card processing system. Give the specification for customer service part of the system using any tool.

6. Describe your university or college as a system. What is the input, output, and boundaries? What are the components, their relationships, constraints, the purpose, and interfaces? Draw a diagram of the system.

7. A car is a system with several subsystems, including the braking subsystem, the electrical subsystem, the engine, the fuel subsystem, climate control subsystem, and the passenger subsystem. Draw a diagram of a car as a system and label all of its system characteristics.

8. Define each of the following terms.
    (*a*) system
    (*b*) interface
    (*c*) boundary
    (*d*) purpose
    (*e*) modularity

9. What is decomposition? Coupling? Cohesion?

10. **Match the following terms to the appropriate definitions.**

    _____ Closed system   *a.*   systems that interact freely with their environments, taking input and returning output.

    _____ Open system   *b.*   systems that are cut off from their environments and do not interact with them.

    _____ Components   *c.*   everything external to a system.

    _____ Constraints   *d.*   limits to what a system can accomplish.

    _____ Environment   *e.*   the parts or subsystems that make up a system.

CHAPTER 6

Object Oriented Analysis and Design

Objective

The main objective of this chapter is to introduce the **Object-Oriented (OO)** methodologies and its applications in the software design process. The **OO** terminologies are described. The concepts and principles underlying the **OO** approach are discussed. The process of object identifications and class identifications are introduced in this chapter. You will also learn in this chapter that how analysis and design activities are blended in the object-oriented approach. The techniques and associated notations are incorporated into a standard object-oriented language called **Unified Modeling Languages**. The various static and dynamic models are described using **UML** with examples.

Introduction

A more recent approach to system development which is becoming more and more popular is **Object-oriented analysis and design (OOAD)**. **OOAD** is often called the third approach to systems development, after the process-oriented and data-oriented approaches. The object-oriented approach combines data and process (call methods) into a single entity called *object*. Objects usually correspond to the real things, an information system deals with, such as customers, suppliers, contracts, and rental agreements. Putting data and processes together in one place recognizes the fact that there is a limited number of operations for any given data structure. Putting data and processes together makes sense even though typical system development keeps data and processes independent of each other.

An **object-oriented** system is made up of interacting objects that maintain their local state and provide operations on that state. The representation of the state is private and cannot be accessed directly from outside the object. **Object-oriented design** processes involve designing object classes and the relationships between these classes. These classes define the objects in the system and their interactions. When the design is realized as an executing program, the objects are created dynamically from these class definitions.

Object-oriented design is part of object-oriented development where an object-oriented strategy is used throughout the development process:

1. **Object-oriented analysis** is concerned with developing an object-oriented model of the application domain. The objects, in that model, reflect the entities and operations associated with the problem to be solved.

2. **Object-oriented design** is concerned with developing an object-oriented model of a software system to implement the identified requirements. The objects in an object-oriented design are related to the solution of the problem. There may be a close relationship between some problem objects and some solution objects, but the designer inevitably has to add new objects and to transform problem objects to implement the solution.

3. **Object-oriented programming** is concerned with realizing a software design using an object-oriented programming language such as Java. An object-oriented programming language provides constructs to define object classes and a run-time system to create objects from these classes.

The Unified Modeling Language

The **UML** is the brainchild of Grady Brooch, James Rum Baugh, and Invar Jacobson. Dubbed "the Three Amigos", these gentlemen worked in separate organizations through the **1980s** and **early 1990s**, each devising his methodology for **object-oriented analysis and design**. Their methodologies achieved preeminence over those of numerous competitors. By the **mid-1990s,** they began to borrow ideas from each other, so they decided to evolve their work together.

In **1994**, Rum Baugh joined Rational Software Corporation, where Brooch was already working. Jacobson enlisted at Rational a year later.

The rest, as they say, is history. Draft versions of the **UML** began to circulate throughout the software industry, and the resulting feedback brought substantial changes. Because, many corporations felt the **UML** would serve their strategic purposes, a **UML** consortium sprung up. Members included DEC, Hewlett-Packard,

Intellicorp, Microsoft, Oracle, Texas Instruments, Rational, and others. In **1997**, the consortium produced version 1.0 of the UML and submitted it to the **Object Management Group (OMG)** in response to the OMG's request for a proposal for a standard modeling language.

The consortium expanded, generated version 1.1, and submitted it to the **OMG**, who adopted it in the late **1997**. The **OMG** took over the maintenance of the **UML** and produced two more revisions in 1998. The **UML** has become a de facto standard in the software industry, and it continues to evolve. Versions 1.3, 1.4, and 1.5 have come into being, and **OMG** recently put its stamp of approval on version 2.0. The earlier versions, referred to generically as version 1.x, have been the basis of most models.

Object orientation

Object -orientation has taken the software world by storm, and rightfully so. As a way of creating programs, it has a number of advantages. It fosters a component-based approach to software development, so that, you first create a system by creating a set of classes. Then, you can expand the system by adding capabilities to components that you've already built or by components. Finally, you can reuse the classes that you have created when you build a new down substantially on system development time.

Class

First and foremost, an **object** is an instance of a class (a category). You and I, for example, are instances of the *Person* class. An object has *structure*. That is, it has **attributes** (properties) and **behavior** or operations. We also perform these operations: eat, sleep, read, write, talk, go to work, and more (objectspeak, eat(), sleep(), read(), write(), talk(), and goToWork()). An object's behavior consists of the operations it carries out. Attributes and operations taken together are called *features*. Figure 6.1, a washing machine, is an example of an object having attributes and behavior

The concept of a **class** is best understood with an analogy. Out of several objects in a room, let us talk about the pictures on the wall. There is a class, which we can call the class of *pictures* of which the picture on the wall is an *instance* (meaning an example). The room belongs to the class of pictures, which consist of all the pictures in the world.

A **class** is a category or group of things that have the same attributes and the same behaviors. Here's an example: Anything in the **class "washing machines"** has **attributes** such as brand name, model, serial number, and capacity. **Behaviors** for things in this class include the operations "accept clothes," "accept detergent," "turn on", and "turn off". *Figure 6.1,* shows an example of the **UML** notation that captures these attributes and behaviors of a washing machine. A rectangle is an icon that represents the class. It's divided into three areas. The **uppermost** area contains the name, the **middle** area holds the attributes, and the **lowest** area holds the operations.

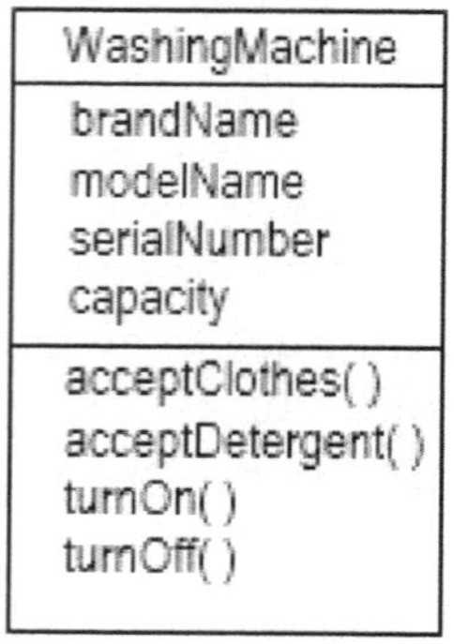

```
┌─────────────────────┐
│ WashingMachine      │
├─────────────────────┤
│ brandName           │
│ modelName           │
│ serialNumber        │
│ capacity            │
├─────────────────────┤
│ acceptClothes( )    │
│ acceptDetergent( )  │
│ turnOn( )           │
│ turnOff( )          │
└─────────────────────┘
```

Figure 6.1: *The UML class icon*

Another example is a **chair** on which I am sitting. We can call it *My Chair*. The chair across the room is also an object. We can call this second chair *Her Chair*. Both these objects share certain common characteristics or **attributes** (associated actions that enable them to be recognized or classified as belonging to a single *Chair Class*). Thus, *My Chair* and *Her Chair* are two examples (instances) of the Chair Class but they exist independent of each other and values of their characteristics or attributes differ. For example, they occupy different positions in the room, their colors are different. Thus, **Chair** is a class, but *My Chair* and *Her Chair* are *objects* or instances of *Chair* class.

As *objects* in the **Person** class, "you" and "I" each have these attributes: height, weight, and age. Each of the persons is unique because of the specific values that each of them has for those attributes. We, also, perform these operations: eat, sleep, read, write, talk, go to work, and more. The operations or functions in object *eat()*, *sleep()*, *read()*, *write()*, *talk()*, and *goToWork()*. If we were to create a system that deals with information on people say, a payroll system or a system for a human resources department, we would likely incorporate some of these attributes and some of these operations in our software.

If we specify that the *WashingMachine* class has the attributes *brandName, modelName, serialNumber,* and *capacity,* along with the operations *acceptClothes(), acceptDetergent(), turnOn(),* and *turnOff()* as shown in *figure 6.2*. You have a mechanism for turning out new instances of the *WashingMachine* class. That is, you can create new objects based on this class.

The more **attributes** and **behaviors** you take into account, the more your model will be in tune with reality. In the **washing machine** example, you'll have a potentially more accurate model if you include the attributes *drumVolume, trap, motor,* and *motorSpeed*. You might also increase the accuracy of the model if you include operations like *acceptBleach()* and *controlWaterLevel()* as shown in *figure 6.3*.

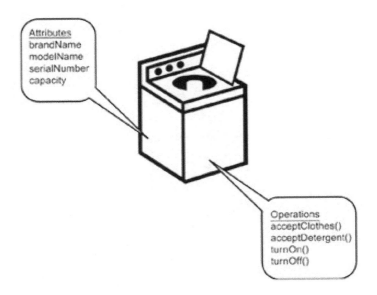

Figure 6.2: *The Washing Machine class (template for creating new washing machines instances)*

If we specify that the **Washing Machine** class has the *attributes - brandName, modelName, serialNumber,* and *capacity,* along with the *operations - acceptClothes(), acceptDetergent(), turnOn(),* and *turnOff().* You have a mechanism for turning out new instances of the **Washing Machine** class. That is, you can create new objects based on this class as in *figure 6.3.*

Object Oriented Paradigm

Object-Oriented Programming (OOP) is a programming paradigm that uses objects and their interactions to design applications and computer programs. Object-orientation goes beyond just modeling *attributes* and *behavior*. It considers other aspects of objects as well. These aspects are called *modularity, abstraction, inheritance, polymorphism,* and *encapsulation.* Three other important parts of object-orientation are *message sending, association* or *aggregation.* It was not commonly used in mainstream software application development until the 1990s. Many modern programming languages now support OOP. Let's examine each of these concepts.

Abstraction

Abstraction means, simply, to filter out an object's properties and operations until just the ones you need are left. What does "just the ones you need" mean? Different types of problems require different amounts of information, even if those problems are in the same general area. In the second pass at building a washing machine class, more attributes and operations emerged than in the first pass. *(Figure 6.3)*

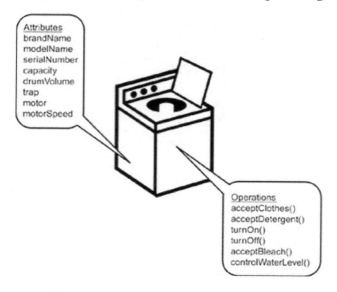

Attributes
brandName
modelName
serialNumber
capacity
drumVolume
trap
motor
motorSpeed

Operations
acceptClothes()
acceptDetergent()
turnOn()
turnOff()
acceptBleach()
controlWaterLevel()

Figure 6.3: Adding attributes and operations brings the model closer to reality.

If you're part of a development team that's ultimately going to create a computer program that simulates exactly how a washing machine does what it does, then it's worth it. A computer program like that (which might be useful to design engineers who are building a washing machine) has to have enough in it to make accurate predictions about what will happen when the washing machine is built, fully functioning, and washing clothes. For this kind of program, you can filter out the *serial Number* attribute because it's probably not going to be very helpful.

What if, on the other hand, you are going to create software to track the transactions in a laundry that has several washing machines? In this program, you probably won't need all the detailed attributes and operations mentioned. You might, however, want to include the serialNumber of each washing machine object.

In any case, what you are left with after you have made your decisions about what to include and exclude, is an abstraction of the washing machine.

Encapsulation

An object is said to **encapsulate** (hide) data and program. The user cannot see the inside of the object but can use the object by calling the program part of the object. For example, you drive a car without knowing much of the internal details. That is, the engine, gear, fuel injection system, etc. of the car are *encapsulated* and the driver need not know the details.

In a TV commercial that aired a few years ago, two people discuss all the money they'll save only if they dial a particular seven-digit prefix before dialing a long-distance phone call.

One of them asks, incredulously, "How does that work?"

The other replies: "How does popcorn pop? Who cares?

That's the essence of *encapsulation*: When an object carries out its operations, those operations are hidden (see *figure 6.4*). When most people watch a television show, they usually don't know or care about the complex electronics components that sit in the back of the TV screen and all the many operations that have to occur to paint the image on the screen. The TV does what it does and hides the process from us. Most other appliances work that way, too. Why this is important? In the software world, *encapsulation* helps cut down on the potential for bad things to happen. In a system that consists of objects, the objects depend on each other in various ways. If one of them happens to malfunction and software engineers have to change it in some way, hiding its operations from other objects means that it probably won't be necessary to change those other objects.

The TV hides its operations from the person watching it.

Figure 6.4: Objects encapsulate what they do

Turning from software to reality, you see the importance of encapsulation in the objects you work with, too. Your computer monitor, in a sense, hides its operations from your computer's CPU. When something goes wrong with your monitor, you either fix the monitor or replace it. You probably won't have to fix or replace the CPU along with it.

While we're on the subject, here's a related concept. Because, **encapsulation** means that an object hides what it does from other objects and the outside world, **encapsulation** is also called **information hiding**. But, an object does have to present a "face" to the outside world, so you can initiate those operations. The TV, for example, has a set of buttons either on the TV itself or on a remote. A washing machine has a set of dials that enable you to set temperature and water level. The TV's buttons and the washing machine's dials are called **interfaces**.

Inheritance

Inheritance is defined as the property of objects by which instances of a class can have access to data and program contained in a previously defined class. Classes are linked together in a hierarchy. They form a tree, whose root is the **class of objects**. Each class (except the root class) will have a *superclass* (a class above it in the hierarchy) and possibly **subclasses**. A class can *inherit* (acquire) methods from its superclass and in turn, can pass methods on its **subclasses**.

Washing machines, refrigerators, microwave ovens, toasters, dishwashers, radios, waffle makers, blenders, and irons are all appliances. In the world of object-orientation, we would say that each one is a **subclass** of the *Appliance* class. Another way to say this is, that, *Appliance* is a **super class** of all those others. Appliance is a **class** that has the attributes *onOffSwitch* and *electricWire*, and the **operations** *turnOn()* and *turnOff()*. Thus, if you know something is an appliance, you know immediately that it has the Appliance class's attributes and operations.

Figure 6.5 shows that *appliances* inherit the *attributes* and *operations* of the appliance class. Each one is a subclass of the appliance class. The appliance class is a superclass of each subclass. Superclass can also be subclasses and inherit from other superclasses. The appliance superclass can also be a subclass of **Householditem** class as shown in *figure 6.6.*

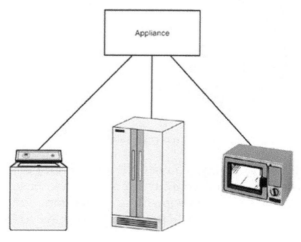

Figure 6.5: *Appliances inherit the attributes and operations of the appliance class*

Inheritance is always transitive. A class can inherit features from superclasses many levels away. For example, if Dog is a subclass of class Mammal, and class Mammal, in turn, a subclass of class Animal, Dog will inherit attributes both from Mammal and from Animal. The characteristics of mammals and animals are automatically included into dog.

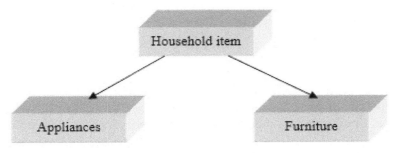

Figure 6.6: Superclass can be a subclass and inherit from other superclass

The concept of *Inheritance* is also known as **Generalization/ Specialization**. Supertype class is known as **Generalization** and the subtype class is known as **Specialization** class. For example, furniture is referred to as a generalization class whereas chair, table, and cupboards are specialization classes.

Polymorphism

Sometimes, an operation has the same name in different classes. For example, you can open a door, you can open a window, and you can open a newspaper, a presentation packet, a bank account, or a conversation. In each case, you're performing a different operation. In object-orientation, each class knows how that operation is supposed to take place. This is called **polymorphism** (see *figure 6.7*). Polymorphism includes the ability to use the same message to objects of different classes and have them behave differently.

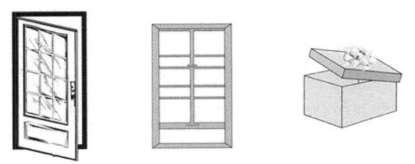

Figure 6.7: "Open", operation can have same name in different classes, and proceed differently in each class.

Thus, we could define the message "+" for both the addition of numbers and the concatenation (joining) of characters/strings, even though, both of these operations are completely different. For example, although, all window objects exhibit the same behavior, that is *open* and *close*. But, all windows do not open and close in the same manner. Some windows "swings shut" while others "slide downwards". Thus, *polymorphism* provides the ability to use the same word to invoke different methods, according to similarity of meaning.

Messages

In a system, objects work together. They do this by sending messages to one another. One object sends another a message, a request to operate and the receiving object performs that operation. A TV and a remote present a nice intuitive example (*figure 6.8*). When you want to watch a TV show, you hunt around for the remote, settle into your favorite chair, and push the "On" button. What happens? The remote object sends a message to the TV object to turn itself on. The TV object receives this message, knows how to perform the turn-on operation, and turns itself on. When you want to watch a different channel, you click the appropriate button on the remote, and the remote-object sends a different message, "change the channel", to the TV object. The remote can also communicate with the TV via other messages for changing the volume, muting the volume, and setting up closed captioning.

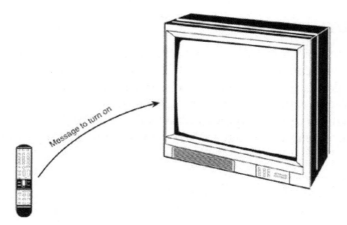

Figure 6.8: *Object sending message to another object and vice versa.*

The above figure is an example of a message sending from one object to another. The remote object sends a message to the TV object to turn itself on. The TV object receives the message through its interface, an infrared receiver.

Association

Another common occurrence is that objects are typically related to one another in some fashion. For example, when you turn on your TV, in object-oriented terms, you're in an *association* with your TV. The "turn-on" association is unidirectional (one-way), as in *figure 6.9*. That is, you turn your TV on. Unless you watch way too much television, however, it doesn't return the favor. Other *associations*, like "is married to," are bidirectional.

Figure 6.9: Unidirectional Association

Objects are often associated with each other in some way. When you turn on your TV, you're in a unidirectional association with it. Sometimes, an object might be associated with another in more than one way. If you and your coworker are friends, that's an example. You're in an "is the friend of" association, as well as an "is the coworker of" association, as shown in *figure 6.10*.

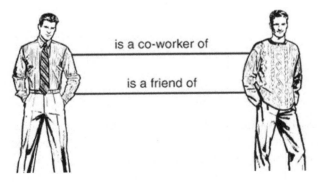

Figure 6.10: Association between objects in more than one way

A class can associate with more than one other class. A person can ride in a car, and a person an also ride in a bus (see *figure 6.11*). **Multiplicity** is an important aspect of associations among objects. It tells the number of objects in one class that relate to a single object of the associated class. For example, in a typical college course, the course is taught by a single instructor. The course and the instructor are in a *one-to-*

one association. In a pro-seminar, however, several instructors might teach the course throughout the semester. In that case, the course and the instructor are in a *one-to-many association.* You can find all kinds of multiplicities if you look hard enough. A bicycle rides on two tires (*one-to-two multiplicity*), a tricycle ride on three, and an 18 -wheeler on 18.

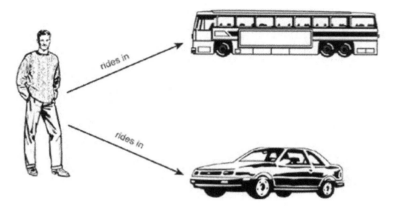

Figure 6.11: *Association of one class with more than one other class*

Diagrammatically, the associations between the two objects can be shown as in *figure 6.12.* Let's examine one - the association between a player and a team. You can characterize this association with the phrase "a player plays on a team". You visualize the association as a line connecting the two classes, with the name of the association ("Plays on") just above the line.

Figure 6.12: *An association between a player and a team.*

Class associates with another, each one usually plays a role within that association. You can show each class's role by writing it near the line next to the class. Let's examine the association between a player and a team, if the team is professional, it's an employer and the player is an employee. *Figure 6.13* shows how to represent these roles.

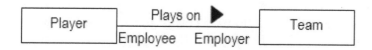

Figure 6.13: *In an association, each class typically plays a role.*

You can imagine an association that you could read in the other direction: A team employs players. You can show both associations in the same diagram, with a filled triangle indicating how to read each association in *figure 6.14*.

Figure 6.14: *Two associations between classes*

Associations may be more complex than just one class connected to another. Several classes can connect to one class. If you consider guards, forwards, and centers, and their associations with the *Team* class, you'll have the diagram in *figure 6.15*.

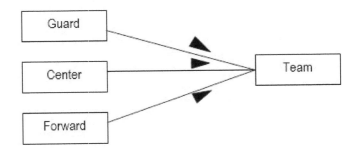

Figure 6.15: *Association of many classes with a particular class*

Sometimes, an association between two classes has to follow a rule. You indicate that rule by putting a constraint near the association line. For example, a *Bank Teller* serves a *Customer*, but each *Customer* is served in the order in which he or she appears in line. You capture this in the model by putting the word ordered inside curly brackets (to indicate the constraint) near the *Customer* class, as in *figure 6.16*.

Figure 6.16: *Constraint on an association.*

In this example, the Serves association is constrained to have the *Bank Teller* serve the *Customer* in the order. The association drawn so far between *Player* and *Team* suggests that the two classes are in **one-to-one** relationship. Common sense tells you that this isn't the case, however. A basketball team has five players (not counting substitutes). The Has association must take this into account. In the other direction, a player can play for just one team, and the *Plays* on association must account for that can relate to one object of an associated class.

Figure 6.17: *Multiplicity shows the number of objects of one class*

These specifications are examples of multiplicity - the number of objects from one class that relates to a single object in an associated class. To represent these numbers in the diagram, you place them near the appropriate class, as in *figure 6.17*.

The **UML** uses an asterisk (*) to represent more and to represent many. In one context, "**or**" is represented by two dots, as in 1. * ("one or more"). In another context, "**or**" is represented by a comma, as in 5, 10 ("5 or 10"). *Figure 6.18* shows, how to visualize possible multiplicities.

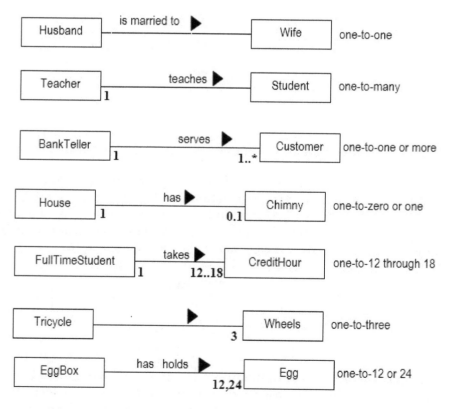

Figure 6.18: *Possible multiplicities and representation in the UML*

Aggregation

Think about your computer system. It consists of a CPU box, a keyboard, a mouse, a monitor, a CD-ROM drive, one or more hard drives, a modem, a disk drive, a printer, and possibly some speakers. Inside the CPU box, along with the aforementioned drives, you have a CPU, a graphics card, a sound card, and some other elements you would undoubtedly find it hard to live without. Your computer is an aggregation, another kind of association among objects. Like many other things worth having, the computer is made from several different types of components (see *figure 6.19*). You can probably come up with numerous examples of aggregations.

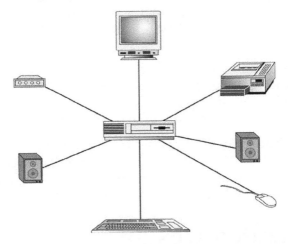

Figure 6.19: Computer system object is made up of a combination of a number of different type of objects

One form of aggregation involves a strong relationship between an aggregate object and its component objects. This is called **composition**. The key to composition is that the component exists as a component only within the composite object. For example, a shirt is a composite of a body, a collar, sleeves, buttons, buttonholes, and cuffs. Do away with the shirt and the collar becomes useless.

Figure 6.20: In a composition, a component can sometimes die out before the composite does

Sometimes, a component in a composite doesn't last as long as the composite itself. The leaves on a tree can die out before the tree does. If you destroy the tree, the leaves also die. On the destruction of the composite, the component is destroyed (see *figure 6.20*).

Object Oriented Analysis

Object-oriented analysis (OOA) looks at the problem domain to produce a conceptual model of the information that exists in the area being analyzed. Analysis models do not consider any implementation constraints that might exist, such as concurrency, distribution, persistence, or how the system is to be built. Implementation constraints are dealt with during *object-oriented design (OOD)*. An analysis is done before the Design.

The sources for the analysis can be a written requirements statement, a formal vision document, and interviews with stakeholders or other interested parties. A system may be divided into multiple domains, representing the different business, technological, or other areas of interest, each of which are analyzed separately.

The result of the object-oriented analysis is a description of *what* the system is functionally required to do, in the form of a conceptual model. That will typically be presented as a set of use cases, one or more UML class diagrams, and a number of interaction diagrams. It may also include some kind of user interface mock-up.

Object Oriented Design
Object oriented software development

Objects and frames share the property that they bring descriptive and behavioral features closely together. This shared feature, phrased from the programming angle, means that the storage structures and the procedural components that operate on them are tightly coupled. The responsibilities of frames go beyond those of objects. Frames are supposed to support complex cognitive operations including reasoning, planning, natural language understanding, and generation. In contrast, objects for software development are most often used for realizing better-understood operations.

On the programming side, the *Simula* programming language is another, even older, historical root of objects. Unsurprisingly, Simula was aimed at supporting simulation activities. Procedures could be attached to a type (a class in Simula's terminology) to represent the behavior of an instance. Simula supported parallelism, in the approximation of co-routines, allowing for many interacting entities in a simulation.

Simula objects share the close coupling of data and procedures. The concurrency in Simula was lost in Smalltalk, Eiffel, Objective-C, C++, and other popular OO programming languages. However, parallelism has reentered the OO paradigm via OO analysis methods and distributed designs. Modeling reality with "active" objects requires giving them a large degree of autonomy.

The notion of whether objects have parallel connotations or not is currently a major difference between OO analysis and OO programming. Since, we expect OO programming languages to evolve to support the implementation of distributed, parallel systems, we expect this difference to decrease. The parallel OO paradigm is well-positioned to meet these upcoming demands.

Before 1975, most software organizations used no specific techniques. Each individual worked in his/her way. The breakthrough was made between approximately 1975 and 1985, with the development of the so-called *structured* or *classical paradigm*. This included structured programming and structured testing. As time passed, this proved to be less successful and less acceptable because of:

1   The technique was unable to cope with the increasing size of software products. The classical technique was adequate for small scale software products up to 5000 lines of code. To-day large scale products of 5,00,000 lines of code is relatively common; even products of 5 million or more lines of code are not considered unusual. The classical techniques frequently could not scale up to handle such large products.

    Delivering large object-oriented software systems routinely and cost-effectively is still a significant challenge. To quote Ed Yourdon: "A system composed of 100,000 lines of C++ is not to be sneezed at, but we don't have that much trouble developing 100,000 lines of COBOL today. The real test of OOP will come when systems of 1 to 10 million lines of code are developed."

    To be fair and accurate, systems of 1,00,000 lines of C++ and those of 10,00,000 lines of **COBOL** are often of the same order of magnitude in complexity.

2   The classical paradigm did not live up to earlier expectations during post-delivery maintenance. In the classical paradigm, the cost of post-delivery maintenance used to be about two-third of the software budget. Many organizations still spend 70 to 80 percent or more of their time and effort on post-delivery maintenance [Yourdon, 1992; Hatton, 1998].

A major reason for the limited success of the classical approach is that classical techniques are either operation oriented or attribute (data) oriented, but not both. In contrast, the object-oriented approach considers both attributes and operations to be equally important. An object may be looked like a unified software artifact that incorporates both attribute and operation (an **artifact** is a component of a software product that may be a specification document, a code module, or a manual).

A **class diagram** shows the static structure of an object-oriented model: the object classes, their internal structure, and the relationship in which they participate. In **UML**, a class is represented by a rectangle with three compartments separated by horizontal lines. The class name appears on the top compartment, the list of attributes in the middle and the list of operations at the bottom compartment of the box. *Figure 6.21* shows two classes, *Student* and *Course*, along with their attributes and operations.

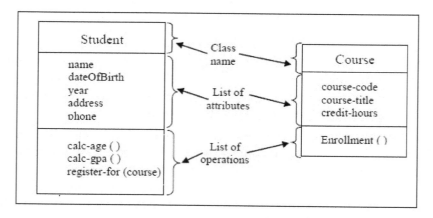

Figure 6.21: Class diagram showing two classes

A class provides a template or schema for its instance. Each object knows that it belongs to the *Student* class. An **object diagram**, also known as instance diagram, is a graph of instances that are compatible with a given class diagram. In *figure 6.22*, we have shown object diagrams with two instances. A **static object diagram** is an instance of a class diagram. In an object diagram, an object is represented as a rectangle with two compartments. The names of the project and its class are underlined and shown in the top compartment using the following syntax: **objectname: classname**. The object's attributes and their values are shown in the second compartment.

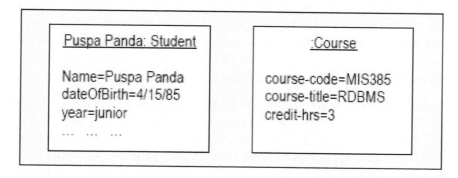

Figure 6.22: Object diagram with two instances

An *operation*, such as calc-gpa ( ), of *Student class* in *figure 6.21* is a function or a service that is provided by all instances of a class. It is only through such operations that other objects can access or manipulate the information stored in an object. It provides an external interface to a class without showing the internal structure or how its operations are implemented. The technique of hiding the internal implementation details of an object from its external view is known as **encapsulation** or information hiding [Booch, 1994; Rumbaug, et al. 1991].

Objects play the central role in all stages of project development. The entire development project becomes evolutionary in nature. Graphical representation of project-oriented version of the software development life-cycle containing overlap and feedback is shown in *figure 6.23*. This figure model shows that the development reaches a higher level only to fall back to a previous level and then again climbing up till completion of the project. Finally, these objects at each stage may need modifications to get the final results to fulfilling the aim of the project.

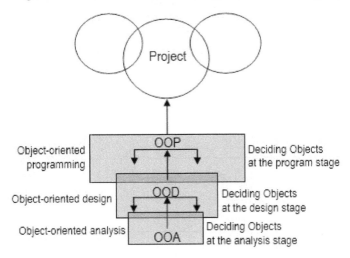

Figure 6.23: *Series of stages in project development*

The project goes through an evolutionary development life cycle containing objects decided at three different stages, namely:

    a) Objects decided at the stage of object-oriented analysis **(OOA)**.

    b) Objects decided at the stage of object-oriented design **(OOD)**.

    c) Objects finalized at the stage of final programming **(OOP)**.

In **OOA**, we decide the objects, their behavior, and their interactions meeting the requirements of the project. In **OOD**, we draw hierarchies from which the objects can be created. Finally, an **OOP**, we implement the programs in **C++** or any other **OOP** languages using objects.

A well-defined project statement will help in deciding the objects at the analysis stage. Further refinements of the objects may need to be added at the implementation stage. At the implementation stage, the objects may have to be further modified so that each object properly fits in to give the result.

In the **OO** method, all three stages work more closely because of the commonality of the object model. In one stage, the problem domain objects are identified while in the next stage; additional objects required for a particular solution are decided. The design process is repeated for these implementation level objects.

The object-oriented development life cycle is shown above, consists of progressively developing an object representation through three phases - *analysis, design, and implementation* – similar to the heart of the systems development LC. In contrast to the **SDLC**, the **OODLC** is more like an onion than a waterfall. In the early stages (or core) of development, the model you build is abstract, focusing on the external qualities of the application system. As the model evolves, it becomes more and more detailed, shifting the focus to how the system will be built and how it should function-system architecture, data structure, and algorithms. Like any information system, the system developer must generate code and database access routines. The emphasis in modeling should be on analysis and design, focusing on front-end conceptual issues, rather than backend implementation issues, which unnecessarily restrict design choices.

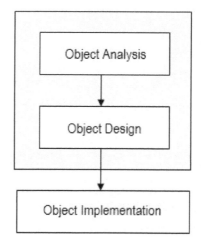

Figure 6.24: Object-Oriented life cycles

The OO development life cycle is shown in *figure 6.24*. The different components are shown in the diagram, namely *object analysis, object design,* and *object implementation* are explained in the following subsections.

Object Analysis

In **OOA**, we identify objects, which are the building blocks of the project to be developed. We perform analysis using these objects. In the module-oriented approach which we studied in previous chapters, we thought in terms of building one large system. In the **OOA**, we identify objects as independent entities with their own local goals. These independent objects are then unified to achieve the global goal of the large system. In **OOA**, we consider the following points:

a) Understand the requirements of the project.

b) Write the specifications of the requirements of the user and the software.

c) Decide the objects and their attributes.

d) Establish the services that each object is expected to provide. In other words, it is called the interface.

e) Determine interconnections among the objects in terms of services required and the services rendered.

All the above-mentioned steps are illustrated in *figure 6.25*. Note that steps c, d, and e, need not be in the order in which they are mentioned above, as they are interdependent.

In object-oriented project analysis, one of the important requirements is to identify the objects. Following are the criteria for identifying objects in a system:

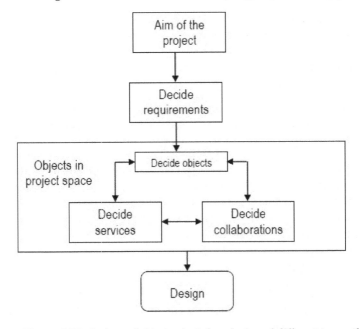

Figure 6.25: *Actions of object-oriented analysis and different types of diagrams and views supported in UML*

a) An object must perform some service in the system. In other words, we should be able to assign specific responsibilities to various objects in the system.

b) An object must have attributes whose values are examined and used in performing the service assigned to it. There must be several relevant attributes.

c) An object must be essential for the functioning of the system. This is judged by examining whether it is essential to remember information about the object.

d) There must be a common set of attributes and operations which are necessary for all occurrences of the object.

Shlaer and **Mellor** suggest classes and objects usually come from one of the following sources:

- **Tangible things** (e.g. Cars, telemetry data, pressure sensors)
- **Roles** (e.g. mother, teacher, politician)
- **Events** (e.g. landing, interrupt, request)
- **Interactions** (e.g. loan, meeting, depositing form)

For example, in a financial management system, we may identify objects like Investment, Account, and Transaction so on. Each of these will be operating with independent responsibilities.

Once the required objects are identified, we may identify their general properties and specialize them. For example, there are many kinds of investment such as investment in real estate, investment in shares, etc. All investments have some features in common like an evaluation of returns on investment as well as some features which are specific to each.

The next step is to determine the responsibilities of each object that is operations it can carry out on its own. Thereafter, determine the operations which will be performed by multiple objects in collaboration.

Thus, we can model the system as a collection of independent objects and allow these objects to communicate with each other. Communication among objects is done through the transfer of messages. A client object sends a message requesting a service from the server object. A message activates a process or method in the receiving object. The message causes the execution of the method program, which will carry out the required processing and return the response. Thus, **OOA** techniques are used to do the following three main activities:

1 Study existing objects to see if they can be reused in the new system.

2 Define new or modified objects that will be combined with the existing objects to develop the system.

3 Define responsibilities or operations for each object.

Object Design

In object design, we are required to specify the components of each object. There are different ways of accomplishing this. One way is to extend the **Entity-Relationship (ER) model**. The other way is to use the new modeling techniques specially devised for designing objects. Parallel to the definition of a relationship for the **ER model**, an association is a relationship among object classes. As in the **ER model**, the degree of an association may be done **one** (unary), **two** (binary) or **three** (ternary), or **higher** (n-ary).

Object-Oriented Entity-Relationship Model

In the **Object-Oriented Entity-Relationship (OOER)** model, we represent each entity as an object. The attributes form the object properties. Also, methods are added to the **OOER** model. These methods, also called *services*, can change object properties or perform some computations.

Object Diagram is similar to the ER diagram. It represents object properties.

Functional Model shows the changes in the object properties. It is modeled similar to **Data Flow Diagram (DFD).**

Dynamic Model represents the states of an object.

Object Design includes the following steps:

1 Refining the objects identified in the analysis phase, so that they can be implemented in the real environment.
2 Modeling the interactions among objects and their behavior.
3 Updating the object model to reflect the implementation environment.

Object Implementation

Other implementations of the systems require that the system be developed as a set of objects, using either object-oriented languages such as **C++** or object-oriented database management systems, such as **Oracle 8i** and above. The implementation is independent of the analysis or design technique followed. Thus, it is possible to perform object implementation of a system that was analyzed using **DFDs** and **ER** diagrams.

Unified Development Process

Object Oriented Development Life Cycle and Modeling:

It is a recent approach to systems development is becoming popular. **Object-Oriented Analysis and Design (OOAD)** are often called the third approach to system development, after the process-oriented and data-oriented approaches. The object-oriented approach combines data and process (cell methods) into single entities called objects. Objects usually correspond to the real things an information system deals with such as customers, suppliers, contracts and rental agreements. Putting data and processes together in one place recognizes the fact that there are a limited number of operations for any given data structure. The goal of **OOAD** is to make system elements more reusable, thus improving system quality and productivity of systems analysis and design.

A software development project can be viewed as a collection of objects that interact together to accomplish certain objectives. Objects may represent data files and functions. In an **object-oriented (OO)** design of a project, we need to decide the objects that encapsulate data and procedures.

The object is an entity that has a well-defined role in the application domain and has state, behavior, and identity. The *state* of an object encompasses its properties (attributes and relationships) and the values those properties have, and its behavior represents how an object acts and reacts [Booch, 1994]. All objects have an identity; that is, no two objects are the same. If there are two Student instances with the same name and date of birth, they are essentially two different objects Even, if those two instances have identical values for all the attributes; the objects maintain their separate identities. You can use *object instance* to refer to an individual object, and *object class* (or simply class) to refer to a set of objects that share a common structure and common behavior.

Object Modeling using UML

UML, the **Unified Modeling Language**, is used to create diagrams describing the various aspects and uses of your application before you start coding, to ensure that you have everything covered. Millions of programmers in all languages have found **UML** to be an invaluable asset to their craft. The **UML** consists of several graphical elements that combine to form diagrams. Because **UML** is a language, it has rules for combining these elements. Expert author **Joe Schmuller** takes you through step-by-step lessons designed to ensure your understanding of **UML** diagrams and syntax. This updated edition includes the new features of **UML 2.0** designed to make **UML** an even better modeling tool for modern object-oriented and component-based programming. **UML** is not a system design or development methodology. It can only be used to document object-oriented analysis and design.

Figure 6.25 above shows the various UML diagrams with their respective views. These are used for object-oriented analysis and design. The diagram shows some of the important views which are used for system development. The different views of a system are used for development by using UML [R Mall, 2003].

1. **User's view:** It defines the functionalities (facilities) made available by the system to its users. It is a *black box* where the internal structure, the dynamic behavior of system components, the implementation is not visible. This can be considered as the central view and all other views are expected to conform to this view.

2. **Structural view:** It defines the kinds of objects (classes) important to the understanding of the working of a system and its implementation. It also captures the relationship among classes (objects). It is a *static model* since the structures of a system do not change with time.

3. **Behavioral view:** It captures how objects interact with each other to realize the system behavior that captures the time dependent (dynamic) behavior of the system.

4. **Implementation view:** It captures the important components of the system and its dependencies.

5. **Environmental view:** This view models how the different components are implemented on different pieces of hardware.

Don't use all UML diagrams and modeling elements while modeling a system [Rosenberge, 2000].

Why is it necessary to have numerous views of a system? Typically, a system has several different stakeholders—people who have interests in different aspects of the system. Let's return to the **washing machine example**. If you're designing a washing machine's motor, you have one view of the system. If you're writing the operating instructions, you have another. If you're designing the machine's overall shape, you see the system differently if you just want to wash your clothes.

Conscientious system design involves all the possible viewpoints, and each UML diagram gives you a way of incorporating a particular view. The **objective** is to communicate clearly with every type of stakeholder.

Modeling Using UML

UML offers several diagrams to model a system. Each UML diagram depicts a different aspect of the system. We will first show how to develop a use-case model during the requirement analysis phase. Next, we will show how to model the static structure of the system using class and object diagrams. Then we shall capture the dynamic aspects using state and interaction diagrams. Finally, we will provide a brief description of the component and deployment diagrams, which are generated during the design and implementation phases. The various UML diagrams are discussed below:

Perform the Detailed Design

Figure 6.26 is constructed from the state chart of *figure 6.25*. For example, the event *button pushed, button unlit* is implemented by two nested **if** statements, at the beginning, *figure 6.26*. The two operations of the state:

```
void elevatorEventLoop (void)
{
   while (TRUE)
    {
      if (a button has been pressed)
          if (button is not on)
          {
             updateRequests;
             button::turnOnButton;
          }
          else if (elevator is moving up)
          {
      if (there is no request to stop at floor f)
          elevator::moveUpOneFloor;
      else
      {
          stop elevator by not sending a message to move;
          elevatorDoors::openDoors;
          startTimer;
          if (elevatorButton is on)
             elevatorButton::turnOffButton;
          updateRequest;
      }
          }
          else if (elevator is moving down)
        [similar to up case]
          else if (elevator is stopped and request is pending)
          {
      elevatorDoors::closeDoors;
```

```
    determine direction of next request;
    if (appropriate floorButton is on)
        floorButton::turnOffButton;
    elevator::moveUp/DownOneFloor;
}
else if (elevator is at rest and not (request is pending))
    elevatorDoors::closeDoors;
else
    there is no requests, elevator is stopped with
elevatorDoors closed, so do nothing;
                }
            }
```

Figure 6.26: The detailed design of method elevator Event Loop

Static and Dynamic Modeling

A **static model** describes the layout of data or arrangement of stored data (i.e. data structure) but it does not show what happens to the various parts of the system. The ER model describes earlier is a static model. In contrast, the **dynamic model** represents the states of an object. *Figure 6.27* exemplifies, the states that an object can assume in its lifetime and the transition between the states.

Dynamic Modeling: The State chart

Note that in *figure 6.27*, an application (object) for sanction of a personal loan in the bank may be received, in which case it is a *received application*. It is then checked, and it becomes *checked application*. Next, the application may be either approved or rejected. In the former case, it becomes an approved application and in the latter case, it becomes a *rejected application*. Thus, the application object goes through several states, namely the received application state, the checked application state, the approved application state and finally the *accepted application* state. The movement from one state to another is known as a *state transition*.

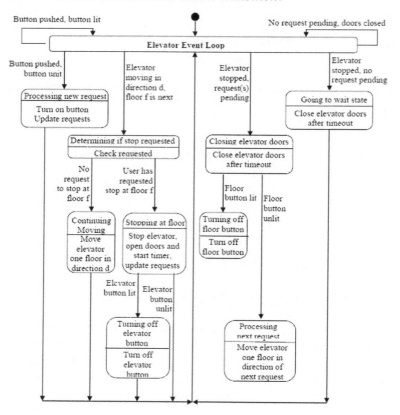

Figure 6.27: *The first iteration of the state chart for elevator controller class*

Figure 6.27 is a dynamic model. Each *state transition* is activated by an internal event or by a message from another object. Each arrow in *figure 6.27* would become a method in the application object. Hence, methods for the application object would be to *receive application, check application, approve application*, etc. The *check application* method causes a state transition from the *received application* state to the checked application state. The transition from the *checked application* state depends on the result of the methods *accept application* or *reject application*.

The Elevator Problem Case Study: Dynamic modeling aims to produce a *State Chart*, a description of the target product similar to a finite state machine, for each class. First, consider the *Elevator Controller Class*. The relevant State chart is in *figure 6.27*. The *state transition* diagrams are not a complete representation of the product to be built.

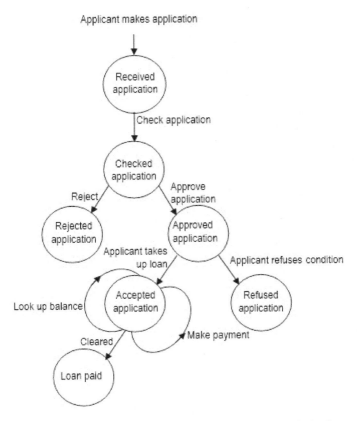

Figure 6.28: *State diagram for personal loan application in bank*

Current state and *event* and *predicate next state*

The three aspects of a state machine **(state, event, and predicate)** are distributed over the UML diagram. For example, the state *Going to wait state,* in *figure 6.27,* is entered, if the present state is *Elevator event loop* and the event elevator stopped, no requests pending is true. When going to wait state has been entered, operation *Close elevator doors after timeout* is to be carried out. The solid circle denotes the start state, which takes the system into state *Elevator event loop.* The arrows represent the events that trigger the object to change from one state to another. The state diagram depicts the life cycle of a single object. State diagrams are not required for all objects. One simpler bank loan application is shown through a UML state diagram in *figure 6.28.*

Dynamic Modeling: Sequence Diagram

A *sequence diagram* depicts the interactions among objects during a certain period. The pattern of interactions varies from one use case to another, each sequence diagram shows only the interactions pertinent to a specific use case. It shows the participating objects by their lifelines, and the interactions among those objects arranged in time sequence by exchanging messages with one another.

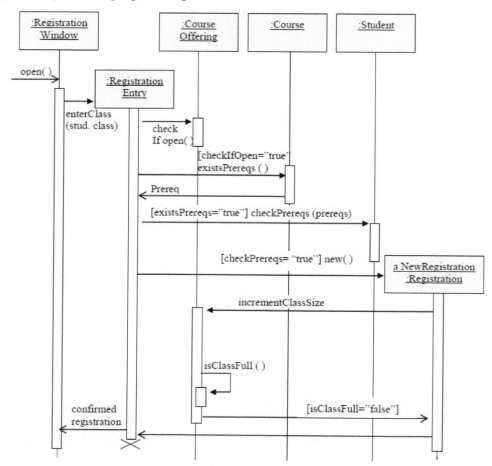

Figure 6.29: *Sequence diagram for a class registration scenario*

A **sequence diagram** may be presented in a generic form or an instance form. The generic form shows all possible sequences of interactions, i.e., the sequences corresponding to all scenarios of a use case. For example, a generic sequence diagram for the Class registration use case (see *figure 6.29*) would capture the sequence interactions for every valid scenario of that *use case*. The instance form, on the other hand, shows the sequence for only one scenario. A scenario in UML refers to a single path, among possibly many different paths, through a use case [Fowler, 1997]. In *figure 6.29*, we have shown a *sequence diagram*, in instance form, for a scenario where a student registers for a course that specifies one or more prerequisite courses as requirements.

The *vertical axis* of the diagram represents time and the *boxes* represent the participating objects. Time increases as we go down the vertical axes. The diagram in *figure 6.29* has got six *objects*, from an instance of Registration Window on the left, to an instance of Registration called a "**New Registration**" on the right. The sequence of objects do not follow any rule, however, one should try to arrange the objects in such a way that the diagram is easy to read and understand. Each object has a vertical dashed line called *lifeline*. The lifeline represents the object's existence over a certain period. An *object symbol* - a box with the object's name underlined- is placed at the head of each lifeline.

A thin rectangle, superimposed on the lifeline of an object, represents an *activation* of the object. *Activation* shows the period during which the object operates. Objects communicate with one another by sending messages. A *message* is shown as a solid arrow from sending the object to the receiving object. For example, check Open message is represented by an arrow from the Registration Entry object to the Course Offering object. Normally the arrow is drawn horizontally, but in some situations (in case of branching) you may draw a sloping message line.

The *synchronous message* shown as a full, solid arrowhead, is one where the caller has to wait for the receiving object to complete executing the called operation before it can resume execution. The synchronous message always has an associated return message. The message may provide the caller with some return value(s), or simply acknowledge to the caller that the operation called has been completed. An example of the synchronous message is checkOpen. When a Registration Entry object sends this message to a Course Offering object, the latter responds by executing an operation called checkIfOpen (same name as the message). After the execution of this operation is completed, control is transferred back to the calling operation within Registration Entry with a return value, "true" or "false". We have not shown the return for the checkIfOpen message; it is implicit. We have explicitly shown the return for the existsPrereq message from Registration Entry to Course.

A *simple message* simply transfers control from the sender to the recipient without describing the details of the communication. In a diagram, the arrowhead for a simple message is drawn as a transverse tick mark. As we have seen, the return of the synchronous message is a simple message. The "open" message in *figure 2.29* is also simple; it simply transfers control to the Registration Window object.

An *asynchronous message*, shown as a half arrowhead in a sequence diagram, is one where the sender does not have to wait for the recipient to handle the message. The sender can continue executing immediately after sending the message. *Asynchronous messages* are common in concurrent, real-time systems, where several objects operate in parallel.

Use Case Diagram

A **use case** is a description of a system's behavior from a user's standpoint. For system developers, the use case is a valuable tool: It's a tried-and-true technique for gathering system requirements from a user's point of view. Obtaining information from the user's point view is important if the goal is to build a system that real people (and not just computer files) can use.

Use-case modeling

Use-case modeling is done in the early stages of system development to help developers gain a clear understanding of the functional requirements of the system. A use-case model consists of actors and use cases. An actor is an external entity that interacts with the system. A *use case* represents a sequence of related actions initiated by an actor. There is a difference between an *actor* and a *user*. A user is anyone who uses the system. An actor, on the other hand, represents a role that a user can play. The actor's name should indicate that role. An actor is a type or class of users. A user is a specific instance of an actor class playing the actor's role. The same user can play multiple roles.

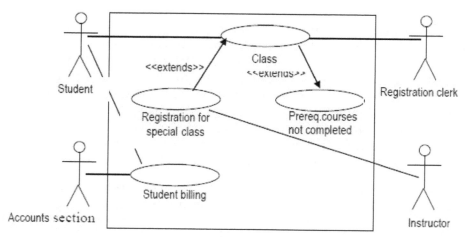

Figure 6.30: Use-case diagram for a university registration

A university registration system has a use case for class registration and another for student billing. In UML, a use-case model depicted diagrammatically as in *figure 6.30*. This *use-case diagram* is for a university registration system, which is shown in a box. Outside the box are four actors - student, registration clerk, instructor, and Accounts office, those interacting with the system. An actor is shown using a stickman symbol with its name below. Inside the box are four use-cases - Class registration, Registration for special class, Prerequisite courses not completed, and student billing. These are shown as ellipses with the name below. These use cases are performed by the actor outside the system. An actor does not necessarily have to be a human user. It could be anything (another system or a hardware device) with which the system interacts or exchanges information.

This use case performs a series of related actions at registering a student for a class. It represents complete functionality. Two actions are performed by the student user, i.e., submit the registration form as the actions of Class registration *use case* and Pay tuition as one of the actions of the Student billing use case. *(see: figure 6.31).* Therefore, a use case is a complete sequence of related actions performed by an actor and the system during a dialog. An *extend* relationship, shown as a line with an arrowhead pointing toward the extended use case and labeled with the <<*extend*>> symbol, extends a use case by adding new behavior or actions. The registration for special class use case extends the Class registration use case by capturing additional actions that need to be performed in registering a student for a special class.

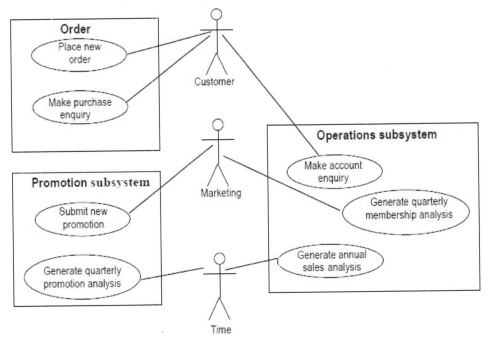

Figure 6.31: A Sample use case diagram of an ordering system

The little stick figure that corresponds to the customer, marketing, or time user is called an actor. The ellipse represents the use case. Note that, the actor, the entity that initiates the use case, can be a person or another system. Note that, the use case is inside a rectangle that represents the system, and the actor is outside the rectangle.

Class Diagram

Think about the things in the world around you. The things that surround you have attributes (properties) and they behave in certain ways. We can think of these behaviors as a set of operations. You'll also see that things naturally fall into categories (automobiles, furniture, washing machines. . .). We refer to these categories as classes. A *class* is a category or group of things that have the same attributes and the same behaviors. Here's an example. Anything in the class of washing machines has attributes such as *brand name, model, serial number,* and *capacity*. Behaviors for things in this class include the operations *"accept clothes," "accept detergent," "turn on,"* and *"turn off."* behaviors of a washing machine. A *rectangle* is an icon that represents the class (see *figure 6.32*). It's divided into three areas. The *uppermost area* contains the name, the *middle area* holds the attributes, and the *lowermost area* holds the operations.

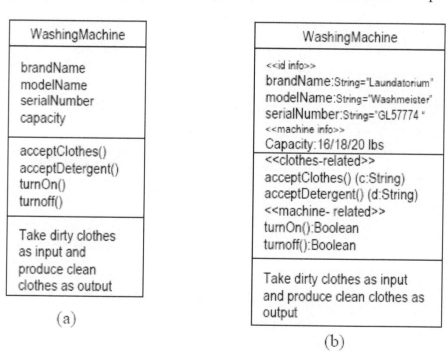

Figure 6.32: *(a) Representation of class icons of washing machine,*

(b) An attribute can show its types and default values.

Class Modeling

The detail of a class diagram is already discussed in previous section. In this section, we shall handle a case study to understand more about it.

Case study of an elevator

A product is to be installed to control n elevators in a building with *m* floors. The problem concerns the logic required to move elevators between floors according to the following constraints:

1) Each elevator has a set of **m** buttons, one for each floor. These illuminate when pressed and cause the elevator to visit the corresponding floor. The illumination is canceled when the corresponding floor is visited by the elevator.

2) Each floor, except the first floor and the top floor, has two buttons, one to request an up-elevator and one to request a down-elevator. These buttons illuminate when pressed. The illumination is canceled when an elevator visits the floor and then moves in the desired direction.

3) When the elevator has no requests, it remains at its current floor with doors closed.

The first step in **OOA** is to model the use cases. A *use case* describes the interaction between the product to be constructed and the *actors*, i.e., the external users of that product. The only interactions possible between a user and an elevator are the user pressing an elevator button to call an elevator or the user pressing a floor button to request the elevator to stop at a specific floor. Hence, two use cases, *Press an Elevator Button* and *Press a Floor Button*. The two use cases are shown in the use-case diagram of *figure 6.33*.

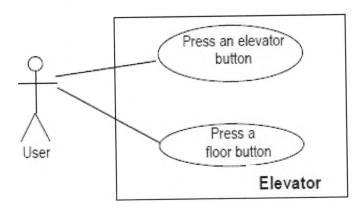

Figure 6.33: Use-case diagrams for the elevator case study

A use case provides a generic description of overall functionality. A scenario is a specific instantiation of a use case, just as an instantiation of a class. In general, there are a large number of scenarios, each representing one specific set of interactions. *Table 6.2* depicts a *normal scenario*; that is, a set of interaction between users and elevators that corresponds to the way we understand elevators should be used. *Table 6.2* is constructed by considering different users interacting with elevators (more precisely with elevator buttons and floor buttons). The 15 numbered event describes in detail the two interactions between *User A* and the buttons of the elevator system (event 1 and event 6) and the operations performed by the components of the elevator system (event 1 through 5 and event 7 through 15). Two items, *User A enters the elevator* and *User A exits from the elevator*, are unnumbered. Such items essentially are comments.

In contrast, *table 6.3* is an *exception scenario*. It depicts what happens when a user presses the Up button on floor 3 but wants to go down to floor 1. This scenario, too, was constructed by observing the actions of many users in elevators; it is unlikely that someone who has never used an elevator would realize that users, sometimes, press the wrong button.

The scenarios of *table 6.1* and *6.2*, plus innumerable others, are specific instances of the use cases as shown in *figure 6.33*. Sufficient scenarios should be studied to give OOA team a comprehensive insight into the system behavior being modeled.

Entity class modeling

The first step is to extract the entity classes and their attributes to be represented in a *UML class diagram*. The attributes of an entity class are determined in OOA. The methods are assigned to the classes during OOD.

1	User A presses the Up-floor button at floor 3 to request an elevator. User A wishes to go to floor 7.
2	The Up-floor button is turned on.
3	An elevator arrives at floor 3. It contains User B, who entered the elevator at floor 1 and pressed the elevator button for floor 9.
4	The elevator doors open.
5	The time starts.
User A enters the elevator	
6	User A presses the elevator button for floor 7.
7	The elevator button for floor 7 is turned on.
8	The elevator doors close after a time out.
9	The Up-floor button is turned off.
10	The elevator travels to floor 7.
11	The elevator button for floor 7 is turned off.
12	The elevator doors open to allow User A to exit from the elevator.
13	The time starts.

User A exits from the elevator	
14	The elevator doors close after a time out.
15	The elevator proceeds to floor 9 with User B.

Table 6.1: The first iteration of a normal scenario

1	User A presses the Up-floor button at floor 3 to request an elevator. User A wishes to go to floor 1.
2	The Up-floor button is turned on.
3	An elevator arrives at floor 3. It contains User B, who entered the elevator at floor 1 and pressed the elevator button for floor 9.
4	The elevator doors open.
5	The time starts.
User A enters the elevator	
6	User A presses the elevator button for floor 1.
7	The elevator button for floor 1 is turned on.
8	The elevator doors close after a time out.
9	The Up-floor button is turned off.
10	The elevator travels to floor 9.
11	The elevator button for floor 9 is turned off.
12	The elevator doors open to allow User B to exit from the elevator.
13	The time starts.
Table 6.3: An exception scenario	
14	The elevator doors close after a time out.
15	The elevator proceeds to floor 1 with User A.

Table 6.2: An exception scenario

One method of determining the entity classes is to deduce them from the use cases. The developers carefully study the scenarios, both normal and exception, and identify the components that play a role in the use case. From the scenarios of *tables 6.2* and *6.3*, candidate entity classes are elevator buttons, floor buttons, elevators, doors, and timers. These candidate entity classes are close to the actual classes extracted during entity class modeling. An experienced developer may be able to determine the candidate entity classes from the scenarios.

Another approach is to use noun extraction. For the developers with no domain, expertise can use two-stage *noun extraction methods* to extract candidate entity classes and then refine the solution.

Stage 1. Describe the software product in a single paragraph.

The elevator problem can be written as:

Buttons in an elevator and on the floors control the movement of **n** elevators in a building with **m** floors. Buttons illuminate when pressed to request the elevator to stop at a specific floor; the illumination is canceled when the request has been satisfied. When an elevator has no requests, it remains at its current floor with its doors closed.

Stage 2. Identify the Nouns

Identify the nouns in the informal strategy (excluding those are outside the problem boundary, and then use these nouns as candidate entity classes.

Buttons in the elevator and on the *floors* control the *movement* of n *elevators* in a *building* with **m** floors. Buttons illuminate when pressed to request the elevator to stop at a specific floor; the *illumination* is canceled when the *request* has been satisfied. When an elevator has no requests, it remains at its current floor with its doors closed.

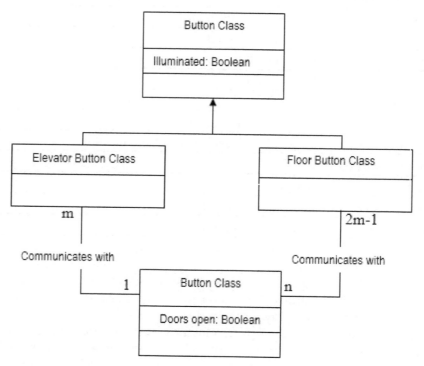

Figure 6.34: The first iteration of the class diagram

There are eight different nouns: button, elevator, floor, movement, building, illumination, request, and door. *Floor, building,* and *door* lie outside the problem boundary and therefore may be ignored. Three of the remaining nouns- *movement, illumination*, and *request* are *abstract nouns;* which identity having no physical existence. A thumb rule that abstract nouns rarely end up corresponding to classes. Instead, they frequently are attributes of classes. For example, illumination is an *attribute of button*. This leaves two nouns and, therefore two candidate classes: *Elevator Class* and *Button Class.*

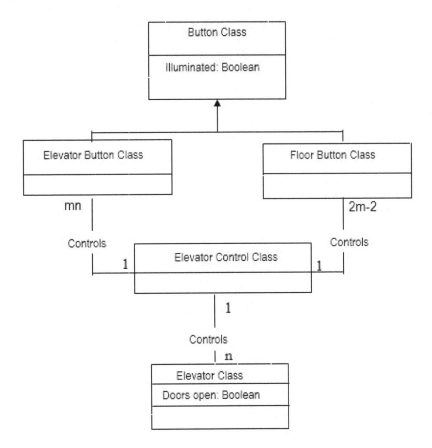

Figure 6.35: *The second iteration of the class diagram*

This is not a good beginning. In a real elevator, the buttons do not directly communicate with the elevator. An elevator controller is needed if only to decide which elevator to dispatch in response to a particular request. Adding the *Elevator Control Class* to *figure 6.34* it yields *figure 6.35*. There are now one-to-many relationships in *figure 6.34*, as opposed to the previous *figure 6.35* having a many-to-many relationship.

It, therefore, seems reasonable to go on to step 3 at this point, bearing in mind that it is possible to return to entity class modeling at any time, even as late as the implementation workflow.

Complete class diagram

Two additional operations (methods) are added (*figure 6.36*) as it used to be in Java implementation, adding two more classes. **Elevator Application Class** corresponds to the C++ main function, and **Elevator Utilities Class** contains Java routines that correspond to the C++ functions declared external to the C++ classes. The methods *closeDoor* and *openDoor* are assigned to *Elevator Door Class*. That is, a client of *Elevator Door Class* sends a message to an object of elevator door class to close or open the doors of the elevator, and that request is then carried out by the relevant method.

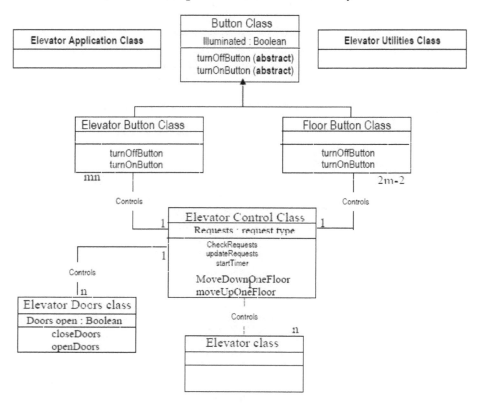

Figure 6.36: *The detailed class diagram of elevator problem*

Every aspect of those two methods is encapsulated within **Elevator Doors Class.** Also, information hiding results in a truly independent **Elevator Doors Class**, instances of which can undergo detailed design and implementation independently and be reused later in other products. The same two design principles are applied to methods *moveDownOneFloor*, and they are assigned to **Elevator Class**. Finally, methods turnOnButton and turnOffButton are assigned to both **Elevator Button Class** and **Floor Button Class**. The reasoning here is the same as for the methods assigned to **Elevator Door Class** and **Elevator Class.**

State-Chart Diagram

State diagram

At any given time, an *object* is in a particular state. A person can be a newborn, infant, child, adolescent, teenager, or adult. An elevator is either moving or stationary. A washing machine can be either in the soaking, washing, rinsing, spinning, or off state. The **UML state diagram** shown in *figure 6.37* captures this bit of reality. The figure shows that the washing machine transitions from one state to the next. The symbol at the top of the figure represents the start state and the symbol at the bottom represents the end state.

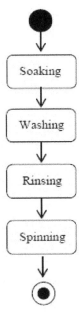

Figure 6.37: The UML state diagram

Interaction diagram / sequence diagram

Class diagrams and object diagrams represent static information. In a functioning system, however, objects interact with one another, and these interactions occur over time. The UML sequence diagram shows the time-based dynamics of the interaction. Continuing with the washing machine example, the components of the machine include a timer, a water pipe (for fresh water input), and a drum (the part that holds the clothes and the water). These, of course, are also objects (as you'll see, an object can consist of other objects) **UML, the Unified Modeling Language,** to create diagrams describing the various aspects and uses of your application before you start coding, to ensure that you have everything. What happens when you invoke the "Wash clothes" use case? Assuming you have completed the covered. "add clothes," "add_detergent," and "turn_on" operations, the sequence of steps goes something like this:

1. At the beginning of "Soaking", water enters the drum via the water pipe.
2. Remains stationary for 5 minutes.
3. At the end of "Soaking", water stops entering the drum.
4. At the beginning of "Washing", the drum rotates back and forth and continues doing this for 15 minutes.
5. At the end of "Washing", the drum pumps out the soapy water.
6. The drum stops rotating.
7. At the beginning of "Rinsing", water entry restarts.
8. The drum rotates back and forth.
9. After 15 minutes of water, entry stops.
10. At the end of "Rinsing", the drum pumps out the rinse water.
11. The drum stops rotating.
12. At the beginning of "Spinning", the drum rotates clockwise and continues for 5 minutes.
13. At the end of "Spinning", the drum rotation stops.
14. The wash is done.

Imagine that *the timer, the water pipe,* and *the drum* are objects. Assume, each object has one or more operations. The objects work together by sending messages to each other. Each message is a request from the sender-object to the receiver-object. The request asks the receiver to complete one of its (the receiver's) operations.

Let's get specific about the operations.

The timer can:

- Time the soaking
- Time the washing
- Time the rinsing
- Time the spinning

The water pipe can:

- Start a flow
- Stop a flow

The drum can:

- Store water
- Rotate back and forth
- Rotate clockwise
- Stop rotating
- Pump water

Figure 6.38 shows how to use these operations to create a sequence diagram that captures the timer, water pipe, drum, and drain represented as anonymous objects at the top of the diagram. Each *arrow* represents a message that goes from one object to another. Time, in this diagram, proceeds from top to bottom. So, the first message is timeSoak(), which the timer sends to itself. The second message is sendWater(), which the timer sends to the water pipe. The final message, stopRotating(), goes from the timer to the drum.

Collaboration diagram/ communication diagram

A *collaboration diagram* has both properties of **structural** and **behavioral** views. Within a collaboration diagram, the example objects are shown in icons. As on a sequence diagram, arrows indicate the messages within the given use case. In this case, the sequence is indicated by numbering the messages. Numbering the messages makes it more difficult to see the sequence than putting the lines down the page. In this diagram, an object is also called a **collaborator**. The behavioral aspect is described by a set of messages exchanged among different collaborators. You can see, how the objects are linked together with solid lines to send messages between two objects. You can see the various forms of UML's object naming scheme (*figure 6.38*). This takes the form *objectName:ClassName,* where the object name or the class name may be omitted. Note that, if you omit the object name, you must retain the colon, so that it is clear that it is the class name and not the object name. *(See figure 6.39)*

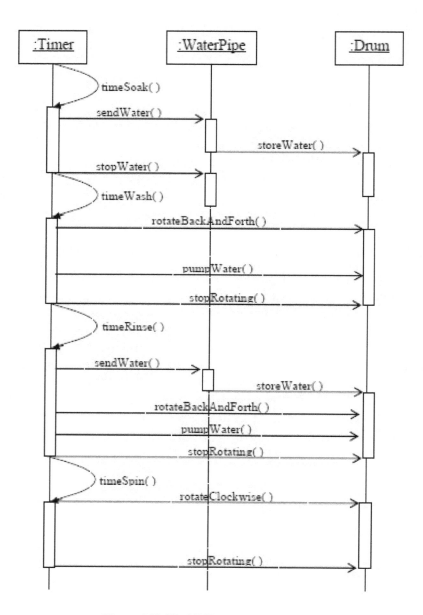

Figure 6.38: *The UML sequence diagram*

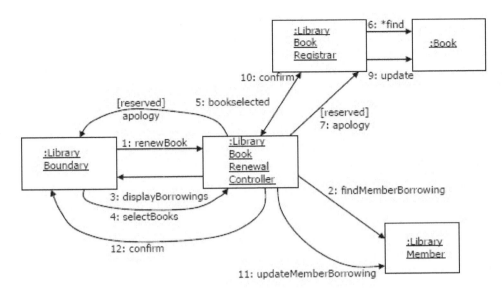

Figure 6.39: *Collaboration diagram for book renewal use case*

Communication diagram

The elements of a system work together to accomplish the system's objectives, and a modeling language must have a way of representing this. The aforementioned sequence diagram does this. The **UML communication diagram** is shown in *figure 6.40* also does this but in a slightly different way. Rather than show you the communication diagram that's equivalent to the sequence diagram in *figure 6.38*, *figure 6.40* shows you one that captures just the first few messages among *the timer*, *the water pipe*, and *the drum*. Rather than represent time in the vertical dimension, this diagram shows the order of messages by attaching a number to the message label.

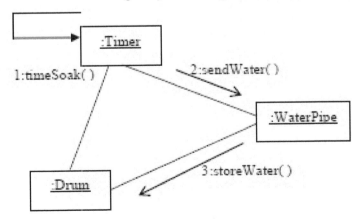

Figure 6.40: *The UML communication diagram*

The *communication diagram* shows the interaction among objects, but it does so in a way that's slightly different from the sequence diagram. In the *sequence diagram*, the *communication diagram* shows how objects interact. It shows the objects along with the messages that travel from one object to another. So, now you may be asking yourself, "If the sequence diagram does that, why does the UML need another gram? Don't they do the same thing? Is this just overkill?"

The two types of diagrams are similar. In fact, they're *semantically equivalent*. That is, they present the same information, and you can turn a sequence diagram into an equivalent communication diagram and vice versa.

As it turns out, it is helpful to have both forms. The *sequence diagram* emphasizes the time ordering of interactions. The *communication diagram* emphasizes the context and overall of the objects that interact. Here, another way to look at the distinction: The *sequence diagram* is arranged according to time, the *communication diagram* according to space. Both deal with interactions among objects, and for that reason, each one is a type of *interaction diagram*.

What is a communication diagram?

An *object diagram* shows objects and their relationships with one another. A *communication diagram* is an extension of the object diagram. In addition to the links among objects, the *communication diagram* shows the messages, the objects send each other. You, usually, omit the names of the links because they would add clutter.

One way to think of the relationship between the *object diagram* and the *communication diagram* is to imagine the difference between a snapshot and a movie. The object diagram is the snapshot: It shows how instances of classes are linked together in an instant of time ("Instants and instances". . . Remember?). The communication diagram is the movie: It shows interactions among those instances over time.

To represent a message, you draw an arrow near the link between two objects. The arrow points to the receiving object. A label near the arrow shows what the message is. The message typically tells the receiving object to execute one of its (the receiver's) operations. Arrowheads have the same meaning as in the sequence diagram.

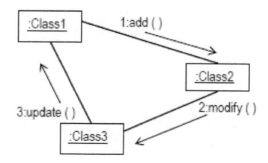

Figure 6.41: *The symbol set for the communication diagram*

To represent a message, you can turn any *sequence diagram* into a *communication diagram*, and vice versa. Thus, you have to be able to represent sequential information in a communication diagram. To do this, you add a number to the label of a message, with the number and uses of your application before you start coding, to ensure that you have everything corresponding to the message's order in the sequence. A colon separates the number from the message.

You might be familiar with the kind of car key that allows you to remotely lock and unlock a car. It also lets you open the car's trunk. If you have one of these keys, you know what happens when you push the "lock" button. The car locks itself, and then it blinks its lights and beeps to let you know it's finished locking its doors.

Let us capture all this in a class diagram. *Figure 6.41* shows the relationships among the *CarOwner*, Car, and *CarKey* classes, as well as some other concepts. The Car processes a message from the key and causes the appropriate behavior to take place.

Notice a couple of things about this diagram. In the *CarKey* class, I've shown the signature of *getButtonPress()*. This operation works with a button name ("lock," "unlock," or "openTrunk"). The idea is that the Car receives a message from the *CarKey*, processes that message, and implements the operation corresponding to the name of the pressed button.

The diagram also shows the two signals *BlinkLights* and *Beep*. You model a signal as a class with the keyword *«signal»* added. The dependency arrows between Car and each signal show that the Car sends these signals. Once again, the UML has no symbol for sending, so you add the keyword *«send»* to the dependency arrow.

Note that the *CarOwner* class shows something you haven't seen before in a class icon—the two occurrences of the «signal» keyword. These show you that *CarOwner* is capable of receiving these signals. The signals don't request the *CarOwner* to do anything. Because the Car (the sender) isn't making a request when it sends those signals, it certainly isn't waiting for the *CarOwner* to do anything. Hence, the sequence diagram uses the asynchronous message symbol to model signals.

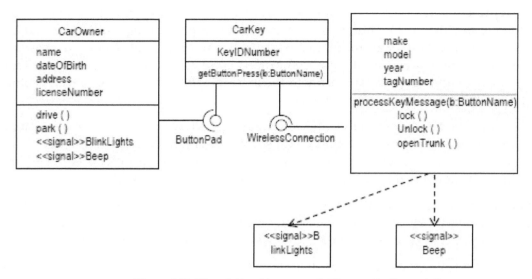

Figure 6.42: *The relationship among CarOwner, CarKey and Car*

This diagram appears in figure 6.42 and is the foundation for a communication diagram.

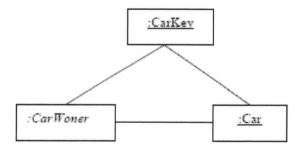

Figure 6.43: *An object diagram that models' instances of the classes in figure 6.42.*

Now, you can add messages to figure 6.43. *Figure 6.44*, shows one way of dealing with multiple messages that pass between two objects. As you can see, messages 4 and 5 are signals that go from the *Car* to the *CarOwner*. They have separate labels but not separate arrows.

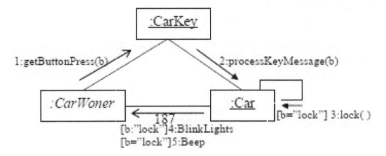

Figure 6.44: Communication diagram with messages between objects

The corresponding sequence diagram is, shown in *figure 6.45*, where the messages are sent from lifeline to lifeline. The first message (the one highest in the vertical dimension) is a request from *CarOwner* to *CarKey*. The request is for *CarKey* to implement its *getKeyPress()* operation, registering the button the *CarOwner* has pressed

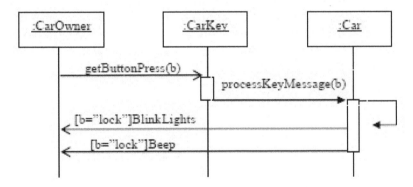

Figure 6.45: The equivalent sequence diagram of figure 6.44 with complete messages.

(generically referred to as b). The stick arrowhead indicates that *CarOwner* is transferring control to *CarKey*. *CarKey* then sends a message to *Car*, calling on *Car* to implement its *processKeyMessage()* operation, depending on the specified button. After it processes the message from *CarKey*, Car sends itself a message to implement the operation that corresponds to the pressed button. Note the expression in the bracket. That's a guard condition. It's the UML's way of saying *"if"*. So, if the pressed button is "locked", the car sends itself a request to carry out the *lock ()* operation. Then *Car* sends a message to *CarOwner* to blink the lights or beeping the light. The first message and the signals are examples of the two usages of the stick arrowhead.

Changing States and Nesting Messages

Suppose, Car has an attribute, locked, whose values are either True or False. Thinking that, "Working with State Diagrams," you can imagine two states, locked and unlocked for Car, as shown in *figure 6.46*.

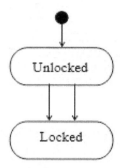

Figure 6.46: Modeling the Unlocked and Locked states of a car.

You can show a change of state in a communication diagram. To do that in this example, *figure 6.47*, you show the value of *locked* in the *Car* object. Then, you duplicate the *Car* object with the new value of *locked*. Connect the two, and then show a message going from the first to the second. Label the message with the keyword <<*become*>>.

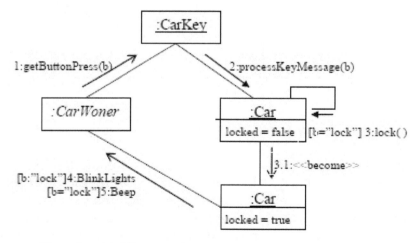

Figure 6.47: Modeling state changes in a communication diagram.

Activity diagram

The activities that occur within a use case or an object's behavior typically occur in a sequence, as in the steps listed in the preceding subsection. *Figure 6.48* shows how the UML activity diagram represents steps of that sequence.

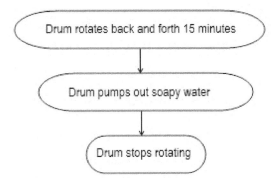

Figure 6.48: The UML activity diagram.

Activity Diagram

UML *activity diagram, figure 6.48* is much like the flowcharts of old. It's steps (called, appropriately enough, *activities*) as well as decision points and branches. It's useful for showing what happens in a business process or operation. You'll find it an integral part of system analysis. First and foremost, an *activity diagram* is designed to be a simplified look at what happens during an operation or a process.

Each activity is represented by a rounded rectangle - narrower and more oval - shaped than the state icon you saw "Working with State Diagrams." The processing within an activity goes to completion and then an automatic transmission to the next activity occurs. An *arrow* represents the transition from one activity to the next. Like the state diagram, the *activity diagram* as a starting point represented by a filled-in circle and an *endpoint* represented by a bull's-eye shown in *figure 6.49.*

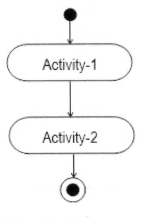

Figure 6.49: Transitioning from one activity to other

A sequence of activities almost always comes to a point where a decision has to take place. One set of conditions leads to one path, another set of conditions to another path, and the two paths are mutually exclusive.

You can represent a decision point in either of two ways: One way is to show the possible paths coming directly out of an activity and the other is to have the activity transition to a small diamond—reminiscent of the decision symbol in a flowchart—and have the possible paths flow out of the diamond. Either way, you indicate the condition with a bracketed condition statement near the appropriate path. *Figure 6.50* shows you the possibilities.

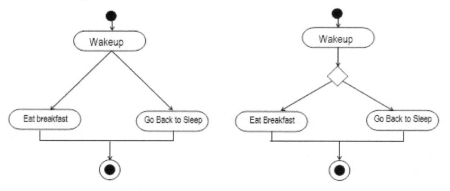

Figure 6.50: The two ways of showing a decision.

Concurrent paths

As you model activities, you'll occasionally have to separate a transition into two separate paths that run at the same time (that is, concurrently) and then come together. To represent split, you use a solid bold line perpendicular to the transition and show the paths coming out of the line. To represent the merge, show the paths pointing at another solid bold line (see *figure 6.51*).

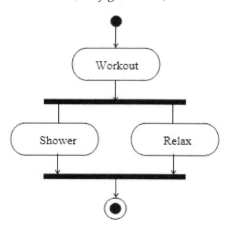

Figure 6.51: Representing a transition split into two paths that run concurrently and then come together.

Signals

During a sequence of activities, it's possible to send a signal. When received, the signal causes an activity to take place. The symbol for sending a signal is a convex polygon, and the symbol for receiving a signal is a concave polygon. *Figure 6.52* will clarify this.

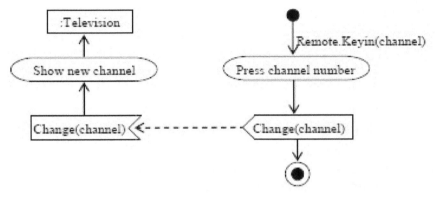

***Figure 6.52:** Sending and receiving a signal.*

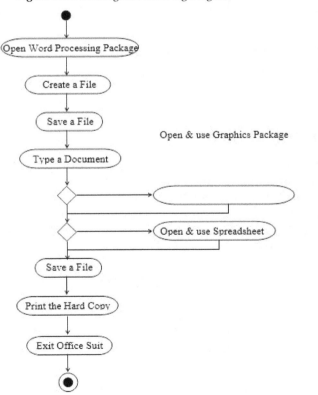

***Figure 6.53:** An activity diagram for the process of creating a document*

During a sequence of activities, it is possible to send a signal. When received, the signal causes an activity to take place. The symbol for sending a signal is a convex polygon, and the symbol for receiving a signal is a concave polygon. *Figure 6.52* will clarify this. In **UML** terms, the convex polygon symbolizes an *output event*; the concave polygon symbolizes an *input event*.

Applying Activity Diagrams

Let's look at an example that uses an activity diagram to model a process.

A process: Creating a document

1. Open the word processing package.
2. Create a file.
3. Save the file under a unique name within its directory.
4. Type the document.
5. If graphics are necessary, open the graphics package, create the graphics, and paste the graphics into the document.
6. If a spreadsheet is necessary, open the spreadsheet package, create a spreadsheet, and paste the spreadsheet into the document.
7. Save the file.
8. Print the hard copy of the document.
9. Exit the office suit.

The *activity* diagram for this sequence is in *figure 6.53*.

Component diagram

This diagram and the next one move away from the world of washing machines because the component diagram and the deployment diagram are geared expressly toward computer systems. Modern software development proceeds via components, which is particularly important in team-based development efforts. Without elaborating too much at this point, *figure 6.54* shows how the **UML version 1.x** represents a software component.

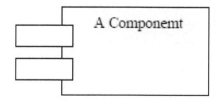

Figure 6.54: *The software component icon in UML 1.x.*

The **UML 2.0** makes an entry here. In response to the many modelers who felt this symbol as awkward, **UML 2.0** provides a revised symbol. *Figure 6.55* shows the new way to represent a software component.

Component Diagrams

A software component is a modular part of a system. Because it's the software implementation of one or more classes, a component resides in a computer, not in the mind of an analyst. A component provides interfaces to other components.

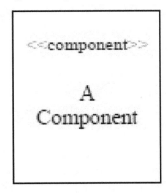

Figure 6.55: The software component icon in UML 2.0.

In **UML 1.x**, data files, tables, executables, documents, and dynamic link libraries were defined as components. Modelers used to classify these kinds of items as deployment components, work product components, and execution components. **UML 2.0** refers to them instead as *artifacts*—pieces of information that a system uses or produces.

A *component*, by contrast, defines a system's functionality. When you deal with components, you have to deal with their interfaces. The *object* has to present a "face" to the outside world so that other objects (including, potentially, humans) can ask the object to execute its operations. This face is the object's interface.

In **UML 1.x**, the component diagram's main icon is a rectangle that has two rectangles overlaid on its left side. Many modelers found the 1.x symbol too cumbersome, particularly when they had to show a connection to the left side. For this reason, **UML 2.0** provides a new component icon. In **UML 2.0**, the icon is a rectangle with the keyword «*component*» near the top. For continuity over the near-term, you can include the 1.x icon inside the 2.0 icon. *Figure 6.56* shows these icons.

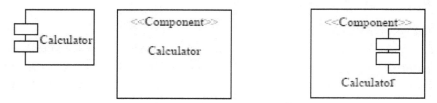

Figure 6.56: *The component icon in UML 1.x and the two versions of the component icon in UML 2.0.*

A component diagram contains, appropriately enough, components, along with interfaces and relationships. Other types of symbols that you've already seen can also appear in a component diagram. *Figure 6.57* shows that if the component is a member of a package, you can prefix the component's name with the name of the package. You can also show the component's operations in a separate panel.

Speaking of artifacts, *figure 6.58* shows a couple of ways to represent them, and it also shows how to model the *relationship* between a particular kind of artifact (an executable) and the component it implements. As you can see, you can place a notation symbol in the artifact on, analogous to the **UML 1.x** component symbol in the component icon, and uses of your application before you start coding, to ensure that you have everything covered.

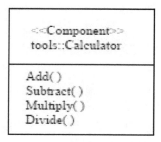

Figure 6.57: *Adding information to the component icon.*

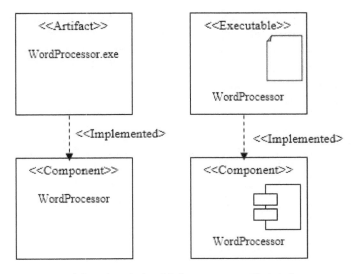

Figure 6.58: *Modeling the relationship between an artifact and a component*

A *component* and the *interfaces* its realization can be represented in two ways. The first shows the *interface* as a rectangle that contains interface-related information. It's connected to the component by the dashed line and large open triangle that indicate realization. (See *figure 6.59*)

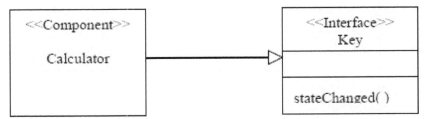

Figure 6.59: *You can represent an interface as a rectangle that contains information, connected to the component by a realization arrow.*

Figure 6.60 shows the second way. It's iconic: You represent the interface as a small circle connected to the component by a solid line.

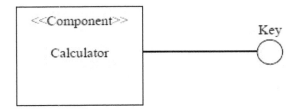

Figure 6.60: *You can represent an interface as a small circle connected to the component by a solid line.*

In addition to realization, you can represent dependency—the relationship between a component and an interface through which it accesses another component. As you'll recall, the dependency is visualized as a dashed line with an arrowhead. You can show realization and dependency on the same diagram, as in the upper diagram of *figure 6.61*. The lower diagram of *figure 6.61* shows the equivalent ball-and-socket notation. The "ball" represents a provided interface and the "socket" represents a required interface.

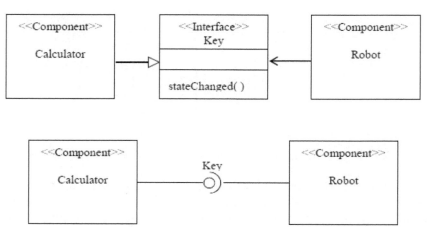

Figure 6.61: *Two ways of showing realization and dependency in the same diagram.*

When you model a component's interfaces as in *figure 6.61*, you show what UML calls an external, or "black box," view. You also have the option of showing an internal, or "white box," view. This view shows interfaces listed inside the component icon and organized by keywords. *Figure 6.62* shows a white box view of the components in *figure 6.61*.

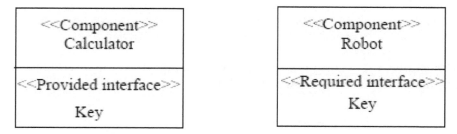

Figure 6.62: *A white box view of the components*

Deployment diagram

The *UML deployment diagram* shows the physical architecture of a computer-based system. It can depict the computers, show their connections with one another, and show the software that sits on each machine. Each computer is represented as a cube, with interconnections between computers drawn as lines connecting the cubes. *Figure 6.63* presents an example.

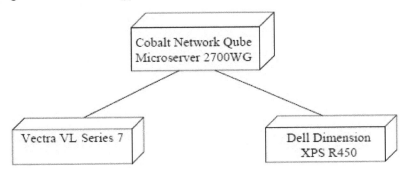

Figure 6.63: The UML deployment diagram.

A *deployment diagram* shows how artifacts (which you met in "Working with Component Diagrams") are deployed on system hardware, and how the pieces of hardware connect. The main hardware item is a node, a generic name for a computing.

In **UML 1.x**, many modelers (including me) distinguished between two types of nodes—a processor (a node that can execute a component) and a device (a peripheral piece of hardware that doesn't execute components but typically interfaces in some way with the outside world). Although that distinction wasn't formalized in **UML 1.x**, it was useful.

UML 2.0, now, formally defines a device as a node that executes artifacts (an executable is now classified as an artifact). In **UML 2 .0**, a cube represents a node (as was the case in **UML 1.x**). You supply a name for the node, and you can add the keyword «Device», although it's usually not necessary. I still think it's a good idea to distinguish between devices and peripherals, as you'll see. *Figure 6.64* shows a node.

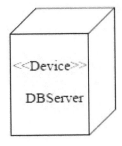

Figure 6.64: Representing a node in the UML.

Figure 6.65 shows three ways to model the artifacts deployed on a node.

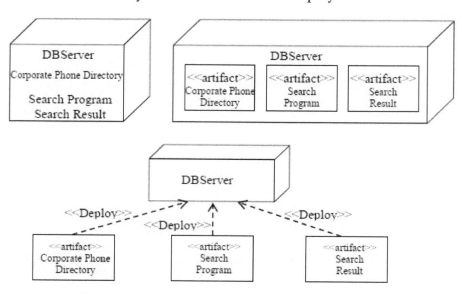

Figure 6.65: *Three ways to model the deployment of artifacts on a node.*

A line joining two cubes represents a connection between two nodes. Bear in mind that a connection isn't necessarily a piece of wire or cable. You can also represent wireless connections, such as infrared and satellite. *Figure 6.66* shows an example of an inter-nodes' connection.

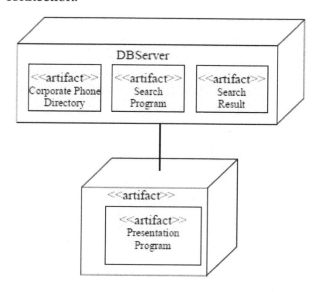

Figure 6.66: *Representing the connection between nodes.*

UML 2.0's emphasis on artifacts brings a set of new artifact-related concepts. One of these concepts is the *deployment specification*, an artifact that provides parameters for another artifact. A good example of this is the initialization command that some modem connections require. This is a string of characters that sets values for certain characteristics of the modem. *Figure 6.67* shows how to model a deployment specification.

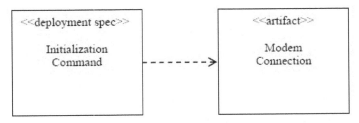

Figure 6.67: Representing a deployment specification and its relationship with an artifact it parameterizes.

For clarity, one could add the keyword «parameterize» to the arrow, although this keyword doesn't come with **UML 2.0** —that is, it's not part of the UML specification.

A Conceptual Sample Project

If you have visited Ram Lila sites a day or two before the Dussehra festival in North India, you would find the parts of Ravana effigy spread on the ground for assembly and erection, on Dussehra day, for burning. The complete design and assembly of each of the components of the Ravana effigy is a good example of *object-oriented analysis and design*.

Project Specification

In the *first phase – Specification* - of the project, the specifications of the effigy may be the height of the effigy and the money to be spent on the preparation and burning of the demon.

Project Analysis

In the *analysis phase*, the height of different parts and the width and shape of each part will be analyzed. The number of crackers to be stuffed inside the effigy and the exact location on the Ram Lila ground where the effigy will be finally erected need to be analyzed so that the whole project succeeds on the Dussehra day without causing any harm/loss to anybody or property.

Project Design

In the *design* stage, the different objects, namely hands, legs, head, and the belly and their proper sizes are decided, so that, the total height of the effigy and money spent on the model are within the laid down limits. If due to any reason, the objects at the analysis stage cannot be exactly matched, then they may need to be modified. For example, if the specified height of the demon is 25 feet and readily available parts when assembled amount to a height of 27 feet, then the original specification of the height of 25 feet has to be modified at the design stage. Similarly, the total amount to be spent on the construction of the project may need to be increased.

Project Implementation

Once each component of the Ravana effigy is either designed or bought from different vendors, the assembly of the effigy is done. It may so happen that any part may not exactly fit according to the need. For example, you may find that due to faulty design, one hand of the effigy holding sword is not strong enough to be fitted with the rest of the structure. In such a case, the hand may have to be modified by reducing the size of the sword or by adding some more bamboo pieces to the end of the hand for strengthening the structure. In this manner, the different parts will be joined together to form the effigy. The *final phase* would be the erection of the effigy at the place where spectators cannot enter or move near effigy.

After the effigy is erected, the crackers may be stuffed in various parts of the skeleton. Depending upon the estimates given earlier and modified later, the crackers may be stuffed all over the effigy keeping in mind that crackers should not cause any damage to the viewers who would surround the place for viewing the effigy burning. Thus, even at the last stage of the implementation, the modification, and interaction may take place between the objects decided at the analysis stage and the erection of the effigy stage.

Maintenance

As regards the maintenance, you may find that some paper on the leg or hand gets torn at the time of the erection of the effigy. In such a case, one needs to paste the new paper to make the effigy look presentable. The above explanation describes the project theoretically but presents an object-oriented project conceptually.

Table 6.3 gives a comparative study of the **object-oriented (OO) approach** and **module-oriented (MO) approach.**

	Object-Oriented approach	Module-Oriented approach
1	In this approach, a system is seen as a collection of objects, each with a functional purpose. These objects are interconnected to achieve a common objective.	In this approach, a system is seen as a set of functions, data and processes and their interrelationship.
2	It facilitates easy maintenance of the system and at a low cost. This is because a change in algorithms used by an object does not affect other objects.	Maintenance is a costlier affair in this approach. Proper and detailed documentation is needed for modification of the system.

3	Repairing faults in the system is much easier in this approach.	Repairing faults may require changes in more than one module. Also, fault identification is difficult.
4	Since objects can e reused in different applications, it promotes reuse of code in large systems.	The reuse of code is limited and infrequent.
5	It is simpler to implement in distributed systems since independent objects communicate through messages. One object can invoke methods of some other object located on a remote computer.	Difficult to implement in distributed systems.
6	Ideal for fully exploiting object technologies like C++, Java, CORBA, GUI, COM, DCOM, etc.	Not as efficient as OO tools and techniques in implementing new technologies.
7	This leads to systems that are more flexible to change.	Leads to less flexible systems.
8	Performance and start-up costs are greater. This is because the cost is involved in sending a message from one object to another. Developers have to start from scratch in the initial stage of OO system development.	Initial costs and overheads are not so high. Trained manpower is available at a cheaper price.
9	Ideal for large systems.	Ideal for small systems.

Table 6.3: Comparison of the OO and MO approach for system design

Summary

The *object-oriented modeling approach* is becoming more and more popular since it allows you to model a real-world application, both in terms of data and process, using a common underlying representation. The seamless nature of the transitions that an *object-oriented model* undergoes from analysis to design to implementation has been discussed. We have discussed the concept of object-oriented programming with a different type of terminologies. How to use different types of **UML** model has been discussed. The requirement analysis model is developed using use-case diagrams. The use-case diagram shows the interaction between external actors and actions performed within the system. How to model the static structure of objects in the problem domain using class diagrams is discussed. Objects having both states (conditions) and behavior (operations) are encapsulated. Associations exist between objects, like entity relationships, which are discussed. A state diagram for capturing the dynamic state transitions in an object is discussed. State transitions occur when events trigger changes in an object. Also, a detailed elaboration has been made on how to develop a dynamic model of interactions among objects using a sequence diagram. A *sequence diagram* shows the passing of messages between objects. Messages activate operations within objects, causing the system to perform the desired functions.

Questions and Answers

State True or False

1. Object modeling is the identification of objects and their relationships.

2. During object-oriented system development, objects are identified in the system-implementation stage.

3. The terms object class and class are not similar.

4. Encapsulation is the packaging of several items together into one unit.

5. Object-oriented techniques promote the reuse of code.

Answers

1. True   2. False   3. False   4. True   5. True

1. Multiple Choice

1.1 Objects are

   (*a*) tangible entities   (*b*) intangible entities

   (*c*) none of these   (*d*) both (a) and (b)

1.2 A class is a

   (*a*) group of objects

   (*b*) template for objects of a particular type

   (*c*) class of objects

   (*d*) classification of objects

1.3 In object-oriented design

   (*a*) operations and methods are identical

   (*b*) methods specify algorithms whereas operations only state what is to be done

   (*c*) methods do not change the values of attributes

   (*d*) methods and constructor are the same

1.4 By encapsulation, we mean

    (*a*) encapsulating data and programs

    (*b*) hiding attributes of an object from users

    (*c*) hiding operations on an object from users

    (*d*) hiding implementation details of methods from users of objects

1.5 Encapsulation in object modeling is useful as

    (*a*) it allows improving methods of an object independent of other parts of the system

    (*b*) it hides implementation details of methods

    (*c*) it allows easy designing

    (*d*) encapsulates attributes and operations of an object

1.6 An object is selected for modeling, if

    (*a*) its attributes are invariant during operation of the system

    (*b*) its attributes change during operation of the system

    (*c*) it has numerous attributes

    (*d*) it has no attributes relevant to the system

1.7 Inheritance in object modeling can be used to

    (*a*) generalize classes

    (*b*) specialize classes

    (*c*) generalize and specialize classes

    (*d*) create new classes

1.8 Objects may be viewed as

    (a) clients in a system

    (b) servers in a system

    (c) as both clients and servers in a system

    (d) neither as both clients nor as servers in a system

1.9 The advantages of object-oriented modeling are claimed by some like the following:

    (*i*)   it allows easy integration of sub-systems

    (*ii*) it promotes reuse of code

    (*iii*) it allows modification of some objects by other objects

    (*iv*) it allows data structures in objects to be modified by other objects.

State whether-

(*a*) (*i*) and (*ii*) are true   (b) (*i*), (*ii*) and (*iv*) are true

(*c*) (*ii*), (*iii*) and (*iv*) are true   (d) (*i*), (*ii*), (*iii*) and (*iv*) are true

    1.10 In UML diagram of a class

        (*a*) state of an object cannot be represented

        (*b*) state is irrelevant

        (*c*) the state is represented as an attribute

        (*d*) the state is represented as a result of the operation

2. **State whether the following statements are TRUE or FALSE**

    2.1 State diagrams represent dynamic models of how objects change their states in response to events.

    2.2 Object-oriented techniques promote reuse of code.

    2.3 Objects are identified in the System Design phase.

    2.4 Object diagrams and class diagrams are alike.

    2.5 Complexity of software systems exceeds the human intellectual capacity.

    2.6 Object-oriented design defines a notation for constructing complex software systems.

    2.7 Anything that smells are an object in computer science parlance.

    2.8 The state of an object encompasses all the static as well as dynamic properties of objects.

    2.9 In a horse class, there is a method calledriding(). An object of this class will automatically inherit riding as its behavior.

    2.10 The identification and analysis of classes and objects is the fundamental issue in object-oriented design.

3. Match words/phrases in the two columns

3.1	generalization	a. method replacement
3.2	polymorphism	b. not performed by itself
3.3	event	c. instances
3.4	objects	d. the operation applied in different ways
3.5.	overriding	e. sequence diagram
3.6	specialization	f. encourages reuse of software components
3.7	interactions between system and environment	g. separating interface from implementation
		h. a noteworthy occurrence
3.8	interactions within the system	i. use case diagram
3.9	Encapsulation	j. Subclasses
3.10	Object-oriented development	k. Super classes

4. Fill in the blanks out of the following

a. Modularity	b. asynchronous message	c. object
d. multiplicity	e. actor	f. simple message
g. UML	h. association	i. polymorphism
j. encapsulation	k. generalization	1. specialization

4.1 In_____, the sender does not have to wait for the recipient to handle the message.

4.2 In_____the control is transferred from the sender to the recipient without describing the details of the communication.

4.3 _____ is the property of a system that has been decomposed into a set of cohesive and loosely coupled modules.

4.4 The object-oriented design activity consists of system design and_____design.

4.5 In a system, customer is an_____

4.6 Hiding internal implementation of an object from its external view is known as _____

4.7 _____indicates how many objects participate in a relation.

4.8 Applying same operation to two or more classes in different ways is known as_____

4.9 Mammal class is _____ of Dog class.

4.10 Just as relationships exist between entities in an E-R diagram _____ exist between objects.

Answers to multiple choice questions

1. 1.1 (d) 1.2 (b) 1.3 (b) 1.4 (d) 1.5 (a) 1.6 (b)
   1.7 (c) 1.8 (c) 1.9 (a) 1.10 (c)'

2. 2.1 (T) 2.2 (F) 2.3 (F) 2.4 (F) 2.5 (T) 2.6 (T)
   2.7 (F) 2.8 (T) 2.9 (F) 2.10 (T)

3. 3.1 (k) 3.2 (d) 3.3 (h) 3.4 (c) 3.5 (a) 3.6 (j)
   3.7 (i) 3.8 (e) 3.9 (g) 3.10 (f)

4. 4.1 (b) 4.2 (f) 4.3 (a) 4.4 (c) 4.5 (e) 4.6 (j)
   4.7 (d) 4.8 (i) 4.9 (k) 4.10 (h)

Short questions

6. **What is information hiding?**

   Information hiding is a design approach where software is split up into modules that hide the design decisions.

7. **What are off-the-self components?**

   Off-the-self components are existing software that can be acquired from a third party or was developed internally for a past project.

8. **What are Data Objects?**

   A data object is a representation of almost any component information that must be understood by software.

9. **What is an attribute?**

   Attributes are properties of a data object. They are of three different characteristics. They can be used to name an instance of the data objects; describe the instances, or refer to another instance.

10. **What is cardinality?**

    Cardinality is the specifications of the number of occurrences of one (object) that can be related to the number of occurrences of another (object). The combinations of one and many are: One-to-one, one-to-many, and many-to-many.

11. What is procedural abstraction?

Procedural abstraction is a name sequence of instruction that has specific and limited functions. For example, open a door, where open is a procedural abstraction.

12. What is data abstraction?

Data abstraction is the name of a collection of data that describes the data object. For example, the door in the above question.

13. What do you mean by operation? Name different types of operations.

Operations define the behavior of an object and change the object attributes in some way. The types of operations are:

- Operations that manipulate data in some way (adding, deleting, reformatting, selecting).
- Operations that perform a composition.
- Operations that monitor an object for the occurrence of a control event.

14. What is an object-oriented analysis?

Object-Oriented analysis is concerned with devising a precise, concise, understandable and correct model of the real world.

15. Define modeling.

Modeling provides a simple means to identify and organize classes that are relevant to the system or product requirement.

16. What are the characteristics according to which classes can be categorized?

Tangibility, Inclusiveness, Sequentially, Persistence, Integrity.

17. What is Unified Modeling Language?

A unified modeling language (UML) consists of both a modeling language and process. The modeling language is the notation that methods used to express design.

18. What is class diagram?

A class diagram describes the types of objects in the system and the various kinds of state relationships that exist between them. It also shows the attributes of operations of a class and constructs that apply to the way objects are connected.

19. Define association. Name two types of associations.

Association represents relationships between instances of classes (a person works for a company; a company has several persons). In unidirectional association, navigability exists only in one direction. In a bisectional association, navigability is in both directions.

20. What are the primary benefits of object-oriented architecture?

- The internal implementation details of data and procedures are hidden from the outside world.

- Data structures and the operations that manipulate them are placed in a single named entity.

- The interface among encapsulated objects is simple.

21. What is a component system?

A component system is a system product that offers a set of reusable features. In this, features are implemented or related and interconnected in/with the sets of components of various types with associated packages and descriptive documents.

22. Define facade.

A facade is a packaged subset of components or reference to components selected from the component system. Each façade provides public access to only those parts of the component system that have been chosen to be available for reuse.

24. List the diagrams supported by UML.

a. Use-case diagram	*f.* State chart diagram
b. Class diagram	*g.* Activity diagram
c. Object diagram	*h.* Component diagram
d. Sequence diagram	*i.* Development diagram
e. Collaboration diagram	

DESCRIPTIVE QUESTIONS

Q. 1 List the different programming paradigms.

Q. 2 Illustrate the role of CASE tools in system analysis and design.

Q. 3 Compare and contrast the module-oriented and object-oriented approach to system analysis and design.

Q. 4 Define the terms Inheritance and Polymorphism. Give suitable examples.

Q. 5 Define Object Modeling.

Answers to descriptive questions

Ans. 1 The different programming paradigms are:

(a) Procedure-oriented

(b) Object-oriented

(c) Rule-oriented

(d) Logic-oriented

(e) Constraint-oriented

Ans. 2 The objective of **CASE (Computer-Aided Software Engineering)** tools is to aid the system analysts and designers to construct high-quality systems on time and within budget, which can be maintained economically and changed rapidly. CASE tools (for example, Visio, Imagix, etc.) empower the system analysts and designers by freeing them to concentrate upon the truly creative aspects of analysis and design. There are some things that these tools can do and some things that they cannot do. For example, when we use an object program to show a scene with a message being passed from one object to another, a tool can ensure that the message is, in fact, part of the object's protocol. That is, a tool can perform consistency checking. For example, if we say that there are no more than three instances of this class, a tool can enforce this statement. Similarly, a tool can tell us if certain classes or methods are never used (completeness checking).

Some sophisticated tools can also tell us how long it takes to complete a certain operation, or whether or not a certain state in a state-transition diagram is reachable. But a tool cannot tell us that we need to invent a new class to simplify our class structure, which requires human intellect.

Visual development tools allow system developers to build user interfaces, reports and other features in a fraction of time. Development tools like Visual Basic, PowerBuilder, Delphi, etc. allow the development of new systems by piecing together predefined "visual" objects rather than by typing crude programming commands. As a result, more powerful systems could be developed in a fraction of the time previously required.

Ans. 3 *Table 6.4* gives a comparative study of the **object-oriented (OO)** approach and **module-oriented (MO)** approach.

	Object-Oriented approach	Module-Oriented approach
1	In this approach, a system is seen as a collection of objects, each with a functional purpose. These objects are interconnected to achieve a common objective.	In this approach, a system is seen as a set of functions, data and processes and their interrelationship.
2	It facilitates easy maintenance of the system and at a low cost. This is because a change in algorithms used by an object does not affect other objects.	Maintenance is a costlier affair in this approach. Proper and detailed documentation is needed for modification of the system.

3	Repairing faults in the system is much easier in this approach.	Repairing faults may require changes in more than one module. Also, fault identification is difficult.
4	Since objects can e reused in different applications, it promotes reuse of code in large systems.	The reuse of code is limited and infrequent.
5	It is simpler to implement in distributed systems since independent objects communicate through messages. One object can invoke methods of some other object located on a remote computer.	Difficult to implement in distributed systems.
6	Ideal for fully exploiting object technologies like C++, Java, CORBA, GUI, COM, DCOM etc.	Not as efficient as OO tools and techniques in implementing new technologies.
7	This leads to systems that are more flexible to change.	This leads to less flexible systems.
8	Performance and start-up costs are greater. This is because the cost is involved in sending a message from one object to another. Developers have to start from scratch in the initial stage of OO system development.	Initial costs and overheads are not so high. Trained manpower is available at a cheaper price.
9	Ideal for large systems.	Ideal for small systems.

Table 6.4: Comparison of the OO and MO approach for system design

Ans. 4 *Inheritance* is defined as the property of objects by which instances of a class can have access to data and programs contained in a previously defined class, without those definitions being restated. Classes are linked together in a hierarchy. They form a tree; whose root is the class of *objects*. Each class, except the root class, will have a superclass (a class above it in the hierarchy) and possibly subclasses. A class can inherit (i.e. acquire) methods on to its subclasses. Inheritance is always transitive. A class can *inherit* features from super classes many levels away. For example, the tiger is a subclass of class mammal, and class mammal is a subclass of class animal, then the tiger will inherit attributes both from mammal and from an animal.

Polymorphism includes the ability to use the same message to objects of different classes and have them behave differently. Thus, we could define the message "+" for both the addition of numbers and the concatenation (joining) of characters, even though both these operations are completely different. For example, although all *window* objects exhibit the same behavior that is open and close. But, not all windows open and close in the same manner. Some windows swing shut while others slide downwards. Thus, polymorphism provides the ability to use the same word to evoke different methods, according to the similarity of meaning.

Ans. 5 An Object Model is defined as a collection of principles that form the foundation of object-oriented design; a software engineering paradigm emphasizing the principles of abstraction, encapsulation, modularity, hierarchy, typing, concurrency and persistence.

Exercise

1. **Explain Object-oriented Analysis. Is it better than module-oriented analysis? If so, how?**

2. **Write short notes on the following object-oriented concepts giving suitable examples:**

   (*a*) Encapsulation

   (*b*) Inheritance

   (*c*) Messages

   (*d*) Polymorphism

3. **Define each of the following terms:**

a. Actor	*b*. Use case	*c*. Object class
d. State	*e*. Behavior	*f*. Encapsulation
g. Operation	*h*. Method	*i*. Constructor operation
j. Query operation	*k*. Update operation	*l*. Abstract class
m. Multiplicity	*n*. association class	*o*. Class-scope attribute
p. Overriding	*q*. Event	*r*. State transition

4. **Contrast the following terms:**

   a. actor with use case

   b. extends relationship with
       use relationship

   c. object class with object
   d. attribute with operation

   e. state with behavior

   f. operation with method

   g. query operation with update
       operation

   h. an abstract class with concrete

   k. generalization with aggregation

   l. aggregation with composition

   m. overriding for an extension with
       overriding for restriction

   n. state with event

   o. event with action

   p. entry action with exit action

   r. generic sequence diagram with
       class instance sequence diagram

i. class diagram with object diagram

j. association with aggregation   s. synchronous message with asynchronous message

5. Compare and contrast the Object-oriented Analysis with Structured Analysis.

6. What exactly are classes and objects? How does one identify the classes and objects that are relevant to a particular application?

7. State the activities involved in each of the following phases of the object-oriented development life cycle: object-oriented analysis, object-oriented design, and object-oriented implementation.

8. State the conditions under which the extends relationship should be used between use cases.

9. State the conditions under which the uses relationship should be used between use cases.

10. Give an example of an abstract use case. The example should involve at least two other use cases and show how they are related to the abstract use case.

10. State the conditions under which a designer should model an association relationship as an association class.

11. Give an example of aggregation. The example should include at least one aggregation object and three component objects. Specify the multiplicities at each end of all the aggregation relationship.

12. Give an example of generalization. The example should include at least one superclass and three subclasses, and a minimum of one attribute and one operation for each of the classes. Indicate the discriminator and specify the semantic constraints among subclasses.

13. Give an example of state transition. The example should show the state of the object undergoes a transition based on some event.

14. Name any five UML diagrams and taking any real-world example, describe them individually.

15. A student whose attributes include studentName, Address, Phone, and Age, may engage in multiple campus-based activities. The university keeps track of the number of years a given student has participated in a specific activity and; end at the end of each academic year, mails an activity report to the student showing his participation in various activities. Draw a class diagram for this situation.

16. Draw a class diagram, showing the relevant classes, attributes, operations, and relationships, for each of the following situations:

   a. **A company has several employees.** The attributes of Employee include employeeID (primary key), name, address, and birthdate. The company also has several projects. Attributes of the Project include projectName and startDate. Each employee may be assigned to one or more projects, or may not be assigned to a project. A project must have at least one employee assigned, and may have any number of employees assigned. An employee's billing rate may vary by projects, and the company wishes to record the applicable billing rate for each employee when assigned to a particular project. At the end of each month, the company mails a cheque to each employee who has worked on a project during that month. The cheque amount is based on the billing rate and the hours logged for each project assigned to the employee.

   b. A university has a large number of courses in its catalog. Attributes, of Course, include courseNumber (primary key), courseName, and units. Each course may have one or more different courses as prerequisites or may have no prerequisites. Similarly, a particular course may be a prerequisite for any other course or may not be a prerequisite for any other course. The university adds or drops a prerequisite for a course only when the director for the course makes a formal request to that effect.

   c. A college course may have one or more scheduled sections, or may not have a scheduled section. Attributes, of Course, include courseID, courseName, and units. Attributes of Section include sectionNumber and semester. The value of sectionNumber is an integer (such as 1 or 2), which distinguishes one section from another for the same course, but does not uniquely identify a section. There is an operation called findNumSections, which finds the number of sections offered for a given course in a given semester.

Minicase

PROBLEM

A deluxe restaurant in Rohini enclave functions as follows: When a customer walks into the restaurant, the customer is asked whether he made a reservation or not. The people with reservations are seated as quickly as possible. Those who do not have a reservation are made to wait in a well-furnished waiting room. Before the waiting customer's turn comes or the reservation customer arrives, the table is cleaned and neatly set by a buzzer. When the table is ready, customers walk to their table and call for a waiter.

The waiter shows them a menu card and asks whether they want to order a drink while they decide what to order. If someone orders a drink, the waiter goes and gets it. The waiter allows the customers five to ten minutes for making a selection from the menu. After some time, the waiter comes back to take the orders. Each waiter is allotted an area that consists of several tables. Waiters are rotated through all the different areas. The selections made by the customer are noted down on a form, which the waiter gives to the Chef. The form consists of the table number, selection and time. The time is mentioned for the Chef to prioritize his efforts in terms of when an order has arrived.

The Chef cooks the food and the waiter picks it up and brings it to the table. The people then eat their meals. When the people finish their meals, the waiter comes by and asks whether they want anything else. If they do, the waiter takes their order. If they don't want anything more, he goes and brings the bill. After a few minutes, he comes by and collects the cash or credit card. Then, after some time the waiter brings the change or credit card receipts. The customer leaves a tip and goes out.

The restaurant management has now decided to provide a technological backbone to the restaurant so that the customers are treated better and served in time. That is, they propose to computerize the restaurant's functioning.

Answer the following:

1. Draw an activity diagram for the restaurant.
2. Suggest locations where terminals would be required and other optional locations. Also, mention how your suggestion would improve the functioning of the restaurant. Draw a deployment diagram.
3. Draw a class diagram that shows the relevant object classes, attributes, operations, relationships, and multiplicities.
4. Identify all the use cases for the waiter, chef, and the buzzer.
5. Design a user interface for the system.

SOLUTION

1. *Figure 6.77* shows the Activity diagram for the restaurant.
2. A local area network should be set up in the restaurant. A wireless network is preferable because, in a wired network, the waiters would be jumping over wires to get to the terminals, and sometimes may entangle with the laid down wires.

The network will improve communication between the waiter, chef and the buzzer. For example, communicating orders from customers to chefs, enquiring about the status of the meal preparation from the kitchen, etc. Also, the waiter can send a message to the buzzer to come and clean the table when a customer in leaves.

Each buzzer and waiter will carry a terminal on his palm (palmtops). One desktop PC will be installed in the kitchen and another one in the manager's office. The kitchen PC will store the databases namely, the Order database, and the Recipe Database. Kitchen will have one or more screens for easy viewing by all the chefs working there.

When the customer makes an order, the waiter could enter them into his palmtop and the order would go to the kitchen PC. This eliminates the time required to walk from the serving area to the kitchen to communicate orders. Also, the waiter can enquire about the status of a meal by pressing a button on the palmtop. The chef can reply to it by providing an estimate of the time required for the meal to get ready.

When an order is prepared, the chef can send a message to the waiter's palmtop. The waiter can then come and collect the meals. This eliminates the time required for repeatedly coming to the kitchen to check whether the order is ready or not.

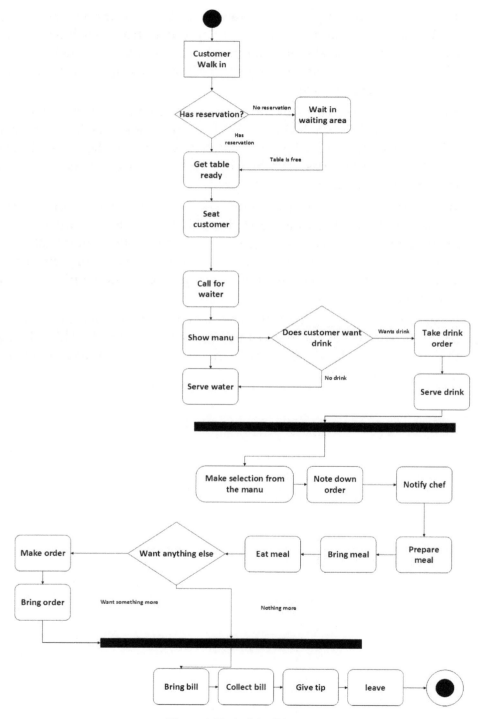

Figure 6.68: Activity Diagram

The kitchen and manager's PC will be connected to a printer. Each serving area will have a printer so that the waiters can print bills without having to walk to the cash collecting counters. Since the kitchen is away from the Manager's office, a repeater is placed in between so that the signals do not get attenuated with distance.

The deployment diagram is shown in figure 6.78.

The Access Point receives and transmits messages from and to devices. The users will make the connection via the wireless-LAN adapters which are integrated with their palmtops.

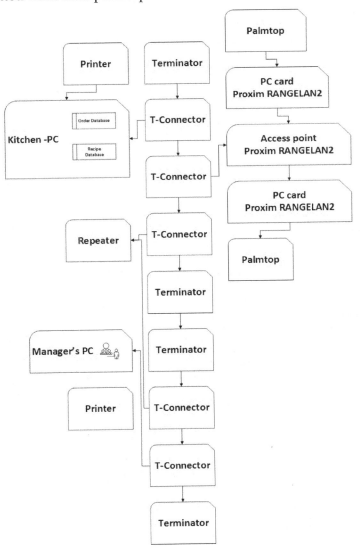

Figure 6.69: Deployment Diagram

3. **Following Classes are identified for the system:**

Employee, Manager, Waiter, Chef, Buzzer, Customer, Bill.

The manager, Waiter, Buzzer and Chef classes will be subclasses of the superclass Employee.

Associations:

Customer is served by a Waiter

Customer places an Order

Customer pays a Bill

The Manager operates the restaurant

The Manager monitors the Employees

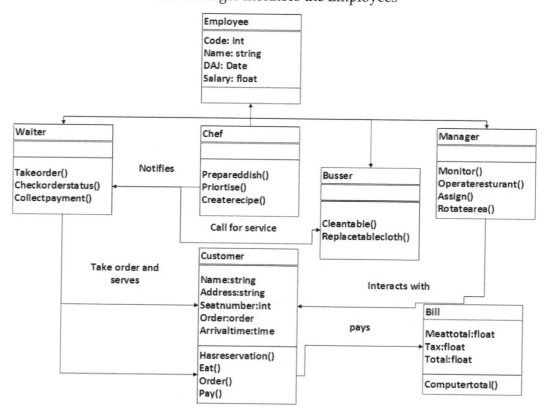

Figure 6.70: Class Diagram

The Manager interacts with the Customer Chef takes orders from the Waiter. *Figure 6.70* shows the class diagram:

4. For the Waiter, the use-cases are:

a) Take an Order

b) Transmit the order to the kitchen

c) Receive notification from kitchen

d) Track Order status

e) Print bill

f) Cass a Busser

g) Receive Acknowledgement

for the Chef, the use cases are:

a) Store a recipe

b) Retrieve a recipe

c) Receive order from Waiter

d) Acknowledge Waiter request

e) Notify the Waiter

The use cases for the Busser are:

a) Receive a call from the Wasiter

b) Acknowledge the request.

5.(a) The screen in *figure 6.71* is for order entry. This screen appears when the waiter clicks on the orders button. The large white box will contain a list of dishes along with check boxes which the waiter will click to indicate the customer's selection. When the waiter clicks the OK button, the order is sent to the kitchen through the wireless LAN.

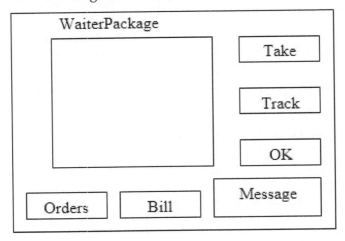

Figure 6.71: Order Entry Screen

5.(b) *Figure 6.81* shows the screen which appears when the bill button is clicked

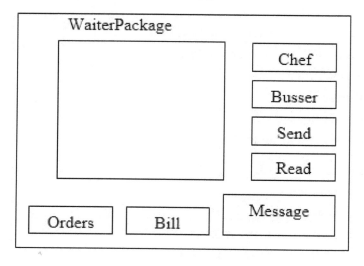

Figure 6.72: Bill Screen

5.(c) The user interface for the chef is shown in *figure 6.72*

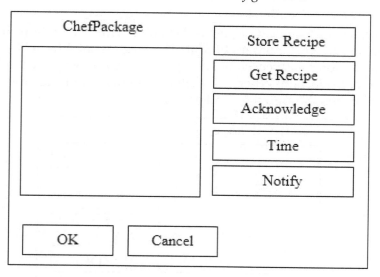

Figure 6.73: User Interface

CHAPTER 7
Designing Interfaces & Dialogues and Database Design

Objectives

In this chapter, we are going to discuss:

- Basics of system interface and dialogue design.
- How the information is provided to and is captured from users?
- Sequences of interface display.
- Rules for designing the interfaces and dialogues.
- Navigation between forms and reports, deliverables.
- Data requirements of the system while using the interfaces, databases, forms, and reports **Entity relationship (E-R)** diagrams along with the graphical notations.

The E-R data models are used to represent a conceptual view of organizational data independence of any particular database processing technology. We will learn about structuring the description of data through logical data modeling.

The purpose of logical data modeling:

a. Data to be normalized for a stable structure that does not change over the time and minimal redundancy. Database to be simple, efficient, and less susceptible to problems.

b. To develop a logical data modeling which will help in building a physical database. The database discussed in this chapter is a relational database. We will discuss about the basic principles of the relational data models from E-R models.

c. The aim is to develop a data model which will reflects the actual data requirement which exist in the forms and reports of an information system.

User Interface Design

The design of forms and reports are the design of **human-computer interface**. The logical design of system files and databases is required for interfaces. Designing the forms, reports, interfaces, dialogues, or databases are to be critically viewed. These activities can be developed in parallel.

Process of Designing Interfaces and Dialogues

Similar to designing of forms and reports, the process of designing interfaces and dialogues is a user focused activity. Follow a prototyping methodology of iteratively collecting information, constructing a prototype, assessing usability, and making refinements. To design a usable interfaces and dialogues, one must answer who, what, when, where, and how; questions used to guide the design of forms and reports.

Deliverables and Outcomes

The deliverables and outcome from a system interface and dialogue design is the creation of a design specification. The specification is similar to the specification produced for form and report designs. The sections are:

a. Narrative overview

b. Sample design

c. Testing and usability assessment

For interface and dialogue designs, one additional subsection is included, which is:

- A section outlining the dialogue sequence;
- The way a user can move from one display to another.

The sequence can be shown by using a dialogue diagram and state transition diagram. An outline for a design specification for interface and dialogue is shown in *figure 7.1*.

```
┌─────────────────────────────────────────────────────┐
│              DESIGN SPECIFICATION                      │
│                                                       │
│   1.  Narrative overview                              │
│          a.  Interface/Dialogue name                  │
│          b.  User characteristics                     │
│          c.  Task characteristics                     │
│          d.  System characteristics                   │
│          e.  Environment characteristics              │
│   2.  Interface/Dialogue design                       │
│          a.  Form/Report design                       │
│          b.  Dialogue sequene, narrative description  │
│   3.  Testing and usability assessment                │
│          a.  Testing objectives                       │
│          b.  Testing procedures                       │
│          c.  Testing results                          │
│                  i)    Time to learn                  │
│                  ii)   Speed ofperformance            │
│                  iii)  Rate of errors                 │
│                  iv)   Retention over time            │
│                  v)    User satisfaction and perceptions │
│                                                       │
└─────────────────────────────────────────────────────┘
```

Figure 7.1: Specification outline design for interface and dialogue

Interaction Methods and Devices

The **human-computer interface** defines the way in which users interact with an information system. All human-computer interfaces must have an interaction style and use some hardware devices for supporting this interaction. Various interaction method and guidelines for designing usable interfaces are described.

When designing the user interface, the most fundamental decision is made that relates to methods used to interact with the system. There are numerous approaches for designing the interactions, basics of five widely used styles are command language, menu, form, object, and natural language.

Command Language Interaction

In **command language interaction**, the user enters explicit statements to invoke operations within a system. This type of interaction requires users to remember the command syntax and semantics. Example: COPY C: LETTER.DOC A: LETTERNEW. DOC.

Command language interaction places a substantial burden on the user to remember names, syntax, and operations.

Menu Interaction

Menu Interaction is a means by which many designers have accomplished the ease of use and understandability. *A menu is simply a list of options; which when selected by the user, a specific command is invoked, or another menu is activated.* Menus have become the most widely used interface method because the user only needs to understand simple signposts and route option to effectively navigate through the system. To develop a menu system, complexity in design is encountered. The development environment, the skill of the developer, and the size of complexity are main factors for developing a menu-based system. For large and complex systems, the menu hierarchy provides a navigation between menus.

In a *pop-up-menu* (dialogue box), menus are displayed near the current cursor position, so user don't have to move the position. A pop-up-menu shows a list of commands relevant to the current cursor position (delete, clear, copy, and so on.). In a list of possible values, one can select the desired one by navigating and clicking the mouse. In a drop-down menu, menus drop down from the top line of the display. *Drop-down* menu has become very popular as it provides consistency in menu location and operation.

Form Interaction

Form interaction allows the users to fill in the blanks when working with a system. Form interaction is effective for both input and presentation of information. A good designed form includes a self-explanatory title and field headings organized into logical groups and distinct boundaries. Form interaction is the most commonly used method for data entry and retrieval in business-based systems.

Object-Based Interaction

Object-Bases interaction is the most common method for implementing through the use of icons. Icons are the graphic symbols that look like the processing option they are meant to represent. Users select operations by pointing to the appropriate icon with some type of pointing device. The primary advantage of using icon is that it takes a little space and is easily understood by the user. An icon may also look like a button, when selected or pressed, causes the system to take an action. Example: save, edit a record, cancel, and so on.

Natural Language Interaction

A branch of artificial intelligence research studies techniques for allowing systems to accept inputs and produce outputs in a conventional language like English. This method of interaction is referred to as **Natural Language Interaction**. Natural language interaction is being applied within both keyboard and voice entry system.

Hardware Option for System Interaction

There is also a growing number of hardware devices employed to support interaction. The most fundamental and widely used is the keyboard, which is mainstay of most computer-based applications for entry of alphanumeric information. The growth of graphical user environment has facilitated the use of pointing devices such as, mice, joystick, trackballs, and so on. The creation of notebook and pen-based computers has got this type devices to interface.

Interface Design

To ease the job of the data recording, a standard format for computer-based forms and reports similar to paper-based forms and reports is essential. The form should have:

- Header information
- Sequence and time-related information
- Instruction or formatting information
- Body or data details
- Totals or data summary
- Authorization or signatures
- Comments

When designing the layouts to record or display an information, one should try to make similar with paper-based forms. The data entry displays should be consistently formatted across applications to speed up the data entry and reduce errors.

The navigation between fields, while designing the layout, should be considered. Standard screen navigation should flow from left to right and top to bottom as one works on a paper. If necessary, the grouping of data fields into logical categories with labels should be added. In the design process, the navigation procedures should have flexibility and consistency to move forward and backward. The data should not be permanently saved by the system until the user makes an explicit request to do so. A functional and consistent interface is required to move the cursor to different places on the form, editing characters, and fields, moving among form displays, and obtaining help. These functions may be provided by keystrokes, mouse clicks, menu selection, or button activation. A good form layout design also provides data validation and verification.

Structuring Data Entry

To minimize the data entry errors, never allow the user to enter data which are available in the system. The unit of measurement of a value need not to be entered. This should be provided on the screen. The data entered into the form should automatically justify in a standard format (ex. date, time, money, or phone number).

Controlling Input Data

In designing the interface, care must be taken to reduce the data entry errors. Steps must be taken to ensure the data validity. Avoid, detect, and correct data entry mistakes. Data errors, during appending (adding additional characters to a field), truncating (losing characters from a field), transcripting (entering invalid data into a field), and transposing (reversing the sequence of one or more characters in a field), are to be handled at the time of data entry.

Providing Feedback

While designing the system interfaces, provide appropriate feedback to the user from time to time to make the user's job more enjoyable. The feedback should be relevant to the process like status information, prompting cues, errors, or warning message. Not providing the feedback information to user is frustrating.

Providing Help

Providing the help feature during interface is very important. The user may face problems which should be answered immediately without abandoning the screen. The help message should be short and simple. The help message needs to be organized which should be easily absorbed by the user. After leaving the help screen, users should always return back to the original screen from where the request was initiated.

Controlling User Access

When the data is very sensitive and vulnerable to unwanted access some restrictions are to be imposed at the interface stage. Several techniques are available to control user access, which are:

- **Views:** This is one form of user access control for a system interfaces, which is use to provide a customized version of the system data to the user. A view is a subset of the database that is presented to one or more users. Views promote security by restricting user access to limited data, views are not adequate security measures, as unauthorized persons gain knowledge of or access to a particular view. Many may read the data but few can update.

- **Authentication Rules:** Controls are incorporated into the system that restrict access to data and actions that people may take on accessed data. Using **user identification (ID)** and password is to authenticate a user to use the computer.

- **Encryption Procedure:** For very sensitive data, such as data related to defense and finance, encryption can be used. The encrypted data cannot be read by human beings, special software and hardware are used along with an algorithm to convert the data into encrypted one. The encryption routines automatically encode the data. The encryption facility provides the complementary routines to decode the data. This method provides adequate security.

The human-computer interfaces and dialogs are important for a software design process. Understanding various characteristics of interaction methods is a fundamental skill you should master. The techniques for structuring and controlling the data entry were presented along with guidelines for providing feedback, prompting, and error message.

Database Design

The database design is a conceptual level before the physical database is made. This is basically a logical design which concerns with the specifications of major data features of the system that would meet the objectives. The logical design can be called as the **blueprint** of the database. A conceptual data model is a representative of organizational data. The purpose is to show as many rules about the meaning and inter-relationships among data as possible. The data information is gathered through interview, questionnaires, and JAD sessions. After this, the team members work in coordination and shares the project dictionary or repository. The repository is often maintained by a common **CASE tool**.

Database Models

Database models are of three types. Although **relational database** is ruling **Information Technology**, so it is worthwhile to know about other models. Almost all **data administrators** know about database management system well, but they have little knowledge about data center. The different database models are:

Hierarchal model

A hierarchical model is created to eliminate redundancy and is use with smaller components which are added to a larger one until all components are together. Its structure resembles to an upside-down tree. A hierarchy of segments (nodes) is similar to record types. Layers of segments include root, parent, children, leaves, and so on. Each parent can have many children, but each child must have only one parent. It follows a sequence method beginning with a root and going down leftmost side of a segment, proceeding right until all segments are visited.

Advantages:

- Database can be shared easily.
- Security is enforced.
- Creates environment for data independence.

- Database integrity promoted by link between parent and child segments.
- Very efficient for large amount of data using fix relationship.
- Installed base is large.

Disadvantages:

- Requires knowledge of physical level of storage.
- Difficult to implement many-to-many relationships.
- Multiple parent conditions occur in real world.
- Complex to manage, not very flexible.
- Requires extensive application programming, not user friendly.
- Support tools must be invoked separately.
- No common standard.

Network model

Network data model has been created to represent the complex data relationships more efficiently than in hierarchical model, improve database performance, and impose database standard. A 3-Level architecture originated with this model, DDL and DML are introduced. They are:

a. **Subschema:** External view description (view of application programmer)

b. **Schema:** Conceptual view (as viewed by database administrator)

c. **Data Storage Definition Language:** Specified internal models and physical details of storage.

Data Manipulation Language (DML) characteristics data and data structures and provide a way to manipulate the data. **Data Base Task Group (DBTG)** uses sets to express relationships (owner: member) 1: M. A set consists of an owner record (parent) and a member (child). One major difference here is that a member can have two parents (owners).

Network is a directed graph of nodes connected by links or directed arcs nodes correspond to record types and link to pointers. Network Database has record types described in the schema and has data items (fields), which are the smallest unit of data. Each data item has a specific type and relates to an attribute as the record correspond to an entity.

Advantages:

- Many-to-many relationships and is easier to implement than hierarchical model.
- More flexible and better data access method.
- Data integrity is enforced because owner record is defined first and then member.

- Achieves data independence by isolating program from physical details.

    Disadvantages:
    - Difficult to design and use since in-depth understanding of record is needed.
    - Difficult to make changes because it is not structurally independent.
    - Complex structure from program point of view.
    - Provides navigational data access like the hierarchical model.

Relational model

In Relational model the relationships between the entities in a database are considered. Relationships are the glue that hold various components together. A relationship is an association between the instances of one or more entity types that is of interest to the organization. An **association** usually means an event that has occurred due to the natural linkage between entity instances. This model is widely used and is more popular than other models.

    Advantages:
    - Data and structural independence.
    - Single data repository whose contents are easier to manage.
    - Powerful yet flexible query capability, especially for ad-hoc queries.
    - **Structured Query Language (SQL)** requires less programming and is standard.
    - System's physical complexity hidden from designer and end user.

    Disadvantages:
    - Substantial amount of hardware and software overhead slows the system.
    - Large database may slow down the system with certain operations like **JOIN** and so on.

Entity Relationship Diagram

P.P. Chen introduced the **Entity-Relationship (E-R) models** and the corresponding diagrams. The overall logic structure of a database can be expressed graphically by an E-R Diagram. While drawing the entity-relationship diagram, entity names are represented by a rectangle, relationships are represented by a diamond and oval shapes are used for representing attributes.

Entity Relationship Analysis

It involves capturing and analyzing of maximum possible details on data required for building an information system for an organization. **Entity-Relationship (E-R)** modeling is concerned with the structure of data. Structure of data involves details on

- Data entities
- Relationships
- Associated Attributes

ER model is expressed in terms of entities in the business environment, the associations among those entities, and the attributes or properties of both entities and their relationships

E-R analysis involves the following:

- Determining what type of people, places, things, and material interact with the business and which objects the data must be maintained. These objects form entities.

- Determining different characteristics (attributes) of each entity. This involves identifying only those characteristics which are of interest to the organization and for which the system is being built.

- Determining what unique feature such as the primary key can be used to identify entity in an entity list.

- Determining the associations (relationship) among identified objects.

Entity

An entity is a person, location, object, or event about which the organization wishes to maintain data. An entity has its own identity which distinguishes it from each other entity. Examples:

Person	:	EMPLOYEE, STUDENT, PATIENT
Place	:	STATE, REGION, COUNTRY, BRANCH
Object	:	MACHINE, BUILDING, AUTOMOBILE
Event	:	SALE, REGISTRATION, RENEWAL
Concept	:	ACCOUNTING, COURSE, WORKCENTRE

Entity Type: (entity class)

Entity type is a collection of entities that share common properties or characteristics. Each entity type in an E-R model is given a name, it is an object and use capital letters in naming. It is place inside a rectangle representing an entity.

Entity Instance: (or instance)

Entity Instance is a single occurrence of an entity type. An entity type with one instance is described in a data model while many instances of that entity type may be represented by data stored in the database. Consider an example: There is one EMPLOYEE entity type in most organization, but there may be hundreds (or even thousands) of instances of this entity type stored in the database.

Basic Symbols

Rectangle	Represents entity set
Oval	Represents attributes
Diamond	Represents relationship Among entity sets
Line	Links attributes to entity Sets to relationship

Figure 7.2: Basic Symbols

Attributes

An attribute is a property or characteristics of an entity which is of interest to the organization. An entity has set of attributes associated with it. Examples:

STUDENT: Student_id, Stud_nm, Addr, Ph_no, Major

AUTOMOBILE: Vehicle_id, colour, Weight, HP

EMPLOYEE: Emp_id, Emp_name, Address, Skill

While naming an entity, make first letter a capital followed by lowercase letters, and use nouns in naming an attribute. An attribute is placed inside an ellipse with a line connecting to the associated entity. The attributes of an entity are listed in the repository, then each attribute may be separately defined as another object in the repository.

Candidate Key and Identifiers

A candidate key is an attribute (or combination of attributes) that uniquely identifies each instance of an entity type. A candidate key for a STUDENT entity type might be Student_id.

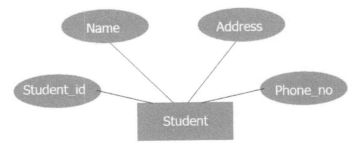

Figure 7.3: Candidate Keys for Student

Multi-valued Attribute

Multi-valued Attribute may take more than one value for each entity instance. Suppose skill is one of the attributes of EMPLOYEE. Each employee can have more than one skill; so, Skill is a multi-valued attribute.

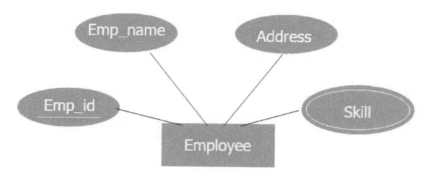

Figure 7.4: Candidate Keys for Employee

Attribute Entity

Degree of a Relationship

An association among entities leads to **relationship**. The degree of a relationship is the number of entity types that participate in that relationship, there are two types entity in a 2-degree relationship.

Crow foot notation is used to show the association between the entities. They are:

        One-to-one   (1:1)

        One-to-many (1:M)

        Many-to-many (M:M)

1:1 Relationship

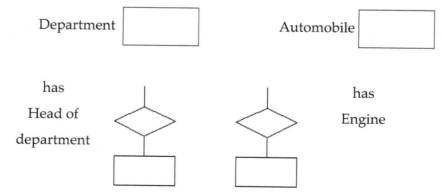

1:M Relationship

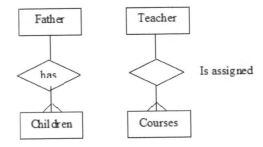

M:M Relationship

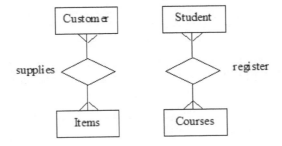

Figure 7.5: *Relationship*

Data Normalization

Concepts of Normalization

Normalization is a process of simplifying the relationship among the data elements in a record. By normalization, a collection of data in a record structure is replaced by simpler records that are more predictable and manageable.

1st step: Convert E-R model into *Tables* or *Relations*.

2nd step: Examine the tables for redundancy and if necessary, change them to non-redundant forms.

This non-redundant model is then converted to a database definition, which achieves the objective of the database *Design Phase*.

The goal of data base design is to generate a set of schemes which allow us to store information without redundant data and to retrieve information easily and efficiently. The design schemes are in appropriate form is known as **Normalization**.

Need for Normalization

Redundancy is the unnecessary repetition of data. It can cause problems with storage and retrieval of data. Normalization reduces redundancy. Redundant can lead to:

a. Inconsistencies: errors are more likely to occur when facts are repeated.

b. Update anomalies: inserting, modifying and deleting data may cause inconsistencies. While updating and deleting data in one relation, you may forget to make corresponding changes in other relations.

Normalization helps to simplify the structure of tables. A fully normalized record consists of:

a. A primary key that identifies the entities.

b. A set of attributes that describes the entity.

1st Normal Form (1NF)

The repeating columns or fields in an un-normalized *Table 7.1* are removed and put them into separate tables. The key to these tables must be a part of the parent table, so that the parent tables and derived tables *(table 7.2)* can be related to each other. Isolate repeating groups from an entity because they are easier to process separately.

Salesperson				Sales		
Emp_ no	Emp_name	Store_Br.	Department	Item_no	Item_desc.	Sale_Price
201	Anand K	Delhi	Production	TR10	Router	35.00
				SA51	Saw	19.00
				PT6	Drill	21.00
				A16	Lawn mower	245.00
301	Zadoo S	Noida	Research	TT01	Humidfier	114.00
				DO10	Dish washer	262.00
419	Balwant	Gurgaon	Accounts	C16	New tire	85.00
				AT146	Alternator	65.00
				BH90	Battery	49.50
612	Bhagwan	Faridabad	Marketing	S10	Suit	215.00

Table 7.1: Unnormalized File

2nd Normal Form (2NF)

A table is in the **Second Normal Form** if all its non-key fields are fully dependent on the whole key. It means that each field in a table must depend upon the entire key. Those fields, which does not depend upon the combination key are moved to another table on whose key they depend on. Structures which do not contain combination keys are automatically in the **2NF**.

Non-key attributes that do not meet this condition are split into simpler entities. To solve the problem, we create a new independent entity for *"Item description"* and *"Sales price"*. In one file, we create the item description attribute with item number keys from the salesperson item file. The remaining attributes (Employee number, Item number, and Sales price) become the second relation or file. (*table 7.3*)

*Emp_no	Emp_name	Store_Br	Dept
201	Anand K	Delhi	Production
301	Zadoo S	Noida	Research
419	Balwant	Gurgaon	Accounts
612	Bhagwan	Faidabad	Marketing

*Emp_no	*Item_no	Item_des	Sale_Price
201	TR10	Router	35.00
201	SA51	Saw	19.00
201	PT6	Drill	21.00
201	A16	Lawnmowr	245.00
301	TT01	Humidfier	114.00
301	DO10	Dishwasher	262.00
419	C16	Snow tire	85.00
419	AT146	Alternator	65.00
419	BH90	Battery	49.50
612	S10	Suit	215.00
* Key			

Table 7.2: First Normalized File

*Emp_no	Emp_name	Store_Br	Dept
201	Anand K	Delhi	Production
301	Zadoo S	Noida	Research
419	Balwant	Gurgaon	Accounts
612	Bhagwan	Faridabad	Marketing
Sales Person Data File			

Emp_no	*Item_no	Sale_Price		*Item_no	Item_des
201	TR10	35.00		TR10	Router
201	SA51	19.00		SA51	Saw
201	PT6	21.00		PT6	Drill
201	A16	245.00		A16	Lawnmower
301	TT01	114.00		TT01	Humidifier
301	DO10	262.00		DO10	Dishwasher
419	C16	85.00		C16	New tire
419	AT146	65.00		AT146	Alternator
419	BH90	49.50		BH90	Battery
612	S10	215.00		S10	Suit
Salesperson Item File				Item File	

Table 7.3: Second Normalization

3rd Normal Form (3NF)

A table is said to be in the **Third Normal Form**, if all the non-key fields of the table are independent of all other non-key fields of the same fields. A relation is in the third normal form provided it is in second normal form and no non-prime attribute is functionally dependent on other prime attributes

We find further room for improvement. In the salesperson data file, the attribute *"Stores branch"* is tagged to the primary key *"Employee number"*, while the attribute *"Department"* is related to *"Store branch"*, which is a non-key attribute. Making *"Store branch"*, as a key attribute requires isolating *"Department"* along with *"Store branch"* in a new relation. With the 3rd normalization, we can store branch information independent of the salespersons in the branch. We can make changes in the *"Department"* without having to update the record of the employee in it.

For Store branch, the system goes through three steps:

a. Computes total sales for each salesperson from the salesperson item file.

b. Goes to the employee data file to look up the store branch to which the salesperson is assigned.

c. Accumulate each salespersons sale in a specifies field. (table 7.4)

*Emp_no	Emp_name	Store_Br
201	Anand K	Delhi
301	Zadoo S	Noida
419	Balwant	Gurgaon
612	Bhagwan	Faridabad
Salesperson Data File		

Store_Br	Dept
Delhi	Hardware
Noida	Home Appliance
Gurgaon	Auto parts
Faridabad	Men's clothing
Store Branch File	

*Espino	*Item_no	Sale_Price
201	TR10	35.00
201	SA51	19.00
201	PT6	21.00
201	A16	245.00
301	TT01	114.00
301	DO10	262.00
419	C16	85.00
419	AT146	65.00
419	BH90	49.50
612	S10	215.00
Salesperson Item File		

*Item_no	Item_des
TR10	Router
SA51	Saw
PT6	Drill
A16	Lawnmower
TT01	Humidifier
DO10	Dishwasher
C16	New tire
AT146	Alternator
BH90	Battery
S10	Suit
Item File	

Table 7.4: *Third Normalization*

This procedure is repeated for each salesperson in the file. *Table 7.5* illustrates the processing cycle for salesperson 201.

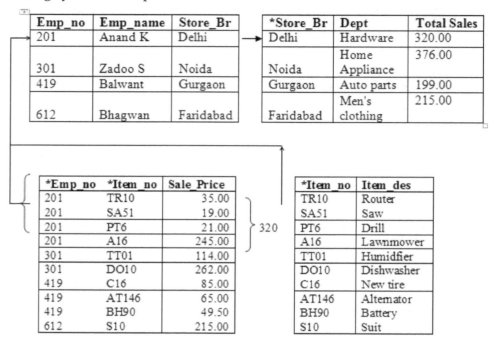

Emp_no	Emp_name	Store_Br
201	Anand K	Delhi
301	Zadoo S	Noida
419	Balwant	Gurgaon
612	Bhagwan	Faridabad

*Store_Br	Dept	Total Sales
Delhi	Hardware	320.00
Noida	Home Appliance	376.00
Gurgaon	Auto parts	199.00
Faridabad	Men's clothing	215.00

*Emp_no	*Item_no	Sale_Price
201	TR10	35.00
201	SA51	19.00
201	PT6	21.00
201	A16	245.00
301	TT01	114.00
301	DO10	262.00
419	C16	85.00
419	AT146	65.00
419	BH90	49.50
612	S10	215.00

320

*Item_no	Item_des
TR10	Router
SA51	Saw
PT6	Drill
A16	Lawnmower
TT01	Humidfier
DO10	Dishwasher
C16	New tire
AT146	Alternator
BH90	Battery
S10	Suit

Table 7.5: Processing Cycle

Summary

Physical file and database design take, as input, the normalized relations from logical data modeling as well as other models that explain how data in files and databases will be accessed. Physical file and database design involve designing fields, records, files, and databases. Designing a field includes selecting a data type, coding, and compression methods to reduce the storage space and improve data accuracy, the format for primary keys, and data integrity control to ease data entry and reduce errors. Designing physical records involves grouping fields together based on a shared primary key and an affinity of usage. Records are also designed to minimize the wasted space in secondary memory storage units called **pages**. **CASE tools** can help in physical and database design by storing the results of file and database design in a **CASE repository**, generating file, or database definition code, reverse engineering existing file and database definitions for elements of current systems that will be reused in the new application.

Exercises

1. **Define the followings:**
   a. dialogue
   b. drop-down menu
   c. icon
   d. authorization rule
   e. view
   f. pop-up-menu

2. **Contrast the following terms:**
   a. Dialogue, interface
   b. Command language interaction, form interaction, menu interaction, natural language interaction, object-based interaction.
   c. Drop-down menu, pop-up-menu
   d. Authorization rules, view

3. Describe the process of designing interfaces and dialogues. What deliverables are produced from this process?

4. Describe five methods of interacting with a system. Is one method better than all others? Why or why not?

5. Describe the general guidelines for the design of menus. Can you think of any instances when it would be appropriate to violate these guidelines?

6. List and describe the functional capabilities needed in an interface for effective entry and navigation. Which capabilities are most important? Why?

7. Describe four types of data errors.

8. Describe four ways to control user access to a system or data.

9. **Define the followings:**
   a. data type
   b. file organization
   c. index
   d. page
   e. record
   f. null value

10. Describe the inputs to physical file and database design.

11. What is normalization? Explain its objective.

12. **Write short notes on:**
   a. Entity
   b. Relationship
   c. 2NF
   d. Data dictionary
   e. Key

CHAPTER 8
Coding and Debugging

Objectives

Programming is a sequence of statements, called **code**, which can be executed by a computer. Coding is translating the detailed design of the product into a series of statements. The design specifications are translated into codes in the design phase.

In this chapter, we are going to discuss:

- Guideline to write programming statements with clarity, efficiency and low cost
- Code testing and implementing
- Selecting criteria for a suitable programming language
- Style rules to produce a good code
- Types of languages suitable for writing a program

Introduction

In a **software development life cycle**, the product takes the least time in comparison to other phases. A well-structured code will help in:

- Reducing the testing and integration time.
- Maintaining a good documentation.

- Improving the maintainability of the software product after implementation.

The maintenance phase of the product life is the highest of all. In order to have a very smooth operation during software maintenance phase, we should not compromise the cost, time, and size of software code. The coding phase of a **software development cycle** represents only about 10% to 15% of total software cost. *A 20% increase in the cost coding will increase the total cost by 2% to 3% of total development cost [Ali Behforooz].* If this additional effort results in a better-structured, better-documented, and more readable code, the benefits that occur during test, integration, implementation, and operational phase will be more than the additional cost during coding. The criteria for deciding the quality of a software program is the size (**KLOC**), memory utilization, readability, execution time, cyclomatic complexity, and algorithmic complexity.

Programming Language Characteristics

The followings are the indication of the extent of language support for the characteristics. Programs written in a particular language will vary widely with respect to these characteristics, depending on the support provided by language, skill, and discipline of the programmers.

a. **Clarity of source code:** The extent to which inherent language features support source code which is readable and understandable and that clearly reflects the underlying logical structure of the program.

   Most of the life cycle cost of a software system (usually between 60% and 80%) will come during the time after its initial development has been completed **[Schach] [Sommerville]**. This includes all the efforts to change the software, whether it is to fix the problems or to add new capabilities. Regardless of the purpose, changing the software implies that a significant cost will be associated with understanding the program and its structure. This is the first step before any changes can be made. Although it is always possible to use techniques to make a program easier to understand. Language support for source code clarity can facilitate this process considerably. Note that clarity is a readability issue. It is not unusual for languages with good readability to be somewhat more verbose than less readable languages.

b. **Complexity management (architecture support):** The extent to which inherent language features support the management of system complexity, in terms of addressing issues of data, algorithm, interface, and architectural complexity.

   The more complex a system get, the more important its complexity to be managed. Properly structuring a system from beginning, as well as using appropriate supporting tools, is essential. However, complexity management is always difficult, and it is very helpful if the language can facilitate this goal.

c. **Concurrency support:** The extent to which inherent language features support the construction of code with multiple threads of control (also known parallel processing).

For many types of applications, multiple threads of control are very useful. This is particularly true for real-time systems and those running on hardware with multiple processors. Concurrency is rarely directly supported by a language, and, in fact, the philosophy of some languages is that it should be a separate issue for the operating system to deal with. However, the language support can make concurrent processing more straightforward and understandable, and it can also provide the programmer with more control over how it is implemented.

d. **Distributed system support:** The extent to which inherent language features support the construction of code to be distributed across multiple platforms on a network.

It is becoming more and more common for the software components of systems, particularly for a very large software systems, to be distributed across multiple platforms on a network. In this networked configuration, each platform performs some portion of the system functions. This makes sense for various reasons, with performance right at the top of the list. However, distribution creates many new problems, not the least of which is that the multiple platforms are generally heterogeneous (different hardware and/or operating systems). The problems of distribution can be dealt with by tools rather than language. Some newer languages also address the issues of distribution.

e. **Maintainability:** The extent to which inherent language features support the construction of code that can be readily modified to satisfy the new requirements or to correct the deficiencies.

Support for clarity has been mentioned above as one type of support for maintainability. Maintainability is facilitated by many of the language characteristics, those which make it easier to understand and then change the software. The structure of the code also has a significant impact on how easy the code is to change. The technique of encapsulating units and limiting their access through well defined interfaces greatly facilitates the maintainability. Hence, language features which facilitate encapsulation can be very beneficial.

f. **Mixed language support:** The extent to which inherent language features support interfacing to other languages.

This should not be confused with the complementary product support that provides calling **interfaces** (bindings) for specific languages. Binding is the product characteristic tool support for interfacing with other languages. Mixed language support, from the perspective of the language, means the provision of specific capabilities to interface with other languages. This type of support can have a significant impact on the reliability of the data which is exchanged between languages. Without specific language support, no checking may be done on the form, or even the existence, of data exchanged on a call between units of different languages, and the potential for unreliability is high. Specific language support can provide the expected reliability.

g. **Object-oriented programming support:** The extent to which inherent language features support the construction of object-oriented code.

There is general agreement that **object-oriented programming** support means specific language support for the creation of code with encapsulated classes and objects, inheritance, and polymorphism. This form of programming is associated with the software that has good maintainability characteristics because of the encapsulation of classes and objects. It also facilitates the creation of reusable software because it encourages well-structured software with well-defined interfaces, and existing abstractions. There are two different ways a language can provide object-oriented programming support. Some languages are strictly object-oriented and do not support any other form of programming. Other languages provide object-oriented capabilities along with more conventional programming capabilities, and the programmer determines whether or not the language is used to create object-oriented software. For this language characteristic, the specific mechanism for providing the capability is not the issue but the extent of support.

h. **Portability:** The extent to which inherent language features support the transfer of a program from one hardware and/or software platform to another.

To make software readily portable, it must be written using **non-system-dependant** constructs except where system dependencies are encapsulated. The system dependent parts, if any, must be re-accomplished for the new platform, but if those parts of the software are encapsulated, a relatively small amount of new code is required to run the software on the new platform. Language support for portability come from support for encapsulation, and it can also come from support for expressing constructs in a non-system-dependent manner. Language standardization has a significant impact on the portability because non-standard language constructs can only be ported to systems that support the same non-standard constructs. Consider an example, if both systems have compilers from the same vendor. In some circles, the issue of existing compatible support products, including compilers, on many different platforms is considered in the concept of portability. Note that a language's portability characteristics can be severely compromised by poor programming practices.

i. **Real-time support:** The extent to which inherent language features support the construction of real-time system.

Real-time systems have mandatory time constraints, and often space constraints, that must be met. These will usually tax both the software and the hardware of the system, and system performance predictability becomes an important issue. Language can support real-time systems in two ways. A language can provide specific constructs for specifying the time and space constraints of a system. It can also support streamlined ways to express the program instructions. For example, real-time systems often have unique requirements in areas such as device control and interrupt handling, and a language can support managing these in a straightforward, predictable manner. Since many real-time systems are concurrent systems, real-time support, and concurrency support are closely related.

j. **Reliability:** The extent to which inherent language features support the construction of components that can be expected to perform their intended functions in a satisfactory manner throughout the expected lifetime of the product.

Reliability is concerned with making a system failure free, and thus is concerned with all possible errors. System reliability is suspected when software being stressed to its capacity limits or when it is interfacing with resources outside the system, particularly when receiving input from such resources. One way that interfacing with outside resources occurs is when users operate the system. Reliability problems often surface when novices use the system, because they can provide unexpected input that was not tested. Interfacing with outside resources also occurs when the system is interfacing with devices or other software systems. Language can provide support for this potential reliability problem through consistency checking of data exchanged. Language can also provide the support for robustness with features facilitating the construction of independent (encapsulated) components which do not communicate with the other parts of the software except through well-defined interfaces. Language may also provide support for reliability by supporting explicit mechanisms for dealing with problems that are detected when the system is in operation (exception handling). Note that poor reliability in a safety-oriented portion of the software also becomes a safety issue.

k. **Reusability:** The extent to which inherent language features support the adaptation of code for use in another application.

Code is reusable when it is independent of other code except for communication through well-defined interfaces. This type of construction can occur at many levels. It is very common, for example, to reuse common data structures, such as stacks, queues, and trees. When these have been defined with common operations on the structures, these **abstract data types** are easy to reuse. When reusing larger portion of code, the biggest issue for reusability is whether the interfaces defined for the code to be reused are compatible with the interfaces defined for the system being created. This is facilitated by the definition of software architecture for the domain of the system under construction. If those defining the components to be reused are aware of the architecture definition, then they can follow the standard interfaces defined in the architecture to ensure the code is reusable for other systems by using the same architecture. Reusing at any level can be facilitated by language features that make it easy to write independent (encapsulated) modules with well-defined interfaces.

l. **Safety:** The extent to which inherent language features support the construction of safety-critical systems, yielding systems that are fault-tolerant, fail-safe, or robust in the face of the system failure.

Safety is related to reliability, but it is of great deal. The more reliable a system is, the more it does what is expected. A system is safe if it protects against the physical danger to people, as well as against loss or damage to other physical resources, such as equipment. This implies that the system must always do what is expected from it and be able to recover from any situation that might lead to a mishap or actual system hazard. Thus, safety tries to ensure that any failures that occur are minor consequences, and even potentially dangerous failures are handled in a fail-safe fashion. Language can facilitate this through such features as a rigorous computational model, built-in consistency checking, and exception handling.

m. **Standardization:** The extent to which inherent language definition has been formally standardized (by recognized bodies such as **ANSI** and **ISO**) and the extent to which it can be reasonably expected that this standard will be followed in a language translator.

Most popular languages are standardized through ANSI and ISO, but an important issue here is that the language definition that is supported by a compiler product may not be that which is standardized. Most languages have evolved in a manner that has produced a proliferation of different dialects before the languages was standardized, and the result has been that most compiler product support non-standard features from these dialects in addition to the standard language. Some of these products also support a mode that enforces the use of the standard languages constructs, but programmer discipline is still required to use this mode.

n. **Support for modern engineering methods:** The extent to which inherent language features support the expression of source code that enforces good software engineering principles.

Support for modern software engineering methods is to encourage the use of good engineering practices and discourages poor practices. Hence, support for code clarity, encapsulation, and all forms of consistency checking are Language features that provide this support. Also, support for complexity management and construction of large systems and subsystems support software engineering tenets.

Fundamentals of Computer Language

The first computer codes were specialized for the applications. In the first decades of the twentieth century, numerical calculations were based on the decimal numbers. Eventually, it was realized that logic could be represented with numbers, as well as with words. For example, Alonzo Church was able to express the lambda calculus in a formulaic way.

Like many "*firsts*" in history, the first modern programming language is hard to identify. From the start, the restrictions of the hardware defined the language. Punch cards allowed 80 columns, but some of the columns had to be used for sorting number on each card. **FORTRAN** included some keywords which were the same as English words, such as "IF", "*GOTO*" (go to) and "*CONTINUE*". To some people the answer depends on how much power and human-readability is required before the status of "*programming language*" is granted. Jacquard looms and Charles Babbage's Difference Engine both had simple, extremely limited languages for describing the actions that these machines should perform.

In the 1940s the first recognizably modern, electrically powered computers were created. The limited speed and memory capacity forced programmers to write hand tuned Assembly language programs. It was soon discovered that programming in assembly language required a great deal of intellectual effort and was error-prone.

In the 1950s the first three modern programming languages whose descendants are still in widespread use today were designed:

FORTRAN (1955), the "FORmula TRANslator", invented by John W. Backus et al.;

LISP, the "LISt Processor", invented by John McCarthy et al.;

COBOL, the COmmon Business Oriented Language, created by the Short Range Committee, heavily influenced by Grace Hopper.

Another milestone in the late 1950s was the publication, by a committee of American and European computer scientists, of "a new language for algorithms"; the Algol 60 Report (the "ALGOrithmic Language"). This report consolidated many ideas circulating at the time and featured two key language innovations:

- **Arbitrarily nested block structure:** meaningful chunks of code could be grouped into statement blocks without having to be turned into separate, explicitly named procedures;

- **Lexical scoping:** a block could have its own variables that code outside the chunk cannot access, let alone manipulate.

Another innovation, related to this, was in how the language was described:

- A mathematically exact notation, Backus-Naur Form (BNF), was used to describe the language's syntax. Nearly all subsequent programming languages have used a variant of BNF to describe the context-free portion of their syntax.

Algol 60 was particularly influential in the design of later languages, some of which soon became more popular. The Burroughs large systems were designed to be programmed in an extended subset of Algol.

Algol 68's many little-used language features (concurrent and parallel blocks) and its complex system of syntactic shortcuts and automatic type coercions made it unpopular with implementers and gained it a reputation of being difficult. Niklaus Wirth actually walked out of the design committee to create the simpler Pascal language.

The period from the late 1960s to the late 1970s brought a major flowering of programming languages. Most of the major language paradigms now in use were invented in this period:

- Simula, invented in the late 1960s by Nygaard and Dahl as a superset of Algol 60, was the first language designed to support object-oriented programming.
- C, an early systems programming language, was developed by Dennis Ritchie and Ken Thompson at Bell Labs between 1969 and 1973.
- Smalltalk (mid 1970s) provided a complete ground-up design of an object-oriented language.
- Prolog, designed in 1972 by Colmerauer, Roussel, and Kowalski, was the first logic programming language.
- ML built a polymorphic type system (invented by Robin Milner in 1973) on top of Lisp, pioneering statically typed functional programming languages.

Each of these languages spawned an entire family of descendants, and most modern languages count at least one of them in their ancestry.

The 1960s and 1970s also saw considerable debate over the merits of *"structured programming"*, which essentially meant programming without the use of **GOTO**. This debate was closely related to language design: some languages did not include GOTO, which forced *structured programming* on the programmer. Although the debate raged hotly at the time, nearly all programmers now agree that, even in languages that provide GOTO, it is bad style to use it except in rare circumstances. As a result, later generations of language designers have found the structured programming debate tedious and even bewildering.

The 1980s was the year of relative consolidation. C++ combined object-oriented and systems programming. The United States government standardized Ada, a systems programming language intended for use by defense contractors. In Japan and elsewhere, vast sums were spent investigating so-called "fifth generation" languages that incorporated logic programming constructs. The functional languages community moved to standardize ML and Lisp. Rather than inventing new paradigms, all of these movements elaborated upon the ideas invented in the previous decade.

However, one new important new trend in language design was an increased focus on programming for large-scale systems through the use of modules, or large-scale organizational units of code. Modula, Ada, and ML all developed notable module systems in the 1980s. Module systems were often wedded to generic programming constructs---generics being, in essence, parameterized modules.

Although major new paradigms for programming languages did not appear, many researchers expanded their ideas of prior languages and adapted them to new contexts. For example, the languages of the **Argus** and **Emerald** systems adapted **object-oriented programming** to distributed systems.

The 1980s also brought advances in programming language implementation. The RISC movement in computer architecture postulated that hardware should be designed for compilers rather than for human assembly programmers. Aided by processor speed improvements that enabled increasingly aggressive compilation techniques, the RISC movement sparked greater interest in compilation technology for high-level languages.

The 1990s saw no fundamental novelty, but much recombination as well as maturation of old ideas. A big driving philosophy was programmer productivity. Many "rapid application development" languages emerged, which usually came with an Integrated development environment (IDE), garbage collection, and were descendants of older languages. All such languages were object-oriented. These included Object Pascal, Visual Basic, and C#. Java was a more conservative language that also featured garbage collection and received much attention. More radical and innovative than the RAD languages were the new scripting languages. These did not directly descend from other languages and featured new syntaxes and more liberal incorporation of features. Many consider these scripting languages to be more productive than even the RAD languages, but often because of choices that make small programs simpler but large programs more difficult to write and maintain. Nevertheless, scripting languages came to be the most prominent ones used in connection with the Web.

Haskell (1990). Python (1991), Java (1991), Ruby (1993), Lua (1993), ANSI Common Lisp (1994), JavaScript (1995), PHP (1995), C# (2000), and JavaFX Script (2008) are some of the languages are in use.

Programming language evolution continues, in both industry and research. Some of the current trends include:

- **Mechanisms for adding security and reliability verification to the language:** extended static checking, information flow control, and static thread safety.

- **Alternative mechanisms for modularity:** mixins, delegates, aspects.

- Component-oriented software development.

- Meta-programming, reflection, or access to the abstract syntax tree

- Increased emphasis on distribution and mobility.

- Integration with databases, including XML and relational databases.

- Support for Unicode so that source code (program text) is not restricted to those characters contained in the ASCII character set; allowing, for example, use of non-Latin-based scripts or extended punctuation.

- XML for graphical interface (XUL, XAML).

Computer Languages

Around more than 250 languages have been used till today. Computer languages can be categorized as procedural, nonprocedural, imperative, declarative, functional, logic, object oriented, fourth generation, and fifth generation. Some of the categories overlap, and some languages belong to more than one category.

Categories of Computer Languages

1. **Procedural Languages:** The programmer can precisely define each step to perform a task. Through the language the programmer can give step by step instruction on how the task is going to be accomplished. The programmer can specify language statements to perform a sequence of algorithmic steps. To find the average of three numbers, the procedural language will direct the computer through language statements to add the three numbers by adding the first two, then adding the third one to the result and then dividing the sum by three to obtain the average of the three numbers. Such languages are Ada, Algol, BASIC, C, C++, COBOL, FORTRAN, Pascal, and so on.

2. **Nonprocedural Languages:** The programmer tells the computer through language, what must be done, but leaves the details of how to perform the task to the language itself. To compute the average of three numbers, a nonprocedural language will require the programmer to state: Compute average of X, Y, Z. Some of the nonprocedural languages are SQL, dBase, and Paradox. Fourth generation languages are nonprocedural.

3. **Imperative Languages:** In this the expressions are computed and results are stored as variables. Language control statements direct the computer to execute an exact sequence of statements. Most of the procedural languages

are high-level languages. Some of the imperative languages are COBOL, FORTRAN, BASIC, Pascal, C, C++, and Ada.

4. **Declarative Languages:** Most logic programming languages are considered as declarative languages. The semantic definitions in declarative languages are called declarative semantics. In an imperative language the programmer is required to keep the track of many elements that may be distributed throughout the program; example: type definition, data structure definition, and scoping. Where as in a declarative semantic the meaning of an expression is contained within expression itself.

5. **Functional Languages:** In functional Language every entity is a function. A function in functional language has the same meaning as a function in mathematics. In mathematics a function has a name and one or more arguments. So, it is with a functional programming language. LISP is one of the oldest and most widely used functional language. Other functional programming languages are FP, Miranda, ML, and FQL. Both functional and imperative languages are mainly procedural language.

6. **Logic Languages:** The design of the logic programming languages is based on mathematical propositions to define the objects and operations on objects. The language is designed around mathematical logic, predicate calculus, and lambda calculus. Languages used for logic programming are usually declarative languages. Prolog is a widely used logic programming language. Other languages are SASL, HASL, and LOGLISP.

7. **Object-Oriented Languages:** Smalltalk is the first truly object-oriented programming language. The object-oriented languages define and use classes, inheritance and polymorphism. Ada95, C++, JAVA are some of the most widely used languages among many available products today. One of the goals of object-oriented programming language is to achieve both reusability and evolvability.

8. **Visual Languages:** This has got a wide acceptability by the users due to its graphic user interface capability. The languages under this category are Visual Basic, Visual C++, Visual FoxPro, and Visual Pascal. Its graphic interactive communication with user made it popular.

9. **Fourth-Generation Languages (4GL):** In early 1980s many such languages were developed. These are very easy to learn and use. The main goal was to develop a nonprocedural language. These languages were put into a new category called fourth generation languages. The main emphasis was to give novice users the capability to define, design, and develop application software without involving a professional programmer. The combination of 4GLs and databases created a powerful database management system. Microsoft and Oracle have developed such languages and became popular. Languages of this category are ADF, ADS, APL, DMS, Focus, Intellect, Natural, and SQL. Many of these languages are available on PC platforms.

10. **Fifth-Generation Languages:** Till today there is no such distinct language available on computer. Some of the 4GLs showed an extended capability. The 5GLs are supposed to make communications with computers as easy as like human communicate with each other and possibly with the same tools through voice and vision.

Some Important Languages

The chronological evolution of programming language was discussed in the previous section. The details of some of the important languages are:

Machine Language refers to the *"ones and zeroes"* that digital processors use as instructions. Give it one pattern of bits (11001001) and it will add two numbers, give it a different pattern (11001010), it will instead subtract one from the other in as little as a billionth of second. The instruction sets within a CPU family are usually compatible, but not between product lines. For example, Intel's x86/Pentium language and Motorola's PPC/Gx language are completely incompatible. Machine Language is painfully difficult to work with, and almost never worth the effort anymore. Instead programmers use the higher-level languages, which are either compiled or interpreted into machine language by the computer itself with the help of compiler or interpreter.

Assembly Language is as close as you can come to writing in machine language, but has the advantage that it's also human-readable, using a small vocabulary of words with one syllable. Each written instruction (such as MOV A,B) typically corresponds to a single machine-language instruction (such as 11001001). An assembler makes the translation before the program is executed. Back when CPU speed was measured in Kilo-Hertz and storage space was measured in Kilo-Bytes, Assembly language was the most cost-efficient way to implement a program. It is used less often now (with all those kilo's replaced by *mega's* or *giga's*, and even *tera's* on the horizon, it seems no one cares anymore about efficiency), but if you need speed and/or compactness above all else, Assembly language is the solution.

C [successor to the language "*B*"] offers an elegant compromise between the efficiency of coding in assembly language and the convenience and portability of writing in a structured, high-level language. By keeping many of its commands and syntax analogous to those of common machine languages, and with several generations of optimizing compilers behind it, C makes it easy to write fast code without necessarily sacrificing readability. But it still tempts you to write code that only a machine can follow, which can be a problem when it comes time to debug it or make changes. Free and commercial tools (most of which now also support C++) are available from various sources for just about every operating system.

C++ ["C" with the C instruction to "*increment*"] is probably the most widely-supported language today, and most commercial software is written in **C++**. The name reflects why: when it was introduced it took all the benefits of the then-reigning development language (C) and incrementally added the next set of features programmers were looking for (*Object Oriented Programming-OOP*). So, programmers didn't have to throw anything out and re-do it; but they could add those techniques to their repertoire as needed. OO purists hate the results, but it's difficult to argue with that success. Free and commercial tools are available from various sources for just about every operating system. Objective-C is an alternate approach to adding OO characteristics to C (borrowing directly from SmallTalk), which hasn't attracted large community of users.

C# ["C++" with the plus signs overlapping, pronounced "*C sharp*"] is actually Microsoft's answer to Java. They originally tried to release "*Java*" development tools that would produce applications that weren't truly portable; you could only use them on Windows. But this violated their licensing agreement with Sun (creators of Java), who successfully put a stop to that. So, Microsoft turned around and produced a language with similar features that effectively is tied to Windows. Although they are submitting the language to a standard-setting body, for all practical purposes it's just a proprietary variant of C++ whose specs they'll dictate, available only from Microsoft, and practical only for Windows.

Java [slang for "*coffee*"] is kind of a streamlined version of C++, designed for portability. Its key advantage is that the Java programs can be run on any operating system for which a Java "*virtual environment*" is available. (Programs in most other languages have to be modified and recompiled to go from one Operating System to another.) The language is defined by Sun and widely licensed to other companies, making it possible to run Java applications in web browsers, portable phones, desktop computers, web servers, and so on. It isn't as fast as applications written in a compiled language like **C++**. However, free, and commercial tools are available from various sources for most current operating systems. Although Microsoft is removing support for Java from the default setup of new versions of Windows, it can easily be added back in.

Pascal [mathematician/philosopher Blaise Pascal] was designed primarily as a tool for teaching good programming skills, but - thanks largely to the availability of Borland's inexpensive Pascal compiler for the early **IBM PC** - it has become popular outside of the classroom. Unlike many languages, Pascal requires a fairly structured approach, which prevents the kinds of indecipherable "spaghetti code" and easily-overlooked mistakes that plague programmers using languages such as **Fortran** or **C**. Free and commercial tools are available from various sources for DOS, Windows, Mac, OS/2, AmigaOS, and Unix-like systems. The web site editor BBEdit is written in Pascal.

Delphi [home of the Greek oracle Pythia] is a non-standard, object-oriented version of **Pascal** developed by **Borland** for their rapid application development tool of the same name. The Delphi environment was designed to compete with Microsoft's

Visual Basic tools, freeing the programmer from having to write all the code for the user interface by letting her drag and drop objects and attach functions to various buttons and other on-screen elements. Its ability to manipulate databases is another strength. Commercial tools are available from Borland for Windows and Linux.

BASIC ["*Beginner's All-purpose Symbolic Instruction Code*"] is the first language that most early microcomputer users learned. The BASIC interpreters on those machines weren't very sophisticated or fast, largely due to the memory and speed limitations of the hardware, and the language encouraged sloppy coding. "*BASIC is to computer languages what Roman numerals are to arithmetic*". Modern versions of BASIC are more structured. They often include compilers for greater speed. Free and commercial tools are available from various sources for DOS, Windows, Mac, and Unix-like systems.

Visual Basic [a version of "*BASIC*" for graphical environments] is Microsoft's Jack of all Trades language. It's a cross between BASIC, the various macro languages of Microsoft Office, and some **rapid application development** tools. The idea was to get people started writing macros using **VBA (Visual Basic for Applications),** then sell them the whole VB programming tool when they run into the limits of that approach. Unfortunately, VB applications are impossible to port to other environments, and you're at the mercy of Microsoft's changing specs for the language. Programs written in **VB6** or earlier will not run properly in **VB.NET.** It is available only from Microsoft and run in Windows.

SmallTalk ["*easy conversation*"] is object-oriented. Graphical Smalltalk development environment is what inspired Steve Jobs and later Bill Gates to "*invent*" the Mac OS and Windows interfaces. Focusing on the superficial aspects of it (windows and mice) they missed the real gem: the language.

Squeak [the sound a mouse makes] is a variant of **SmallTalk**, created by alumni of the **Xerox PARC** (where SmallTalk and the computer mouse were invented) and of Apple, who are now working at Disney (home of a famous mouse). It's a deliberately open system, with even the Squeak interpreter itself written in **Squeak**. This makes it highly portable, and it isavailable for Mac OS, Windows (95 and later), WinCE, Unix-like systems, BeOS, OS/2, and RISC OS. Squeak makes it possible for a programmer to modify the language itself. The interpreter, optional compiler, and everything else are free.

PERL ["*Practical Extraction and Report Language*"] is often treated as synonymous with "*CGI scripting*". In fact, Perl is even older than the Web itself; it got its nose into the Web-scripting tent and thrived due to its strong text-processing abilities, incredible flexibility (its creator likens it to duct tape), portability (it's available for nearly every modern operating system), and price (free). The Internet Movie Database and Yahoo both run on it.

Ruby [the birthstone for July (following "*PERL*" for June)] combines some of the best features of several other languages, leaving behind many of their shortcomings. It's a pure object-oriented language like **SmallTalk**, but with clearer syntax (inspired by Eiffel). It has powerful text-handling like Perl, but is better structured and more consistent. It borrows ideas (but not the parentheses) from Lisp. Those who've tried it seem to love it, and rarely switch back to their previous languages. A free interpreter is available for Windows, Unix-like, Mac, OS/2, and BeOS systems.

Python [comedy troupe **Monty Python**] is an open-source, interpreted object-oriented language developed for Unix and now available for everything from DOS to Mac OS to OS/2 to Windows to Unix-like systems. It shares many positive attributes with Ruby, and adds the ability to run it on any machine that supports Java. It is often criticized, however, for not being as purely **object-oriented** as other languages.

[Director and **Flash]** are the de facto tools of choice for developing web sites featuring dynamic media. They are not really "*languages*", though both include a bit of their own scripting. Instead they are GUI development environments for producing "*source code*" modules containing both data and instructions, which can in turn be "*compiled*" into executable programs. As tools for creating snazzy graphical user interfaces, they are top-notch, but they require some separate back-end programming for anything that will require processing or manipulating data.

LISP ["*LISt Processing*"] is "*a programmable programming language*", built on the concept of recursion and highly adaptable to vague specifications. Avoid it if you find parentheses unappealing (its syntax tends toward a proliferation of nested parentheses), but its ability to handle problems that other languages cannot is one of the reasons that this more than year-old language is still in use. There's an entire cross-platform web server written in it.

PROLOG ["*PROgramming in LOGic*"] is an independent study project in college, written a Prolog application which evaluated and proved (if possible) arguments in propositional logic (example, "*A implies B, and A is true, therefore B is true*") a task which would have been much more difficult using a procedural language.

ToonTalk is a highly-visual environment designed to teach children the principles of programming. Rather than typing instructions, the programmer manipulates various objects (LEGO-looking toy items that come to life when used) to define how the system is supposed to work. Unlike "*educational*" puzzle-solving computer games, ToonTalk encourages its users to create their own puzzles. Experienced C++ programmers will hate it, but then, most 4th-graders wouldn't care for C++). It's available for Windows only.

COBOL ["*Common Business-Oriented Language*"] is the language which modern programmers love to hate and ridicule. Although it is nearly as old as commercial computing itself, improperly blamed for Y2K issues, and its imminent extinction is frequently predicted, it is still in widespread use due to its usefulness for traditional business uses of processing data and producing reports. A version with object-oriented tools has been created, with an inexpensive **integrated development environment** for Linux and Windows available. It is very verbose, designed so that its commands would describe in English exactly what it was doing. Example, ADD SHIPPING-CHARGE TO INVOICE-SUBTOTAL.

FORTRAN ["*FORmula TRANslation*"] is the oldest language but still in general use, dating back to 1957, the year the Space Age began. It excels at the first task computers were called on for: number-crunching. This is the language that literally put a man on the moon, and some of the features it developed in the process of that project (and other less glamorous ones) have yet to be duplicated in other, more "*modern*" languages.

DBASE ["*DataBASE*"] (renamed "*Xbase*" to avoid trademark issues) was the command language for Ashton-Tate's ground-breaking database management program (the first such tool for microcomputers). As the program grew, so did the language, until it became an application development tool in its own right. At its zenith, various competing implementations and compilers were available and the language became standardized. Xbase didn't make the transition to Windows very well, but it's still being used and supported (kind of the **COBOL** of the microcomputer age).

Coding Style

The followings are some rules and guidelines that will lead to a better programming style:

a. The identifiers should be as simple as possible and meaningful which need not to be explained. Use as much as comment lines for proper understanding. Avoid using identifiers like SUB1, SUB2, TOTAL_1, or TOTAL_2, and so on. These may cause typographical errors to mistype SUB2 for SUB1 which may not be noticed during compilation or execution.

b. Same names not to be used for two different variables. Same name for both global and local variables may cause disasters and confusion in debugging. Use more local definitions, data types, and identifiers. Don't clutter with more global variables to save few lines of code.

c. Use simple key elements for a successful completion of a program. Shortcuts, tricky code, and complicated algorithms will conceal errors, and reduce readability.

d. Function should be simple and should compute one value. Use the function that returns a value and the function that returns no value (void) appropriately. The function in mathematics has one or more than one argument and produce one value and does not redefine or change the value of its arguments during computation. Function arguments should not be used to return values to calling **program**. Avoid using a function without an argument *e.* Use a procedure subprogram to perform a simple task as we know the **procedure** is a **task oriented** and a **function** is **value oriented**. At the beginning of each subprogram, define the arguments and their initial values. Also, for those arguments that return values to the calling program, define the value they must return.

f. For control structures, the program control pointer must enter the structure at its entry point and leave it at its exit point. Do not create a conditional jump from the middle of a control structure to a point outside the structure. This shortcut may save execution time but it may also result in the loss of readability, understandability, and comprehension. If necessary to use nested control structures, limit the direct nesting to no more than three levels. Nested loops and if-then-else statements reduce the readability of the program. Too many nested subprograms make it extremely difficult to follow the program logic.

g. Use of GOTO, a BREAK, or EXIT statements can clarify a control structure or divide a long control structure to small ones. Limit the use of GOTO statements to only these kinds of situations.

h. Avoid defining subprograms whose execution may create confusion. Try to describe it clearly. Limit the number of arguments in a subprogram up to five. Too many arguments reduce clarity and readability.

i. A better program is simple, clear, easy to understand, and maintain. The fastest program is not necessarily the shortest program. Therefore, while developing a program avoid using difficult and tricky statements to shorten the program.

j. Use abstraction in the design and coding programs only to the extent program readability is preserved. The use of abstraction helps to create reusable code.

k. While writing code use more indentation for better clarity and readability.

l. To improve the portability of the program, use minimum system utilities.

m. Effective use of comment statements strategically located in the code can enhance program understanding greatly.

Coding Quality

The coding consumes a small fraction (10% to 15%) of the entire software development cost and schedule. A poorly written program can have very bad effect at the time of testing and maintenance. A good program has certain measurable attributes. These attributes can be specified in the **Software Requirements Specification (SRS)** and tested during **test** and **integration** phases. Subsequently these attributes can become quality assurance parameters for the program. The attributes include:

- **Readability, Understandability, and Comprehensibility (RUC):** The most important characteristics of a program are smooth readability, following the logic and its structure. RUC refers to all these features and assists in debugging and maintenance of a program.

- **Logical Structure:** Application of structured programming rules help to create a logically and structurally sound coding. A well designed and structured program will have low level of coupling and high level of cohesion among its subprograms and will not allow multiple entry and exit points in subprograms. A logically designed program will become stronger and long lasting.

- **Physical Layout:** It refers to the actual listing of the source code of a program. Good use of indentation, separation of key words from identifiers, use of meaningful identifiers, extensive use of comment statements, minimum use of explanatory comment statements, proper beginning, and end of each block are some of the features of physical layout of a good programming.

- **Robustness:** It means how well a program can withstand at the time of handling incorrect input data. A software product must be protected against the misuse and be designed to deal with bad input data. On encountering a bad input data, the execution should not stop and on the other hand sufficient warning should be given on validation or self-correcting capability should be provided. This attribute should be specified in user manual, operation manual, and SRS.

- **Memory and Execution Efficiency:** This refers how fast the program works and how much computer memory is used. A program must use fast and efficient algorithms. Appropriate file, data structures, and access methods should be used. Since the memory of a computer is very expensive, care must be taken to minimize the use of memory without sacrificing the execution efficiency.

- **Complexity:** Both algorithmic complexity and cyclomatic or structural complexity will make the program difficult to understand and implement. Less complexity with less branching of program needs to be used for a good coding.

- **Human Factors:** Proper care must be given in developing the human-to-computer interface. For example, an input screen that is hard to read, has more fields than a person can easily comprehend, is not laid out properly, and is not robust with regard to human error will be rejected by the users. This effect will be an economic failure of the software product.

- **Reusable Code:** Segments of code are available in the libraries or market. In order to reduce the cost of the software product and make it available in shortest possible time these segments are used in different parts of the program. Hence, the reusability attribute of a program segment could be a measure of segment quality.

Art of Debugging

Art of Debugging is a process of locating and correcting the causes of known **errors**. Commonly used debugging methods include induction, deduction, and backtracking.

- Debugging by Induction method involves the following steps:

  a. **Collect the available information.** Enumerate known facts about the observed failure and known facts concerning successful test cases. What are the observed symptoms? When did the error occur? How does the failure case differ from successful cases?

  b. **Look for patterns.** Examine the collected information for conditions that differentiate the failure case from successful cases.

  c. **Form one or more hypothesis.** Derive one or more hypothesis from the observed relationships. If no hypotheses are apparent, re-examine the available information and collect additional information. If several hypotheses emerge, rank them in order of most likely to least likely.

  d. **Prove or disapprove each hypothesis.** Re-examine the available information to determine whether the hypotheses explain all aspects of the observed problem. Do not proceed to steps until step-4 is completed.

  e. **Implement appropriate corrections.** Make the corrections to back-up your copy of the code in case the modifications are not correct.

  f. **Verify the correction.** Rerun the failure case to be sure that the fix corrects the observed symptom. If the fix is not successful, then go to **step a.**

- Debugging by **deduction** method proceeds as follows:

  a. List possible causes for the observed failure.

  b. Use the available information to eliminate various hypotheses.

  c. Elaborate the remaining hypotheses.

  d. Prove or disapprove each hypothesis.

  e. Determine the appropriate correctness.

  f. Verify the corrections.

- Debugging by **backtracking** involves working backward in the source code from the point where the error was observed in an attempt to identify the exact point where the error occurred.

Traditional Debugging

Traditional debugging techniques utilize:

a. **Diagnostic output statements:** These can be embedded in the source code as specially formatted comment statement that are activated using a special translator option.

b. **Snap shot dumps:** A snapshot dump is a machine level representation of the partial or total program state at a particular point in the execution sequence.

c. **Trace facility:** A trace facility lists changes in selected state components.

d. **Traditional breakpoint:** This facility interrupts program execution and transfers control to the programmer's terminal when execution reaches a specified break instruction in the source code.

Modern Debugging

Modern debugging tools utilize:

a. **Assertion-driven debugging:** Assertions are logical predicates written in the source code level to describe relationships among the components of current program state and relationships between program states. An assertion violation can alter the execution sequence. Assertion violation that transfer control to the programmer's terminal are called **conditional break points.** They become unconditional break points under assertion such as $0 = 1$ or false. Conditional break points are state dependent while unconditional break points are instruction dependent.

   Consider an example: For an assertion-driven debugging and unit testing tool is AL ADD IN (Assembly language Assertion Driven Debugging Interpreter).

b. **Execution histories:** An execution history is a record of execution events collected from an executing program. The history is typically stored in a database for post-mortem examination after the program has terminated execution. A trace back facility uses the execution history to trace the control flow and data flow both forward and backward in execution time.

In this approach, only changes in execution state are recorded as the program executes. This approach is use to reduce the unreasonable overhead in execution time and memory space that would be required to maintain a complete copy of the execution state at each step in the execution sequence. **Executable Debugging and Monitoring System (EXDAMS)** and **Interactive Semantic Modeling System (ISMS)** are the examples for this approach.

Debugging Process

Debugging is done when a failure occurs during the execution of a software program. The failure symptoms are examined through a debugging process. Testing and debugging are of different activities with different objectives. In testing, the primary objective is to produce failures due to the software faults. The testing team finds a way to make the software to fail. The objective of debugging is to locate and remove the identified fault in a module. **The debugging process consists of six steps:**

a. Information gathering

b. Fault location

c. Confirmation

d. Documentation

e. Fault removal

f. Retesting.

For the failure the related data and information should be collected. The fault must be localized within a small segment of the software like a function, a procedure, or a small block of code. The fault must be uncovered that is causing failure. The debugging process and remedial actions taken must be documented.

Information Gathering

The software engineer, during debugging, tries to collect as much information as it can on the failure. He may refer to test logs, test anomaly report, hearsay, and eye witness accounts, and so on.. Frequent feedback from debugging will help in improving the quality of the software. The debugging activity is supported by the test log and anomaly reports. To debug a software, it is essential to learn more about it so that the debugging process is easier and smooth.

Fault Isolation

It is necessary to isolate the failure to a specific statement, a block of statements, a control structure, and so on. There are different types of approaches to isolate failure. The first approach is **binary approach** by which an attempt is made to bracket the statements or control structures those are the sources of failure. The second approach is the **structured question and answer approach** where a set of questions is posed and answered. The third approach is based by **inducing other people into failure analysis**. The fourth approach relies on the **development of new test cases** specifically designed to isolate the known faults.

Fault Confirmation

Once the fault isolation process identifies a function, a procedure, a control structure, a block of statements, or a single statement as fault, the error must be confirmed. Using additional special testing, desk checking, reviews, walk-through, and other methods, the cause of failure must be fully verified. The fault must be confirmed as the sole cause of failure.

Documentation

A proper documentation is required on every correction, updating, modification, and addition. The abnormal behavior of the program under new test cases must be recorded. A structured documentation of the debugging process helps in testing process. A large program may run perfectly at test site but may not run properly at operation site. In such cases the embedded software is blamed for the problems. Therefore, based on the documentation, all the system engineer, software engineer, hardware engineer, and tester must work together to sort out the problem.

Fixing the Fault

On confirmation of the fault with its exact nature, location, remedial action can be initiated. Changing one part of the program may influence other part immediately or remain latent for the future. The software must be evaluated carefully. The best way is to re-run the selected portion of the program during acceptance test.

Test after Correction

After each modification, change, or correction in the module the full software needs to be tested. Change in a specific path may cause failures in another place. Execute new test cases to ensure the affected area is working without any further failure. The test and integration team must work together to ensure the correctness of the unexecuted portion.

Debugging Tools

The debugging tools are generally embedded with the compiler which help the software engineer to locate the logical errors in the program. This helps in identifying and removing the errors effectively. The debugging tools facilitates a structured walk through, while the program is in execution mode. There are a variety of debuggers that works differently with different levels of sophistication. The debuggers show the errors on the screen in the form of a visual trace of execution. The programmer is able to see the statement with an indication of the error. The statement under execution will show all types of errors directly or indirectly. An experienced programmer can use the debugger to reduce the debugging time effectively. The debugger is especially helpful in isolating the source of the reported error.

Summary

This chapter describes the evolution of coding language and different languages widely used for writing a program. The chapter has also discussed on the characteristics of a language that can be used in coding effectively. The difference in testing and debugging can be realized here. The debugging process is discussed here, and the steps involved are:

a. Investigating the different errors thoroughly to isolate the failure causing faults

b. Confirming the identified faults by additional tests

c. Correcting the faults with same degree of discipline and control as in the original development process

d. Performing the regression testing on the software product.

This ensures that the program is fully corrected and bug free.

Questions and Answers

What is debugging?

1. In software development, debugging involves locating and correcting code errors in a computer program. Debugging is part of the software testing process and is an integral part of the entire software development lifecycle.

What are the outcomes of debugging process?

2. The cause will be found, corrected, and removed.

3. What are the categories of debugging?

4. Brute force, backtracking, cause elimination.

Define defect removal efficiency

5. Defect removal efficiency is a quality metric that provides the benefit of both project and process level. It is the ratio between the defects removed to the total number of defects.

6. **List some categories of faults**

a. **Logic problems:** Duplicate logic, forgotten steps, extreme conditions neglected, unnecessary functions, missing condition, using wrong variables, iterating loops incorrectly, computational problems, incorrect or insufficient equations, precision loss.

b. **Interface/timing problem:** Interrupts handled incorrectly, I/O timing incorrect, subroutine/module mismatch, data handling problems, access data incorrectly, incorrect units of data, scope of data incorrect.

   c. **Data problem:** Incorrect or missing sensor data, incorrect or missing operator data, embedded data in table incorrect, I/O data incorrect or missing.

   d. **Documentation problem:** Ambiguous statement, incomplete or incorrect or missing items, conflicting or redundant or confusing items, illogical or non-verifiable or unachievable items.

   e. **Document quality problems:** Application standards not met, inconsistency, incomplete, not traceable.

   f. **Enhancements:** Change in program requirements, improve comments, improve code efficiency, improve usability, improve code efficiency, software fix of a hardware problem, other enhancements.

7. **Define software error, software fault and software failure.**

   Software error is an observed difference between computed values and required values. A software fault occurs whenever it has an incorrect step, process, or data definition. Software failure occurs whenever a software is unable to perform its required function.

8. **What is error tracking?**

   Error tracking allows us to compare the current work with the past efforts and provides a quantitative indication of the work being conducted.

Exercise

1. **Take a newly written program of around 1000 lines and perform the following steps:**

   a. Identify the faults if any in the program.

   b. Isolate the cause of each fault using a debugger.

   c. Remove the failure causing code by replacing a new statement.

   d. At the time of isolating the faults and correcting, other failures may occur. Make a report of them.

2. **While performing the tasks in the above problem collect the data as given:**

   a. Number of faults

   b. Number of errors

   c. Number of failures causing errors found during debugging

   d. Density of faults per 100 line of code.

   e. Test time spent debugging the program

CHAPTER 9
Software Testing

Objective

The objectives of testing a system is to identify all defects existing in software, remove them, and achieve error-free operation under stated conditions for a stated period of time. Testing is vital to the success of a system. System testing makes a logical assumption that if all the parts of the system are correct, the goal will be successfully achieved. Inadequate testing or non-testing leads to errors which may not appear until months later. **This creates two problems**:

   a. The time lag between the cause and the appearance of the problem (the longer the time interval, the more complicated the problem has become).

   b. The effect of the system errors on files and records within the system.

Small system error can conceivably explode into a much larger problem. Effective testing early in the process translates directly into long-term cost savings from a reduced number of errors.

Another objective of system testing is its utility as **a user-oriented** vehicle before implementation. The best program is worthless if it does not meet user needs. Unfortunately, the user's demands are often compromised by the efforts to facilitate program or design efficiency in terms of processing time or memory utilization. Often the computer technician and the user have communication barriers due to different backgrounds, interests, priorities, and languages. The system tester (designer, programmer, or user) who has developed some computer mastery can bridge this barrier.

In **Software Development Life Cycle (SWDLC),** testing is the most important phase. The testing is carried out along with system integration. All types of issues found are unresolved during requirement analysis, design, and coding stage. Many unforeseen problems are handled.

In this chapter, we are going to discuss:
- The dynamics of test and integration during the software development
- Strategies, techniques, and tools used in testing
- Importance of test planning activity
- Identify the types of testing during a test plan.

The testing activity is described here as a part of the system development.

Introduction

The system development phases involve many activities where chances for the occurrence of human errors are enormous. Logical error, carelessness, improper communication, the need to hurry through the whole process of software development due to time constraint, cost constraint, and so on; provide ways for errors to creep in. The system must be tested thoroughly so that such errors are detected and corrected as early as possible. A successful test is the one that uncovers every possible error.

The analyst prepares system specifications that are passed to programmers for coding. The coding takes considerable effort and skill of the programmer to convert the charts, tables, and instructions into program statements. These need to be tested at various intervals. Testing software begins earlier in the systems development life cycle, even though many of the actual testing activities are carried out during implementation. During analysis, a master test plan is developed. The indicative test plan is shown in **Table 9.1**. During design, you develop a unit test plan, an integration test plan, and a system test plan. During implementation, these various plans are put into effect and the actual testing is performed.

Test Plan

The purpose of the written test plans is to improve the communication among all the people involved in testing application software. The plan specifies each person's role during testing. The test plan also serves as a checklist, which you can use to determine whether the entire master test plan has been completed or not. The master test plan is not just a single document but a collection of documents. A master test plan is a project within the overall system development project. The Overall Plan and Testing Requirements sections are like a baseline project plan for testing, with a schedule of events, resource requirements, and standards of practice outlined. Procedure Control explains how testing to be conducted, how to fix errors will be documented.

Testing managers are responsible for developing test plans, establishing testing standards, integrating testing, and development activities in the life cycle, and ensuring the test plans are completed. Testing specialists help in developing test plans, create test cases, and scenarios, execute the actual tests, and analyze report test results.

		Introduction			Procedure control
1	a	Description of the system to be tested	4	a	Test initiation
	b	Objective of the test plan		b	Test execution
	c	Method of testing		c	Test failure
	d	Supporting documents		d	Access/change control
		Overall Plan		e	Document control
2	a	Mile stone, schedule & locations	5		Test specific/component test plans
	b	Test material		a	Objectives
		1. Test plans		b	Software description
		2. Test cases		c	Method
		3. Test scenario		d	Milestone, schedule, location
		4. Test log		e	Requirements
3		Testing requirements		f	Criteria for passing tests
	a	Hardware		g	Resulting test material
	b	Software		h	Execution control
	c	Personnel		i	Attachments

Table: 9.1: Table of Content of a Master Test Plan

Software application testing is an umbrella term that covers several types of tests. **Mosley (1993)** organizes the types of tests according to whether they employ static or dynamic techniques and whether the test is automated or manual. *Static testing* means that the code being tested is not executed. The results of running the code are not an issue for that particular test. *Dynamic testing,* on the other hand, involves execution of code. Automated testing means the computer conducts the test while

Manual testing means that people do. Using this framework, we can categorize type of tests as shown in *Table 9.2* below:

	Manual	**Automated**
Static	Inspections	Syntax checking
Dynamic	Walkthrough	Unit test
	Desk checking	Integration test
		System test

Table: 9.2: A Categorization of Test Types

Inspections

Inspections are formal group of activities where participants manually examine the code for the occurrences of well-known errors. Syntax, grammar, and some other routine errors can be checked by automated inspection software, so manual inspection checks are used for more subtle errors. This detects 60 to 90 percent of all software defects and provides feedback to the programmers with the feedback that enables them to avoid making the same type of errors in future work. It is a testing technique in which participants examine the program code for predictable language-specific errors.

Walkthrough

Walkthrough, in a structured manner, is a very effective method of detecting errors in code. Structured walkthrough is used to review many system development deliverables, including logical and physical design specifications as well as code. The specification walkthrough tends to be formal reviews, code walkthroughs tend to be informal. According to **Yourdon (1989),** code walkthroughs should be done frequently when the pieces of work reviewed are relatively small and before the work is formally tested. Different organizations conduct the walkthrough differently. There is a basic structure you can follow, that works well.

Guidelines for Conducting a Code Walkthrough:

a. Have the review meeting chaired by the project manager or chief programmer, who is also responsible for scheduling the meeting, reserving a room, setting the agenda, inviting participants, and so on.

b. The programmer presents his or her work to the reviewers. Discussion should be general during the presentation.

c. Following the general discussion, the programmer walks through the code in detail, focusing on the logic of the code rather than on specific test cases.

d. Reviewers ask to walk through specific cases.

e. The chair resolves disagreement if the review team cannot reach agreement among themselves and assign duties, usually to the programmer, for making specific changes.

f. A second walkthrough is then scheduled if needed.

Desk Checking

Walkthrough is another testing technique in which the program code is sequentially executed manually by the reviewer. What the code does is also important in desk checking, an informal process where the programmer or some one else, who understands the logic of the program works through the code with a paper and pencil. The programmer executes each instruction by using test cases that may or may not be written down. In one sense, the reviewer acts as the computer, mentally checking each step, and its results for the entire set of computer instructions.

Among the list of automated checking in *Table 9.2*, there is only one *static* technique which checks syntax. Syntax checking is typically done by a compiler. Errors in syntax are uncovered but the code is not executed. For the other three automated techniques, the code is executed.

Unit Testing

Unit testing, sometimes called **module testing** is an automated technique. In unit testing, each module is tested alone in an attempt to discover any error that may exist in the module's code. Since modules coexist and work with other modules in programs and systems, they must be tested together in large groups.

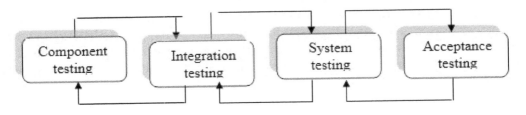

Figure 9.1: Testing process

Except for small programs, system should not be tested as a single, monolithic unit. *Figure 9.1* shows a four-stage testing process where system components are tested, the integrated system is tested and, finally system is tested with the customer's data. On completion of acceptance testing the sign-on procedure takes place between the developer and customer where the handing over of the application system takes place.

Integration Testing

Integration testing is done by combining the modules and testing them together. Integration testing is gradual. The integration plan is guided by the module dependency graph of the structure chart. The structure chart shows the chronological arrangement of various modules calling each other. Hence, by examining the structure chart the integration plan is developed. The structure chart is shown in *Figure 9.2*. First you test the coordinating module (the root module in a structure chart tree) and only one of its subordinate modules. After the first test, you add one or two other subordinate modules from the same level. Once the program has been tested with the coordinating module and all of its immediately subordinate modules, you add modules from the next level and then test the program. The modules are typically integrated in a top-down, incremental order. You continue this procedure until the entire program has been tested as a unit. Some of the popular methods are used in making an integrated test plan.

Top-down approach

Integration starts with the root module and one or two sub modules followed by testing. After the top-level modules are tested, the immediate module is combined and become ready for testing. It is suitable for small systems. It causes problem for testing if there are no lower level routines which may be called by top level one.

Bottom-up approach

In Bottom-up approach, all the sub modules are tested separately and finally the full system is tested. The purpose of testing each sub module is to test the interfaces among them. In this situation control and data interfaces between modules are tested. Lower level sub systems are tested and are combined with the higher-level modules for further testing. The advantage is, many sub systems, having no dependency, can be tested simultaneously. The disadvantage is that during testing of a number of sub systems makes the situation complex. This extreme condition calls for big bang approach.

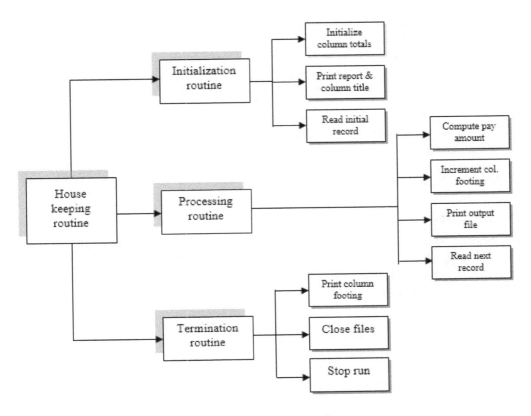

Figure 9.2: *Structure chart of a program*

Big-bang approach

All the sub modules are integrated in a single step and tested together. This approach is convenient for a small system where on one go the errors are fixed. The disadvantage is to spot the error found in the exact module during integration testing. To remove the error during integration testing is costly and time consuming.

Mixed approach

Mixed approach is a combination of both top-down and bottom-up approaches. The disadvantages of both the approaches are reduced to a great extent. The testing is possible from both top and bottom level, wherever the modules are available. This is common approach for integration testing.

System Testing

System testing is a similar process, but instead of integrating modules into programs for testing, you integrate programs into systems. System testing follows the same incremental logic that does the integration testing. Programs are typically integrated in top-down, incremental fashion. Under both integration and system testing, the individual modules and programs get tested many times as well as interfaces between modules and programs also get tested. Considering the testing location and data; two types of testing are conducted.

Alpha testing

Tests performed at the developer's site before the system is finally installed in the real working environment (user's site) is known as **alpha testing**. It involves testing the system with live data supplied by the organization rather than by the test data used by the system designer. Some times it called as *acceptance testing*.

Beta testing

In beta testing, the system is delivered to a number of potential users who agree to use that system and provide feedback to the designers. Testing should be repeated if any modification is done based on the feedback given by the users. Some times it called as regression testing.

Stub testing

Stub testing is a technique used in testing modules, where modules are written and tested in a top-down fashion, where a few lines of code are used to substitute the subordinate modules. Under a top-down approach, the coordinating module is written first. Then the modules at the next level in structure chart are written, followed by the modules at the next level, and so on, until all the modules in the system are done. Each module is tested as it is written. Since top-level modules contain many calls to subordinate modules, you may wonder how they can be tested if the lower level modules haven't been written yet. The answer is stub testing, which is a two to three lines of code written by a programmer to stand for the missing modules. During the testing, the coordinating module calls the stub instead of subordinate module. The stub accepts control and then returns it to the coordinating module.

Acceptance Testing

Acceptance testing is the final stage in the testing process before the system is accepted for operational use by the client. The system is tested with data supplied by the user rather than with simulated data. Acceptance testing may reveal errors and omissions in the system requirement definition because real data exercise the system in different ways from the test data. Acceptance testing may also reveal requirements problems where the system's facilities do not really meet the user's needs or the system performance is not acceptable. (*figure 9.3*)

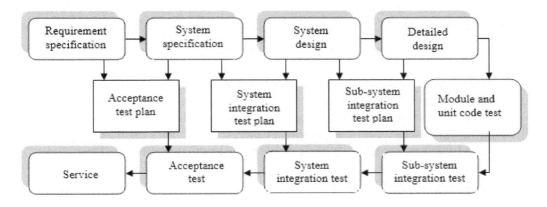

Figure 9.3: *Testing phases in the software process*

Normally, component (unit) development and testing are interleaved. Programmers make up their own test data and incrementally test the code as it is developed. This is an economically sensible approach, as the programmer knows the component best and is therefore the best person to generate test cases.

Static Testing

The static testing refers to **non-executable** files like requirement analysis, audits, desk checks, inspections, and walkthroughs. It is employed to verify the correctness of requirements, designs, and code before execution of the test cases.

The static testing functions are performed in code auditing, consistency checking, cross referencing, interface analysis, input and output specification analysis, data flow analysis, error checking, type analysis, unit analysis, walkthroughs, and clean-room correctness verification.

Dynamic Testing

Dynamic testing is used to describe the development and execution of test cases, test procedures, structures, use of test logs, and so on. The two common ways to perform dynamic testing are **black box and white box testing**. Both the methods require a set of well-developed and well-structured test cases. The dynamic testing can not prove absolute correctness of a software product unless it is performed in an exhaustive manner. The exhaustive testing takes a lot of time to cover up all the possible module paths, combination of paths, and the combination of inputs.

The exhaustive testing of a small system is not practical. For example, suppose one is required to test an integer addition algorithm by employing an exhaustive testing approach. It will include approximately 2^{64} test executions (assuming integers are stored in 32 bits). For a computer that performs 2^{24} operations per second, it will take 240 seconds or approximately 35,000 years to complete an exhaustive test of addition algorithm. Hence an exhaustive testing is not a viable approach.

Test data for unit testing can be constructed systematically in two basic ways. The first is to **test to specifications**. The technique also is called **black-box, behavioral, data-driven, functional,** and **input/output-driven testing**. In this approach, the code itself is ignored. The only information used in drawing up test cases is the specification document. The other extreme is to **test to code** and to ignore the specification document when selecting test cases. Other names for this technique are **glass-box, white-box, structural, logic-driven,** and **path-oriented testing**.

Black-Box Testing

Black-box testing is concerned with the proper execution of the program specification. In this testing, each function or sub-program used in the main program is first identified. For example, in a payroll system Calc_grosspay( ), Print_payslips( ) may be the functions, used to calculate the gross pay and printing of pay slips. Test cases are devised to test each function or sub-program separately. Test-cases are decided solely on the basis of the requirements or specifications of the program and not on the basis of coding (data structure used) of the modules.

Black-box testing is complementary to **white-box** technique. It uncovers a different class of errors which are not discovered by white-box methods. This type of testing attempts to find the following errors:

- Interface error
- Incorrect or missing functions
- Errors in external database access
- Performance errors
- Initialization and termination errors

Feasibility of black-box

Consider the following example. Suppose that the specifications for a certain data-processing product state that five types of commission and seven types of discount must be incorporated. Testing every possible combination of just commission and discount requires 35 test cases. It is no use of saying that commission and discount are computed in two entirely separate code artifacts and hence may be tested independently. On the contrary, in black-box testing, the product is treated as a black box, and it's internal structure therefore is completely irrelevant.

This example contains only two factors, commission and discount, taking on five and seven different values respectively. Any realistic product has hundreds, if not thousands of different factors. Even if there are only 20 factors, each taking on only four different values, a total of 4^{20} or 1.1×10^{12} different test cases must be examined.

To see the implication of over a trillion test cases, consider how long it would take to test them all. If a team of programmers could be found that could generate, run, and exam test cases at an average rate of one every 30 second, then it would take more than a million years to test the product exhaustively. Therefore, exhaustive testing to specifications is impossible in practice because of the combinatorial explosion. There are simply too many test cases to consider.

Black-box unit-testing techniques

Exhaustive black-box testing generally requires billions and billions of test cases. The art of testing is to devise a small, manageable set of test cases to maximize the chances of detecting a fault while minimizing the chances of wasting a set of case by having the same fault detected by more than one test case. Every test case must be chosen to detect a previously undetected fault. One such black-box technique is *equivalence testing combined* with *boundary value analysis*.

Equivalence testing and boundary value analysis

Suppose the specification for a database product state that the product must be able to handle any number of records from 1 through 16,383 ($2^{14} - 1$). If the product can handle 34 records and 14,870 records, then the chances are good that it will work fine.. In fact, the chances of detecting a fault, if present, are likely to be equally good if any test case from 1 to 16,383 records is selected. Conversely, if the product works correctly for any one test case in the range from 1 through 16,383, then it probably will work for any other test case in the range. The range from 1 to 16,383 constitutes an *equivalence class*, that is, a set of test cases such that any one member of the class is as good a test case as any other. To be more precise, the specified range of numbers of records that the product must be able to handle defines three equivalence classes:

- *a.* Equivalence class   1. Less than 1 record.
- *b.* Equivalence class   2. From 1 to 16,383 records.
- *c.* Equivalence class   3. More than 16,383 records.

Testing the database product by using the technique of equivalence classes requires that one test case from each equivalence class is selected. The test case from equivalence class 2 should be handled correctly, where as error messages should be printed for the test cases from class 1 and class 3. A successful test case detects a previously undetected fault. To maximize the chances of finding such a fault, a high-payoff technique is **boundary value analysis**. Experience has shown that, when a test case on or just to one side of the boundary of an equivalence class is selected, the probability of detecting a fault increase. Therefore, when testing the database product, seven test cases should be selected.

Test case 1.   0 record: Member of equivalence class 1 and adjacent to boundary value.

Test case 2.	1 record:	Boundary value.
Test case 3.	2 records:	Adjacent to boundary value.
Test case 4.	723 records:	Member of equivalence class 2.
Test case 5.	16,383 records:	Adjacent to boundary value.
Test case 6.	16,383 records:	Boundary value.
Test case 7.	16,383 records:	Member of equivalence class 3 and adjacent to boundary value.

For each range (R_1, R_2) listed in either the input or the output specifications, five test cases should be selected, corresponding to values less than R_1, equal to R_1, greater than R_1 but less than R_2, equal to R_2, and greater than R_2. Where it is specified that an item has to be a member of a certain set, two equivalence classes must be tested, a member of the specified set and a non-member of the set. The use of equivalence classes, together with boundary value analysis, to test both the input specifications and the output specifications is a valuable technique for generating a relatively small set of test data with potential of uncovering a number of faults that might well remain hidden if less powerful techniques for test data selection were used.

Functional testing

An alternative form of black-box testing is to base the test data on the functionality of a code artifact. In functional testing [Howden, 1987], each item of functionality or function implemented in code artifact is identified. Typical functions in a classical module for a computerized warehouse product might be **get_next_ database_ record** or determine whether **quantity_on_hand** is below the reorder point. In a weapon control system, a module might include the function **compute_trajectory**. In a module of an operating system, one function might be **determine_whether_ file_is_ empty**.

After determining all the functions of a code artifact, test data are devised to test each function separately. Now, the functional testing is taken a step further. If code artifact consists of a hierarchy of power-level functions, connected by control structures of structured programming, then functional testing proceeds recursively. For example, if a higher-level function is of the form

```
<higher-level function> :: =      if <conditional expression>
                                      <lower-level function 1>;
                              else
                                      <lower-level function 2>;
```

Then, because   <conditional expression>, <lower-level function 1>, and <lower-level function 2> have been subjected to functional testing,

`<higher-level function>` can be tested, byusing branch coverage which is a **glass-box technique**. Note that this form of structural testing is a **hybrid technique**, where the lower-level functions are tested using a glass-box technique.

In practice, however, higher-level functions are not constructed in such a structured fashion from lower-level functions. Instead, the lower-level functions usually are inter-twined in some way. To determine faults in this situation, *functional analysis* is required, a somewhat complex procedure.

White-Box Testing

White-box testing is concerned with the implementation of the program. In this type of testing different programming structures and data structures used in the program are tested for proper operations. This test concentrates on the examination of the coding. The system software engineers and programmers coin test-cases and test-data. The system designer creates test-cases that have likelihood of finding out the possible errors.

Feasibility of white-box testing (testing to code)

The most common form of testing code requires that each path through code artifact to be executed at least once. Consider the code fragment of *figure 9.4*. The corresponding flowchart is shown in *figure 9.5*. Even though the flowchart appears to be almost trivial, it has over 1012 different paths. There are five possible paths through the central group of six shaded boxes, and the total number of possible paths through the flowchart therefore is

$$5^1 + 5^2 + 5^3 + \cdots + 5^{18} = \frac{5X(5^{18}-1)}{(5-1)} = 4.77 X 10^{12}$$

If there can be these many paths through a simple flowchart containing a single loop, it is not difficult to imagine the total number of different paths in a code artifact of reasonable size and complexity.. In short, the huge number of possible paths renders exhaustive testing to code as infeasible as exhaustive testing to specifications.

```
read(kmax)    //kmax is an integer between 1 and 18

for (k=0; k < kmax; k++) do

{

read(myChar) //myChar is the character A, B, or C

        switch(myChar)

        {

                case 'A':
```

```
        blockA;
        if(cond1) blockC
        break;
    case 'B':
        blockB;
        if(cond2) blockC
        break;
    case 'C':
        blockC;
        break;
    }
    blockD;
}
```

Figure 9.4: A code fragment

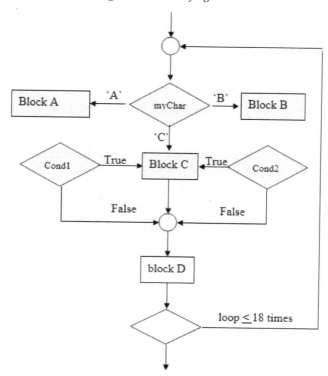

Figure 9.5: A flowchart with over 1012 possible paths

White-box unit-testing techniques

In white-box or glass-box techniques, test cases are selected on the basis of examination of the code rather than the specifications. There are a number of different forms of glass-box testing, including statement, branch, and path coverage.

Structural testing: Statement, branch, and path coverage

Statement coverage is the simplest form of glass-box testing, in which a series of test cases is run during which every statement is executed at least once. To keep the track of which statements are still to be executed, a **CASE tool** keeps a record of how many times each statement has been executed over the series of tests

A weakness of this approach is that there is no guarantee that all outcomes of branches are properly tested. To see this, consider the code fragment of *figure 9.6*. The programmers made a mistake; the compound conditional $s > 1$ && $t == 0$ should read $s > 1 \; || \; t = 0$. The test data shown in the *figure 9.6* allow the statement $x = 9$ to be executed without the fault being highlighted.

if (s > 1 && t == 0)

X=9;

Test case: s = 2, t = 0.

Figure 9.6: Code fragment with test data

An improvement over statement coverage is **branch coverage**, that is, running a series of tests to ensure that all branches are tested at least once. Again, a tool usually is needed to help the tester to keep the track of which branches have or have not been tested. **Generic Coverage Tool (GCT)** is an example of a branch coverage tool for C programs. Techniques such as statement or branch coverage are termed **structural tests**.

The most powerful form of structural testing is *path coverage*, which is testing all paths. As shown previously, in a product with loops, the number of paths can be very large. The researchers have been investigating ways of reducing the number of paths to be examined while uncovering more faults than would be possible by using branch coverage.

When using *structural testing*, the tester simply might not come up with a test case that exercises a specific statement, branch, or path. What may have happened is that an infeasible path (dead code) is in the code artifact, that is, a path that cannot be possibly executed for any input data. *Figure 9.7* shows two examples of infeasible paths. In *figure 9.7(a)* the programmer omitted a minus sign. If k is less than 2, then k cannot possibly be greater than 3, so the statement $x = x * k$ cannot be reached.

```
if (k < 2)

{

        If (k > 3)          // should be k > -3

            x = x * k;

}
```

Figure 9.7(a): 1st example of infeasible path

Similarly in *figure 9.7(b)*, j is never less than 0, so the statement total = total + value[j] can never reached. The programmer had intended the test to be j < 10, but made a typing mistake. A tester using statement coverage would soon realize that neither statement could be reached, and the fault would be found.

```
for (j = 0; j < 0; j+ +)     // should be j < 10

    total = total + value [ j];
```

Figure 9.7(b): 2nd example of infeasible path

Complexity Metrics

Complexity metrices is another glass-box unit approach being used in quality assurance viewpoint. Suppose a manager is told that code artifact **m1** is more complex than code artifact **m2**. Irrespective of the precise way in which the term complex is defined, the manager intuitively believes that **m1** is likely to have more faults than **m2**. Following this idea, computer scientists have developed a number metrics of software complexity as an aid in determining which code artifacts are most likely to have faults. If the complexity of a code artifact is found to be reasonably high, a manager may direct that the artifact be redesigned and re-implemented on the ground that is less costly and faster to start from scratch than to attempt to debug a fault-prone code artifact.

A simple metric for predicting number of faults is line of code. The underlying assumption is that there is a constant probability, p, that a line of code contains a fault. If a tester believes that, on average, a line of code has a 2% chance of containing a fault, and the artifact under test is 100 lines long, then it implies that the artifact is expected to contain 2 faults; and an artifact that is twice as long is likely to have 4 faults.

Attempts have been made to find more sophisticated predictors of fault based on the measures of product complexity. McCabe's cyclomatic complexity is a measure through a number of binary decisions (predicates) plus 1. The cyclomatic complexity essentially is the number of branches in the code artifact. Accordingly, cyclomatic complexity can be used as a metrics for the number of test cases needed for branch coverage of a code artifact. This is the basis for so-called **structured testing**.

McCabe's metrics can be computed almost as easy as lines of code. In some cases, it has been shown to be a good metric for predicting faults; the higher the value of M, the greater is the chance that a code artifact contains a fault. However, the validity of McCabe's metric has been questioned seriously on both theoretical and experimental grounds.

Various Testing Strategies

Let us first understand, what do we test for? The first test of a system is to see whether it produces the correct output or not. Follow the given steps to see a variety of other tests which are conducted:

a. **Online response:** Online systems have a response time that will not cause a hardship to the user. One way to test this is to input the transactions on as many input screens as would normally be used in peak hours and time the response to each online function to establish a true performance level.

b. **Volume:** In this test, we create as many records as would normally be introduced to verify that the hardware and software will function correctly. The user is usually asked to provide test data for volume testing.

c. **Stress testing:** The purpose of stress testing is to prove that the candidate system does not malfunction under the peak loads. Unlike volume testing, where time is not a factor, we subject the system to a high volume of data over a short time period. This simulates an online environment where a high volume of activities occurs in spurts.

d. **Recover and security:** A forced system failure is induced to test a backup recovery procedure for file integrity. Inaccurate data are entered to see how the system responds in terms of error detection and protection. Related to file integrity is a test to demonstrate that data and programs are secure from unauthorized access.

e. **Usability documentation and procedure:** The usability test verifies the user-friendly nature of the system. This relates to normal operating and error-handling procedures. Consider an example, One aspect of user friendliness is accurate and complete documentation. The user is asked to use only the documentation and procedures as a guide to determine whether the system can be run smoothly.

The Nature of Test Data

The proper choice of test data is as important as the test itself. If test data as input are not valid or representative of the data to be provided by the user, then the reliability of the output is suspected. Test data may be artificial or live. Properly created artificial test data should provide all combinations of values and formats and make it possible to test all logics and transaction path subroutines

The Test Strategy

The first step in system testing is to check out strategy and prepare a plan that will test all the aspects of system in a way that promotes its credibility among potential users. There is a psychology in testing:

- Programmers usually do a better job in unit testing because they are expected to document and report on method and extent of their testing.
- Users are involved, which means communication is improved between users and designer group.
- Programmers are involved when they become aware of user problems and expectations. The user also becomes more aware of the complexity of programming and testing. The outcome of all this is a more realistic and cooperative user for successful testing.

Activity network for system testing

A test strategy entails the following activities (Figure 9.8):

- Prepare test plan.
- Specify conditions for user acceptance testing.
- Prepare test data for program testing.
- Prepare test data for transaction path testing.
- Plan user training.
- Compile/assemble programs.
- Prepare job performance aids.
- Prepare operational documents.

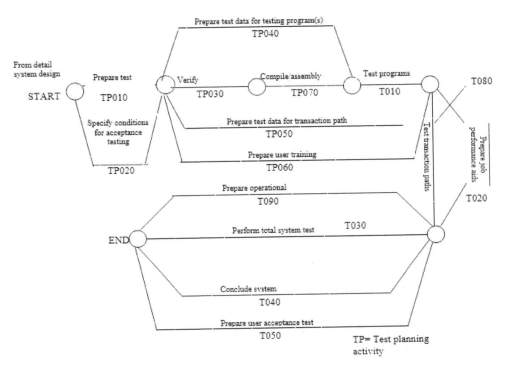

Figure 9.8: Activity network for system testing

Prepare test strategies

A workable test strategy must be prepared in accordance with the established design specifications. It includes:

- Outputs expected from the system
- Criteria for evaluating outputs
- A volume of test data
- Procedure for using test data
- Personnel and training requirements

Prepare test plan

A workable test plan must be prepared in accordance with the established design specifications. It includes:

- Outputs expected from the system
- Criteria for evaluating outputs
- A volume of test data

- Procedure for using test data
- Personnel and training requirements

Specify conditions for user acceptance testing

Planning for user acceptance testing, calls for the analyst and the user to agree on the conditions for the test. Many of these conditions may be derived from the test plan. Others are an agreement on the test schedule, the test duration, and the persons designated for the test. The start and termination dates for the test should also be specified in advance.

Prepare test data for program testing

As each program is coded, test data are prepared and documented to ensure that all aspects of the program are properly tested. After the testing the data are filed for future reference.

Prepare test data for transition path testing

This activity develops the data required for testing every condition and transaction to be introduced into the system. The path of each transaction from origin to destination is carefully tested for reliable results. The test verifies that the test data are virtually comparable to live data used after conversion.

Plan for user training

User training is designed to prepare the user for testing and converting the system. User involvement and training take place parallel with programming for three reasons:

a. The system group has time available to spend on training while the programs are being written.

b. Initiating a user-training program gives the systems group a clearer image of the user's interest in the new system.

c. A trained user participates more effectively in system testing.

For user training, preparation of a checklist is useful which is shown in *Figure 9.9*. The provisions for developing training materials and other document to complete the training activity are included. In effect, the checklist calls for a commitment of personnel, facilities, and efforts for implementing the candidate system.

The training plan is followed by the preparation of user training manual and other text materials. Facility requirements and the necessary hardware are specified and documented. A common procedure is to train the supervisors and department heads who, in turn, train their staff. The reasons are:

- User supervisors are knowledgeable about the capabilities of their staff and the overall preparation.
- Staff members usually respond more favorably and accept instructions better from supervisors than from outsiders.
- Familiarity of users with their particular problems (bugs) makes them better candidates for handling user training than the system analyst. The analyst gets the feedback to ensure that proper training is provided.

Company_____   Analyst _____

Project Name_____   Date --/--/----

	Activity	Start date	End date	Staff in-charge	Department in-charge	
	Notification	mm/dd	mm/dd			
1	Announcement to the officers	10/06	10/20	P K Mohanty	Sr. Vice. Prez	
	Announcement to the employees	10/06	10/20	R C Munde	Auditing	
	Coordinated customer activities	10/06	10/29	Shanket Paul	Casier	
	Coordinate computer service	10/06	10/29	Trina Dwivedi	PersonnelMgr.	
	Procedures					
2	Inter-departmental	10/14	11/01	Arjun Sethy	Auditing	
	Inter-departmental	10/14	11/01	Amit Raina	Systems	
	Forms					
3	Design	11/01	11/14	Madan Pai	Systems	
	Printing	11/01	11/20	P V Srinivas	Systems	
	Equipment					
4	P Cs, Printers, UPS & network	11/01	12/15	S K Mishra	HW engineer	
	Training & Orientation					
5	Manuals	12/01	12/16	Sudhir Sen	Systems	
	Training aids	12/01	12/16	Bikash Jain	Systems	
	Special workshops	12/10	12/14	Sweta Sudha	Systems	
6	**Lobby Layout**	12/10	12/30	S K Bebortha	President	
7	Supplies	12/10	12/15	Ranjan Sahoo	Purchase mgr.	

	Personnel					
8	Transfers	12/10	12/12	Naresh Jha	PersonnelMgr.	
	New hires	12/12	12/30	M Anthony	PersonnelMgr.	

Figure 9.9: A check list for user training

Compile/assemble program

All programs have to be compiled/assembled for testing. Before this, a complete program description should be available. Program and system flowcharts of the project should be available. Before actual program testing, run order schedule and test schemes are finalized. A *run order schedule* specifies the transactions to test and the order in which they should be tested. The bottom-up (linking small-scale modules to higher level modules) or top-down (after testing the general program and then adding one lower level programs) approaches can be used.

Prepare job performance aids

In this activity the materials to be used by personnel to run the system are specified and scheduled. This includes a display of materials such as program codes, a list of input codes attached to the computer screen, and a posted instruction schedule to load to the disk drive or to a help menu. These aids reduce the training time and employ personnel at lower level.

Prepare operational documents

During the test plan stage, all the operational documents are finalized, including copies of the operational formats required by the candidate system. During operational documentation of the new system operation, the personnel with proper experience, training, and educational qualification are to be involved.

During the system testing, some of the performances criteria need to be used are planned in advance. A substandard performance or service interruptions may cause system failure and are checked during the test. Some of the performance criteria being used during testing are:

* **Turnaround time** is the elapsed time between the receipt of the input and the availability of the output. In an online system, high priority processing is handled during the peak hours, while low priority processing is done later. The objective is to decide on and evaluate all the factors that might have bearing on the turnaround time for handling all applications.
* **Backup** relates to procedures to be used when the system is down. Backup plans might call for the use of another computer. The software for the candidate system must be tested for compatibility with a backup computer.

Many times, a server with a **RAID** control system can be tested for backups in case the main hard disk drive fails.

- **File protection** pertains to storing files in a separate area for protection against fire, flood, or natural disaster. Strategy should be established for reconstructing files though a hardware malfunction. Fortress, cold backup, warm backup, mutual backup approaches can be planned to meet the disaster recovery.

- The **human factor** applies to the personnel involved in the candidate system. During system testing, lighting, air conditioning, noise, and other environmental factors are evaluated. Hardware should be designed to match human comfort with consideration of agronomy.

Guidelines For Module Testing

To emphasize the importance and applicability to module testing the following guidelines are to be followed:

a. Try to design module tests so that failure to pass one test case will not move to the next test case.

b. Under stressful load and conditions, test the modules at their performance limit and beyond.

c. The performance characteristics like throughput accuracy, input and output capacities, and timings should be measured for each module.

d. A log book may be maintained to provide information to debug a failure.

e. Concurrently many problems should not be solved. They should be handled one after the other so that the source of error can be traced easily.

f. Conduct a critical analysis after each module test to ensure doing better next time.

Conclusion

Software testing is done to ensure that it runs correctly, including hardware and other software linked to it. Planning, discipline, control, and documentations are very important factors for a successful software testing. Software testing is the most important phase in the **SDLC**. Planning for the test phase should begin early in the development life cycle and should be constant concern throughout the development cycle. The activity network or flow graphs should be prepared to determine the distinct and independent paths through the program module. Execution every line in the program and performing black-box test on each path are necessary. When a program module is tested, it is important to test for all required internal and external interfaces.

Questions and Answers

1. The term used to refer to the checking of outputs of a computer with corresponding input document is called

    a. Auditing through computer   *c*. Auditing around the computer

    b. Process control   *d*. Beta testing

2. **What is a software error, software fault, and software failure?**

    Software error is the difference between computed value and the desired value. A software fault appears when there is an incorrect step in the program. The software failure occurs when the program is unable to perform in a desired way.

3. **What are the types of failure cost?**

    One is internal failure cost that occurs when errors in a product are detected prior to shipment. The other one is external failure cost that is associated with the defects found after the product is shipped to the customer. The internal failure costs are reworking, repair, and failure mode analysis. The external failure costs are complaint resolution, product return, and replacements, helpline support, and warranty work.

4. **Why do error removal costs increase as a project progress?**

    As the projects starts rolling, testing becomes more complex and costlier. Documentation of changes becomes more frequent and testing becomes costly. Communicating the problem downward and making necessary changes involving many people becomes more. Repeating previous tests consumes more time and man power.

5. **What is the difference between verification and validation?**

    Verification is to check that the product is designed and developed in accordance with the required specifications and development standards. Validation involves requirements that satisfy client or customer needs.

6. **What is a system acceptance test? What are the levels of acceptance testing?**

    System acceptance test is the test by which the end-users, management, and information system operations management will either accept the system or reject the system. A system acceptance test performed by end-users using real data over a certain period. It is an expensive test that addresses three levels of acceptance testing as follows:

    a. **Verification testing:** Where the system runs in a simulated environment using simulated data.

   b. **Validation testing:** The system runs in a live environment using real data. This is sometimes called beta testing.

   c. **Audit testing:** Audit testing certifies that the system is free of errors and is ready to be placed into operation.

7. Who are the role players in the system testing?

The role players in system testing process are the system analysis, owners, users, and builders. The system analyst typically communicates testing problems and issues with the project team members. The system owners and the system users hold ultimate authority on whether a system is operating correctly or not. System builders are involved in the testing process. System builders include the application programmers, database administrator, and networking specialists. They are needed to solve problems that arise during the testing phase.

8. Define system testing.

System testing is using a series of tools whose primary purpose is to fully exercise the computer-based system.

9. What is security testing?

Security testing attempts to verify that protection mechanism is built into a system such that improper penetration of errors is avoided.

10. Define stress testing.

Stress testing helps in executing a system in a manner to upgrade the resource status with proper quality, frequency of running, and proper volume of the module.

11. Define performance testing.

Performance testing is designed to test the run-time performance of software in the context of an integrated system.

12. What is debugging?

Debugging is to remove the errors found during testing. The outcomes of debugging are to find the cause of error and remove it by correction. The types of debugging are bruit force, backtracking, and cause elimination.

13. What is the goal of the software tester?

The goal of the software tester is to find bugs, find them at the earliest and make sure they are fixed.

14. What errors are found during black-box testing?

The errors found are incorrect or missing functions, interface errors, errors in data base structure, performance errors, initialization, and termination errors.

15. Define loop testing.

Loop testing is a white box testing technique that focuses exclusively on the validity of loop constructs.

16. Name the different categories of system testing.

Different categories of system testing are operation test, full scale test, negative test, tests based on the requirement specification, and test of user documentation.

17. When to stop testing?

It not possible to test a program completely. There is no correct answer to when to stop testing. Each project is different starting from a leave record system to missile system. The testing to remove the bugs depend on the types of testing done, which one to evaluate and to fix the bugs. Mostly the product is validated against the user requirement.

18. Why is it impossible to test a program completely?

Any software program other than smaller ones, there are too many inputs, outputs, and too many path combinations to be tested fully. Also, the software specifications can be subjective and can be interpreted in different ways. Therefore, it is not right to say the testing is complete.

19. Can a software tester perform white box testing on a specification?

Yes, if the tester is involved with the process used in defining the specification. He could attend the focus groups, usability studies, and marketing meeting to understand the underlying process being used to design the features and overall product. There is a risk, though, the information could bias the tester into assuming that the specification is correct.

20. You can perform dynamic black box testing without a product specification or requirement document. True or False.

True. The technique is called **exploratory testing**, and you essentially use the software as though it is a product specification. It is not an ideal process but can work fine in a pinch. The largest risk is that you will not even know if a feature is missing.

21. It is unfair to perform stress testing at the same time as you are performing load testing. True or False.

False. No test is ever unfair. Your job is to find bugs.

22. Name several advantages of performing static white box testing.

Static white box testing finds bugs early in the development cycle, making them less time consuming, and less costly to fix. The software testers can get information about how the software testers can get information about how the software works, what potential weakness and risky areas exist, and can build a better working relationship with the programmers. Project status can be communicated to all the team members who participate in the testing.

23. White box testing can find missing items as well as problems. True or False.

True. Missing items are more important than normal problems and can be found through static white box testing. When code is checked against the published standards, and guidelines are correctly analyzed in formal reviews, missing items become important to consider.

24. What is the difference between dynamic white box testing and debugging?

Both the processes overlap. The goal of dynamic white box testing is to find bugs and the goal of debugging is to fix them. The overlap occurs in the area of isolating exactly where and why the bug occurs.

25. Why a testing in big-bang software development model is nearly impossible?

The software delivered is a big one. It is difficult, if not possible, to figure out why a bug occurs- the needle-in-a haystack problem. Moreover, there are so many bugs, that hide the others. While integrating and testing the modules find the bugs and fix them before they hide or pile on each other.

26. What is Ad Hoc testing?

Ad hoc testing is a testing without a plan. It is easy and cozy but not organized. It can not be tracked, and when it is over, there is no proof that it was ever done.

27. Who are the role players in the system testing process?

The role players in the system testing process are the system analyst, owners, users, and builders. The system analyst typically communicates testing problems and issues with the project team members. The system owners and the system users hold ultimate authority on whether a system is operating correctly or not. System builders are involved in the testing process. System builders include the application programmers, database operators, and networking specialists. They are needed to solve problems that arise during the testing phase.

Exercise

1. Distinguish between system testing and system acceptance testing.

2. Discuss how both the white box and black box testing can be used together.

3. Discuss the difference between black box (functional) and white box (structural) testing models.

4. Why a real time software system that has been tested in a simulated environment is not always reliable?

5. What are the deliverables from coding, testing, and installation?

6. What are structured walkthroughs for code? What is their purpose? How are they conducted?

7. What are activities take place in a testing process?

8. What is cyclomatic complexity? Where it is used?

CHAPTER 10

System Implementation and Maintenance

Objectives

In this chapter, we are going to discuss:

- Software development tasks required for implementation and maintenance of a software system.
- Steps for implementation and maintenance of the system.
- Factors that influence the implementation and maintenance process.
- Guide lines for carrying out the implementation and maintenance procedures.

This chapter deals with both system implementation and maintenance.

Introduction

Once the application modules are coded with **high level languages**, the next job is to assemble them into a computer software system. This is known as **software system implementation**. The successful implementation of the new software package is the most important part of the **system development life cycle**. We have to buy the equipment, plan individual sub-system, and hire people to implement the whole system. The implementation depends on the available resources and the type of hardware equipment available. It can be more complex, because an equipment may be shared among multiple systems. One has to do a lot of planning before implementing a system.

Implementation Procedures

The process of ensuring that the information system is operational and then allowing users to take its operation for use and evaluation is called **system implementation**. Implementation includes all those activities that take place to convert from old system to the new one. The new system may be totally new, replacing an existing manual, or automatic system, or it may be a major modification in the existing system. In either case, proper implementation is essential to provide a reliable system to meet the organizational requirements. Successful implementation may not guarantee the improvement in the organization by using the new system but improper installation will prevent it. There are four aspects of implementation:

  a. Equipment installation
  b. Training the personnel
  c. Conversion procedures
  d. Post-implementation evaluation

Equipment Installation

The hardware required to support the new system is selected prior to the implementation phase. The necessary hardware should be ordered in time to allow for installation and testing of equipment during the implementation phase. An installation checklist should be developed at this time with operating advice from vendor and system development team. In those installations where people are experienced in the installation of same or similar equipment, adequate time should be scheduled to allow the completion of the following activities:

  i. **Site preparation:** An appropriate location must be found to provide an operating environment for the equipment that will meet the vendor's temperature, humidity, and dust control specifications. It is very important to lay down a proper procedure for acquiring and planning space layout in the systems implementation. It would be foolish to be stingy on layout expenses and human environment when so much is spent on system analysis, design and development. A bad layout can not only drastically reduce the productivity of the data processing department but also that of the entire organization as a whole.

  If the system is a small computer, little layout and site preparation work is needed. However, the electric lines should be checked to ensure that they are free of static or power fluctuation. It will be better to install a dedicated line that is not shared by other equipments. In case of a medium or large mainframe computer, the project manager should prepare a rough layout, make cost estimates, and get budget approval from top management. Layout planning must be done in advance in order to permit acquisition for long lead-time items like air conditioning equipments, electrical earthing, fire/smoke detection systems, and so on. The following factors should be taken into considerations for space planning:

- Space occupied by equipments
- Space occupied by people
- Movement of equipment and people

The site layout should allow ample space for moving the equipment in and setting it for normal operation. Vendors will provide clearance requirement for performing service, maintenance, and air circulation. These requirements must be strictly adhered; Otherwise warranties may become void and maintenance discontinued until specifications are met. Carpets should be avoided whenever possible in computer room because they catch dust and create static power which may damage the data stored in magnetic medium. Highly waxed floors may cause same type of effects. It is best to have the site preparation completed prior to the delivery of the equipment, since many vendors are reluctant to deliver equipment when construction work is still in progress.

ii. **Equipment installation:** The equipment must be physically installed by the manufacturer, connected to the power source, and wired to communication lines if required.

iii. **Equipment check out:** The equipment must be turned on for testing under normal operating conditions. Not only the routine *diagnostic test* should be run by the vendor, but also the implementation team should devise and run extensive tests of its own to ensure that the equipment's are in proper working condition.

Training the Personnel

A system can succeed or fail depending on the way it is operated and used. The quality of training received by the personnel involved with the system in various capacities, help to hinders the successful implementation of information system. Thus, training is becoming a major component of system implementation. When a new system is acquired which often involves new hardware and software, both users and computer professionals generally need some type of training. Often this is imparted through classes, which are organized by vendor, and through hands-on learning techniques.

i. **Training the Systems operators:** Many systems depend on the computer-centre personnel, who are responsible for keeping the equipment running and for providing the necessary support services. Their training must ensure that they are able to handle all the possible operations, both routine and extra-ordinary. Operator training must also involve the data entry personnel. If the system calls for the installation of new equipment like computers, printers, special terminal for data entry equipment's, and so on. The operator training should include such fundamentals as how to turn the equipment on and use it with the knowledge of normal operation. The operators should also be instructed in what common malfunctioning may occur, how to recognize them, and what steps to take when they arise. As a part of their training, operators should be given both a trouble shooting list that identifies possible problems and remedies for them, as well as the names and telephone numbers of the contact persons in case of unexpected or unusual problems arise. Training also involves familiarization with run procedures, which involve working through the sequence of activities needed to use a new system on an on-going basis.

ii.   **User training:** User training may involve the equipment use, particularly in the case where a personal computer is in use and the individual involved as both operator and user. In these cases, user must be instructed to operate the equipment. User training must also instruct individuals involved in trouble shooting of the system, determining whether the problem is caused by the equipment or software or something they have done in using the system. Most user training deals with the operation of the system itself. Training in data coding emphasizes the methods to be followed in capturing data from transactions or preparing data for decision activities. Users should be trained on data handling activities such as handling input/output screens, editing data, formulating inquiries (finding specific records or getting response to questions), and deleting records of data. From time to time, users will have to prepare disks, load papers into printers or change cartridge/ribbons on printers. Some training time should be devoted to such system maintenance activities.

Training is often seen as a necessary evil by managers. While reorganizing its importance, many managers have to release employees from their regular job activities so that they can be trained. When managers are actively involved in determining training needs, they are usually more supportive of training efforts. It is common to have managers directly involved in evaluating the effectiveness of training activities because training deficiencies can translate into reduced user productivity level.

Conversion from Manual to Computerized System

Conversion or changeover is the process of changing from the old system (manual system) to the new system. It requires careful planning to establish the basic approach to be used in the actual changeover. There are many conversion strategies available to the analyst, regrading who has to consider for several organizational variables in deciding which conversion strategy to use. There is no single best way to proceed with conversion. It may be noted that adequate planning and scheduling of conversion as well as adequate security are more important for a successful changeover.

   i.   **Conversion strategies:** There are five strategies for converting from the old system to new system.

       a.   **Direct changeover:** Conversion by direct changeover means that on a specified date, the old system is dropped and the new system is put into use. Direct changeover can only be successful if extensive testing is done beforehand. An advantage of the direct changeover is that users have no possibility of using the old system other than the new adaptation.

          Direct changeover is considered a risky approach to conversion, and disadvantages are numerous. For instance, long delays might ensure if errors occur, since there is no other way to accomplish processing. Additionally, users may resent being forced into using an unfamiliar system without recourse. Finally, there is no adequate way to compare new results with old.

       b.   **Parallel conversion:** This refers to running the old system at the same time, in parallel. This is the most frequently used conversion approach, but its popularity may be in decline because it works best when a computerized system replaces a manual one. Both systems are run simultaneously for a specified period of time and the reliability of results is examined. When the same results are gained over time, the new system is put into use and the old system is ceased.

          The advantage of running both systems in parallel includes the possibility of checking new data against old data in order to catch any errors in processing the new system. Parallel processing also offers a feeling of security to users, who are not forced to make an abrupt change to the new system.

          There are many disadvantages to parallel conversion. These include the cost of running two systems at the same time, and the burden on employees of virtually doubling their workload during conversion. Another disadvantage is that unless the system being replaced is a manual one, it is difficult to make comparison between the output of the new system and the old one. Supposedly, the new system was created to improve on the old one. Therefore, outputs from the system should differ. Finally, it is understandable that employees who are faced with a choice between two systems will continue using the old one because of their familiarity with it.

b. **Gradual conversion:** Gradual conversion attempts to combine the best features of the earlier two plans, without incurring the risks. In this plan, the volume of transaction is gradually increased as the system is phased in. The disadvantages include allowing users to get involved with the system gradually and the possibility of detecting and recovering from errors without a lot of downtime. Disadvantages of gradual conversion include taking too long to get the new system in place and its inappropriateness for conversion of small, uncomplicated systems.

c. **Modular prototype conversion:** This approach to conversion uses the building of modular, operational prototype to change from old system to new in a gradual manner. As each module is modified and accepted, it is put into use. One advantage is that each module is thoroughly tested before being used. Another advantage is that users are familiar with each module as it becomes operational.

The fact that many times prototype is not feasible and automatically rules out this approach for many conversions. Another disadvantage is that special attention must be paid to interfaces so that the modules being built actually work as a system.

d. **Distributed conversion:** This refers to a situation in which many installations of the same system are contemplated, like in banking or in franchises such as restaurants or clothing stores. One entire conversion is done (with any of the four approaches considered already) at one site. When that conversion is successfully completed, other conversions are done for other sites.

An advantage of the distributed conversion is that problems can be detected (and contained) rather than inflicting them, in succession, on all sites. A disadvantage is that even when one conversion is successful, each site will have its own peculiarities to work through and these must be handled.

e. **Activities involved in conversion:** Conversion includes all those activities which must be completed to successfully convert from the previous system to the new information system. Fundamentally these activities can be classified as follows:

- **Procedure conversion:** Operating procedure should be completely documented for the new system. This applies to both computer operations and functional area operations. Before any parallel or conversion activities can start, operating procedures must be clearly spelled out for personnel in the functional areas undergoing changes. Information on input, data files, methods, procedures, output, and internal control must be presented in clear, concise, and understandable terms for the average reader. Written operating procedures must be supplemented by oral communication during the training sessions on the system change.

Despite many hours of training, many questions will have to be answered during the conversion activities. Brief meetings must be held when changes are taking place in order to inform all operating employees of any change initiated. Qualified system personnel must be in the conversion area to communicate and coordinate new developments as they occur. Likewise, revisions to operating procedures should be issued as quickly as possible. These efforts enhance the chances of successful conversion.

Once the new system is completely operational, the system implementation group should spend several days checking with all supervisory personnel about their respective areas. As with every new installation, minor adjustments should be expected. Channels of communication should be open between the systems development team members and all the supervisory personnel so that necessary changes can be initiated as conditions change. There is no need to get locked into a rigid system when it would be beneficial for the organization to make necessary changes. Thus, the proper machinery for making changes must be set in place.

- **File conversion:** In this phase many large files of information are going to be converted from one medium to other. Therefore, programming and testing are to be completed long before. The cost and related problems of file conversion are significant whether they involve on-line files or off-line files. Present manual files are likely to be inaccurate and incomplete where deviations from the accepted format are common. These files suffer from the shortcomings of inexperienced and at times, indifferent personnel whose jobs are to maintain them. Computer generated files tend to be more accurate and consistent. If the existing system is operating on a computer but of different configurations, the formats of the present computer files are generally unacceptable for the new system.

Besides the need to provide a compatible format, there are several other reasons for file conversion. The files may require character translation that is acceptable to the character set of the new computer system. Data from one magnetic storage to another media is to be placed in order to construct an on-line common database. Also, the rearrangement of certain data fields for more efficient programming may be desired.

In order for the conversion to be as accurate as possible, file conversion programs must be thoroughly tested. Adequate control, such as record counts and control totals, should be required output of the conversion program. The existing computer files should be kept for a period of time until sufficient files are accumulated for backup. This is necessary in case the files must be reconstructed from scratch after a bug is discovered later in the conversion routine.

- **System conversion:** After the files have been converted and the reliability has been confirmed for a functional area, daily processing can be shifted from the existing information system to the new one. A cut-point is established so that database and other data requirements can be updated to the cut-off point. All transactions initiated after this time are processed on the new system. System development team members should be present to assist and to answer any questions that might develop. Consideration should be given to the old system for some more time to permit checking and balancing the total results of both systems. All differences must be reconciled. If necessary, appropriate changes are made to the new system and its computer programs. The old system can be dropped as soon as the data processing group is satisfied with the new system's performance.

- **Scheduling personnel and equipment:** Scheduling data processing operations of a new information system for the first time is a difficult task for the system manager. As users become more familiar with the new system, the job becomes more routine. Before the new design project is complete, it is necessary to schedule the new equipment. Some program will be operational while others will be in various stages of compiling and testing. Since production runs tend to push aside new program testing, the system manager must assign ample time for all individuals involved. This generally means second shift for those working on programs.

Schedules should be set up by the system manager in conjunction with the department of operational units serviced by the equipment. The master schedule for next month should provide sufficient computer time to handle all the required processing. Daily schedules should be prepared in accordance with the master schedule and should include time necessary for reruns, program testing, special non-recurring reports and other necessary runs. Hence, schedule should be as realistic as possible.

Just as the equipment must be scheduled for its maximum utilization, so must be personnel who operate the equipment. It is also imperative that personnel who enter input data and handle output data be included in the data processing schedule. Otherwise, data will not be available when the equipment needs it for processing. It is essential that each person follow the methods and procedures set forth by the management. Non-compliance with established norms will have an adverse effect on the entire system.

Implementation Techniques

Implementation of software system can be done in the following two ways:

a. Traditional approach

b. Incremental approach

Traditional Approach

In the traditional approach the following sequence is followed:

i. Each module or small group of modules is coded, tested, and debugged.

ii. After all the module of the whole system are debugged, these modules are grouped in sub-systems.

iii. Subsequently, each sub-system is tested and debugged.

iv. Next, the sub-systems are combined to form the whole system. This is known as **system integration**.

v. Finally, the whole system is tested and debugged.

The traditional system is not very popular these days, as the system as a whole is tested very late in the project. By then there would be little time left to correct the problems, which are sure to occur. Therefore, the development team is unable to meet the project deadline. The team continues to get stuck until the problems are over. Such problems occur because of the reluctance of implementers to begin the testing as soon as possible. When the project deadline approaches the team hurriedly tests the module. This leads to lack of some resources for testing. Due to the lack of time the team decides to perform testing without using all the required resources. This leads to major defects going undetected. Major faults are known only when the system as a whole is tested, wherein the bug passes from module to another.

Incremental Approach

In the incremental approach to implementation, the first module is first coded, tested, and debugged. Subsequently further modules are added to it one by one or in small groups. In this approach the system begins as a small unit but eventually with additions, builds into a complete system. The system is implemented from bottom to top. One can incrementally implement a system from top to bottom, from bottom to top, from left to right, or from right to left. Such a system provides enough time for major changes.

System Acceptance

System testing is done after all programs are completed. Acceptance testing puts the system through a procedure design to convince the user that the system will meet the stated requirement. Acceptance testing is technically similar to system testing, but politically it is different. In system testing, bugs are found and corrected. Acceptance testing is conducted in the presence of the user, audit representative, or the entire staff.

Both system testing and acceptance testing may share test cases; system testing may be viewed as a dress rehearsal for the acceptance test. The criteria or plan for acceptance should be available in the structured specification.

System Evaluation & Performance

Application systems may be evaluated in terms of measures of system value. These may also be compared with the reports of technical, operational, and economic feasibility where they were originally and initially justified.

a. **Evaluation of system value**

- Significant task relevance
- Willingness to pay
- System usage
- User information satisfaction

b. **Technical evaluation**

- Data transmission is fast to handle data?
- Sufficient secondary storage to hold data?
- CPU responds well to all requests?

c. **Operational evaluation**

Operational considerations relate to whether the input data is properly provided and the output is usable and used appropriately. Evaluation of application should examine how well they operate with special reference to input, error rates, and timeliness of output and utilization of reports.

d. **Economic evaluation**

Actual costs are compared with actual benefits. It is easy to calculate cost but not benefits. Hence, we may make estimates to evaluate. It may aid future decision making to identify the cost of applications for which an economic return was not expected. It shows the **return-on-investment (ROI).** An economic analysis is required to decide whether or not to drop the application uses.

e. **Evaluation by use of performance monitors**

- **Hardware monitors:** Use of sensor to measure the time of the CPU in wait state. Read/write time in Floppy/Hard disk.

- **Software monitors:** They reside in main memory and require execution time; they interrupt the program being executed to record data about the execution. These can identify particular program or programs modules within the operating system environment.

f. **Evaluation by the use of system logs and observations**

- Small installations maintain simple logs of jobs, job times. An analysis of the system may indicate problems with returns, variation in job running times or excessive machine failures. The log may be used to develop a distribution of jobs by time required. Observations of computer operations are useful in detecting in efficient scheduling of resource use and inefficient applications.

System Acceptance Criteria

A system must posses some basic desirable features for acceptance. In the following sub-sections, we will be discussing these qualities.

a. **Correctness:** Correctness means that the system meets the organizational desired goals. In other words, correctness is the degree to which the system performs required functions. The most common measure for correctness is **defects per thousand lines of code (KLOC)** where defect is defined as lack of conformance to requirements.

b. **Reliability:** A system is reliable if the user can trust the results given by the system. Reliability is defined as *the* **probability of failure-free operation of a system in a specified environment for a specified time**. For example, if we say that a program 'A' has a reliability of 0.90 over 10 hours, it means that when the program runs 100 times, it will work without failure 90 times in 10 hours of execution time. A simple measure of reliability is:

MTBF = MTTF + MTTR

Where:

- **MTBF** is Mean Time Between Failures
- **MTTF** is Mean Time to Failure
- **MTTR** is Mean Time to Repair

c. **Robustness:** A system is said to be robust if it can adapt to an unanticipated change in the environment such as *disk crash* or *incorrect input data*. For example, a system is said to be robust if it provides some standby (duplicate data file in the backup hard disk) to recover from hard disk failure.

d. **Performance:** Performance of a system is measured in terms of the following parameters:

- processing speed
- response time
- resource consumption
- throughput and efficiency

If a system is too slow it reduces the productivity. If a computer-based system uses too much disk space it may be very expensive to run. Also, it may affect other applications. Hence, performance parameters are important from system's function point of view.

e. **User Friendliness:** If a system is not user friendly it is sure to lose the support of the user. User Friendliness can be measured in terms of:

- The physical and/or intellectual skill required to learn the system.
- The time required to become moderately efficient in using the system.
- Measure of user's attitude towards a system.

The user interface is an important component of the user friendliness. A software system that presents the novice user with a windows interface and a mouse is friendly than one requires the user to use a set of textual commands.

f. **Maintainability:** Maintainability of a system is measured as a function of the effort required to locate and fix an error in the system. A system is maintainable if it allows corrections of its defects with a limited amount of work. Maintenance involves corrective, adaptive, and perfective practices.

g. **Testability:** Testability is a measure of effort required to test the system in order to ensure its accurate performance.

h. **Reusability:** Reusability is the creation and reuse of the system building blocks. As in an automobile industry, the engine specification and design are reused in different models, the same software modules can be used for the development of other modules. This saves production cost, time, and labor. The reuse of a system can be considered at a number of different levels like system reuse, sub-system reuse, object, or module reuse, and function reuse.

i. **Interoperability:** Interoperability refers to the ability of the system to co-exist and co-operate with other systems. For example a word processing software can incorporate a chart produced by a spreadsheet package. Interoperability has become a key characteristic of many systems. New systems must communicate with the existing old system.

Maintenance, Reliability, and Availability

The software production was viewed, in seventies, as consisting of two distinct activities which are performed sequentially:

a. Development

b. Maintenance

Starting from the scratch, the software product was developed, and then installed on the client's computer. Any change to the software after installation on the client's computer and acceptance by the client, whether to fix a residual fault or extend the functionality, constituted classical maintenance. Hence the way that software was developed classically can be described as the **development-then-maintenance model**. The post delivery maintenance refers to the 1990 IEEE definition of maintenance as any change to the software after it has been delivered and installed on the client's computer. The modern maintenance or just maintenance refers to the 1995 ISO/IEC definition of corrective, perfective, or adaptive activities performed at any time. Post delivery maintenance is therefore a subset of (modern) maintenance.

System availability and *reliability* are closely related properties that can be expressed as a numerical probability. The reliability of a system is the probability that the system's services will be correctly delivered as specified. The availability of a system will be up and running to deliver these services to users when they request them.

So, *System reliability* is the probability of failure-free operation over a specified time in a given environment for a specific purpose. *System availability* is the probability that a system, at a point of time, will be operational and able to deliver the requested service.

Maintenance

Maintenance means restoring something to its original condition. It covers a wide range of activities, including correcting coding, design errors, updating documentation, test data, and upgrading user support. Many activities are classified as maintenance are actually enhancements. Enhancement means adding, modifying, or redeveloping the code to support the changes in specifications. It is necessary to keep up with changing user needs and operational environment.

Although software does not wear out like a piece of hardware, it *ages* and eventually fails to perform because of cumulative maintenance. Over the time, the integrity of the program, test data, and documentation degenerates as a result of modifications. Eventually, it takes more effort to maintain the application than to rewrite it.

Characteristics

The obsolescence of hardware is very fast as compared to the software. The user wants to see the existing software is running smoothly on the new hardware platform. If the software performs a low-level function, maintenance is necessary. The software product needs re-work to cope with new interface. Therefore, every software product continues to evolve after its development through the maintenance efforts.

Types of Software Maintenance

There are several types of maintenance that one can perform on an information system. By maintenance, we mean fixing or enhancing of an information system.

a. **Corrective maintenance** refers to the changes made to repair defects in the design, coding, or implementation of the system. Most corrective maintenance problems surface soon after installation. When corrective maintenance problems surface, they are typically urgent and need to be resolved to curtail possible interruptions in normal business activities. Of all types of maintenance, corrective accounts for as much as 75% of all maintenance activity (**Andrews and Leventhal, 1993**). This is unfortunate because corrective maintenance adds little or no value to the organization. It simply focuses on removing defects from an existing system without adding new functionality.

b. **Adaptive maintenance** involves making changes to an information system to evolve its functionality to changing business needs or to migrate to a different operating environment. Adaptive maintenance is usually less urgent than corrective maintenance because business and technical changes typically occur over some period of time. Contrary to corrective maintenance, adaptive maintenance is generally a small part of an organization's maintenance effort but does add value to the organization.

c. **Perfective maintenance** involves making enhancements to improve processing performance, interface usability, or to add desired but not necessarily required, system failures (*"bells and whistles"*). For example, perfective maintenance would be adding a new room to our home. Many system professionals feel that perfective maintenance is not really maintenance but new development.

d. **Preventive maintenance** involves changes made to a system to reduce the chance of future system failure. An example of preventive maintenance might be to increase the number of records that a system can process far beyond what is currently needed or to generalize how a system sends report information to a printer so that the system can easily adapt to changes in printer technology. Consider an example, in a home the preventive maintenance could be painting the exterior to protect the home from severe weather conditions. As with adaptive maintenance, both perfective and preventive maintenance are of much lower priority than corrective maintenance. Over the life of a system, corrective maintenance is most likely to occur after initial system installation or after major system changes. This means that adaptive, perfective, and preventive maintenance activities can lead to corrective maintenance activities if not carefully designed and implemented. (*Table 10.1*)

TYPE	DESCRIPTION
Corrective	Repair design and programming errors.
Adaptive	Modify system to environmental changes. Changes made to a system to evolve its functionality to changing business needs or technologies.
Perfective	Evolve system to solve new problems or take advantage of new opportunities. Changes made to a system to add new features or to improve performance.
Preventive	Safeguard system from future problems. Changes made to a system to avoid possible future problems.

Table 10.1: Types of Maintenance

Maintenance Tasks

There is always required a plan to solve the ever-growing problem of software maintenance. Many organizations have done this through a maintenance reduction task. They are:

a. **Maintenance management audit,** which is done through interviews and questionnaires. It evaluates the quality of maintenance effort. Some of the questions asked are:

- Are maintenance requests logged in?
- What percent of total hours are spent on an error corrections, additions/changes/deletions, and improvements?
- Does your organization currently have a well-defined maintenance reduction program?
- The data gathered are used to develop a diagnostic study to provide the management with an assessment of the software maintenance function.

b. **Software system audit**, which entails:

- An overall view of the system documentation and an assessment of the quality of data files, databases and system maintainability, reliability, and efficiency.

- Functional information gathered on all the programs in the system to determine how well they do the job. Each program is assigned a preliminary ranking value.
- A detailed program audit, which considers the ranking value, **mean time between failure (MTBF),** and size of the maintenance backlog. MTBF determines system availability to users.

  c. **Software modification**, which consists of the following steps:
  - Program rewrites, which include logic simplification, documentation updates, and error correction.
  - System level update, which completes system level documentation, brings up to date the data flow diagrams or system flowcharts, and cross-reference programs.
  - Re-audit of low-ranking programs to make sure that the errors have been corrected.

Side Effects

The effect of such maintenance reduction task is that a system is a more reliable software, a reduced maintenance backlog, improved response time in correcting errors, improved user satisfaction, higher morale among maintenance staff. The maintenance demands more orientation and training than any other programming activities, especially for entry-level programmers.

Measuring Maintenance Effectiveness

The measurement of maintenance activities is fundamental to understanding the quality of development and maintenance efforts. To measure the effectiveness, you must measure these factors:

- Number of failures
- Time between each failure
- Type of failure

Measuring the number and time between failures will provide you the basis to calculate a widely used measure of system quality. This metric is referred to as the **Mean Time Between Failures (MTBF).** As its name implies, the MTBF measure the average length of time between the identification of one system failure until the next. Over the time, you should expect the MTBF value to rapidly increase after a few months of use (corrective maintenance) of the system. If the MTBF does not rapidly increase over a time, it will be a signal to management that major problems exist within the system that are not being adequately resolved through the maintenance process.

A more revealing method of measurement is to examine the failures that are occurring. Over time, logging the types of failures will provide a very clear picture of where, when, and how failures occur. For example, knowing that a system repeatedly fails in logging new account information to the database when a particular customer is using the system can provide invaluable information to the maintenance personnel. Were the users adequately trained? Is there something unique about this user? Is there something unique about an installation that is causing the failure? What activities were being performed when the system failed?

Tracking these failures also provides important management information for future projects. If a higher frequency of errors occurs when a particular development environment is used, such information can help to guide personnel assignments, training courses, or the avoidance of a particular package or language during future development.

Reverse Engineering

Reverse engineering is the process of creating design specifications for a system or program module from program code and data definitions. For example, **CASE** tools that support reverse engineering read program source as input, perform analysis, and extract information such as program control structures, data structures, logic, and data flow. Once a program is represented at a design level by using both graphical and textual representations, the system analyst can more effectively restructure the code according to the current business needs or programming practices. This tool provides analysts with a powerful method to quickly explore and understand a system. The tool many times shows a mapping between the variables and program procedures. This high-level view of a program allows the programmers to see more quickly the interrelationships and structure of a program, thus making it easier to understand and maintain. As with many legacy systems, only the source code may exist, yet additional documentation is necessary to make program maintenance productive. *Reverse engineering is an automated tool that reads program source code as input and creates graphical and textual representations of program design-level information such as program control structures, logical flow, and data flow.*

Reengineerinmg

Reengineering tools are similar to the reverse engineering tools but include analysis features that can automatically or interactively with a system analyst, alter an existing system in an effort to improve its quality or performance. Although most organizations may have numerous systems that are candidates for reverse engineering or reengineering, the complexity, and effort in using these tools have limited their widespread use. Additionally, most CASE environments do not yet have reverse or reengineering capabilities. However, as automated development environments evolve to support these features, CASE should evolve to have greater impact beyond what the technology has experienced, so far.

The critical distinction between reengineering and a new software development is the starting point for the development. Rather than starting with a written specification, the old system acts as a specification for the new system. Chikofsky and Cross call conventional development forward engineering to distinguish it from the software reengineering. Forward engineering starts with a system specification and involves the design and implementation of a new system. Reengineering starts with an existing system and the development process for the replacement, which is based on understanding and transforming the original system. (*See Figure 10.1*)

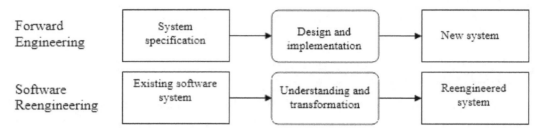

Figure 10.1: *Forward and Re-engineering processes*

Figure 10.2 illustrates the reengineering process. The input to the process is a legacy program and the output is a structured, and the modularized version of the same program. During program reengineering, the data for the system may also be reengineered.

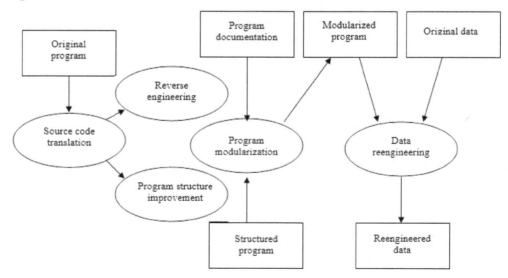

Figure 10.2: *Reengineering Process*

The activities in this reengineering process are:

- **Source code translation:** The program is converted from an old programming language to a more modern version of the same language or to a different language.
- **Reverse engineering:** The program is analyzed and information extracted from it. This helps to document its organization and functionality.
- **Program structure improvement:** The control structure of the program is analyzed and modified to make it easier to read and understand.
- **Program modularization:** Related parts of the program are grouped together and, where appropriate the redundancy is removed. In some cases, this stage may involve architectural transformation where a centralized system intended for a single computer is modified to run on a distributed platform.
- **Data reengineering:** The data processes by the program are changed to reflect program changes.

To summarize, reengineering is the automated tool (*figure 10.2*) that read program source code as input, perform an analysis of the program's data, and logic, and then automatically, or interactively with a system analyst, alter an existing system in an effort to improve its quality or performance.

Business Process Reengineering

Sometimes it is understood that a system reengineering and a **business process reengineering (BPR)** are synonyms. To make the organization more profitable or systematic the BPR is initiated. Along with the BPR, the system reengineering is automatically invoked. The BPR is the popular term for re-optimization of organizational processes and structures following the introduction of new information technology into an organization.

There are seven *principles of reengineering* suggested by Michael Hammer and James Champy to streamline the work-process and thereby achieve significant levels improvement in quality, time-management, and cost:

a. Organize around outcomes and cost.

b. Identify all the processes in an organization and prioritize them in order of redesign urgency.

c. Integrate information processing work into the real work that produces the information.

d. Treat geographically dispersed resources as they were centralized.

e. Link parallel activities in workflow instead of just integrating their results.

f. Put the decision point where the work is performed, and build control into the process.

g. Capture information once and catch the source for improvement.

Questions and Answers

1. **Define maintainability.**

   Maintainability is the ease with which a program can be corrected if an error is encountered, adapted if the environment changes, or changed if the customer desires a change of requirements.

2. **State true or false**

   a. User training stage is known as the system implementation stage. (false)

   b. The organization's infrastructure needs not be changed for implementing a new system. (true)

   c. Planning is an iterative process. (true)

   d. The steps followed in incremental approach to system design is module testing, sub-system testing, and system testing. (false)

   e. In dual system method two new systems are implemented. The one that meets the user requirements is chosen as final system. (false)

   f. Multimedia can be harnessed for end-user training in the implementation phase of SDLC. (true)

   g. Maintainability is one of the factors that determines system quality. (true)

   h. The system review is carried out periodically even after the system is successfully implemented. (true)

   i. Since all the users belong to the organization and familiar with its working, training after system acceptance can be done away with. (false)

3. **Discuss the two main implementation techniques**

   Refer section 10.4

4. **Discuss the different steps which should be followed while converting from old system to a new system.**

   The following steps are followed when converting an old system to a new one:

   a. Conversion begins with a review of the project plan, implementation plan, and system test documentation. Review of these documents is done by the project team and programmers along with users and operators.

   b. The conversion portion of the implementation plan is finalized and approved.

  c. The conversion method (discussed) to be followed is decided.

  d. Required files are converted.

  e. Outputs generated and operations by the new system are recorded on a special form. These are documented for future reference.

  f. If no difficulties are encountered with the new system, it is allowed to continue its operation in the organization.

  g. With this the conversion is completed and plans for the post implementation review are prepared.

  h. Following the review, the new system will be declared to be officially operational.

5. What is a system acceptance test? What are the three levels of acceptance testing?

System acceptance test is the test by which the end users, management, and information system operations management will either accept the system or reject. A system acceptance test is the final test performed by end users using the real data over a certain period. It is an extensive test that addresses three levels of acceptance testing, namely verification testing and validation testing, and audit testing.

  a. **Verification testing:** In verification testing, the system is run in a simulated environment using simulated data.

  b. **Validation testing:** In validation testing, the system is run in a live environment using real data. This is sometimes called a beta testing.

  c. **Audit testing:** Audit testing certifies that the system is free of errors and is ready to be placed into operation.

6. Discuss the human psychological factors that can hamper the system implementation process.

Human behavioral factors should not be overlooked in the system implementation phase. System changes can produce unnecessary psychological impact among the staff. The staff in the target organization may show signs of resistance to the new system. This is because of one or more of the following reasons:

  a. Prospective change in nature of job or job profile due to the introduction of the new system.

  b. Possible loss of self esteem relative to the new job.

  c. Possible loss of one's job.

  d. Possible loss of control one's job content.

In order to overcome the human resistance to system change, the following initial steps can be taken before starting off with conversion phase.

a. The deficiencies of the present system should be discussed with the staff.

b. They may be shown how the changeover will improve that quality of life at work place.

c. The user and the technical staff need to work together and answer questions and follow up on difficulties that may occur after implementation.

d. Employee participation must be encouraged during all phases of conversion process.

Exercise

1. Write a short note on planning for system implementation

2. Explain briefly the parallel running (or conversion) in implementation.

3. Would you like to have a career for yourself in software maintenance? Describe the career path.

4. Develop a means to quantify and measure the maintainability attribute of a software product.

5. What is the appropriate set of tools and documents required to maintain a large software product?

6. If a software product or part of it spends 60% of its operational life cycle in maintenance, why do you pay so little attention to maintainability during design phase?

7. Is it practical to specify maintainability in the SRS? How would you specify it?

8. What is the conventional wisdom about implementation success?

9. What are the different types of maintenance and how do they differ?

10. What types of measurements must be taken to gain an understanding of the effectiveness of maintenance? Why is tracking mean time between failures an important measurement?

11. What is the difference between reverse engineering and re-engineering CASE tools?

CHAPTER 11
Reliability

Objectives

In this chapter, we are going to discuss:

- Reliability required while developing a software package used by public.
- Need of the reliability for the developers to apply the concept for a smooth running of the product.
- Important properties of good reliability models for software measurement.

Introduction

Reliability is defined as the probability of a software system to perform its specified functions correctly over a long period of time or for different input sets under the usage environment similar to that of its input target customers (*Goel, 1985; Musa et al, 1987, Titan,1995*). **Software reliability engineering (SRE)** is the branch of software engineering that studies the issues related to the measurement, modeling, and improvement of software reliability. Reliability is a measure of the frequency and criticality of product failure. A failure is an unacceptable effect or behavior, under permissible operating conditions that occurs as a consequence of a fault. The product must be stable.

Reliability may be defined as:

- The idea that something is fit for the purpose with respect to time;
- The capacity of a device or system to perform as designed;
- The resistance to failure of a device or system;
- The ability of a device or a system to perform a required function under the stated conditions for a specified period of <u>time;</u>
- The probability that a <u>functional unit</u> will perform its required function for a specified interval of time under stated conditions.

It is a paradox that more effort is given to increase the hardware reliability, but it is ignored in the case of software. A failure in software may cause more damage than a hardware failure. The characteristics of a product failure take the shape of a bath tub Shown in *figure 11.1*. When the product is launched it fails more frequently at the initial stage, while correcting the fault, it slowly stabilizes with a constant failure rate. At the end of the product life cycle due to wear and tear, aging effect, and technology obsolescence the product encounters more failures and needs rejuvenation.

The major goal of reliability and quality assurance is to identify all the possible influences on failure rates and take an appropriate step to reduce and eliminate those influences.

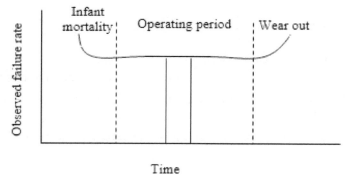

Figure 11.1: Bath Tub Curve on Failure

The Myth of Stable Requirements

Stable requirements are the holy grail of software development. With stable requirements, a project can proceed from an architecture to design to coding to testing in a way that's orderly, predictable, and calm. This is **software heaven!** You have predictable expenses, and you never have to worry about a feature costing 100 times as much as to implement as it would otherwise because your user didn't think of it until you were finished **debugging**. It's fine to hope that once your customer has accepted a requirements document, no changes will be needed. On a typical project, however, the customer can't reliably describe what is needed before the code is written. The problem isn't that the customers are a lower life-form. Just as the more you work with the project, the better you understand it, the more they work with it, the better they understand it.

Concepts

Reliability is defined as the **probability** that a device will perform its intended function during a specified period of time under the stated conditions. If the reliability of a system or device is 0.95 for a 100-hour operating period, the device will operate successfully for 100 hours with the probability of 0.95. If in an experiment employing 100 such devices, at the end of 100 hours it is expected that 5 of the 100 devices will experienced a failure. We sometimes say that the device has a 95 percent chance of surviving 100 hours of operation.

Reliability, R(t), is defined as the probability that a device, component, unit, module, or system will function correctly for a specified period of time in a specified operating environment. If **T** is a continuous random variable representing the specified failure-free service life, then the reliability as a function of the length of any operating time t is defined by:

$$R(t) = P(T>t)$$

The probability that the successful operating time will be greater than the specified service life, T, is often referred to as the probability of survival. The function R(t) is a decreasing function of time and

$$0 < R(t) < 1$$

$$R(0) = 1 \text{ and } R(\infty) = 0$$

The unreliability or probability of failure, F(t), is obtained as:

$$F(t) = 1 - R(t) = P(T<t)$$

F(t) is an increasing function of time and is often referred to as *cumulative distribution* function of the service life, T. The derivative of F(t) with respect to t is:

$$f(t) = \frac{dF(t)}{dt}$$

is the probability density function of the continuous random variable T, service life.

Any product, in service, may fail from time to time. It is necessary to know how often the product fails **Mean time between failures (MTBF)** and how bad the effects of that failure can be. When a product fails, an important issue is how long it takes, to repair it **Mean time to repair (MTTR).** It is important to know that how long it takes to repair the result of the failure. This last point frequently is overlooked.

Suppose that the software running on a communication front fails, on an average, only once every 6 months. When it fails, it completely wipes out a database. At best, the database can be re-initialized to its status when the last checkpoint dump was taken, and the audit trail can then be used to put the database into a state that is virtually up to date. But, if this recovery process takes two days, during which time the database and communication front end are inoperative. In this case the reliability of the product is low, notwithstanding that the MTBF is 6 months.

Probability of failure = $F(t) = 1 - R(t)$

Where, $R(t)$ is the probability of failure free operation in time period t, *i.e.* the reliability. The reliability function, $R(t)$, and the probability density function, $f(t)$, can be expressed explicitly in terms of hazard function $Z(t)$. Differentiating $F(t) = 1 - R(t)$ with respect to t yields:

$$\frac{dF(t)}{dt} = \frac{-dR(t)}{dt}$$

or

$$F'(t) = -R'(t)$$

On the other hand, we had $Z(t) = F'(t)/R'(t)$. Substituting for $F'(t)$ we get

$$Z(t) = \frac{R'(t)}{R(t)}$$

Integrating this equation with respect to t we obtain:

$$\int Z(t)dt = -\int \frac{R'(t)}{R(t)}dt = -\ln R(t)$$

And from this we have:

$$R(t) = e^{-\int_0^t Z(u)du}$$

and

$$f(t) = Z(t)R(t) = Z(t)e^{-\int_0^t Z(u)du}$$

$Z(t)$ for hardware failure can be closely approximately by a constant failure rate. A constant failure rate model has been used quite successfully in the system and subsystem reliability work including computer hardware reliability. Substituting in the just above equation for $Z(t)$ the constant λ, have:

$$R(t) = e^{-\int_0^1 \lambda du} \quad \text{since} \quad \int_0^1 \lambda du = \lambda t \quad \text{we conclude that } R(t)=e^{-\lambda t}$$

Therefore, $\quad f(t)= e^{-\int_0^1 \lambda du} \lambda e^{-\lambda t} \quad$ where λ is the mean failure rate.

At the time of system failure there is a cost associated to the software which is dependent on the probability of failure. The equation is:

$$Cf = cf \cdot pf$$

Cf is the total failure cost and cf is average single failure cost. In order to minimize Cf, one has to minimize either cf or pf.

cf is determined by the nature of software applications and overall environment, the software is used. More cannot be done to reduce cf. To minimize pf, one has to improve the reliability. This needs additional development cost, additional testing time, and the use of additional quality assurance techniques.

Reliability design begins with the development of a model. Reliability models use *block diagrams* and *fault trees* to provide a graphical means of evaluating the relationships between the different parts of the system. These models incorporate predictions based on the parts-count failure rates, which are taken from the historical data. While the predictions are not often accurate in an absolute sense, they are valuable to assess relative differences in design alternatives.

One of the most important design techniques is *redundancy*. This means that if one part of the system fails, there is an alternate success path, such as a backup system. An automobile brake light might use two light bulbs. If one bulb fails, the brake light still operates using the other bulb. Redundancy significantly increases system reliability, and is often the only viable means of doing so. However, redundancy is difficult and expensive, and is therefore limited to critical parts of the system. Another design technique, *physics of failure*, relies on understanding the physical processes of stress, strength, and failure at a very detailed level. Then the material or component can be re-designed to reduce the probability of failure.

Errors

While writing the program or handling data, various errors are committed and they are encountered during the software testing or running the system. When designing the system interfaces, try to provide an appropriate feedback on encountering errors. The system feedback can consist of three types:

a. Status information

b. Prompting cues

c. Error or warning messages

Providing *status information* is a simple technique for keeping user informed of what is going on within a system. For example, relevant status information such as displaying the current customer name or time, placing appropriate titles on a menu or screen, or identifying the number of screens following the current one, and so on; are the feed backs needed by the user. The second feedback method is to display *prompting cues*. When prompting the user for information or action, it is useful to be specific in your request. For example, suppose a system prompted users with the following request:

READY FOR INPUT: _____

With such a prompt, the designer assumes that the user knows exactly what to enter. A better design would be specific in its request, possibly providing an example, default value, or formatting information. A final method available to the user for providing system feedback is using *error* and *warning* messages. Practical experience has found that a few simple guidelines can greatly improve their usefulness.

Error Tolerance

Error tolerance property can be considered as a part of usability and reflects the extent to which the system has been designed so that user input error is avoided and tolerated. When user errors occur, the system should, as far as possible, detect these errors and either fixes them automatically or request the user to re-input their data.

Error Processing

Error processing is turning out to be one of the thorniest problems of modern computer science, and you cannot afford to deal with it haphazardly. Some people have estimated that as much as 90 percent of a program's code is written for exceptional, error-processing cases, or housekeeping, implying that only 10 percent is written for nominal cases (Shaw in Bentley 1982). With so much code dedicated to handling errors, a strategy for handling them consistently should be spelled out in the architecture.

Error handling is often treated as a **coding-convention-level** issue, if it's treated at all. But because it has system-wide implications, it is best treated at the architectural level. Here are some questions to consider:

- **Is error detection active or passive?** The system can actively anticipate errors or example, by checking user input for validity or it can passively respond to them only when it can't avoid them. For example, when a combination of user input produces a numeric overflow. It can clear the way or clean up the mess. Again, in either case, the choice has user interface implications

- **How does the program propagate errors?** Once it detects an error, it can immediately discard the data that caused the error, it can treat the error as an error and enter an error-processing state, or it can wait until all processing is complete and notify the user that errors were detected (somewhere).

- **What are the conventions for handling error messages?** If the architecture doesn't specify a single, consistent strategy, the user interface will appear to be a confusing macaroni-and-dried-bean collage of different interfaces in different parts of the program. To avoid such an appearance, the architecture should establish conventions for error messages.

- **Is error processing corrective or merely detective?** If corrective, the program can attempt to recover from errors. If it's merely detective, the program can continue processing as if nothing had happened, or it can quit. In either case, it should notify the user that it detected an error.

- **Inside the program, at what level are errors handled?** You can handle them at the point of detection, pass them off to an error-handling class, or pass them up the call chain.

- **Is error detection active passive?** The system can actively anticipate errors for example, by checking user input for validity or it can passively respond to them only when it can't avoid them. For example, when a combination of user input produces a numeric overflow. It can clear the way or clean up the mess. Again, in either case, the choice has user-interface implications.

- **How does the program propagate errors?** Once it detects an error, it can immediately discard the data that caused the error, it can treat the error as an error and enter an error-processing state, or it can wait until all the processing is complete and notify the user that errors were detected (somewhere).

- **What are the conventions for handling error messages?** If the architecture doesn't specify a single, consistent strategy, the user interface will appear to be a confusing macaroni-and-dried-bean collage of different interfaces in different parts of the program. To avoid such an appearance, the architecture should establish conventions for error messages.

- **What is the level of responsibility of each class for validating its input data?** Is each class being responsible for validating its own data, or is there a group of classes responsible for validating the system's data? Can classes at any level assume that the data they're receiving is clean?

- **Do you want to use your environment's built-in exception handling mechanism, or build your own?** The fact that an environment has a particular error handling approach doesn't mean that it's the best approach for your requirements.

System Faults

It is a characteristic of a software system that can lead to a system error. For example, failure to initialize a variable could lead to that variable having the wrong value when it is used. A **fault** is injected into the software when a human makes a *mistake*. One mistake on part of the software professional may cause several faults; conversely various mistakes may cause the identical fault. A **failure** is the observed incorrect behavior of the software product as a consequence of a fault, and the **error** is the amount by which a result is incorrect.

The distinction between the terms helps us to identify three complementary approaches that are used to improve the reliability of a system, are:

- **Fault avoidance:** Development techniques are used that either minimize the possibility or mistakes and/or that trap the mistakes before they result in the introduction of system faults. Examples of such techniques include avoiding error-prone programming language constructs such as pointers and the use of static analysis to detect the program anomalies.

- **Fault detection and removal:** The use of verification and validation techniques that increase the chances that faults will be detected and removed before the system is used. Systematic system testing and debugging is an example of a fault-detection technique.

- **Fault tolerance:** Techniques that ensure faults in a system do not result in system errors or that ensure system errors do not result in system failures. The incorporation of self-checking facilities in a system and use of redundant system modules are the example of fault tolerance techniques.

Fault Tolerance

The architecture should indicate the kind of fault tolerance expected. Fault tolerance is a collection of techniques that increase a system's reliability by detecting errors, and recovering from them if possible, and containing their bad effects if not.

There are four aspects to fault tolerance:

- *a.* **Fault detection:** The system must detect a fault that could lead to a system failure. Generally, this involves checking that the system state is consistent.

- *b.* **Damage assessment:** The parts of the system state that have been affected by the fault must be detected.

- *c.* **Fault recovery:** The system must restore its state to a known *safe* state. This may be achieved by correcting the damaged state (forward error recovery) or by restoring the system to a known *safe* state (backward error recovery).

- *d.* **Fault repair:** This involves modifying the system so that the fault does not recur. However, many software faults manifest themselves as transient states. They are due to a peculiar combination of system inputs. No repair is necessary and normal processing can resume immediately after fault recovery.

You might think that fault-tolerance facilities are unnecessary in systems that have been developed by using techniques that avoid the introduction of faults. If there are no faults in the system, there would not seem to be any chance of system failure.

For example, a system could make the computation of the square root of a number fault tolerant in any of several ways:

- The system might back up and try again when it detects a fault. If the first answer is wrong, it would back up to a point at which it knew everything was all right and continue from there.

- The system might have auxiliary code to use if it detects a fault in the primary code. In the example, if the first answer appears to be wrong, the system switches over to an alternative square-root routine and uses it instead.

- The system might use a voting algorithm. It might have three square-root classes that each use a different method. Each class computes the square root, and then the system compares the results. Depending on the kind of fault tolerance built into the system, it then uses the mean, the median, or the mode of the three results.

- The system might replace the erroneous value with a phony value that it knows to have a benign effect on the rest of the system.

- Other fault-tolerance approaches include having the system change to a state of partial operation or a state of degraded functionality when it detects an error. It can shut itself down or automatically restart itself. These examples are necessarily simplistic. Fault tolerance is a fascinating and complex subject.

Reliability Models

A model is required to predict the future behavior of a system accurately. The model is a representation of a real-world problem based on the mathematical equations with one or more measurable parameters. The model takes the observation data and then analyze to predict the future behavior. The model is either confirmed or modified to better match with the reality by comparing both actual observed performance and predicted performance. Some desirable model characteristics include the following:

- **Simplicity:** The model may be simple to understand easily the observed data and explain the analyzed output. The important parameters responsible to measure the performance are included in the model.

- **Completeness:** The parameters those are important to performance are identified and include in the model. The constraints and limitations are clearly stated and observed.

- **Accuracy:** Matching to the performance of real-world problem with the desired accuracy level.

- **Utility:** The model may predict the desired future behavior accurately with the better understanding of reality. It may be as close to reality during experiment.

- **Validity:** Model performance confirmed through exhaustive testing and constraints carefully defined to limit the model application to the area where model is valid.

The software reliability is yet to catch up with the hardware reliability. Much to be learned about software reliability. While hardware reliability models have been predicted on an observed constant failure rate. Software reliability have been based more on logically or analytically derived failure rate. Figure 11.2 shows a cumulative software failure rate.

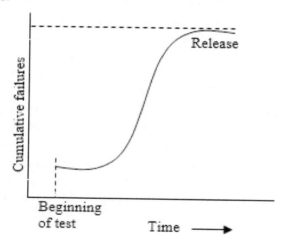

Figure 11.2: *Cumulative software failure rate*

The figure 11.2 shows that initially, when a software product is introduced to the system test environment, reported failure rates are low because the testers are not familiar with the product and have difficulty separating failures from test operator errors, errors in test cases, and sources other than the test objects. The period is followed by a test period in which failure rates are initially high but decline as testing continues and faults are removed. The failure rate declines until the software product is released. The failure rate behavior is a learning curve for the testers. Once the testers become familiar with product, the resident faults in the software product are more easily detected. Software products are released when failure rates reach some established threshold. Shortly after the release, the failure rate increases due to more users, different environment, and different test cases. The scenario is followed by a declining failure rate. The following equation:

$$R(t) = e^{-\int_0^1 Z(u)\,du}$$

represents a family of software reliability modules, in which $Z(u)$ is the hazard function. The simplest $Z(u)$ is when $Z(u)$ is a constant value equal to an average software failure rate. This will result in a reliability model represented by the following equation:

$$R(t) = e^{-\lambda t}$$

Reliability Systems

Reliability models are basically computed with a series or parallel systems. The parallel systems are called **redundant systems**. The cost of a redundant system is greater than the cost of a simplex system. Reliability modeling for redundant systems is straightforward application of probability theory. The total reliability of a string of n subsystems or components connected in a series (*figure 11.3*) configuration. In the series model, a failure in any one of the components results in loss of entire system's capability, which reliability is determined by the product of the n individual subsystem reliability.

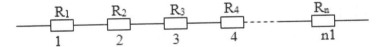

Figure 11.3: *Components are in series*

The reliability of the system where the components are in series is:

$$R(t) = \prod_{i=1}^{i=n} R_i$$

When two subsystems are connected in parallel shown in *figure 11.4*, the total reliability of this redundant system is represented as union of R_1 and R_2.

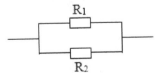

Figure 11.4: *A parallel system with two components*

The total reliability of the parallel system is $R(t) = R_1 + (1 - R_1) * R_2$

Another configuration having both serial and parallel connections of components, which is having a complex nature is given in *figure 11.5*. In the figure the configuration shows two parallel configurations connected in series.

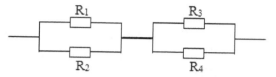

Figure 11.5: *A combined configuration*

The reliability of this configuration is given by:

$$R(t) = (R_1 + (1 - R_1) * R_2) * (R_3 + (1 - R_3) * R_4)$$

Systematic application of elementary series and parallel results can be used to reduce the complex configuration and obtain a single reliability value for the entire configuration.

Availability

Another parameter to reliability is **availability** which is a more meaningful performance parameter. Availability is ability to repair a system and restore it to operating condition. It is the probability that a system is fit for operation at a time *t*. This can be stated as the amount of expected downtime over a specified time interval. The availability has got two terms, **mean time to failure (MTTF)** and **mean time to repair (MTTR)**. If *R(t)* is the reliability function for the system, then:

$$MTTF = \int_0^\infty R(t)dt$$

If it is known that there have been *n* failures occurring at times $t_1, t_2, ..., t_n$, then we have:

$$MTTF = \frac{1}{n} \sum_{i=1}^{i=n} t_i$$

The reciprocal of MTTF is called **hazard function**. For example, if *R(t)* is as shown in previous equation, then MTTF is $1/\lambda = 1/Z$.

Mean time to repair is defined as the **average time** required to affect a maintenance action. Its reciprocal *r(t)*, is called the **repaired hazard**. Therefore,

$$MTTF = \frac{1}{Z(t)} \text{ and } MTTR = \frac{1}{r(t)}$$

The probability that the system is operational, $p(t)$, is the desired availability expression. As t increases, the first term dominates and eventually a steady state availability is reached. At this point

$$p(t) = \frac{r(t)}{Z(t) + r(t)}$$

or in terms of MTTF and MTTR, we have

$$p(t) = A = \frac{MTTF}{MTTF + MTTR}$$

where A is the availability, the probability that the system is in service.

Example 1:

One can respond to combined reliability and availability specification, assume that an availability of 0.999 per year (2000 hours of operation) in system service is acceptable, which translates into an availability

or $r = 999 * Z$

There are many combinations of failure rate and repair hazards that can meet this requirement. However, if a reasonable system reliability for one year, 2000 hours of operation, is set to be 0.9, and the hazard functions considered to be a constant failure rate, λ, then failure rate of 5.3E-5 is obtained form equation $R(t) = e^{-\lambda t}$

$$0.9 = R(t) = e^{-\lambda 2000}$$

$$\lambda = \frac{-\ln 0.9}{2000} = 0.000053 = 5.3E - 5$$

to compute r from $r = 999 * Z$

$$r = 999 * 5.3E\text{-}5$$

$$= 5.3E\text{-}2 = 0.053$$

Therefore, **MTTR** is approximately 19 hours (18.1). Mean time to repair and mean time to failure values can be traded to achieve realistic design goal. The availability based on the combination of a mean time to repair of 19 hours and a reliability for one year of 0.9 yields a probability of the system being in service of 99.9%.

Example 2:

A requirement for a 0.975 probability of no interruption of service greater than 10 seconds might be imposed on certain air traffic control function. To meet this requirement with hardware/software reliability of say 0.37 for one year of period of continuous operation (8766 hours) implies an availability of 0.999999842 and a mean time to repair of approximately is 5 seconds. The 5 second MTTR is needed to assure that 97.5% of the interruption will not exceed 10 seconds. The following computations confirm these numbers.

$$R(t) = e^{-\lambda t}$$

$$R(t) = 0.37$$

$$T = 8766$$

$$0.37 = e^{-\lambda 8766}$$

$$Z(t) = \lambda = 0.000113421$$

$$\text{MTTF} = 1/Z(t) = 8816.676002 \text{ hours}$$

$$A = \frac{MTTF}{MTTF + MTTR}$$

Since, the probability of no service interruption over a full year of continuous service is 0.975, we must have an MTTR of 5 to 6 seconds to guarantee that 97.5% of the time the repair takes less than 10 seconds. With assumption we have:

$$A = \frac{8816.676002}{8816.676002 + \dfrac{5}{3600}} = 0.999999842$$

Redundancy offers a way to improve both reliability and availability. In the air traffic control system, the need to make repairs in less than 5 seconds implies automatic error detection and correction for both the hardware and software failures.

Questions and Answers

1. **Define MTTF.**

   The mean time to failure (MTTF) is the mean of the probability density function. It is also called the expected value of t. We can compute the mean pdf $f(t)$ as:

$$E(t) = \int t.f(t)dt$$

   The mean time to failure is the point in time t at which the probability of failure after t is same as the probability failure before t. It follows that we can calculate the value by finding the m satisfying $F(m) = \frac{1}{2}$.

2. **Define MTBF.**

   The mean time between failure (MTBF) is simply the addition of mean time to failure and mean time to repair. i.e. MTBF = MTTF + MTTR. The measures tell us when the system is available for use.

3. **Define availability.**

   Availability is the probability that a component is operating at a given point in time. It is also defined as:

   $$Availabilty = \frac{MTTF}{MTTF + MTTR} * 100$$

Exercise

1. Ten units are placed in a test environment. Failures and failure times are recorded. The results are as follows:

Failure number	1	2	3	4	5	6	7	8	9	10
Operating time	8	20	34	46	63	86	111	141	186	266

   Using the tables as raw data, plot failure density and hazard rate as a function of time. Also plot failure distribution and reliability as a function of time.

2. A four-hour computation process involving a computer operating system, and an application software product must run from initialization to completion with a very low probability of error. Describe in detail the you would follow to allocate failure rates to individual subsystems. List the questions you would ask and the issues that would need resolution in order to complete the allocation process. Where would you expect to get your answer?

3. Determine the required mean time to repair for a system with an availability requirement of 99.9% and a mean time to failure of 5000 hours. What observation would you make?

4. Compute the end-to-end reliability (A to B) for the configuration below. Assume probability of failure detection, switchover, and recovery is unity.

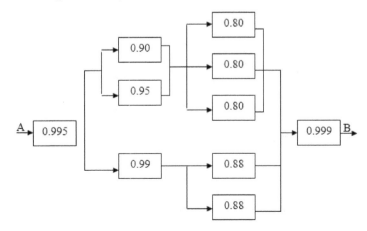

Figure 11.6: A four-hour computation process

CHAPTER 12
Software Quality

Objective

"What is software quality?" the question is bound to generate many different answers, depending on whom you ask, and under what circumstances, for what kind of software systems, and so on. An alternative question that is probably easier for us to get more informative answers is: *"What are the characteristics for high-quality software?"*

In this chapter, we are going to discuss:

- Software quality by defining the expected characteristics or properties of high-quality software
- Examine the different perspectives and expectations of users as well as other people involved with the development, management, marketing, and maintenance of the software product
- Individual characteristics associated with quality and their inter-relationship
- Critical characteristics of functional correctness.

Concept

The different views of quality in a systematic manner, based on the different roles, responsibilities, and quality expectations of different people, are laid down here. A small set of views and related properties are discussed.

Five major views according to (P Fleeger et al., 2002) are: transcendental, user, manufacturing, product, and value-based views, are:

- In the transcendental view, quality is hard to define or describe in abstract terms, but can be recognized if it is present. It is generally associated with some intangible properties that delight users.

- In the user view, quality is fitness for the purpose or meeting user's needs.

- In the manufacturing view, quality means conformance to process the standards.

- In the product view, the focus is on the inherent characteristics in the product itself in the hope that controlling these internal quality indicators (product-internal metrics) will result in improved external product behavior (quality in use).

- In the value-based view, quality is the customers' willingness to pay for software.

- **People's roles and responsibilities**

  When software quality is concerned, different people would have different views and expectations based on their roles and responsibilities. With the **quality assurance (QA)** and quality engineering focus of this book, we can divide the people into two broad groups:

  o Consumers of software products or services, including customers and users, either internally or externally. Sometime we also make the distinction between the customers, who are responsible for the acquisition of software products or services, and the users, who use the software products or services for various purposes, although the dual roles of customers and users are quite common. We can also extend the concept of users to include such non-human or "invisible" users as other software, embedded hardware, and the overall operational environment that the software operates under and interacts with **(Whittaker, 2001)**.

  o Producers of software products, or anyone involved with the development, management, maintenance, marketing, and service of software products. We adopt a broad definition of producers, which also include third-party participants who may be involved in add-on products and services, software packaging, software certification, fulfilling independent verification and validation (IV&V) responsibilities, and so on.

- **Quality expectations on the consumer side**

  The basic quality expectations of a user are that a software system performs useful functions as it is specified. There are two basic elements to this expectation:

a. It performs right functions as specified, which, hopefully fits the user's needs.

b. It performs these specified functions correctly over repeated use or over a long period of time, or performs its functions reliably.

These two elements are related to the validation and verification aspects of QA

- **Quality in software engineering**

  Within software engineering, quality has been one of the most important factor, including cost, schedule, and functionality, which have been studied by researchers and practitioners. These factors determine the success or failure of a software product in evolving market environments, but may have varying importance for different time periods and different market segments.

  In **Musa and Everett (1990),** these varying primary concerns were conveniently used to divide software engineering into four progressive stages:

  a. In the functional stage, the focus was on providing the automated functions to replace what had been done manually before.

  b. In the schedule stage, the focus was on introducing the important features and new systems on a timely and orderly basis to satisfy the urgent user needs.

  c. In the cost stage, the focus was on reducing the price to stay competitive accompanied by the widespread use of personal computers.

  d. In the reliability stage, the focus was managing users' quality expectations under the increased dependency on software and high cost or severe damages associated with software failures.

  We can see a gradual increase in the importance of quality within software engineering. This general characterization is in agreement with what we have discussed so far, namely, the importance of focusing on correctness-centered quality attributes in our software QA effort for modern software systems.

  In summary the **Software Quality Engineering (SQE)** is a process that evaluates, assesses, and improves the quality of software. Software quality is often defined as the degree to which software meets requirements for reliability, maintainability, transportability, and so on; as contrasted with functional, performance, and interface requirements that are satisfied as a result of software engineering.

  Quality must be built into a software product during its development to satisfy the quality requirements as established for it. SQE ensures that the process of incorporating quality in the software is done properly, and that the resulting software product meets the quality requirements and is usually must be determined by analysis while functional requirements are demonstrated by testing. SQE performs a function complementary to software development engineering. Their common goal is to ensure that a safe, reliable, and quality engineered software product is developed.

Software Qualities

Qualities for which an SQE evaluation is to be done must first be selected and then the requirements are set for them. Some commonly used qualities are:

a. **Reliability:** Hardware reliability often defined in terms of the **Mean-Time-To-Failure (MTTF),** of a given set of equipment. An analogous notion is useful for software, although the failure mechanisms are different and the mathematical predictions used for hardware have not yet been usefully applied to software. Software reliability is often defined as the extent to which a program can be expected to perform intended functions with the required precision over a given period of time. Software reliability engineering is concerned with the detection and correction of errors in the software; even more, it is concerned with the techniques to compensate for unknown software errors and for problems in the hardware and data environments in which the software must operate.

b. **Maintainability:** Software maintainability is defined as the ease of finding and correcting errors in the software. It is analogous to the hardware quality of **Mean-Time-To-Repair (MTTR).** While there is as yet no way to directly measure or predict the software maintainability, there is a significant body of knowledge about software attributes that make software easier to maintain. These include modularity, self (internal) documentation, code readability, and structured coding techniques. These same attributes also improve sustainability, the ability to make improvements to the software.

c. **Transportability:** Transportability is defined as the ease of transporting a given set of software to a new hardware and/or operating system environment.

d. **Interoperability:** Software interoperability is the ability of two or more software systems used to exchange information and to mutually use the exchanged information.

e. **Efficiency:** Efficiency is the extent to which software uses the minimum hardware resources to perform its functions.

Some of the software quality requirements one would look for are outlined below:

- **Specific Non-Functional (Quality) Requirements**
    - o Is the expected response time, from the user's point of view, specified for all necessary operations?

o Are other timing considerations specified, such as processing time, data-transfer rate, and system throughput?

o Is the level of security specified?

o Is the reliability specified, including the consequences of software failure, the vital information that needs to be protected from failure, and the strategy for error detection and recovery?

o Is maximum memory specified?

o Is the maximum storage specified?

o Is the maintainability of the system specified, including its ability to adapt the changes in specific functionality, changes in the operating environment, and changes in its interfaces with other software?

o Is the definition of success included? Of failure?

- **Requirements Quality**

  o Are the requirements written in the user's language? Do the users think so?

  o Does each requirement avoid the conflicts with other requirements?

  o Are acceptable trade-offs are there between competing attributes specified, for example, between robustness and correctness?

  o Do the requirements avoid specifying the design?

  o Are the requirements at a fairly consistent level of detail? Should any requirement be specified in more detail? Should any requirement be specified in less detail?

  o Are the requirements clear enough to be turned over to an independent group for construction and still be understood?

  o Is each item relevant to the problem and its solution? Can each item be traced to its origin in the problem environment?

  o Is each requirement testable? Will it be possible for independent testing to determine whether each requirement has been satisfied?

  o Are all possible changes to the requirements specified, including the likelihood of each change?

There are many other software qualities. Some of them are not important to a specific software system, thus no activities will be performed to assess or improve them. Maximizing some qualities may cause others to be decreased. For example, increasing the efficiency of a piece of software may require writing parts of it in assembly language. This will decrease the transportability and maintainability of the software.

Metrics

Metrics are the quantitative values, usually computed from the design or code, that measures the quality in question, or some attribute of the software related to the quality. Many metrics have been invented, and a number of them have been successfully used in specific environment, but none has gained widespread acceptance.

A Software Quality Engineering Program

The two software qualities which command the most attention are reliability and maintainability. Some practical programs and techniques have been developed to improve the reliability and maintainability of the software, even if they are not measurable or predictable. The types of activities that might be included in an SQE program are described in terms of these two qualities. These activities could be used as a model for the SQE activities for additional qualities.

a. **Qualities and Attributes**

- An initial step in laying out an SQE program is to select the qualities that are important in the context of the use of the software which is being developed. For example, the highest priority qualities for flight software are usually reliability and efficiency. If revised flight software can be up-linked during flight, maintainability may be of interest, but considerations like transportability will not drive the design or implementation. On the other hand, the use of science analysis software might require ease of change and maintainability, with reliability a concern and efficiency not a driver at all.

- After the software qualities are selected and ranked, specific attributes of the software which help to increase those qualities should be identified. For example, modularity is an attribute that tends to increase both reliability and maintainability. Modular software is designed to result in code that is apportioned into small, self-contained, functionally unique components, or units. Modular code is easier to maintain, because of the interactions between units of code are easily understood, and low-level functions are contained in few units of code. Modular code is also more reliable, because it is easier to completely test a small, self-contained unit.

- Not all software qualities are simply related to measurable design and code attributes, and no quality is so simple that it can be easily measured. The idea is to select or devise measurable, analyzable, or testable design and code attributes that will increase the desired qualities. Attributes like information hiding, strength, cohesion, and coupling should be considered.

b. **Quality Evaluations**

- Once some decisions have been made about the quality objectives and software attributes, quality evaluations can be done. The intent in an evaluation is to measure the effectiveness of a standard or procedure in promoting the desired attributes of the software product. Consider an example, the design and coding standards should undergo a quality evaluation. If modularity is desired, the standards should clearly say so and should set standards for the size of units or components. Since internal documentation is linked to maintainability, the documentation standards should be clear and require good internal documentation.

- Quality of designs and code should also be evaluated. This can be done as a part of the walkthrough or inspection process, or a quality audit can be done. In either case the implementation is evaluated against the standard and the evaluator's knowledge of good software engineering practices and example of poor quality in the product are identified for possible correction.

c. **Nonconformance Analysis**

- One very useful SQE activity is an analysis of a project's nonconformance records. The nonconformance should be analyzed for unexpectedly high numbers of events in specific sections or modules of code. If areas of code are found that have had an unusually high error count (assuming it is not because the code in question has been tested more thoroughly), then the code should be examined. The high error count may be due to poor quality code, an inappropriate design, or requirements that are not well understood or defined. In any case, the analysis may indicate changes and rework that can improve the reliability of the completed software. In addition to code problems, the analysis may also reveal software development or maintenance processes that allow or cause a high proportion of errors to be introduced into the software. If so, an audit may discover that the procedures are not being followed.

d. **Fault Tolerance Engineering**

- For software that must be of high reliability, a fault tolerance activity should be established. It should identify the software which provides and accomplishes critical functions and requirements. For this software, the engineering activity should determine and develop techniques which will ensure that the needed reliability or fault tolerance will be attained. Some of the techniques that have been developed for high reliability environments include:

  o **Input data checking and error tolerance**: Consider an example, if out-of-range or missing input data can affect reliability, then sophisticated error checking and data interpolation/extrapolation schemes may significantly improve the reliability.

o **Proof of correctness:** For limited amounts of code, formal *"Proof of correctness"* methods may be able to demonstrate that no errors exist.

o **N-Item voting:** This is a design and implementation scheme where a number of independent sets of software and hardware operate on the same input. Some comparison (voting) scheme is used to determine which output to use. This is especially effective where subtle timing or hardware errors may be present.

o **Independent development:** In this scheme, more or more of the N-items are independently developed units of software. This helps to prevent the simultaneous failure of all items due to a common coding error.

Tools and Techniques

Some of the useful fault-tolerance techniques are described under subsection D, above. Standard statistical techniques can be used to manipulate nonconformance data. In addition, there is considerable experimentation with the **Failure Modes and Effect Analysis (FMEA)** technique adapted from hardware reliability engineering. In particular, the FMEA can be used to identify the failure modes or other assemble (hardware) system states which can then lead the quality engineer to an analysis of the software that controls the system as it assumes those states.

There are also tools that are useful for quality engineering. They include system and software simulators, which allow the modeling of system behavior; dynamic analyzers, which detect the portions of the code that are used most intensively; software tools that are used to compute metrics from code or designs; and a host of special purpose tools that can, for example, detect all system calls to help decide on portability limits.

Characteristics of Software Quality

Software has both external and internal quality characteristics. External characteristics are the characteristics that a user of the software product is aware of, and it includes:

- **Correctness:** The degree to which a system is free from faults in its specification, design, and implementation.

- **Usability:** The ease with which users can learn and use a system.

- **Efficiency:** Minimal use of system resources, including memory, and execution time.

- **Reliability:** The ability of a system to perform its required functions understated conditions whenever required—having a long mean time between failures.

- **Integrity:** The degree to which a system prevents unauthorized or improper access to its programs and its data. The idea of integrity includes restricting unauthorized user accesses as well as ensuring that data is accessed properly—that is, that tables with parallel data are modified in parallel, that date fields contain only valid dates, and so on.

- **Adaptability:** The extent to which a system can be used, without modification, in applications or environments other than those for which it was specifically designed.

- **Accuracy:** The degree to which a system built, is free from error, especially with respect to quantitative outputs. Accuracy differs from correctness; it is a determination of how well a system does the job it's built for rather than whether it was built correctly.

- **Robustness:** The degree to which a system continues to function in the presence of invalid inputs or stressful environmental conditions.

  Some of these characteristics overlap, but all have different shades of meaning that are applicable more in some cases, less in others.

External characteristics of quality are the only kind of software characteristics that users care about. Users care about whether the software is easy to use, or whether it's easy for you to modify. They care about whether the software works correctly, not about whether the code is readable or well structured.

Programmers care about the internal characteristics of the software as well as the external ones. We try here to be code-centered. therefore, it focuses on the internal quality characteristics. They include:

- **Maintainability:** The ease with which you can modify a software system to change or add capabilities, improve performance, or correct defects.

- **Flexibility:** The extent to which you can modify a system for use or environments other than those for which it was specifically designed.

- **Portability:** The ease with which you can modify a system to operate in an environment different from that for which it was specifically designed.

- **Reusability:** The extent to which and the ease with which you can use parts of a system in other systems.

- **Readability:** The ease with which you can read and understand the source code of a system, especially at the detailed-statement level.

- **Testability:** The degree to which you can unit-test and system-test a system; the degree to which you can verify that the system meets its requirements.

- **Understandability:** The ease with which you can comprehend a system at both the system-organizational and detailed-statement levels. Understandability has to do with the coherence of the system at a more general level than readability does.

As in the list of external quality characteristics, some of these internal characteristics overlap, but they too each have different shades of meaning that are valuable.

The internal aspects of system quality are the main subject. The difference between internal and external characteristics isn't completely clear-cut because at some level internal characteristics affect external ones. Software that isn't internally understandable or maintainable impairs your ability to correct defects, which in turn affects the external characteristics of correctness and reliability. Software that isn't flexible cannot be enhanced in response to user requests, which in turn affects the external characteristic of usability. The point is that some quality characteristics are emphasized to make life easier for the user and some are emphasized to make life easier for the programmer.

The attempt to maximize certain characteristics invariably conflicts with the attempt to maximize others. Finding an optimal solution from a set of competing objectives is one activity that makes software development a true engineering discipline. The kinds of relationships can be found among the internal characteristics of software quality.

 The most interesting aspect of this chart is that it focusses on a specific characteristic that doesn't always mean a trade-off with another characteristic. Sometimes one hurts another, sometimes one helps another, and sometimes one neither hurts nor helps another. For example, correctness is the characteristic of functioning exactly to specification. Robustness is the ability to continue functioning even under the unanticipated conditions. Sometimes focusing on correctness hurts robustness of the software and vice versa. In contrast, focusing on adaptability helps robustness and vice versa

Techniques for Improving Software Quality

Software quality assurance is a planned and systematic program of activities designed to ensure that a system has the desired characteristics. Although it might seem that the best way to develop a high-quality product would be to focus on the product itself, in software quality assurance the best place is on the process. Here are some of the elements of a software quality program:

Software quality objectives: One powerful technique for improving software quality is setting explicit quality objectives from among the external characteristics described in the last section. Without explicit goals, programmers can work to maximize characteristics different from the ones you expect them to maximize. The power of setting explicit goals is discussed in more detail later in this section.

Explicit quality-assurance activity: One common problem in assuring quality is that quality is perceived as a secondary goal. Indeed, in some organizations, quick and dirty programming is the rule rather than the exception. Programmers who litter their code with defects and "complete" their programs quickly, are rewarded more than programmers who write excellent programs and make sure that they are usable before releasing them. In such organizations, it shouldn't be surprising that programmers don't make quality their first priority. The organization must show programmers that quality is a priority. Making the quality-assurance activity independent makes the priority clear, and programmers will respond accordingly.

Testing strategy: Execution testing can provide a detailed assessment of product reliability. Developers on many projects rely on testing as the primary method of both quality assessment and quality improvement. Testing does have a role in the construction of high-quality software, however, and part of quality assurance is developing a test strategy in conjunction with the product requirements, the architecture, and the design.

Software-engineering guidelines: These are the guidelines that control the technical character of the software as it is developed. Such guidelines apply to all software development activities including problem definition, requirements development, architecture, construction, and system testing. The guidelines in this book are, in one sense, a set of software-engineering guidelines for construction (detailed design, coding, unit testing, and integration).

Informal technical reviews: Many software developers review their work before turning it over for formal review. Informal reviews include desk-checking the design or the code or walking through the code with a few peers.

Formal technical reviews: One part of managing a software-engineering process is catching problems at the *"lowest-value"* stage—that is, at the stage in which problems cost the least to correct. To achieve such goal, developers on most software-engineering projects use *"quality gates,"* periodic tests that determine whether the quality of the product at one stage is sufficient to support moving on to the next. Quality gates are usually used to transition between requirements development and architecture, architecture, detailed design, and construction, system testing. The *"gate"* can be a peer review, a customer review, an inspection, a walkthrough, or an audit.

A *"gate"* does not mean that architecture or requirements need to be 100 percent complete or frozen; it does mean that you will use the gate to determine whether the requirements or architecture are good enough to support downstream development. *"Good enough"* might mean that you have sketched out the most critical 20 percent of the requirements or architecture, or it might mean you have specified 95 percent in excruciating detail which end of the scale you should aim for depends on the nature of your specific project.

External audits: An external audit is a specific kind of technical review used to determine the status of a project or the quality of a product being developed. An audit team is brought in from outside the organization and reports its findings to whoever commissioned the audit, usually management.

Development process: Each of the elements mentioned so far has something to do explicitly with assuring software quality and implicitly with the process of software development. Development efforts that include quality-assurance activities produce better software than those that do not. Other processes that aren't explicitly quality-assurance activities also affect software quality

Change-control procedures: One big obstacle to acheive software quality is uncontrolled changes. Uncontrolled requirements changes can result in disruption to design and coding. Uncontrolled changes in architecture or design can result in code that doesn't agree with its design, inconsistencies in the code, or the use of more time in modifying code to meet the changing design than in moving the project forward. Uncontrolled changes in the code itself can result in internal inconsistencies and uncertainties about which code has been fully reviewed and tested and which hasn't. Uncontrolled changes in requirements, architecture, design, or code can have all of these effects. Consequently, handling changes effectively is a key to effective product development.

Measurement of results: Unless results of a quality-assurance plan are measured, you'll have no way of knowing whether the plan is working. Measurement tells you whether your plan is a success or a failure and also allows you to vary your process in a controlled way to see whether it can be improved.

Measurement has a second, motivational, effect. People pay attention to whatever is measured, assuming that it is used to evaluate them. Choose what you measure carefully. People tend to focus on work that's measured and to ignore work that isn't.

Prototyping: Prototyping is the development of realistic models of a system's key functions. A developer can prototype parts of a user interface to determine usability, critical calculations to determine execution time, or typical data sets to determine the memory requirements. A survey of 16 published and 8 unpublished case studies compared prototyping to traditional, specification-development methods. The comparison revealed that prototyping can lead to better designs, better matches with user needs, and improved maintainability (Gordon and Bieman 1991).

Setting Objectives: Explicitly setting quality objectives is a simple, obvious step in achieving quality software, but it is easy to overlook. You might wonder whether, if you set quality objectives, programmers will actually work to achieve them. The answer is, yes, they will, if they know what the objectives are and the objectives are reasonable. Programmers can't respond to a set of objectives that change daily or those are impossible to meet.

Software Quality Assurance (SQA)

Software Quality Assurance consists of a means of monitoring the software engineering processes and methods used to ensure the quality. It does this by means of audits of the quality management system under which the software system is created. The audits are backed by one or more standards, usually **ISO 9000** series.

It is distinct from software quality control which includes reviewing requirements documents, and software testing. SQA encompasses the entire software development process, which includes processes such as software design, coding, source code control, code reviews, change management, configuration management, and release management. Whereas software quality control is a control of products, software quality assurance is control of processes.

Software quality assurance is related to the practice of quality assurance in the product manufacturing. There are, however, some notable differences between software and a manufactured product. These differences state from the fact that the manufactured product is physical and can be seen whereas the software product is not visible. Therefore, its function, benefit, and costs are not as easily measured. What's more, when a manufactured product rolls off the assembly line, it is essentially a complete, finished product, whereas software is never finished. Software lives, grows, evolves, and metamorphoses, unlike its tangible counterparts. Therefore, the processes and methods to manage, monitor, and measure its ongoing quality are as fluid and sometimes elusive as are the defects that they are meant to keep in check.

The quality system has undergone through four stages of evolution as shown in *figure 12.1*. **Inspection** used to be carried out earlier with finished product. The process used to ensure quality product by eliminating the defective once. Inspection was done after the jobs were produced. The *rejection* of the defective products used to be costly affair for the organization. The initial product inspection method gave way to *Quality Control (QC)*. The QC was detecting the defective products and eliminating them and at the same time it was able to determine the cause of defects. The process is called **error detection**. The cause of defect in the production process was removed to produce good products thereafter. The QC method was found to be a better solution than inspection.

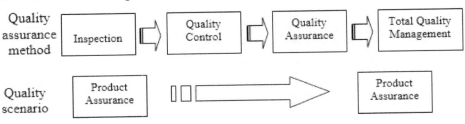

***Figure 12.1:** Evolution of quality concept and quality paradigm*

The next breakthrough in quality system was *Quality Assurance (QA)*. The process of QA was to give more emphasis on the production process to prevent errors. If the process is good and closely monitored, the product being processed are bound to be non-defective and of good quality. The process is called **error prevention**.

This modern quality procedure includes the procedures for recognizing, defining, analyzing, and improving the production process. From the organizational view point **Total Quality Management (TQM)** was adopted instead of process control. This would ensure organization improvement as a whole by achieving continuous process improvement.

Inspection is most commonly applied to code, but it could also be applied to requirement specifications, designs, test plans, and test cases, user manuals, and other documents or software artifacts. Therefore, inspection can be used throughout the development process, particularly early in the software development before anything can be tested. Consequently, inspection can be an effective and economical QA alternative because of the much-increased cost of fixing late defects as compared to fixing early ones. These causal analysis results can be used to guide defect prevention activities by removing identified error sources or correcting identified missing/incorrect human actions.

According to the different ways different QA alternatives deal with defects, they can be classified into three general categories:

a. **Defect prevention** through error source elimination and error blocking activities, such as education and training, formal specification and verification, and proper selection and application of appropriate technologies, tools, processes, or standards.

b. **Defect reduction** through inspection, testing, and other static analyses or dynamic activities, to detect and remove faults from software. As one of the most important and widely used alternatives, is testing

c. **Defect containment** through fault tolerance, failure prevention, or failure impact minimization, to assure the software reliability and safety. Existing software quality literature generally covers defect reduction techniques such as testing and inspection in more details than defect prevention activities, while largely ignore the role of defect containment in QA.

QA in Software Development and Maintenance Processes

In the software maintenance process, the focus of QA is on defect handling, to make sure that each problem reported by customers from field operations is logged, analyzed, resolved, and a complete tracking record is kept so that we can learn from past problems for future quality improvement. In addition, such defect information can be used as an additional input in planning for future releases of the same product or for replacement products. Among the different QA activities, defect containment activities play an important role in post-release product operations and maintenance support.

QA in the Waterfall Process

Most commonly used waterfall process for large software projects, development activities are typically grouped into different sequential stages to form a waterfall, although overlaps are common among successive pairs of stages (**Zelkowitz, 1988**). A typical sequence includes, in chronological order: product planning, requirement analysis, specification, design, coding, testing, release, and post-release product support. As a central part of QA activities, testing is an integral part of the waterfall development process, forming an important link in the overall development chain. Other QA activities, although not explicitly stated in the description process, can be carried out throughout other phases and in the transition from one phase to another. Consider an example, part of the criteria to move on from each phase to the next is quality, typically in the form of checking to see if certain quality plans or standards have been completed or followed, as demonstrated by the results from various forms or reviews or inspections.

Various defect prevention activities are typically concentrated in the earlier phases of software development, before actual faults have been injected into the software systems. There are several important reasons for this focus on early development phases:

- The error sources are typically associated with activities in these early phases, such as conceptual mistakes by designers and programmers, unfamiliarity with the product domain, inexperience with the specific development methodologies, and so on. Therefore, error source removal, a primary method of defect preventions, is closely associated with these early development phases.

- Although some faults could be injected into the software systems during testing and other late development phases, the experience tells us that the vast majority of faults are injected in the early development phases, particularly in detailed design and implementation phases. Therefore, effective defect prevention through error blocking needs to be carried out during these phases.

Because of the possibilities of defect propagations and the increasing cost over time or successive development phases to fix the defects once they are injected into the system, we need to reduce the number of faults in software systems by the combination of defect prevention and application of QA techniques that can help to remove software faults early. Some defect detection and removal techniques, such as inspection, can be applied to early phases, such as inspecting requirement documents, product specifications, and different levels of product designs. On the other hand, there are practical obstacles to the early fixing of injected defects. For example, dynamic problems may only become apparent during execution; and inter-dependency only becomes apparent with the implementation of related components or modules. Because of these reasons, other fault detection and removal activities, such as testing, are typically concentrated in the middle to late phases of software development.

Finally, failure prevention and containment activities, such as fault tolerance and safety assurance, typically focus the operational phases. However, their planning, design, and implementation need to be carried out throughout the software development process. In some sense, they are equivalent to adding some necessary functions or features into the existing product to make them safe or fault tolerant.

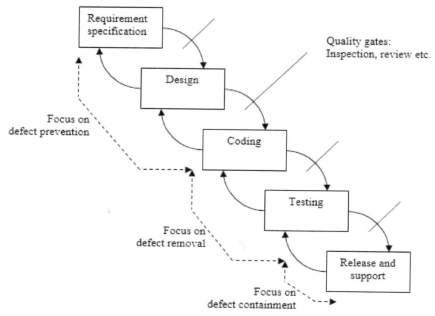

Figure 12.2: *Quality Assurance activities on waterfall model*

Figure 12.2 above illustrate how the different QA activities fit into the waterfall process.

Three key characteristics of this activity distribution are as follows:

   a.   The phase with QA as the focus: Testing phase.

   b.   QA activities, typically includes inspections and reviews, carried out at the transitions from one phase to the next are shown as barriers or gates to pass. The exception to this is between testing and release, where the reviews are typically accompanied by the acceptance testing.

   c.   Other QA activities scatter over other development phases: The general distribution scope is shown by the dotted bracket, with a focus on defect prevention in the early phases, a focus on defect removal during coding and testing phases, and a focus on defect containment in operational support.

ISO-9001

History of ISO 9000

During World War II, there were quality problems in many British industries such as munitions, where bombs were exploding in factories during assembly. The adopted solution was to require factories to document their manufacturing procedures and to prove by record-keeping that the procedures were being followed. The name of the standard was **BS 5750**, and it was known as a management standard because it specified not what to manufacture, but how the manufacturing process was to be managed. According to Seddon, "*In 1987, the British Government persuaded the International Organization for Standardization to adopt BS 5750 as an international standard. BS 5750 became ISO 9000.*"

ISO 9000

ISO 9000 is a family of *standards for quality management systems*. ISO 9000 is maintained by ISO, the *International Organization for Standardization* and is administered by accreditation and certification bodies. It was published its 9000 series of standards in 1987. ISO is a consortium of around 100 exporting countries established to formulate and foster standardization. The ISO 9000 standards have been adopted by many countries including all members of the European Community, Canada, Mexico, the United States, Australia, New Zealand, and the Pacific Rim. Countries in Latin and South America have also shown interest in the standards.

After adopting the standards, a country typically permits only ISO registered companies to supply goods and services to government agencies and public utilities. Telecommunication equipment and medical devices are the examples of product categories that must be supplied by ISO registered companies. In turn, manufacturers of these products often require their suppliers to become registered. Private companies such as automobile and computer manufacturers frequently require their suppliers to be ISO registered as well.

To register to one of the quality assurance system models contained in ISO 9000, a company's quality system and operations are scrutinized by third party auditors for compliance to the standard and for effective operation. Upon successful registration, a company issued a certificate from a registration body represented by the auditors. Semi-annual surveillance audits ensure continued compliance to the standard.

ISO 9000 describes the elements of a quality assurance system in general terms. These elements include the organizational structure, procedures, processes, and resources needed to implement quality planning, quality control, quality assurance, and quality improvement. However, ISO 9000 does not describe how an organization should implement these quality system elements. Consequently, the challenge lies in designing and implementing a quality assurance system that meets the standard and fits the company's products, services, and culture.

Requirements of ISO 9001

Some of the requirements in ISO 9001 (which is one of the standards in the ISO 9000 family) include:

- A set of procedures that cover all the key processes in the business;
- Monitoring processes to ensure they are effective;
- Keeping adequate records;
- Checking output for defects, with appropriate and corrective action where necessary;
- Regularly reviewing individual processes and the quality system itself for effectiveness; and
- Facilitating continual improvement

A company or organization that has been independently audited and certified to be in conformance with ISO 9001 may publicly state that it is *"ISO 9001 certified"* or *"ISO 9001 registered."* Certification to an ISO 9000 standard does not guarantee the compliance (and therefore the quality) of end products and services; rather, it certifies that consistent business processes are being applied. Indeed, some companies enter the ISO 9001 certification as a marketing tool.

Although the standards originated in *manufacturing*, they are now employed across a wide range of other types of organizations. A *"product"*, in ISO vocabulary, can mean a physical object, or services, or software. In fact, according to ISO in 2004, *"service sectors now account by far for the highest number of ISO 9001:2000 certificates - about 31% of the total."*

ISO 9001:2000 Quality management systems – Requirements is intended for use in any organization which designs, develops, manufactures, installs, and/or services any product or provides any form of service. It provides a number of requirements which an organization needs to fulfill if it is to achieve customer satisfaction through consistent products and services which meet customer expectations. It includes a requirement for the continual (i.e. planned) improvement of the Quality Management System, for which ISO 9004:2000 provides many hints. This is the only implementation for which third-party auditors may grant certification.

Note that the previous members of the ISO 9000 family, 9001, 9002, and 9003, have all been integrated into 9001. In most cases, an organization claiming to be "ISO 9000 registered" is referring to ISO 9001.

ISO 9000:1987 Version

ISO 9000:1987 had the same structure as the UK Standard BS 5750, with three '*models*' for quality management systems, the selection of which was based on the scope of activities of the organization:

- **ISO 9001:1987** *Model for quality assurance in design, development, production, installation, and servicing* was for companies and organizations whose activities included the creation of new products.

- **ISO 9002:1987** *Model for quality assurance in production, installation, and servicing* had basically the same material as ISO 9001 but without covering the creation of new products.

- **ISO 9003:1987** *Model for quality assurance in final inspection and test* covered only the final inspection of finished product, with no concern for how the product was produced.

- **ISO 9000:1987** was also influenced by existing U.S. and other *Defense Standards ("MIL SPECS")*, and so was well-suited to manufacturing. The emphasis tended to be placed on conformance with procedures rather than the overall process of management — which was likely the actual intent.

ISO 9000:1994 Version

ISO 9000:1994 emphasized *quality assurance* via preventive actions, instead of just checking final product, and continued to require evidence of compliance with documented procedures. As with the first edition, the down-side was that companies tended to implement its requirements by creating shelf-loads of procedure manuals, and becoming burdened with an ISO bureaucracy. In some companies, adapting and improving processes could actually be impeded by the quality system.

ISO 9000:2000 Version

ISO 9001:2000 combines the three standards **9001, 9002, and 9003** into one, now called 9001. Design and development procedures are required only if a company does in fact engage in the creation of new products. The 2000 version sought to make a radical change in thinking by actually placing the concept of process management front and center ("*Process management*" was the monitoring and optimizing of a company's tasks and activities, instead of just inspecting the final product). The 2000 version also demands the involvement of upper executives, in order to integrate quality into the business system and avoid delegation of quality functions to junior administrators. Another goal is to improve effectiveness via process performance metrics, numerical measurement of the effectiveness of tasks and activities. Expectations of continual *process improvement* and tracking customer satisfaction were made explicit.

ISO 9000:2008 Version

The ISO 9001 technical committee reviewed on the next version of ISO 9001, which will in all likelihood be termed the **ISO 9001:2008** standard, assuming its planned release date of 2008 is met. Early reports are that the standard will not be substantially changed from its 2000 version. As with the release of previous versions, organizations registered to ISO 9001 will be given a substantial period to transit to the new version of the standard, assuming changes are needed. Organizations registered to 9001:1994 had until December of 2003 to undergo upgrade audits.

Certification

ISO does not itself certify organizations. Many countries have formed accreditation bodies to authorize certification bodies, which audit organizations applying for ISO 9001 compliance certification. Although commonly referred to as ISO 9000:2000 certifications, the actual standard to which an organization's quality management can be certified is **ISO 9001:2000**. Both the accreditation bodies and the certification bodies charge fees for their services. The various accreditation bodies have mutual agreements with each other to ensure that certificates issued by one of the **Accredited Certification Bodies (CB)** are accepted world-wide.

The applying organization is assessed based on an extensive sample of its sites, functions, products, services, and processes; a list of problems (*"action requests"* or *"non-compliances"*) is made known to the management. If there are no major problems on this list, the certification body will issue an **ISO 9001** certificate for each geographical site it has visited, once it receives a satisfactory improvement plan from the management showing how any problems will be resolved.

An ISO certificate is not a once-and-for-all award, but must be renewed at regular intervals recommended by the certification body, usually around three years. In contrast to the *Capability Maturity Model* there are no grades of competence within ISO 9001.

Auditing

Two types of *auditing* are required to become registered to the standard:

    a.   Auditing by an external *certification body (external audit)*

    b.   Audits by internal staff trained for this process (*internal audits*).

The aim is a continual process of review and assessment, to verify that the system is working as it's supposed to, find out where it can improve and to correct or prevent problems identified. It is considered healthier for internal auditors to audit outside their usual management line, so as to bring a degree of independence to their judgments.

Under the 1994 standard, the auditing process could be adequately addressed by performing *"compliance auditing"*. The 2000 standard uses the process approach. While auditors perform similar functions, they are expected to go beyond mere auditing for *"compliance"* by focusing on risk, status, and importance. This means they are expected to make more judgments on what is effective, rather than merely adhering to what is formally prescribed.

Under the 1994 version, the question was *"Are you doing what the manual says you should be doing?"*, whereas under the 2000 version, the question is *"Will this process help you achieve your stated objectives? Is it a good process or is there a way to do it better?"*

The *ISO 19011* standard for auditing applies to ISO 9001 besides other management systems like EMS (ISO 14001), FSMS (ISO 22000), and so on.

Advantages

It is widely acknowledged that proper quality management improves business, often having a positive effect on investment, market share, sales growth, sales margins, competitive advantage, and avoidance of litigation. The quality principles **in ISO 9000:2000** are also sound. ISO 9000 guidelines provide a comprehensive model for quality management systems that can make any company competitive [Wade and Barnes]. According to the Providence Business News, implementing ISO often gives the following advantages:

a. Create a more efficient, effective operation

b. Increase customer satisfaction and retention

c. Reduce audits

d. Enhance marketing

e. Improve employee motivation, awareness, and morale

f. Promote international trade

g. Increases profit

h. Reduce waste and increases productivity

In today's service-sector driven economy, more and more companies are using ISO 9000 as a business tool. Through the use of properly stated quality objectives, customer satisfaction surveys and a well-defined continual improvement program companies are using ISO 9000 processes to increase their efficiency and profitability.

Problems

A common criticism of ISO 9001 is the amount of money, time, and paperwork required for registration. Opponents claim that it is only for documentation. Proponents believe that if a company has documented its quality systems, then most of the paperwork has already been completed [Barnes].

ISO 9001 promotes specification, control, and procedures rather than understanding and improvement [Seddon]. Wade argues that ISO 9000 is effective as a guideline, but that promoting it as a standard helps to mislead companies into thinking that certification means better quality. An organization needs to set its own quality standards. Blind reliance on the specifications of ISO 9001 does not guarantee a successful quality system.

The standard is seen especially prone to failure when a company is interested in certification before quality. Certifications are in fact often based on customer contractual requirements rather than a desire to actually improve quality. *"If you just want the certificate on the wall, chances are, you will create a paper system that doesn't have much to do with the way you actually run your business."* Certification by an independent auditor is often seen as the problem area, and has become a vehicle to increase consulting services. In fact, ISO itself advises that ISO 9001 can be implemented without certification, simply for the quality benefits that can be achieved. Another problem reported is the competition among the numerous certifying bodies, leading to a softer approach to the defects noticed in the operation of the Quality System of a firm.

Quality Planning for Software

Develop quality plans to control your software development projects.

- The quality plans should control project implementation, project schedules, project resources, project approvals, project phases (the beginning and end).
- Your quality plans should define the quality requirements, responsibilities, authorities, life cycle model, review methods, testing methods, verification methods, and validation methods.
- Develop detailed quality plans and procedures, define specific responsibilities and authorities to control the configuration management, product verification, product validation, nonconforming products, and corrective actions.
- Your quality plans may include or refer to generic/special project, product, or contract procedures.
- Your quality plan can be a separate document or it can be part of another larger document. Or, it can be made up of several specific documents.
- Your quality plan should be updated and refined as your software development plan is implemented.
- Make sure that all participating groups and organizations get a chance to review and approve the quality plan before it is implemented.

Contract Review

Develop and document procedures to coordinate the review of software development contracts. Develop procedures to coordinate the review of contracts that the software will be developed for a customer or for a market sector or for your internal use or the software will be embedded in a hardware product. The contract review procedures should ensure that all contractual requirements are acceptable before you agree to provide products to your customers. Specifically, your procedures should make sure that the data and facilities to be provided by the customer, to carry out the joint product development, life cycle processes to be imposed by the customer, deployment of software product, the changes to be handled during software development and software maintenance, handling of software problems after acceptance and training of users, and so on.

Software Development And Design

Develop and document procedures to control the product design and development process. These procedures must ensure that all requirements are being met.

Software Development

Control your software development project and make sure that it is executed in a disciplined manner. Use one or more life cycle models to organize your software development project. Develop and document your software development procedures. These procedures should ensure that:

- Software products meet all requirements.
- Software development follows your:
    o Quality plan.
    o Development plan.

Software Design

Control your software design process and make sure that it is performed in a systematic way. Use a suitable software design method. Study previous software design projects to avoid repeating old mistakes. Design software that is easy to test, install, use, and maintain. Develop and document rules to control the coding activities, naming conventions, commentary practices, and programming languages. Apply configuration management techniques to document, and control the use and review of all analysis tools, design techniques, compilers, and assemblers. Train personnel in the use of such tools and techniques.

Design and Development Planning

Create design and development planning procedures. The product planning procedures should ensure that plans are prepared for each design activity. Responsibility for implementing each plan, activity, or phase is properly defined. Qualified personnel are assigned to the product design and development process.

Adequate resources are allocated to the product design and development process. Plans are updated, and circulated to the appropriate participants, as designs change.

Software Design and Development Planning

Prepare a software development plan. Your plan should be documented and approved before it is implemented. Your plan should control:

- Technical activities like requirements analyses, design processes, coding activities, integration methods, testing techniques, installation work, and acceptance testing.

- Management activities like project supervision, progress reviews, and reporting requirements.

Your software development plan should define your project, identify related plans and projects, list your project objectives, and define project inputs and outputs.

Software Design Input

Design input requirements should be specified by the customer. However, sometimes the customer will expect you to develop the design input specification. In this case, you should:

- Prepare procedures that you can use to develop the design input specification. These procedures should be documented and explain how interviews, surveys, studies, prototypes, and demonstrations will be used to develop your design-input specification. How you and your customer will formally agree to accept the official specification and to accept changes to the official specification. The method to change of specification, evaluation of product demonstration, input requirements to be met through the use of hardware, software, and interface technologies are to be laid down. The procedures of review, evaluation, and discussions need to be recorded.

- Work closely with your customer in order to avoid misunderstandings and to ensure that the specification meets the customer's needs.

- Express your specification by using terms that will make it easy to validate during product acceptance.

- Ask your customer to formally approve the resulting design input specification.

Your design input specification may address the following kinds of characteristics or requirements like functionality, reliability, usability, efficiency, maintainability, portability, and hardware/software interfaces.

Your design input specification may also need to address the following kinds of requirements:

- Operational requirements
- Safety requirements
- Security requirements
- Statutory requirements

Design Output

Develop procedures to control design outputs.

- Design outputs are usually documents. It includes drawings, parts lists, process specifications, servicing procedures, and storage instructions. These types of documents are used for purchasing, production, installation, inspection, testing, and servicing.
- Design outputs must be expressed in terms that allow them to be compared with design input requirements.
- Design output documents must identify those aspects of the product that are crucial to its safe and effective operation. These aspects include operating, storage, handling, maintenance, and disposal requirements.
- Design output documents must be reviewed and approved before they are distributed.
- Design outputs must be accepted only if they meet official acceptance criteria.

Software Design Output

- Prepare design output documents by using standardized methods and make sure that your documents are correct and complete.
- Software design outputs can include design specifications, source code, user guides, and so on.

Design Review

- Develop procedures that specify how design reviews should be planned and performed.
- Plan and perform design reviews for software development projects.
- Develop and document design review procedures.
- Define the methods that should be used to ensure that all rules and conventions are being followed.
- Define what needs to be done to prepare for a design review.
- Allow design activities to continue only if all deficiencies and nonconformities have been addressed and risks and consequences have been assessed.

Design Verification

Develop procedures that specify how design outputs, at every stage of the product design, and development process, should be verified. Verify design outputs by performing design reviews, performing demonstrations, and performing tests.

Design Validation

Develop procedures that validate the assumption that your newly designed products will meet customer needs. Develop design validation procedures to confirm that your new product performs properly under all real-world operating conditions. It should also confirm that your new product will meet every legitimate customer need and expectation. Ensure that validations are carried out early in the design process whenever this will help to meet the customer needs.

Document and Data Control

Develop procedures to control all the documents and data related to your quality system. These procedures should control internal and external documents with data, electronic, or hardcopy documents with data. Therefore, identify all internal and external documents and data that must be controlled. Develop procedures to control documents and data by using configuration management procedures.

Use the procedures to control the quality documents and data by adopting proper communications, specifications, requirements, descriptions, instructions, procedures, contracts, standards, manuals, reports, and plans. The procedures should control documents and data connected with customer interactions, periodic evaluations, and progress reviews.

SEI CMM

Since 1984, the Carnegie Mellon **Software Engineering Institute (SEI)** has served as a federally funded research and development center. The SEI staff has advanced software engineering principles and practices and has served as a national resource in software engineering, computer security, and process improvement. As a part of Carnegie Mellon University, Pittsburgh, which is well known for its highly rated programs in computer science and engineering, the SEI operates at the leading edge of technical innovation.

The SEI works closely with defense and government organizations, industry, and academia to continually improve our software-intensive systems. To accomplish this, the SEI

- Performs research to explore promising solutions to software engineering problems

- Identifies and codifies technological and methodological solutions
- Tests and refines the solutions through pilot programs that help industry and government solve their problems
- Widely disseminates proven solutions through training, licensing, and publication of best practices

The SEI's core purpose is to help an organization to improve their software engineering capabilities and to develop or acquire the right software, defect free, within budget and on time, every time.

CMM

The **Capability Maturity Model (CMM)** is a process capability maturity model which aids in the definition and understanding of an organization's processes. The CMM was first described in a book *Managing the Software Process by Watts Humphrey and hence was also known as "Humphrey's CMM"*. Active development of this model by the SEI (US Dept. of Defense Software Engineering Institute) began in 1986.

The CMM was originally intended as a tool for objectively assessing the ability of government contractors' *processes* to perform a contracted software project. Though it comes from the area of software development, it can be applied as a generally applicable model to assist in understanding the process capability maturity of organizations in diverse areas. For example, software engineering, system engineering, project management, software maintenance, risk management, system acquisition, information technology (IT), personnel management. It has been used extensively for avionics software and government projects around the world.

The CMM has been superseded by a variant - the **CMMI (Capability Maturity Model Integration)**. The old CMM was renamed to Software Engineering CMM (SE-CMM) and organizations accreditations based on SE-CMM expired on 31 December 2007. Maturity models have been internationally standardized as part of ISO 15504.

Maturity Model

A maturity model can be described as a structured collection of elements that describe certain aspects of maturity in an organization. A maturity model provides:

- A place to start
- The benefit of a community's prior experiences
- A common language and a shared vision
- A framework for prioritizing actions
- A way to define what improvement means for your organization.

A maturity model can be used as a benchmark for comparison and as an aid to understanding. For example, for comparative assessment of different organizations where there is something in common that can be used as a basis for comparison. In the case of the CMM, for example, the basis for comparison would be the organizations' software development processes.

Structure of CMM

The CMM involves the following aspects:

- **Maturity Levels:** A number of levels culminating in the discipline needed to engage in continuous process improvement and optimization.

- **Key Process Areas:** A Key Process Area (KPA) identifies a cluster of related activities that, when performed collectively, achieve a set of goals considered important.

- **Goals:** The goals of a key process area summarize the states that must exist for that key process area to have been implemented in an effective and lasting way. The extent to which the goals have been accomplished is an indicator of how much capability the organization has established at that maturity level. The goals signify the scope, boundaries, and intent of each key process area.

- **Common Features:** Common features include practices that implement and institutionalize a key process area. There are five types of common features: Commitment to Perform, Ability to Perform, Activities Performed, Measurement and Analysis, and Verifying Implementation.

- **Key Practices:** The key practices describe the elements of infrastructure and practice that contribute most effectively to the implementation and institutionalization of the KPAs.

Levels of the CMM

There are five levels defined along the continuum of the CMM, and, according to the SEI: *"Predictability, effectiveness, and control of an organization's software processes are believed to improve as the organization moves up these five levels. While not rigorous, the empirical evidence to date supports this belief."*

Level 1 - Ad hoc (Chaotic)

Level 1 - Ad hoc (Chaotic) is characteristic of processes at this level that they are (typically) un-documented and in a state of dynamic change, tending to be driven in an ad hoc, uncontrolled, and reactive manner by users or events. This provides a chaotic or unstable environment for the processes.

Organizational implications:

   a. Because institutional knowledge tends to be scattered (there being limited structured approach to knowledge management) in such environments, not all of the stakeholders or participants in the processes may know or understand all of the components that make up the processes. Since the software production processes are not defined, different professionals follow their own process and methods and as a result the development effort becomes chaotic. As a result, process performance in such organizations is likely to be variable (inconsistent) and depend heavily on the institutional knowledge, or the competence, or the heroic efforts of relatively few people or small groups.

b. Despite the chaos, such organizations manage to produce products and services. However, in doing so, there is a significant risk that will tend to exceed any estimated budgets or schedules for their projects. It is difficult to estimate what a process will do when you do not fully understand the process in the first place and cannot therefore control it or manage it effectively.

c. Due to the lack of structure and formality, organizations at this level, may over-commit, or abandon processes during a crisis, and be unable to repeat past successes. There tends to be limited planning, limited executive commitment, or buy-in to projects, and limited acceptance of processes.

Level 2-Repeatable is characteristic of processes at this level that some processes are repeatable, possibly with consistent results. The processes may not repeat for all the projects in the organization. The organization may use some basic project management to track cost and schedule. Size and cost estimation techniques such as function point analysis, **Constructive Cost Estimation Model (COCOMO),** and so on are used.

Process discipline is unlikely to be rigorous, but where it exists it may help to ensure that existing practices are retained during times of stress. When these practices are in place, projects are performed and managed according to their documented plans.

Organizational implications:

a. Project status and the delivery of services are visible to management at defined points - for example, at major milestones and at the completion of major tasks and activities.

b. Basic project management processes are established to track cost, schedule, and functionality. The minimum process discipline is in place to repeat earlier successes on projects with similar applications and scope. There is still a significant risk of exceeding cost and time estimates.

Level 3 - Defined is characteristic of processes at this level that there are sets of defined and documented standard processes established and subject to some degree of improvement over time. The processes for both management and development activities are defined and documented. These standard processes are in place (i.e., they are the AS-IS processes) and used to establish consistency of process performance across the organization. Projects establish their defined processes by applying the organization's set of standard processes, tailored, if necessary, within similarly standardized guidelines.

Organizational implications:

The organization's management establishes and mandates process objectives for the organization have set of standard processes, and ensures that these objectives are appropriately addressed.

Level 4 – Managed is characteristic of processes at this level that, using process metrics, management can effectively control the AS-IS process (e.g., for software development). In particular, management can identify ways to adjust and adapt the process to particular projects without measurable losses of quality or deviations from specifications. Process Capability is established from this level. The process metrics reflect the effectiveness of the process being used like average defect correction time, productivity, the average number of defects found per hour of inspection, the average number of failures detected during testing per **line of code (LOC)**.

Organizational implications:

a. Quantitative quality goals tend to set for process output. For example, software or software maintenance. The quantitative quality goals are set for products.

b. Using quantitative/statistical techniques, process performance is measured and monitored, and process performance is thus generally predictable and controllable. Tools like Pareto charts, fishbone diagrams are used to measure the product and process quality.

Level 5 – Optimized is characteristic of processes at this level that the focus is on continually improving process performance through both incremental and innovative technological changes/improvements. The process and product measurement data are analyzed for continuous process improvement. The lessons learned from specific projects are incorporated into the process. Continuous process improvement is achieved both by carefully analyzing the quantitative feedback from the process measurements and from application of innovative ideas and technologies.

Each maturity level is characterized by several **Key Process Areas (KPAs)** that indicate what the organization should focus on to improve its software process to the next level. The focus and key process areas of each level is indicated in the *table 12.1*.

SEI CMM provides a list of key areas on which to focus to take an organization from one level of maturity to the next. It provides a way for gradual quality improvement over several stages. Each stage is carefully designed such that one stage enhances the capability already built up. The major problem faced by an organization adopting CMM based process improvement initiative that they understand *what is needed to be improved, but they need more guidance about how to improve it.*

CMM level	Focus	Key process area
Ad-hoc	Competent people	Nil
Repeatable	Project management	Software project planning
		Software configuration management
Defined	Definition of process	Process definition, Training program, Peer reviews
Managed	Product and process quality	Quantitative process metrics
		Software quality management
Optimizing	Continuous process improvement	Defect prevention
		Process change management
		Technology change management

Table12.1: Level wise focus and KPA

Six Sigmas in Software Engineering

It is concerned to reduce the defects in a process of production or engineering. It cannot be applied to engineering activities. Six Sigmas has been originated in Motorola in the early 1980s in response to achieving 10X reduction in product-failure levels in 5 years. Engineer Bill Smith invented Six Sigma, but died of a heart attack in the Motorola cafeteria in 1993 never knowing the scope of the craze and controversy he had touched off. Six Sigma is based on various quality management theories (e.g.: Deming, Juran). (*table 12.3*)

Six Sigma is a business-driven, multi-dimensional structured approach to improving processes, lowering defects, reducing process variability, reducing costs, increasing customer satisfaction, and profits. (*figure 12.3*)

Six Sigma Dimensions

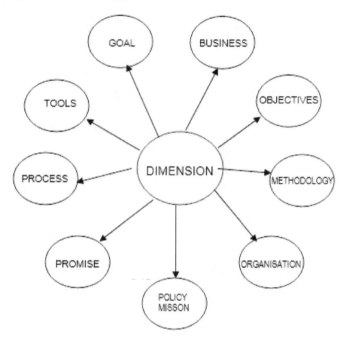

Figure 12.3: Six Sigma Dimension

Mission/Policy

The mission/policy of the organization is doing business smarter and increase profitability. Six Sigma shall be instituted throughout the organization. All employees shall be Six Sigma trained. Provide innovative solutions towards attainment of business goals and objectives. Processes shall be their highest Sigma Level. *(figure 12.4, 12.5)*

Specification Limit	Percentage
+ 1σ	30.23%
+ 2σ	69.13%
+ 3σ	93.32%
+ 4σ	99.3790%
+ 5σ	99.97670%
+ 3σ	99.999660%

Table 12.2: Specification

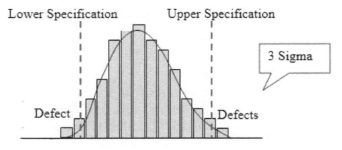

Figure 12.4: *Distribution of 3 Sigma*

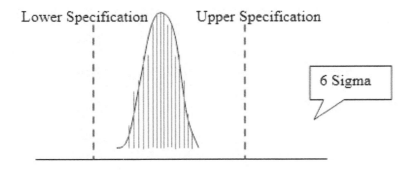

Figure 12.5: *Distribution in 6 Sigma*

3σ (93.32%)	6σ (99.9997%)
20,000 lost articles of mail per hour	1 per hour
Unsafe drinking water for 15 minutes per day	1 minute every 4 years
5,000 incorrect surgical operations per week	1 per month
2 long/short landings at most major airports each day	1 in 28 years
200,000 wrong drug prescriptions each year	10 each year
No electricity for 7 hours each month	1 minute every 4 years

Table 12.3: *The Nature of Six Sigma Quality*

Goal

The goal of six sigma is to realize organization's financial objectives of increasing profits. The initial fundamental goal is to reduce the process output variation to

±6 sigma and attain 3 to 4 **Defects Per Million Opportunities (DPMO).** A Six Sigma defect is defined as anything outside of customer specifications. A Six Sigma opportunity is the total quantity of chances for a defect.

Objectives

The objectives of six sigma, implementation of a measurement-based data/fact driven approach that focuses on continuous process improvement with defect & variation reduction. As the process sigma value increases from zero to six, the variation also decreases to zero. It generates customers satisfaction and increase savings/profitability

Organization

Green Belt

As the Six Sigma quality program evolves, employees include Six Sigma methodology in their daily activities. Employees that are trained in Six Sigma and spend 10% to 50% portion of their time completing projects, but maintain their regular work role and responsibilities.

Black Belt

The black belts coach green belts on their projects and lead quality projects and work full time until they are complete. They are the heart and soul of Six Sigma quality initiative and referred as *Change agents*.

Master Black Belt

Master Black Belt works with process owners and ensure that objectives and targets are set, plans are determined, progress is tracked, and education is provided. He is assigned to a specific area or function of a business/organization.

Process Owner

Process Owner is responsible individuals for a specific process. The process owners are found at all levels of the organization.

Champions

Champions are integrated into the business and help to deploy Six Sigma, remove roadblocks, select projects, adjust, and take the responsibility for implementation. Champions diminish deployment risks.

Quality Leader/Manager

Quality Leader/Manager represent the needs of the customer and to improve the operational effectiveness of the organization. The quality manager sits on the CEO/President's staff, and has equal authority to all other direct reports.

Methodology

Objectives are accomplished through 6σ projects by following one of three defined processes:

DMAIC :	Define – Measure – Analyze – Improve – Control
DMADV :	Define – Measure – Analyze – Design – Verify
DFSS :	Define – Identify – Design – Optimize – Verify

DMAIC vs. DMADV

Main differences between DMAIC and DMADV is:

- DMAIC looks at improving existing processes. DMADV looks at designing new or existing processes.
- DMADV is used when there is no defined process. Incremental changes are not sufficient and the entire process needs to be changed.

(DMAIC vs. DMADV) vs. DFSS

DMAIC and DMADV are used in improving process capability, DFSS primarily focused on the design of the product whose purposes is to increase the product quality by increasing reliability, responding to customer's needs. This increases the profit margin.

Promises

Six sigma technique can reduce costs by 50% or more. It can reduce defects to 6 sigma, increases profitability, increase understanding of customer requirements, improve delivery and quality performance. According to Six Sigma Academy, Black Belts save @ $230,000/project and can complete four to 6 projects per year. General Electric, has estimated benefits on the order of $10 billion during the first five years of implementation.

Conclusion

Software quality control is better than software coding inspection. Software quality assurance is a better approach than software quality control. The quality assurance is applied to each step-in software process. It enforces the procedure for the effective applications of methods and tools, formal technical reviews, testing strategies and techniques, procedures for change control, procedures for assuring compliance to standards, and measurement and reporting mechanism. Software review is one of the most important quality assurance activities. It streamlines the software process and removes error. The ability to ensure quality is a measure of mature engineering discipline.

Questions and Answers

1. **What is software quality management?**

   Quality management provides a quantitative assessment of software product quality according to the goals set for it.

2. **What is defect prevention?**

   Defect prevention identifies causes of defects and carries out procedures to prevent them from recurring.

3. **What is quality of conformance?**

   Quality of conformance is the degree to which design specifications are followed during manufacturing or software development.

4. **Define quality control.**

   Quality control is the series of inspection, reviews, and test throughout the development cycle to ensure that each work product meets the requirements set for it.

5. **What is quality cost?**

   Quality cost includes all costs incurred in maintaining quality of the software and performing quality related activities. They may be incurred on prevention, appraisal or failure.

6. **Define software quality.**

   Software quality is defined as conforming to explicitly stated functional and performance requirements, explicitly documented development standards and implicit characteristics that are expected of all professionally developed software.

7. **Name some characteristics of software product quality.**

Suitability	Reliability	Correctness
Accuracy	Efficiency	Usability
Quality	Maintainability	Understandability
Modularity	Traceability	Testability
Portability	Reusability	Extendibility

8. **What do you mean by formal technical reviews (FTR) and what are the objectives of FTR?**

   FTR is a quality assurance activity that is performed by software engineers.

The objectives of FTR:

- To uncover errors in function, logic or implementation of software.
- To verify that the software under review meets the requirement.
- To ensure that the software is represented according to predefined standards.
- To activate software that is developed in a uniform manner.
- To make the project more manageable.

9. What are the different forms of FTR?

The different forms if FTR are:

- Walkthrough.
- Inspections.
- Round-robin reviews.
- Small group technical assessment of software.

10. What are the guidelines for conducting FTR?

The guidelines for conducting FTR are:

- Review the product, not the producer.
- Set a guideline and maintain it.
- Limit debate and arguments.
- Enumerate problem areas, but do not attempt to solve every problem noted.
- Take written notes.
- Limit the number of participants and insist on advance preparation.
- Develop a checklist.
- Allocate resources and make time schedule.
- Conduct meaningful training for all reviewers.
- Review the earlier reviews.

11. What are the factors involved in prevention cost?

The factors involved in prevention cost are:

Quality planning	Formal technical reviews
Test equipment	Quality related training

12. Define clean room engineering.

Clean room engineering is the scientific application of methods and tools to control the quality of incrementally developed software products. It also certifies the fitness of software products for use at the time of delivery. "Think about it before developing it" is the morale of verification-based inspectors/validation-based inspection.

13. **What processes are involved in clean room technology?**

    Processes are involved in clean room technology are:

    - Management (present during all phases of software development process).
    - Specification (requirement phase).
    - Development (design phase).
    - Certification (statistical control phase).

14. **What is software quality assurance (QA)?**

    Software quality assurance QA provides an independent review of technical and planning work, providing an assurance that work has been done according to plan.

15. **Define a quality assurance system.**

    A quality assurance system is the organizational structure, responsibilities, procedures, processes, and resources involved in implementing quality management.

16. **What are the requirements of a quality assurance system?**

    The requirements of a quality assurance system are:

Management responsibility	Contact review
Design control	Document and data control
Control of customer supplied product	Inspection and testing
Product identification and traceability	Internal quality audits

17. **Mention McCall's quality factors.**

    McCall's quality factors are:

Correctness	Reliability	Efficiency
Integrity	Usability	Flexibility
Testability	Portability	Reusability
Interoperability	Maintainability	Expandability

18. **Define correctness.**

    The extent to which a program satisfies its specification or fulfills customer mission objectives.

19. Define accuracy.

Accuracy is the degree to which the software performs its required function.

20. Define maintainability.

Maintainability is the ease with which a program can be corrected if an error is encountered, adapted if the environment changes or changed when the customer desires a change of requirement.

21. How do you assess quality factors?

Various Quality factor which can be assess are:

- **Functionality** is assessed by evaluating the feature set and capabilities of the program.
- **Reliability** is evaluated by measuring the frequency of failure, the ability to recover from failure and predictability of the program.
- **Performance** is measured by processing speed, response time, resource consumption, throughput, and efficiency.
- **Expandability** is the degree to which architectural data, or procedural design can be extended.
- **Generality** is the breadth of the potential application of program compounds.
- **Modularity** is the functional independence of program components.
- **Operability** is the ease of operation of a program.
- **Traceability** is the ability to trace a design representation of an actual program compounded back to requirements.

22. Define integrity

Software integrity is important from the point of view of hackers and viruses. This attribute measures a system's ability to withstand attacks either accidental or intentional on its security.

23. Define the term maturity.

The term maturity is a measure of the goodness of the organization's process.

24. What is CMM?

The CMM (Capacity Maturity Model) was developed by SEI (Software Engineering Institute). These related group of strategies to improve the software process irrespective of the actual life cycle model.

25. **Name the different categories of CMM.**

    Different categories of CMM are:
    - SW-CMM   :   used for software.
    - P-CMM   :   for managing human resources. P for people.
    - IPD-CMM   :   for integrated product development.
    - SA-CMM   :   for software acquisition.

Exercise

1. Quality and reliability are related concepts but are fundamentally different in many ways. Discuss them.

2. Can a program be correct and still not reliable? Explain.

3. Can a program be correct and still not exhibit quality? Explain.

4. Given the responsibility to improve the quality of the software in your organization, what are the steps you will follow?

5. What do you understand by repeatable software development? At which level of SEI CMM achieve the repeatable software development?

6. What are factors considered for a quality software product?

7. What are the merits of ISO 9001 and SEI CMM certification?

8. What is six sigma quality? What are its organization structures?

CHAPTER 13

CASE and Reuse

Introduction

A good workshop for any craftsperson, whether a mechanic, a carpenter, or a software engineer has three primary characteristics:

a. A collection of useful tools that will help in every step of building a product.

b. An organized layout that enables tools to be found quickly and used efficiently.

c. A skilled artisan who understands how to use the tools in an effective manner.

Software engineers now recognize that they need more and varied tools along with an organized and efficient workshop to place the tools. The software development needs an engineering type discipline. The goal is to concentrate on developing a common technique, standard methodologies, and automated tools in a manner similar to the traditional engineering field. The evolution of using automated tools to support information system development process became **Computer Aided Software Engineering (CASE).**

Objective

The CASE tools to be used to automate and support the system development process with the objective of increasing productivity and improving the overall quality of system. CASE should provide the software engineer an ability to automate manual activities and to improve engineering insight.

Many organizations use CASE to:

- Improve the quality of the system developed
- Increase the speed with which systems are designed and developed
- Ease and improve the testing process through the use of automated checking
- Improve the integration of development activities via common methodologies
- Improve the quality and completeness of documentation
- Help to standardize the development process
- Improve the management of the project
- Simplify program maintenance
- Promote reusability of modules and documentation
- Improve software portability across environments

Driving organizational forces for adaptation of CASE, Organizations adopt CASE to:

- Provide new systems with shorter development time
- Improve the productivity of the system development process
- Improve the quality of the systems development process
- Improve workers skill
- Improve the probability of new system
- Improve the management of the system development process

Resisting organizational forces for adaptation of CASE, Organizations reject CASE because of:

- The high cost of purchasing CASE software
- The high cost of training the personnel
- Low organizational confidence in the **Information System (IS)** department to deliver high-quality systems on time and within the budget
- Lack of methodology standards within the organization
- Viewing CASE as a threat to job security
- Lack of confidence in CASE products

Taxonomy of CASE tools

A number of risks are inherent whenever we attempt to categorize CASE tools. There is a subtle implication that to create an effective CASE environment, one must implement all the categories of tools, is simply not true. Confusion (or antagonism) can be created by placing a specific tool within one category when others might believe that it belongs to another category. It is necessary to create taxonomy of CASE tools, to better understand the breadth of CASE and to better appreciate where such tools can be applied in the software engineering process.

CASE tools can be classified as:

- By function.
- By their role as instruments for managers or technical people.
- By their use in the various steps of the software engineering process.
- By the environment architecture (hardware and software) that supports them.
- By their origin or cost.

The taxonomy presented here uses function as a primary criterion.

Business process engineering tools: By modeling the strategic information requirements of an organization, business process engineering tools provide a "meta-model" from which specific information systems are derived. Rather than focusing on the requirements of a specific application, business information is modeled as it moves between various organizational entities within a company. The primary objective for tools in this category is to represent the business data objects, their relationships, and how these data objects flow between different business areas within a company.

Process modeling and management tools: If an organization works to improve a business (software) process, it must first understand it. Process modeling tools (process technology tools) are used to represent the key elements of a process so that it can be better understood. Such tools can also provide links to process descriptions that help those involved in the process to understand the work tasks that are required to perform it. Process management tools provide links to other tools that provide support to defined process activities.

Project planning tools: Tools in this category focus on two primary areas:

a. Software project effort.
b. Cost estimation and project scheduling.

Estimation tools compute estimated effort, project duration, and recommended number of people for a project. Project scheduling tools enable the manager to define all project tasks (the work breakdown structure), create a task network (usually using graphical input represent task interdependencies, and model the amount of parallelism possible for the project.

Risk analysis tools: Identifying potential risks and developing a plan to mitigate, monitor, and manage them is of paramount importance in large projects. Risk analysis tools enable a project manager to build a risk table by providing detailed guidance in the identification and analysis of risks.

Project management tools: The project schedule and project plan must be tracked and monitored on a continuing basis. In addition, a manager should use tools to collect the metrics that will ultimately provide an indication of software product quality. Tools in the category are often extensions to project planning tools.

Requirements tracing tools: When large systems are developed, things *"fall into the cracks"*. That is, the delivered system does not fully meet customer specified requirements. The objective of requirements tracing tools is to provide a systematic approach to the isolation of requirements, beginning with the customer request for proposal or specification. The typical requirements tracing tool combines human interactive text evaluation with a database management system that stores and categorizes each system requirement.

Metrics and management tools: Software metrics improve a manager's ability to control and coordinate the software engineering process and a practitioner's ability to improve the quality of the software that is produced. Today's metrics or measurement tools focus on the process and product characteristics. Management-oriented tools capture project specific metrics, such as example: LOC/person-month, defects per function point that provide an overall indication of productivity or quality. Technically oriented tools determine the technical metrics that provide greater insight into the quality of design or code.

Documentation tools: This is also called *document generator*. Document production and desktop publishing tools support nearly every aspect of software engineering and represent a substantial *"leverage"* opportunity for all software developers. Most software development organizations spend a substantial amount of time developing documents, and in many cases the documentation process itself is quite inefficient. It is not unusual for a software development organization to spend as much as 20 or 30 percent of all software development effort on documentation. For this reason, documentation tools provide an important opportunity to improve productivity. This helps to produce both technical and user documentation in standard formats.

System software tools: CASE is a workstation technology. Therefore, the CASE environment must accommodate high-quality network system software, object management services, distributed component support, electronic mail, bulletin boards, and, *quality assurance tools*. The majority of CASE tools claim to focus on quality assurance are actually metrics tools that audit source code to determine the compliance with language standards.

Database management tools: Database management software serves as a foundation for the establishment of a CASE database (repository) that we have called the **project database**. Given the emphasis on configuration objects, database management tools for CASE are evolving from relational database management systems to object oriented database management systems. It enables the integrated storage of specification, diagrams, reports, and project management information.

Software configuration management tools: Software configuration management lies at the kernel of every CASE environment. Tools can assist in all five major SCM tasks, which are:

a. Identification

b. Version control

c. Change control

d. Auditing

e. Status accounting.

The CASE database provides a mechanism for identifying each configuration item and relating it to other items; the change control process can be implemented with the aid of specialized tools; easy access to individual configuration items facilitates the auditing process; and CASE communication tools can greatly improve status accounting

Analysis and design tools: Analysis and design tools enable a software engineer to create models of the system to be built. The models contain a representation of data, function, and behavior (at the analysis level) and characterizations of data, architectural, component-level, and interface design. By performing consistency and validity checking on the models, analysis and design tools provide a software engineer with some degree of insight into the analysis representation and help to eliminate the errors before they propagate into the design, or worse, into implementation itself. It automatically checks for incomplete, inconsistent, or incorrect specifications in diagrams, forms, and reports.

Diagramming tools: This enables the system process, data, and control structures to be represented graphically.

PRO/SIM tools: PRO/SIM (prototyping and simulation) tools provide the software engineer with the ability to predict the behavior of a real-time system prior to the time that it is built. In addition, these tools enable the software engineer to develop mock-ups of the real-time system, allowing the customer to gain insight into the function, operation, and response prior to actual implementation.

Interface design and development tools: Interface design and development tools are actually a tool kit of software components (classes) such as menus, buttons, window structures, icons, scrolling mechanisms, device drivers, and so forth. However, these tool kits are being replaced by an interface prototyping tools that enable rapid onscreen creation of sophisticated user interfaces that conform to the interfacing standard that has been adopted for the software.

Prototyping tools: A variety of different prototyping tools can be used. Screen painters enable a software engineer to define screen layout rapidly for interactive applications. More sophisticated CASE prototyping tools enable the creation of a data design, coupled with both screen and report layouts. Many analysis and design tool have extensions that provide a prototyping option. PRO/SIM tools generate skeleton Ada and C source code for engineering (real-time) applications. Finally, a variety of fourth generation tools have prototyping features.

Programming tools: The programming tools category encompasses the compilers, editors, and debuggers that are available to support most conventional programming languages. In addition, object-oriented programming environments, fourth generation languages, graphical programming environments, application generators, and database query languages also reside within this category. The code generators enable the automatic generation of program and database definition code directly from the design document, diagrams, forms, and reports.

Computer display and report generator: The tool helps prototype how systems look and feel to users. Display (or form) and report generators also make it easier for the system analyst to identify data requirements and relationships.

Web development tools: The activities associated with Web engineering are supported by a variety of tools for Web Application development. These include tools that assist in the generation of text, graphics, forms, scripts, applets, and other elements of a Web page.

Integration and testing tools: In their directory of software testing tools, Software Quality Engineering defines the following testing tools categories:

- **Data acquisition:** tools that acquire data to be used during testing.
- **Static measurement:** tools that analyze source code without executing test cases.
- **Dynamic measurement:** tools that analyze source code during execution.
- **Simulation:** tools that simulate function of hardware or other externals.
- **Test management:** tools that assist in the planning, development, and control of testing.
- **Cross-functional tools:** tools that cross the bounds of the preceding categories.

It should be noted that many testing tools have features that span two or more of the categories.

Static analysis tools: Static testing tools assist the software engineer in deriving test cases. Three different types of static testing tools are used in the industry:

- **Code-based testing tools** accept source code (or PDL) as input and perform a number of analyses that result in the generation of test cases.

- **Specialized testing languages** (ATLAS) enable a software engineer to write detailed test specifications that describe each test case and the logistics for its execution.

- **Requirements-based testing tools** isolate specific user requirements and suggest test cases (or classes of tests) that will exercise the requirements.

Dynamic analysis tools: Dynamic testing tools interact with an executing program, checking path coverage, testing assertions about the value of specific variables, and otherwise initiating the execution flow of the program. Dynamic tools can be either intrusive or non-intrusive. An intrusive tool changes the software to be tested by inserting probes (extra instructions) that perform the activities just mentioned. Non-intrusive testing tools use a separate hardware processor that runs in parallel with the processor containing the program that is being tested.

Test management tools: Test management tools are used to control and coordinate software testing for each of the major testing steps. Tools in this category manage and coordinate regression testing, perform comparisons that ascertain differences between actual and expected output, and conduct batch testing of programs with an interactive human/computer interface. In addition to the functions noted, many test management tools also serve as generic test drivers. A test driver reads one or more test cases from a testing file, formats the test data to conform to the needs of the software under test, and then invokes the software to be tested.

Client/server testing tools: The client server environment demands specialized testing tools that exercise the graphical user interface and the network communications requirements for client and server.

Reengineering tools: Tools for legacy software address a set of maintenance activities that currently absorb a significant percentage of all software-related effort. The reengineering tools category can be subdivided into the following functions:

- **Reverse engineering** to specification tools take source code as a input and generate graphical structured analysis and design models, where-used lists, and other design information.

- **Code restructuring and analysis tools** analyze program syntax, generate a control flow graph, and automatically generate a structured program.

- **On-line system reengineering tools** are used to modify on-line database systems (example: convert DB2 files into entity-relationship format).

These tools are limited to a specific programming language (although most major languages are addressed) and require some degree of interaction with the software engineer. Many organizations do not use CASE tools to support all phases of SDLC. Some organizations may extensively use the diagramming features but not use code generators. Table 13.1 summarizes how CASE is commonly used within SDLC phase.

SDLC Phase	Key Activities	CASE Tool Usage
Project identification and selection	Display and structure high-level organizational information	Diagramming and matrix tools to create and structure information
Project initiation and planning	Develop project scope and feasibility	Repository and documentation generators to develop project plans
Analysis	Determine structure system requirements	Diagramming to create process, logic, and data models
Logical and physical designs	Create new system designs	Form and report generators to prototype designs, analysis and documentation generators to define specifications
Implementation	Translate designs into an information system	Code generators and analysis, form, and report generators to develop system; document generators to develop system and user documentation
Maintenance	Evolve information system	All tools are used (repeat life cycle)

Table 13.1: Examples of CASE Usage Within the SDLC

In traditional system development, much of the time is spent on coding and testing. When software changes are approved, the code is first changed and then tested. Once the functionality of the code is assured, the documentation, and the specification documents are updated to reflect the system changes.

Components of CASE

Case tools are used to support a wide variety of SDLC activities. CASE tools can be used to help in the project identification and selection, project initiation, and planning, analysis, and design phases (**upper CASE**) and/or in the implementation and maintenance phases (**lower CASE**) of the SDLC (*figure 13.1*). A third category of CASE, **cross life cycle CASE,** is tools used to support activities that occur across multiple phases of SDLC.

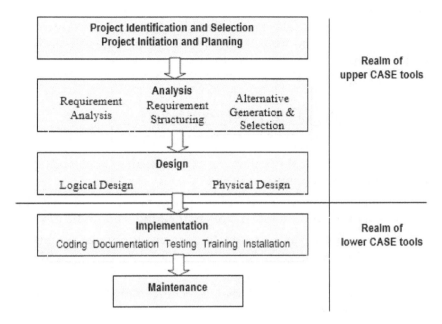

Figure 13.1: Relationship between CASE tools and SDLC

CASE Documentation Generator Tools

Each phase of the SDLC produces documentation. The types of documentation that flow from one phase to the next vary depends upon the organization, methodologies employed, and type of system being built. *Documentation generators* modules can create standard reports based upon the contents of the repository. Typically, SDLC documentation includes textual description needs, solution trade-offs, diagrams of data and processes, prototype forms and reports, program specifications, and user documentation including application, and reference materials. A system that does not have adequate documentation is virtually impossible to use and maintain.

Documentation generators within a CASE environment provide a method for managing the vast amounts of documentation created during the SDLC. Documentation generators allow the creation of master templates that can be used to verify the documentation created for each SDLC phase conforms to a standard and that all required documents have been produced.

CASE Code Generator Tools

Code generators are automated systems that produce high level source code from diagrams and forms which are used to represent the system. As target environments vary on several dimensions, such as hardware, operating system platforms, many code generators are designed to be special-purpose system that produces source code for a particular environment in a particular programming language. Most CASE tools that generate source code take a more flexible approach by producing standard source code and database definitions. Using standard language conventions, CASE-generated code can typically be compiled and executed on numerous hardware and operating system platforms with no, or very minor changes.

Integrated CASE Environment

Although benefits can be derived from individual CASE tools that address separate software engineering activities, the real power of CASE can be achieved only through integration. The benefits of integrated CASE (I-CASE) are:

- Smooth transfer of information (models, programs, documents, data) from one tool to another and one software engineering step to the next

- A reduction in the effort required to perform umbrella activities such as software configuration management, quality assurance, and document production

- An increase in project control that is achieved through better planning, monitoring, and communication

- Improved coordination among staff members who are working on a large software project.

I-CASE also poses significant challenges. Integration demands consistent representations of software engineering information, standardized interfaces between tools, a homogeneous mechanism for communication between the software engineer and each tool, and an effective approach that will enable I-CASE to move among various hardware platforms and operating systems. Comprehensive I-CASE environments have emerged slowly than originally expected. However, integrate environments do exist and becoming more powerful as the years pass.

The term integration implies both combination and closure. I-CASE combines a variety of different tools and a spectrum of information in a way that enables closure of communication among tools, between people, and across the software process. Tools are integrated so that software engineering information is available to each tool that needs it; usage is integrated so that a common look and feel is provided for all tools; a development philosophy is integrated, implying a standardized software engineering approach that applies modern practice and proven methods. To define integration in the context of the software engineering process, it is necessary to establish a set of requirements for I-CASE: An integrated CASE environment should:

- Provide a mechanism for sharing software engineering information among all tools contained in the environment.

- Enable a change to one item of information to be tracked to other related information items.

- Provide version control and overall configuration management for all software engineering information.
- Allow direct, non-sequential access to any tool contained in the environment
- Establish automated support for the software process model that has been chosen, integrating CASE tools and **Software Configuration Items (SCIs)** into a standard work breakdown structure.
- Enable the users of each tool to experience a consistent look and feel at the human/computer interface.
- Support communication among software engineers
- Collect both management and technical metrics that can be used to improve the process and the product.

To achieve these requirements, each of the building blocks of a CASE architecture (*figure 13.2*) must fit together in a seamless fashion. The foundation building blocks including environment architecture, hardware platform, and operating system must be "*joined*" through a set of portability services to an integration framework that achieves these requirements.

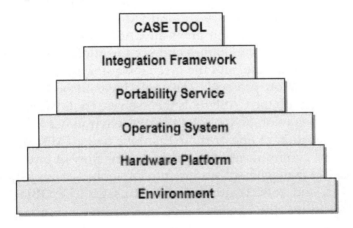

Figure 13.2: CASE building blocks

The Integration Architecture

A software engineering team uses CASE tools, corresponding methods, and a process framework to create a pool of software engineering information. The integration framework facilitates transfer of information into and out of the pool. To accomplish this, the following architectural components must exist; a database must be created to store the information; an object management system must be built to manage changes to the information; a tools control mechanism must be constructed to coordinate the use of CASE tools; a user interface must provide a consistent pathway between actions made by the user and the tools contained in the environment. The user interface layer (figure 13.3) incorporates a standardized interface tool kit with a common presentation protocol.

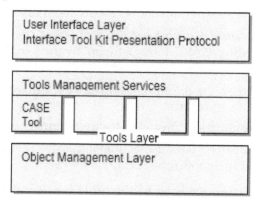

Figure 13.3: User Interface Layer

The interface tool kit contains software for human/computer interface management and a library of display objects. Both provide a consistent mechanism for communication between the interface and individual CASE tools. The presentation protocol is the set of guidelines that gives all CASE tools the same look and feel. Screen layout conventions, menu names and organization, icons, object names, the use of the keyboard and mouse, and the mechanism for tools access are all defined as part of the presentation protocol. The tools layer incorporates a set of tools management services with the CASE tools themselves. **Tools Management Services (TMS)** control the behavior of tools within the environment. If multitasking is used during the execution of one or more than one tools, TMS performs multitask synchronization and communication, coordinates the flow of information from the repository and object management system into the tools, accomplishes security and auditing functions, and collects metrics on tool usage. The **Object Management Layer (OML)** performs the configuration management functions. In essence, software in this layer of the framework architecture provides the mechanism for tools integration. Every CASE tool is "*plugged* into" the object management layer. Working in conjunction with the CASE repository, the OML provides integration services, a set of standard modules that couple tools with the repository. In addition, the OML provides configuration management services by enabling the identification of all configuration objects, performing version control, and providing support for change control, audits, and status accounting. The shared repository layer is the CASE database and the access control functions that enable the object management layer to interact with the database. Data integration is achieved by the object management and shared repository layers.

The CASE Repository

The word repository is *"any thing or person thought of as a center of accumulation or storage"*. During the early history of software development, the repository was indeed a person; the programmer who had to remember the location of all information relevant to software project, who had to recall information that was never written down and reconstruct information that had been lost. Sadly, using a person as *"the center for accumulation and storage"*, does not work very well. Today, the repository is a database that acts as the center for both accumulation and storage of software engineering information. The role of the person (the software engineer) is to interact with the repository by using CASE tools that are integrated with it. The repository holds the complete information needed to create, modify, and evolve a software system from project initiation and planning to code generation and maintenance (figure 13.4) In this book, a number of different terms have been used to refer to the storage place for software engineering information: CASE database, project database, **Integrated Project Support Environment (IPSE) database**, requirements dictionary (a limited database), and repository. Although there are subtle differences between some of these terms, all refer to the center for accumulation and storage. *(figure 13.4)*

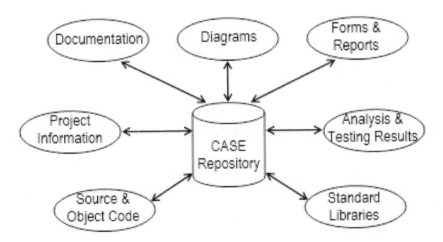

Figure 13.4: System development items stored in the CASE repository

For years, common development repositories have been used to create information systems independent of CASE. *Figure 13.5* reflects the common components of a comprehensive CASE repository. The application development environment is one in which either information specialists or end users use CASE tools, high level languages, and other tools to develop new applications. The production environment is one in which these same people use applications to build databases, keep the data current, and extract data from databases.

The *data dictionary* is a computer software tool which is used to manage and control access to the information repository. It provides facilities for recording, storing, and processing descriptions of an organization's significant data and data processing resources. Data dictionary features within a CASE repository are especially valuable for the system analyst when cross referencing data items. *Cross referencing* enables one description of a data item to be stored and accessed by all individuals (system analyst and end users) so that a single definition for data item is established and used. Such description helps to avoid data duplication and makes systems development and maintenance more efficient.

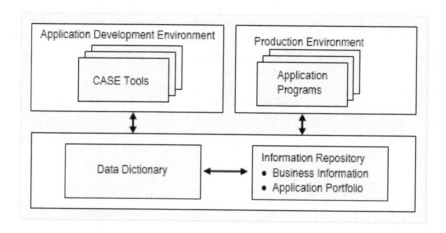

Figure 13.5: Common components of a comprehensive CASE repository

The Role of the Repository in I-CASE

The repository for an I-CASE environment is the set of mechanisms and data structures that achieve data/tool and data/data integration. It provides the obvious functions of a database management system, but in addition, the repository performs or precipitates the following functions:

- **Data integrity** includes functions to validate entries to the repository, ensure consistency among the related objects, and automatically perform "*cascading*" modifications when a change to one object demands some change to objects

- **Information sharing** provides a mechanism for sharing information among multiple developers and between the multiple tools, manages and controls multi user access to data and locks or unlocks objects so that changes are not inadvertently overlaid on one another.

- **Data/tool integration** establishes a data model that can be accessed by all tools in the I-CASE environment, controls access to the data, and performs appropriate configuration management functions.

- **Data/data integration** is the database management system that relates data objects so that other functions can be achieved.

- **Methodology enforcement** defines an entity-relationship model stored in the repository that implies a specific paradigm for software engineering; at a minimum, the relationships and objects define a set of steps that must be conducted to build the contents of the repository.

- **Document standardization** is the definition of objects in the database that leads directly to a standard approach for the creation of software engineering documents.

To achieve these functions, the repository is defined in terms of a meta-model. The meta-model determines how the information is stored in the repository, how data can be accessed by tools and viewed by software engineers, how well data security and integrity can be maintained, and how easily the existing model can be extended to accommodate new needs.

Advantages & Disadvantages of CASE Tools

The advantages of a CASE tool are:

a. Improved speed and reduction in time to develop a software product.

b. Development of diagrams like DFD, Gantt charts, PERT charts.

c. When procedures are coded by a CASE tool, they give a consistent look. It helps in creating a uniform user interface, messaging schemes, standard layout, and documentation plan.

d. In addition to enforcement of consistency, CASE tool ensures completeness.

e. Generation of code out of specifications and standardization of program structure to help in maintaining and reducing errors.

f. It facilitates prototyping as it makes easy to change and adjust specifications in handling screen and report layout with least effort and less time.

g. Use of CASE tools increases the user requirements since CASE tools reduce development time by eliminating users long waiting time. More powerful systems can be developed in much shorter time.

The limitations of CASE tools are:

a. Most CASE tools support structured methods for software development. But many software organizations use mixture of structured approach, modular approach, and object-oriented approach in developing systems.

b. There is no standardization between available CASE tools in the market.

c. The CASE tools do not generate narrative kind of documentation.

d. Different CASE tools have their individual strengths in the area of design, analysis, code generation, documentation, security, and maintenance. No CASE tool is strong in all the areas.

e. CASE tools have limited scope since none of the CASE tools support requirement analysis, feasibility study that require human intellect.

f. A novice driver cannot be an expert driver by using a sophisticated car. Similarly, a bad analyst or designer can never become a good professional by just using sophisticated CASE tools. A CASE tool provides assistance in modeling, verification, clerical data management, and housekeeping that improves efficiency and productivity if they are used by a skilled and intelligent developer.

A software development platform includes three categories of tools.

- The *essential* tools include operating systems, programming languages, assemblers, and compilers.

- *Very useful* tools include editors, linkers, program generators, debuggers, and program definition languages.

The primary tools classified as *useful* tools are known as CASE tools. There are two types of useful tools:

a. Workbench

b. Integrated CASE tools

Functional CASE tools are designed to assist software engineers in a specific phase of the **software development life cycle (SWDLC).** Integrated CASE tools cover the entire SWDLC.

A CASE repository is a large database containing huge amounts of descriptive or numeric information about the details of the software product. The information is kept in a CASE repository helps to build and verify the data dictionary for the software product. It also serves as a cross-reference between the data dictionary and other documents required by the software product.

Though there are some limitations in costing and scheduling, the most benefit of CASE tool is discipline and predefined procedures for the software development process.

Component Model of Software Development

Modern software systems become more and more large-scale, complex, and uneasily controlled, resulting in high development cost, low productivity, unmanageable software quality, and high risk to move to new technology. Consequently, there is a growing demand of searching for a new, efficient, and cost-effective software development paradigm.

One of the most promising solutions today is the component-based software development approach. This approach is based on the idea that software systems can be developed by selecting appropriate off-the-shelf components and then assembling them with well-defined software architecture. This new software development approach is very different from the traditional approach in which software systems can only be implemented from scratch. These **Commercial Off-The Shelf (COTS)** components can be developed by different developers using different languages and different platforms. This can be shown in *figure 13.6*, where COTS components can be checked out from a component repository, and assembled into a target software system.

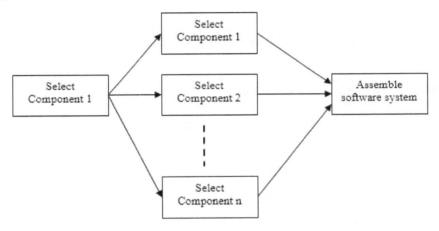

Commercial Off-the-shelf (COTS) components

Figure 13.6: *Component-based software development*

Component-based software development (CBSD) can significantly reduce development cost and time-to-market, improve maintainability, reliability, and overall quality of software systems. This approach has raised a tremendous amount of interests both in the research community and in the software industry. The life cycle and software engineering model of CBSD is much different from that of the traditional ones. This is what the **Component-Based Software Engineering (CBSE)** is focused.

Up to now, software component technologies are emerging technology, which is far from being matured.

Current Component Technologies

Some approaches, such as **Visual Basic Controls (VBX),** ActiveX controls, class libraries, and JavaBeans, make it possible for their related languages, such as Visual Basic, C++, Java, and the supporting tools to share and distribute application pieces. But all of these approaches rely on certain underlying services to provide the communication and coordination necessary for the application. The infrastructure of components (a component model) acts as the "*plumbing*" that allows communication among components. Among the component infrastructure technologies that have been developed, the following have become somewhat standardized:

- OMG's CORBA
- Microsoft's Component Object Model (COM)
- Distributed COM (DCOM)
- Sun's JavaBeans
- Enterprise JavaBeans

Life Cycle of Component-Based Software Systems

Component-based software systems are developed by selecting the various components and assembling them together rather than programming an overall system from scratch, thus the life cycle of component-based software systems is different from that of the traditional software systems. The life cycle of component-based software:

- *a.* Requirements analysis
- *b.* Software architecture selection
- *c.* Component identification and customization
- *d.* System integration

Software Reuse

Although computing power and network bandwidth have increased dramatically in recent years, the design, and implementation of networked applications remains expensive and error-prone. Much of the cost and effort stems from the continual re-discovery and re-invention of the core patterns and framework components throughout the software industry. The heterogeneity of hardware architectures, the diversity of OS and network platforms and stiff global competition are making it increasingly infeasible, however, to build networked applications from scratch with the following qualities:

- **Portability**, to reduce the effort required to support applications across heterogeneous OS platforms, programming languages, and compilers
- **Flexibility**, to support a growing range of multimedia datatypes, traffic patterns, and end-to-end **quality of service (QoS)** requirements
- **Extensibility**, to support successions of quick updates and additions to take advantage of new requirements and emerging markets

- **Predictability and efficiency**, to provide low latency to delay-sensitive real-time applications and high performance to bandwidth-intensive applications and

- **Reliability**, to ensure that applications are robust, fault tolerant, and highly available.

Developing software that achieves these qualities is hard; systematically developing high quality reusable software components and frameworks is even harder [Douglas C. Schmidt]. *Reusable* components and frameworks are inherently abstract, which makes it hard to engineer their quality and to manage their production. Moreover, the skills required to develop, deploy, and support reusable software have traditionally been a *"black art"*, locked in the heads of expert developers. When these technical impediments to reuse are combined with common non-technical organizational, economical, administrative, political, and psychological impediments, achieving significant levels of software reuse throughout an organization becomes decidedly non-trivial.

Software Reuse Assets

Software reuse (code reuse) is the use of existing software, or software knowledge, to build new software. Ad hoc reuse has been practiced from the earliest days of programming. Programmers have always reused sections of code, templates, functions, and procedures. Software reuse is a recognized area of study in software engineering, however, dates only from 1968 when *Douglas McIlroy* of Bell Laboratories proposed basing the software industry on reusable components.

Reusable software, or software knowledge items, is called **reusable assets**. Assets may be designs, requirements, test cases, architectures, knowledge, and so on.

Perhaps the most well-known reusable asset is code. Code reuse is the idea that a partial or complete computer program is written at one time can be, should be, or is being used in another program written at a later time. The reuse of programming code is a common technique which attempts to save time and energy by reducing redundant work.

Usage of Software Reuse

The *software library* is a good example of *abstraction*. Programmers may decide to create internal abstractions so that the certain parts of their program can be re-used, or may create custom libraries for their own use. Some characteristics that make software more easily reusable are *modularity, loose coupling, high cohesion, information hiding, and separation of concerns*.

Many common operations, such as converting information among different well-known formats, accessing external storage, interfacing with external programs, or manipulating information (numbers, words, names, locations, dates, and so on.) in common ways, are needed by many different programs. Authors of new programs can use the code in a software library to perform these tasks, instead of *re-inventing the wheel*, by writing fully new code directly in a program to perform an operation. Library implementations often have the benefit of being well-tested and covering unusual or arcane cases. Disadvantages include the inability to tweak details which may affect performance or the desired output, and the time and cost of acquiring, learning, and configuring the library.

For newly written code to use a piece of existing code, some kind of interface, or means of communication, must be defined. These commonly include a *"call"* or use of a *subroutine, object, class,* or *prototype*. In organizations, such practices are formalized and standardized by *software product line* engineering.

The general practice of using a prior version of an extant program as a starting point for the next version is also a form of software reuse.

Software reuse involves simply copying some or all of the code from an existing program into a new one. While organizations can realize *time to market* benefits for a new product with this approach, they can subsequently be saddled with many of the same code duplication problems caused by cut and paste programming.

Many researchers have worked to make reuse faster, easier, more systematic, and an integral part of the normal process of programming. These are some of the main goals behind the invention of *object-oriented programming*, which became one of the most common forms of formalized reuse. A somewhat later invention is *generic programming*.

Another, newer means is to use software *"generators"*, programs which can create new programs of a certain type, based on a set of parameters that users choose. Fields of study about such systems are *generative programming* and *metaprogramming*.

Why Software Reuse Has Failed Historically

Reuse has been a popular topic of debate and discussion for over 30 years in the software community. Many developers have successfully applied reuse *opportunistically*, example, by cutting and pasting code snippets from existing programs into new programs. Opportunistic reuse works fine in a limited way for individual programmers or small groups. However, it doesn't scale up across business units or enterprises to provide systematic software reuse. *Systematic* software reuse is a promising means to reduce development cycle time and cost, improve software quality, and leverage existing effort by constructing, and applying multi-use assets like architectures, patterns, components, and frameworks.

Like many other promising techniques in the history of software, systematic reuse of software has not universally delivered significant improvements in quality and productivity. There have certainly been successes, example: sophisticated frameworks of reusable components are now available in OO languages running on many OS platforms. In general, however, these frameworks have focused on a relatively small number of domains, such as graphical user-interfaces, or C++ container libraries like STL. Moreover, component reuse is often limited in practice to third-party libraries and tools, rather than being an integral part of an organization's software development processes.

In theory, organizations recognize the value of systematic reuse and reward internal reuse efforts. In practice, many factors conspire to make systematic software reuse hard, particularly in companies with a large installed base of legacy software and developers.

Impediments to Reuse

There are a number of impediments to reuse:

- **Not invented here:** All too many software professionals would rather rewrite a routine from scratch than reuse a routine written by someone else, the implication being that a routine can not be any good unless they wrote it themselves, otherwise **Not Invented Here (NIH)** syndrome [Griss 1993]. NIH is a management issue. Application developers may also perceive *top down* reuse efforts as an indication that management lacks confidence in their technical abilities. If management is aware of the problem, it can be solved, usually by offering financial incentives to promote reuse.

- **No exhaustive testing:** Many developers would be willing to reuse a routine provided they could be sure that the routine in question would not introduce faults into the product. This attitude towards software quality is perfectly easy to understand. After all, every software professional has been faulty software written by others. The solution is to subject potentially reusable routines to exhaustive testing before making them available for reuse.

- **High degree storage/retrieve problem:** A large organization may have hundreds of thousands of potentially useful components. It is hard to catalog, archive, and retrieve reusable assets across multiple business units within large organizations. Although it's common to scavenge small classes or functions opportunistically from existing programs, developers often find it hard to locate suitable reusable assets outside of their immediate workgroups.

- **Reuse is expensive:** In reuse, three costs are involved in it. They are the cost of making something reusable, the cost of reusing it, the cost of defining and implementing a reuse process. Supporting corporate-wide reusable assets requires an economic investment, particularly if reuse groups operate as cost-centers.

- **Political impediments:** Groups that develop reusable middleware platforms are often viewed with suspicion by application developers, who resent the fact that they may no longer be empowered to make key architectural decisions. Likewise, internecine rivalries among business units may stifle reuse of assets developed by other internal product groups, which are perceived as a threat to job security or corporate influence.

- **Violation of legal issues:** It may arise with contract software. In terms of the type of contract usually drawn up between a client and a software development organization, the software product belongs to the client. If the software developer reuses a component of one client's product in a new product for a different client, this essentially constitutes a violation of the first client's copyright. For internal software, that is, when the developers and client members of the same organization, this problem does not arise.

- **Inefficient COTS component:** Another impediment arises when a **commercial off-the-self (COTS)** component is reused. The developers are given a COTS component that is used in the software has limited extensibility and modifiability.

The first five impediments can be overcome, at least in principle. Other than the last two impediments essentially no major impediments prevent implementing reuse within a software organization.

Strive for Successful Systematic Reuse

A systematic software reuse is most effective when the following prerequisites are met:

- **The market is competitive:** In a competitive business environment, such as financial services or wireless networking, time-to-market is crucial. It is therefore essential to leverage the existing software to reduce development effort and cycle time. When a market is not competitive, however, organizations tend to reinvent, rather than reuse, software.

- **The application domain is complex:** Components that are relatively easy to develop, such as generic linked lists, stacks, or queues, are often rewritten from scratch rather than reused. In contrast, developers working in highly complex domains, such as distributed, real-time systems are often willing to reuse components, such as *dynamic scheduling frameworks*, when building equivalent solutions from scratch proves too error-prone, costly, or time-consuming.

- **The corporate culture and development process are supportive:** Not only is it hard to develop high-quality reusable components and frameworks, it's even harder to reap the benefits of reuse immediately. Significant investment must be expended up-front to produce efficient, flexible, and well-documented reusable software assets before they can be leveraged in subsequent generations of a product line. Therefore, organizations must support an appropriate software development process that allows systematic reuse to flourish.

- **Attractive reuse magnets exist:** To attract systematic reuse, it crucial to develop and support *"reuse magnets"*, *i.e.,* well-documented framework and component repositories. These repositories must be well-maintained so that the application developers will have confidence in their quality and assurance that any defects they encounter will be fixed promptly. Likewise, framework and component repositories must be well-supported so that developers can gain experience through hands-on training and mentoring programs.

  The *open-source* development processes are an effective process for creating attractive reuse magnets [Schmidt]. Open-source processes have yielded many widely used software tools and frameworks, such as Linux, Apache, GNU, ACE, and TAO. The open-source model allows users and developers to participate together in evolving software assets. One of the key strengths of this model is that it scales well to large user communities, where application developers and end-users can assist with much of the quality assurance, documentation, and support.

- **Strong leadership and empowerment of skilled architects and developers:** It is observed that the ability of companies and projects to succeed with reuse is highly correlated with the quality and quantity of experienced developers and effective leaders. Conversely, reuse projects that lack a critical mass of developers with the necessarily technical and leadership skills rarely succeed, regardless of the level of managerial and organizational support.

Unfortunately, many organizations lack the five prerequisites as described above. As a result, these organizations often fall victim to the *not-invented-here* syndrome and redevelop many software components from scratch. However, deregulation, global competition, and the general dearth of experienced application, and middleware developers is making it increasingly hard to succeed by building complex networked applications from the ground up.

Types of reuse

- **Opportunistic reuse:** While getting ready to begin a project, the team realizes that there are existing components that they can reuse.

- **Planned reuse:** A team strategically designs components so that they'll be reusable in future projects.

Opportunistic reuse can be categorized further:

- **Internal reuse:** A team reuses its own components. This may be a business decision, since the team may want to control a component critical to the project.

- **External reuse:** A team may choose to buy a third-party component. Buying a third-party component typically costs the team 1 to 20 percent of what it would cost to develop internally [McConnell 1996]. The team must also consider the time it takes to find, learn and integrate the component.

Conclusion

Software reuse and automated software synthesis are the two concepts that have been employed to reduce the development cost and time. Both of these methods follow waterfall model in the development but take the advantage of either software products which is already developed and used to automate many of the waterfall SWDLC steps. Software reuse,, while on the surface sounds like an idea that would lead to substantial cost saving, should be approached skeptically. A software product or element already written, tested, and used cannot be plugged directly into a new application without some analysis to assure that the product meets the actual requirements. Some effort to document requirements and document the reused software product is needed, new interfaces must be confirmed, and the reused product must be tested in its new configuration and in its new operational environment.

Questions and Answers

1. **What are the contents of a CASE repository?**

   The contents of a CASE repository are:

   - Enterprise information
   - Application design
   - Construction
   - Validation and verification
   - Project arrangement information
   - System documentation

2. **What is a component-based software engineering (CBSE)?**

   CBSE is a process that emphasizes the design and construction of computer-based systems, using reusable software components.

3. **What are the CBSE framework activities?**

   The CBSE framework activities are:

- Component qualification
- Component adaptation
- Component composition
- Component update

4. How do we certify a software component?

We can certify a software component by:

- Creating usage scenarios.
- Specifying usage profile.
- Generating test cases from profile.
- Doing Tests, recording and analyzing failure data.
- Computing and certifying reliability.

5. List some CASE tools.

Some CASE tools are:

Information engineering tools	Process modeling and management tools
Project planning tools	Risk analysis tools
Project management tools	Requirement trading tools
Metrics and management tools	Documentation tools
System software tools	Quality assurance tools
Database management tools	SCM tools
Analysis & design tools	PRO/SIM tools
Prototyping tools	Interface design & development tools
Programming tools	Integration and testing tools

6. List the functions of a repository.

The functions of repository are:

Data integrity	Information storage
Data tools integrator	Methodology enforcement
Document standardization	Data security

7. What is a repository and what are the kinds of repository?

Repository is an entity (anything or person) acting as a centre of accumulation or storage of data/information.

The kinds of repository are:

- CASE database

- Project database
- Integrated project supported
- Data dictionary
- environment database

8. **What is a meta-model?**

A meta-model determines how information is stored in the repository, how the data can be accessed by tools and viewed by software engineers, how well data security and integrity can be maintained and how easily the existing model can be extended to accommodate fresh requirements.

Exercises

1. Illustrate the role of CASE tools in system analysis and design. What are its advantages and disadvantages?

2. What is reusability of software? Explain the reuse benefits.

3. What are the hindrances one faces during reuse of software code?

4. What are the merits and demerits of a component-based software system?

5. Why I-CASE environment is mostly favored by the software developer?

CHAPTER 14

Recent Trends and Development in Software Engineering

Introduction

Advances in sensor technologies, wireless communications, and mobile devices have resulted into software applications, usually known as **ubiquitous**, that can be used anywhere and anytime. These applications are sensible to the context in which they operate, which makes them adaptable and responsive to users' profiles and personal requirements. **Context-awareness** is increasingly featured in many instances of application domains such as e-commerce, e-learning, e-healthcare, and so on. Despite this recent flurry of interest in context-awareness, modeling, capturing, and processing contextual information pose a new set of challenges, resulting in high application development overheads. Sensing, localizing, recognizing, profiling, provisioning, discovering, and dealing with the uncertainty and privacy of, contextual information are typical processes associated with such application development overheads. Traditional software engineering and tools have already shown their limitations, which calls for new techniques and tools.

According to Barry Boehm the software engineering future trend 2014 will look towards:

- The increasing integration of software engineering and system engineering.
- An increased emphasis on users and end values.
- Increasing criticality and need for dependability and security.

- Increasing rapid change.
- Increasing SIS globalization and need for interoperability.
- Increasingly complex systems of systems.
- Increasing needs for COTS, reuse, and legacy SIS integration.
- Computational plenty.

This is the second of several levels on the future of software engineering. The first level focused on trends in application programming, particularly related to quality. This level reviews data on programmer staffing and then covers application programming skills. Future levels deal with the trends in system programming and implications of these trends for software engineering and software engineers.

Current Trends in Software Engineering

Software engineering is a young discipline, and is still developing. The directions in which software engineering is developing include:

- **Aspects:** Aspects help software engineers to deal with the abilities by providing tools to add or remove boilerplate code from many areas in the source code. Aspects describe how all objects or functions should behave in a particular circumstance. For example, aspects can add debugging, logging, or locking control into all objects of the particular types. Researchers are currently working to understand how to use aspects to design general-purpose code. Related concepts include generative programming and templates.

- **Agile:** Agile software development guides software development projects that evolve rapidly with the changing expectations and competitive markets. Proponents of this method believe that heavy document driven processes (TickIT, CMM, ISO 9000) are fading in importance. Some people believe that companies and agencies export many of the jobs that can be guided by heavy-weight processes. Related concepts include Extreme Programming and Lean software.

- **Experimental:** Experimental software engineering is a branch of software engineering interested in devising experiments on software, in collecting data from the experiments, and in devising laws and theories from this data. A proponent of this method advocates that the nature of software is such that we can advance the knowledge on software through experiments only.

- **Model-driven:** Model driven software development uses both textual and graphical models as primary development artifacts. By means of model transformation and code generation a part or complete application are generated.

- **Software Product Lines:** It is a systematic way to produce *families* of software systems, instead of creating a succession of completely individual products. This method emphasizes extensive, systematic, formal code reuse to try to industrialize the software development process.

- **Embedded Software:** It increases the variability, configurability, extendibility, and changeability of every product. It allows for a greater variety of function. In the future, embedded software will be in everything like automated home, intelligent automobile, communication infrastructures, medical instruments implants, and ubiquitous control systems. The new energy-related technologies that increase the efficiency of electrical current transmission will provide immediate effective ways to address the energy and climate demands. The embedded system is no longer defined by computing hardware being used. Rather, they will be designed to do any function to achieve multiple and changing objectives, whether on a microcontroller, a microprocessor, a signal processor, a biological assembly, or any other programmable logic device. The more quality of life we desire, the higher living standards we want to establish across the planet, and the more we demand security and safety, the more we need embedded software **[Christol Ebert & Jürgen Salecker]**. Our task is to evolve embedded software engineering to master these grand challenges.

The *Future of Software Engineering conference (FOSE),* held at ICSE 2000, documented the state of the art of SE in 2000 and listed many problems to be solved over the next decade. The FOSE tracks at the ICSE 2000 and the ICSE 2007 conferences to identify the state of art in software engineering.

Adopting SE trends in Artificial Intelligence

Designing and developing reliable, robust, well-architected, and easy-to-extend software applications or tools in any field requires conformance to sound principles and rules of software engineering. Intelligent systems, especially AI development tools, are no exception. Although AI has always been a wellspring of ideas that software engineering has later adopted, most of its gems remain buried in laboratories, available only to a few AI practitioners. We believe AI tools should be integrated with mainstream SE tools and thus become more widely known and used.

We can integrate **Artificial Intelligence (AI)** development environment with model-driven architecture to familiarize the mainstream software technologies and expand them with new functionalities. This integrated environment provides a general modeling and meta-modeling infrastructure for AI systems analysis, system design, and system development.

Software Engineering Trends

Keeping an eye on current Software engineering developments and trends can help us to design more stable AI tools. Some SE trends are general and span many fields and application domains. The specific SE trends, such as agent-oriented SE.

A relatively new, generally applicable SE trend involves application development based on model driven architecture, which has received intensive support from the **Object Management Group (OMG).**

Model Driven Architecture (MDA) interests AI developers because it has much in common with ontology modeling and development. Essentially, MDA defines the following levels of abstraction in system modeling:

- The computation-independent model corresponds to the system's domain model and resembles the domain ontology. It doesn't show details of the system structure.
- The platform-independent model is computationally dependent but unaware of specific computer platform details.

Knowledge Based SE verses Application of Inductive Methods in Software Engineering

The application of artificial intelligence technology to software engineering is known as **Knowledge Based Software Engineering (KBSE)** [Lowry and Duran 1989 p.243]. While this definition is fairly broad, most KBSE systems explicitly encode the knowledge that they employ [McCartney 1991 p. xix]. KBSE systems designed for assisting software engineers in low-level everyday maintenance tasks and have the potential of representing and deducing the relations among components of a software system at the expense of requiring a fairly extensive body of knowledge and employing, sometimes computationally demanding, deductions, and other algorithms. In other words, such systems are fairly *knowledge rich*. KBSE systems tend to employ expert systems or knowledge bases as their underlying technology.

While there has been a fair body of work that has applied deductive methods to different aspects of software engineering, the application of inductive methods (Machine Learning) in software engineering has received far less attention.

It has been argued that learning systems have the potential of going beyond performance of an expert so as to find *new* relations among concepts by examining examples of successfully solved cases. In effect this could allow the incorporation of knowledge into a system without the need for a knowledge engineer. In other words, using inductive methods to extract the knowledge that helps a software engineer in understanding a software system is an alternative to more traditional KBSE techniques. We should point out that this does not mean that one cannot incorporate expert knowledge in the process. On the contrary it is believed that such contribution can increase the potential gain obtained by using inductive methods [Weiss and Kulikowski 1991 p. 3]. Unlike KBSE systems, expert knowledge is not coded in the form of a large knowledge base.

Research Advancement in SE

The conducted research focuses on *software engineering*. Software engineering aims at systematically supporting the different phases of *software production*. Software engineering includes *automated software engineering* and *empirical software engineering*. The scientific research interests include automated and empirical aspects of software engineering as related to *software maintenance and evolution*. Software maintenance is the last part of the software life-cycle. Generally, maintenance is defined to start when the software product has first been delivered to its customers. Software maintenance and evolution is the most expensive and time-consuming phase of the life-cycle. The sub areas of maintenance which have been traditionally studied include the technical aspects of software and also the effects of the attributes of the persons maintaining software. Other areas have traditionally been less studied. In the actual maintenance changing of source code is a central task. Self-evidently the *size and complexity* of the programs to be maintained correlate positively with the problems. Also, problems with the *documentation* (such as non-existent, insufficient, and misleading documentation) complicate maintenance. Problems related to software maintenance can be alleviated in various ways. Proper allocation of resources for achieving sufficient level of *software quality* (and its sub factors, most importantly *maintainability*, and *comprehensibility*) during the initial development of the software is one strategy. In principle, all changes should be made such that no negative *side-effects* emerge. In principle, this goal could be approached via complete *regression testing*. In case of large software, however, complete testing is not possible. Therefore, test cases have to be selected wisely. Reading and interpreting large programs and comprehending their structure, operation, and purpose is a central, problematic, and time-consuming sub-task. Proper comprehension of the relevant issues is a necessary condition for successful fulfilments of maintenance tasks.

Automated Software Engineering

In case of maintaining poorly documented, large or otherwise hard-to-manipulate software, supporting techniques and tools are needed. These include *reverse engineering*, reengineering, restructuring, re-documentation, modernization, renovation, and re-factoring. Specific techniques include static and dynamic *program analysis*, program slicing, simulation, and systematic configuration management. There also exist multiple tools for these purposes.

Hypertext Support for Software Maintenance (Hyper Soft)

Hyper Soft is used for *Automated Hypertext Support for Software Maintenance*. Software maintainers have *situation-dependent information needs* while maintaining the software. Hyper Soft is an automated approach for satisfying these needs. Hyper Soft applies static program analysis and transient hypertext representation. Program comprehension is supported by the formed **Transient Hyper textual Access Structures (THASs).** THASs support *unlinear browsing* of the source code. Hyper Soft applies linear, hyper textual, hierarchical, and graphical views. Potentially cross-linked graphs are also linked to source code. Hypertext has earlier been applied both to manual cross-document linkage and to automated intra-modular linkage in so-called *software hypertext systems*. HyperSoft's specialities include: transient, fully automated cross-module linkage and automated formation of abstracted graphs with hyper textual links to source code. Some of the keywords being used are: software maintenance, program comprehension, reverse engineering, legacy systems, hypertext representation, software hypertext systems, program slicing, impact analysis.

Program Slicing (GRACE)

Program slicing can be used to support various tasks of software maintenance. The two main variants of slicing are backward slicing and forward slicing. Backward slicing is useful in *debugging* and forward slicing in *impact analysis*. The efficiency of slicing is improved by using program dependence graphs as a way to store the needed program information. Some of the keywords being used are: program slicing, program dependence graphs, forward slicing, static analysis, impact analysis, Java, Visual Basic.

Open Source Software Maintenance Support (ASLA)

Open source software development has specific characteristics in terms of maintenance and therefore specific reverse engineering capabilities are needed. These characteristics include software licensing. Keywords: open source software, reverse engineering, software licenses.

Symbolic Evaluation for Program Comprehension Support (SwMaster)

SwMaster is a *Program Comprehension Tools*. SwMaster applies symbolic analysis and program simulation to program comprehension support, reverse engineering and reengineering. Keywords: software maintenance, program comprehension, reverse engineering, legacy systems, symbolic analysis, program simulation, reengineering.

Data Mining

Data mining means nontrivial extraction of implicit, previously unknown, and potentially useful information from data. Research in the intersection of data mining and reverse engineering clearly has good future potential as a basis for sophisticated reverse engineering tools.

Empirical Software Engineering
Evaluation of Software Modernizations (ELTIS)

ELTIS is *Extending the Life-Time of Information Systems*. ELTIS studies decision making support related to the large-scale software evolution choices. Generally, the proportion of software maintenance and evolution activities is 50-75% of the total software life-cycle costs and there seems to be a slightly increasing trend. Nowadays, the proportion can sometimes the case of successful systems with long lifetime but poor maintainability be even as high as 90%. Since the proportion of the maintenance costs is large, so it is important to estimate the induced needed effort and costs of maintenance and modernization activities. There is also a need to evaluate *software evolution alternatives*. Successful systems with long life-time are often problematic in the sense of insufficient *maintainability* and thus modifiability. They are called *legacy systems*. Being large investments with poor flexibility their complete discard is often undesirable but radical modernizations are hard to implement successfully. Main general-level evolution options include: continued conventional maintenance, reduced maintenance, modernization, and replacement. Continued conventional maintenance is a viable option while both the economic and technical values of the system are high. Reduced maintenance is lucrative while the technical value is sufficient but the economic value is low. Modernization is the prime option while the economic value is high but the technical value is low. Finally, replacement is suggested while both the economic and technical values of the system are low. Industrial decision-making processes related to the evaluation of software evolution alternatives should be supported on empirically based methods. ELTIS includes theoretical comparative studies, empirical industrial case studies, and method development and validation activities. Some of the keywords being used are: software evolution, software maintenance, legacy systems, modernization, software benefits, software costs, and **return on investment (ROI)**.

Software Inspections

Software inspections mean peer reviews of software artefacts. Software inspections can be applied to increase the quality of software already prior to testing therefore reducing the needed corrective effort. Both the technical and organizational aspects of inspections have been studied in the scientific literature since 1980s. The studies include different kinds of inspection techniques and some reverse engineering tools for supporting the inspections. We have conducted both the literature survey and empirical industrial case studies related to software inspections.

Software Metrics

Software metrics mean measures of some properties of a piece of software or its specifications. Software metrics cover many quality aspects. They are needed, as a basis for the software evaluation methods. We have gathered empirical data concerning open source software systems and studied the relations between internal and external quality attributes statistically.

Software Maintenance Education

Software Maintenance Education (SME) is a conducted research focuses on software maintenance and evolution, especially on the effects and factors affecting the software maintenance seminars. Despite of its importance, maintenance rarely deserves proper treatment in software maintenance education. One reason to this is the tradition of covering other subject areas; which have been established earlier, instead of maintenance in the past and even current educational curricula. Another related reason is that the general software engineering books deal with the software maintenance and evolution only at a shallow level having typically only 5-10% text coverage as compared to the 50-90% cost proportion. Seminars on the other hand allow motivating interactivity and covers a wide range of scientifically relevant and new theoretical advances. Students need that sort of knowledge in order to become mature enough to commit themselves into large applicative SME work projects. Therefore, seminars and other similar forms of teaching are needed and they should also be studied scientifically.

Decision Making Support

Decision support systems are computer-based information systems that support decision making activities. In addition to the here summarized two branches of specific novel applications, general decision-making theories, and surveys, the earlier described ELTIS-project has extensively studied decision-making support in the context of software evolution.

Fluid Soft. *Fluidity in Software Systems;* The idea is to apply fluid information representations and data transformations in the software engineering context.

Data Modelling

Data modelling is the way toward making an information display for the information to be put away in a database. This information display is a theoretical portrayal of :

- Data objects
- The relationship between various information objects
- The rules.

Data modeling helps in the visual portrayal of information and implements business rules, administrative compliances, and government approaches on the information. Data models guarantee consistency in naming traditions, default esteems, semantics, security while guaranteeing the nature of the information.

Information show accentuates what information is required and how it ought to be sorted out rather than what tasks should be performed on the information. Information model resembles an architect's building plan which fabricates a reasonable model and set the connection between information things.

The two sorts of data models' methods are:

- Entity Relationship (E-R) Model
- UML (Unified Modeling Language)

The Essential Objective of Utilizing Data Models are:

- Ensures that all information objects required by the database are precisely spoken to. Oversight of information will prompt making of faulty reports and deliver erroneous outcomes.
- An information demonstrates to plan the database at the calculated, physical and legitimate dimensions.
- Data model structure characterizes the social tables, essential, and outside keys and put away strategies.
- It gives a reasonable image of the base information and can be utilized by database engineers to make a physical database.
- It is additionally useful to distinguish absent and excess information.

- Though the underlying making of information show is work and tedious, over the long haul, it makes IT framework overhaul.

Types of Data Models:

There are principally three distinct sorts of information models:

a. **Conceptual:** Conceptual data model characterizes WHAT the framework contains. This model is normally made by Business partners and Data Architects. The reason for existing is to sort out, scope, and characterize business ideas and standards.

b. **Logical:** Defines HOW the framework ought to be actualized paying little respect to the DBMS. This model is regularly made by Data Architects and Business Analysts. The reason for existing is to create a specialized guide of tenets and information structures.

c. **Physical:** Physical Data Model portrays HOW the framework will be executed by utilizing a particular DBMS framework. This model is ordinarily made by DBA and engineers. The object is genuine execution of the database. (*figure 14.1*)

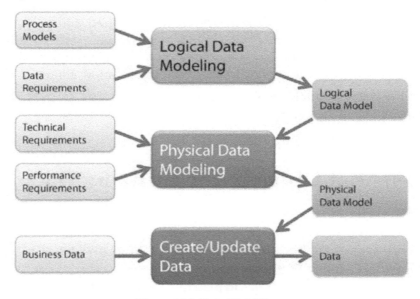

Figure 14.1: Data Model Types

Conceptual Model

The primary goal of this model is to build up the substances, their traits, and their connections. In this Data demonstrating level, there is no detail accessible of the real database structure.

The three fundamental occupants of Data Model are:

- **Entity:** A genuine thing
- **Attribute:** Characteristics or properties of a substance
- **Relationship:** Dependency or relationship between two substances

For instance:

- Customer and Product are two substances. Client number and name are the properties of customer substances.
- Product name and cost are the properties of item substance.
- Sale is the connection between the client and item. *(figure 14.2)*

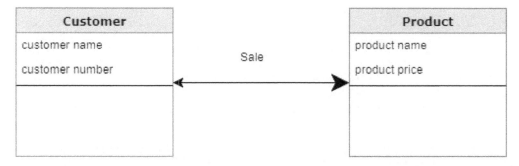

Figure 14.2: Conceptual Model

Attributes of a Reasonable Information Display:

- Offers Organization-wide inclusion of business ideas.
- This sort of Data Models is planned and created for a business group of onlookers.
- The applied model is created autonomously of equipment details like information stockpiling limit, area, or programming particulars like DBMS merchant and innovation. The center is to speak to information as a client will see it in "*this present reality.*"

Reasonable information models known as **domain models** make a typical vocabulary for all partners by setting up essential ideas and degree.

Logical Data Model

Logical Data Models add additional data to the reasonable model components. It characterizes the structure of the information components and set the connections between them. *(figure 14.3)*

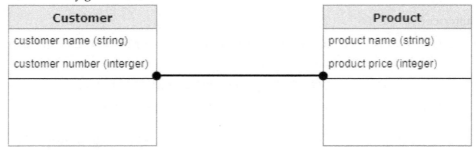

Figure 14.3: *Logical Data Model*

The benefit of the logical information is to frame the base for the physical model. In any case, the demonstrating structure stays conventional. At this data modeling level, no essential or optional key is characterized. At this data demonstrating level, you have to check and change the connector subtitle that were set before connections.

Attributes of a Logical Information Display

- Portrays information requirements for a solitary task yet could be incorporate with other legitimate information models depending on the extent of the venture.
- Planned and grew autonomously from the DBMS.
- Information characteristics will have datatypes with correct precisions and length.
- Standardization procedures to the model is connected normally till 3NF.

Physical Data Model

A Physical Data Model depicts the database explicit execution of the information. It offers a reflection of the database and produces the diagram. This is a direct result of the lavishness of meta-information offered by a **Physical Data Model**. This kind of data demonstrate the database structure. It displays database sections keys, imperatives, files, triggers, and different RDBMS highlights. *(figure 14.4)*

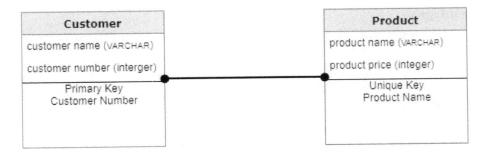

Figure 14.4 *Physical Data Model*

Qualities of a Physical Information Display

- The physical information portrays information requirement for a solitary venture or application however it might be incorporated with other physical information model's dependent on the task scope.

- Information Model contains connections between tables what tends to cardinality and nullability of the connections.

- Produced for a particular adaptation of a DBMS, area, information stockpiling or innovation to be utilized in the task.

- Segments ought to have correct datatypes, lengths allocated and default esteems.

- Essential and Foreign keys, views, indexes, get to profiles, and approvals, and so forth are characterized.

Advantages and Disadvantages of Data Model

Advantages:

- The fundamental objective of a structuring information demonstrate is to verify that information objects offered by the practical group are spoken precisely.

- The information model ought to be point by point enough to be utilized for building the physical database.

- The data in the information model can be utilized for characterizing the connection between tables, essential-outside keys, and put away strategies.

- Data Model causes business to convey the inside and crosswise over associations.

- Data display serves to archives information mappings in ETL process.

- Help to perceive right wellsprings of information to populate the model.

Disadvantages:

- To designer data show one should realize physical information by putting away the qualities.

- This is a navigational framework which produces complex application improvement, the board. Consequently, it requires an information of the true to life truth.

- Even littler change made in structure require an alteration in the whole application.

- There is no set information control dialect in DBMS.

Ontology

Ontologies are utilized for the formal portrayal of domain information. Learning based Applications use Ontologies for information sharing, which shapes the essential utilization of Ontologies. Ontologies improvement is to a great extent gone for AI specialists with learning of different systems starting from the field of AI. This learning is anyway obscure to a vast area of the product business. To overcome any issues between learning of Software Engineering professionals and AI strategies, a few propositions have been made recommending the utilization of Ontologies in the field of Software Engineering. Recommendations incorporate the utilization of UML graphs in the advancement of Ontologies. Indeed, the **Protégé Software** created by Stanford University has a tab which remarkably characterizes the utilization of UML charts in Ontology advancement. This usefulness can be utilized to build up an UML graph from the Ontology created. In any case, it can likewise be seen, that product building approaches themselves don't empower the portrayal of cosmology ideas got from depiction rationales and different ideas incorporated into the **Semantic Web Languages**.

Tools for Ontology Development

A few important ways to deal with applying programming designing systems to ontology advancement lead to UML based instruments that empower the improvement of ontologies utilizing software engineering languages. The list is given below:

Protégé

Protégé is one of the main ontological designing tools. It is an open source. Protégé is known to have a critical design which can additionally be broadened utilizing plug-ins. numerous segments giving interfaces to other learning-based apparatuses (Jess, Argenon, OIL, PAL Constraint, and so forth.) have been actualized and coordinated into Protégé. This meta-model is extensible and versatile. This implies Protégé can be adjusted to help another ontology language by including new meta-classes and meta-openings to the Protégé philosophy. The presentation of these new meta-modeling ideas empowers clients to include the vital metaphysics Primitives.

DUET

DUET empowers the bringing of **DAML Ontologies** into IBM Rational Rose and ArgoUML and the trading of UML models into the DAML ontology language. The apparatus is really actualized as an include for **IBM Rational Rose** and as a module for ArgoUML. Like Protégé it is openly accessible. DUET has a straightforward UML profile that contains generalizations for demonstrating Ontologies (in light of a UML bundle) and properties (in light of a UML class). DUET was the first UML device expansion that empowers sharing of Ontologies between an ontology language (i.e., DAML) and a UML apparatus in the two headings.

XPetal

Ontology tools which change **IBM Rational Rose** models from the mdl configuration to RDF and RDFS Ontologies have been created, better known as **XPetal**. The device has been actualized in Java.

Visual ontology modeler (VOM)

The **Visual Ontology Modeler (VOM)** is an after effect of collective work between Sandpiper Software Inc. and the Knowledge System Laboratory at Stanford University. This instrument was utilized to expand IBM Rational Rose and empower ontology advancement with easy to understand wizards that mechanize the making of a consistent model and related graphs. The apparatus depends on a UML profile for ontology improvement that is firmly identified with Protégé's metamodel for Ontologies.

Data Mining in Software Engineering

Data mining for programming building comprises of gathering programming designing information, removing some learning from it and, if conceivable, utilize this information to enhance the product designing procedure, at the end of the day, "*operationalize*" the mined learning. For example, analysts have removed used patterns from a large number of lines of code of the Linux kernel so as to discover bugs.

Generally, information digging for programming building can be deteriorated along three tomahawks: the objective, the info information utilized, and the mining method utilized. For instance, the objective might be to enhance the code finish frameworks.

The objective: Program building comprises of numerous errands from particular, structure, improvement, checking at runtime, and so on. Each undertaking is deteriorated in numerous littler scale errands. Consider an example, a designer always switches between assignments, such as from exploring code, perusing documentation, composing code, to troubleshooting, and so forth. Amid the most recent decade, it has been appeared the most programming designing assignments, that can make profit by information mining approaches, the errands being whether specialized or more individuals arranged. Moreover, the network, in spite of the fact that favoring solid commitments, likewise delivers exploratory outcomes, elucidating marvels saw in programming designing information.

The information: The product building process completely controls a wide range of information. Obviously, one considers code, however there are likewise many composed records (particulars, documentation), plan archives (charts, equations), runtime reports (logs), and so forth. A large portion of them can be formed utilizing a Version Control System (e.g., CVS, SVN, Git). Contingent upon the focused-on objective, a few curios are pretty much suitable, and mixed methodologies are conceivable (utilizing various types of programming designing ancient rarities related). Additionally, there is typically a decent lot of pre-preparing that is explicit to the relics under thought: characteristic language handling for composed records, static examinations for code, and so forth.

The systems: These days, there is an abundance of information mining and machine learning procedures. They exist, however develop usage are accessible and incredible equipment empowers strategies to scale to extensive datasets. To control programming building information, no one estimate fits-all arrangement. From managed to unsupervised methodologies, numerical or all out, bunch or on the web, numerous systems have been utilized. There are activities, for example, brought together datasets and challenges to empower logical correlations of propriety and execution.

Some Facts

The demand for software engineers is at all-time high, and contuse to increase. The data shows that the number of programmers in the USA doubled from 1986 to 1996. While good data are sparse for such an important field, the demand for programmers has clearly increased in the past ten years, and it is likely to continue increasing in future. Most of the professionals in the fields of engineering and science now write at least some software to do their jobs, the number of people who write, modify, fix, and support software must be very large. If growth trends implied by census data apply to the entire population of casual and full-time programmers, the demand for new programmers in the next ten years is likely to run into millions.

Viewing the last trends, it shows that every industrial organizations will need more people with software application programming skill and that most programming groups will be seriously understaffed. Since many software groups are already understaffed for onshore offshore projects, and the current university graduation rate of software professionals is more; so, there is an ample scope of job opportunity.

Obtaining more software-skilled immigrants into US and other developed countries is an attractive alternative. India alone produces graduates about 1, 00,000 English-speaking software professionals a year. However, the US has tight visa restrictions, and many other groups also have claims on the available slots. Since the demand for software skills is increasing rapidly in India, and since many Indian professionals can now find attractive opportunities at home, the available numbers of Indian immigrants will likely to be limited in the future.

The *packaged applications* are now gaining popularity. Companies are starting to market packaged applications much like those offered by SAP and Oracle. They produce essentially prepackaged application systems that can be configured in prescribed ways. Rather than custom-designing each application, the industry will increasingly develop families of tolerable application systems. By tailoring the system, the users adjust their business procedures to fit the available facilities of the system.

Conclusion

There are many software, becoming popular and many are going out of the market because of their individual efficiency for development of system and maintenance. The systems developed in the specific languages has got merits and demerits that a software developer or user should judge carefully. Users of lightweight J2EE (spring) are becoming more for developing open jobs. The relative growth of Groovy, Ruby, and Scala over the past years is very impressive as they are growing very fast. Is it a hype or are these programming languages of tomorrow? Maybe you ask yourself which computer language you should learn next. Should you learn Groovy, Ruby, Scala or take a look on Microsoft .NET? According to indeed.com Java is the most wanted programming language on the market. We can see the growing *Cloud Computing* trend even better if we view the percentage growth. What about the web framework? JSP and Struts still rock the world. JSP and Struts developers are still most wanted. JBoss is the only open-source application server used in production. What about Java Application Servers? Oracle Application Server is the most wanted, but JBoss is growing fast. Now Tomcat is the dominating web container in comparison to Java web container. Similarly, Flash dominates the web and the job market. Though Silverlight is growing and its growth in the market is impressive.

According to indeed.com you are currently the most valuable IT resource if you are a Java Developer with Spring and Hibernet knowledge. You should know how to develop web applications with JSP, Struts, or Web Flow and how deploy it on

Tomcat or Oracle Application Servers. If you are a rich client developer, you should be able to develop with Swing or Flash. If you want to be the elite of the future, you should take a look at Cloud Computing, Groovy, Spring, JPA, GlassFish, Jetty, ActiveMQ, may be Silverlight.

CHAPTER 15

Model Questions with Answers

1. **Define Software Engineering.**

   Software Engineering:
   - The Application of systematic, disciplined, quantifier approach
   - To the development, operations, and maintenance of software

2. **What is the Process Framework?**

   Process Framework:
   - Establishes the foundation for a complete software process
   - By identifying a small number of framework activities that are applicable for all software projects regardless of their size and complexity

3. **What are the Generic Framework Activities?**

   Generic Framework Activities:
   - Communication
   - Planning
   - Modeling
   - Construction
   - Deployment

4. **Define Stakeholder.**
   - Anyone who has a stake in the successful outcome of Project
   - Business Managers, end-users, software engineer, support people

5. **How the Process Model differ from one another?**
   - Based on the flow of activities
   - Interdependencies between activities
   - Manner of Quality Assurance
   - Manner of Project Tracking
   - Team Organization and Roles
   - Work Products identify a requirement identifier

6. **Write out the reasons for the Failure of Water Fall Model?**
   Reasons for the failure of Water Fall Model:
   - Real Project rarely follow Sequential Flow. Iterations are made in an indirect manner
   - Difficult for the customer to state all requirements explicitly
   - Customer needs more patients as working product reach only at the Deployment phase

7. **What are the Drawbacks of RAD Model?**
   Drawbacks of RAD Model:
   - Require a sufficient number of Human Resources to create enough number of teams
   - Developers and Customers are not committed, system result in failure
   - Not Properly Modularized building component may Problematic
   - Not applicable when there is more possibility for Technical Risk

8. **Why Formal Methods are not widely used?**
   - Quite Time Consuming and Expensive
   - Extensive expertise is needed for developers to apply formal methods
   - Difficult to use as they are technically sophisticated maintenance may become risk

9. **What are Cross-Cutting Concerns?**
   Cross-Cutting Concerns:
   - When concerns cut across multiple functions, features and information

10. **What are the different Phases of Unified Process?**

Different Phases of Unified Process:

- Inception Phase
- Elaboration Phase
- Construction Phase
- Transition Phase
- Production Phase

11. **Define the terms:**

a. Agility *b)* Agile Team

a. **Agility:-**

- Dynamic, Content Specific, Aggressively Change Embracing and Growth Oriented

b. **Agile Team:-**

- Fast Team
- Able to Respond to Changes

12. **Define the terms:**

a. Agile Methods and *b.* Agile Process

a. **Agile Methods:-**

- Methods to overcome perceive and actual weakness in conventional software engineering
- To accommodate changes in environment, requirements and use cases

b. **Agile Process:-**

- Focus on Team Structures, Team Communications, Rapid Delivery of software and it de-emphasis importance of intermediate product

13. **What is the Use of Process Technology Tools?**

Use of Process Technology Tools:

Help Software Organizations

1. Analyze their current process
2. Organize a work task
3. Control And Monitor Progress
4. Manage Technical Quality

14. Define the term Scripts.

Scripts:

- Specific Process Activities and other detailed work functions that are part of the team process

15. What is the Objective of the Project Planning Process?

The objective of the Project Planning Process:

- To provide a framework that enables the manager to make reasonable estimates of resources, cost, and schedule

16. What are Decomposition Techniques?

Decomposition Techniques:

- Software Sizing
- Problem – Based Estimation
- Process-Based Estimation
- Estimation with Use – Cases
- Reconciling Estimates

17. How do we compute the "Expected Value" for Software Size?

- The expected value for estimation variable(size), S, can be computed as Weighted Average of Optimistic (Sopt), most likely (Sm), and Pessimistic(Spess) estimates
- $S = (Sopt+4Sm+Spess)/6$

18. What is an Object Point?

Object Point:

- Count is determined by multiplying the original number of object instances by a weighting factor and summing to obtain total object point count

19. What is the difference between the "Known Risks" and Predictable Risks"?

Known Risks

- That can be uncovered after careful evaluation of the project plan, the business, and technical environment in which the product is being developed
- Example: Unrealistic delivery rate

Predictable Risks

- Extrapolated from past project experience
- Example: Staff turnover

20. **List out the basic principles of software project scheduling?**

Basic Principles Of Software Project Scheduling

- Compartmentalization
- Interdependency
- Time Allocation
- Effort Validation
- Defined Responsibilities
- Defined Outcomes
- Defined Milestones

21. **What are the Classifications of System Engineering?**

Classifications of System Engineering:

- Business Process Engineering [BPE]
- Product Engineering

22. **List out the Elements in Computer-Based System?**

Elements in Computer-Based System:

- Software
- Hardware
- People
- Database
- Documentation
- Procedures

23. **What are the Factors to be considered in the System Model Construction?**

- Assumption
- Simplification
- Limitation
- Constraints
- Preferences

24. **What does a System Engineering Model accomplish?**

- Define Processes that serve needs of view
- Represent behavior of process and assumption
- Explicitly define Exogenous and Endogenous Input
- Represent all Linkages that enable the engineer to better understand view

25. Name the architectures defined and developed as part of BPE.

- Data Architecture
- Applications Architecture
- Technology Architecture

26. What is meant by Cardinality and Modality?

Cardinality

- The number of occurrence of one object related to the number of occurrence of another object
- One to One [1: 1]
- One to Many [1: N]
- Many to Many [M: N]

Modality

- Whether or not a particular Data Object must participate in the relationship

27. What are the Objectives of Requirement Analysis?

Objectives of Requirement Analysis:

- Describe what the customer requires
- Establish a basis for the creation of software design
- Define a set of requirements that can be validated once the software design is built

28. What is the two additional features of Hayley Pirbhai Model?

- User Interface Processing
- Maintenance and Self-test Processing

29. Define System Context Diagram [SCD].

System Context Diagram [SCD]:

- Establish information boundary between System being implemented and Environment which system operates
- Defines all external producers, external consumers, and entities that communicate through User Interface

30. Define System Flow Diagram [SFD].

System Flow Diagram[SFD]:

- Indicates information flow across SCD region
- Used to guide system engineer in developing a system

31. What are the Requirements Engineering Process Functions?

- Inception
- Elicitation
- Elaboration
- Negotiation
- Specification
- Validation
- Management

32. What are the Difficulties in Elicitation?

Difficulties in Elicitation:

- Problem Of Scope
- Problem Of Understanding
- Problem Of Volatility

33. List out the Types of Traceability Table.

Types of Traceability Table:

- Features Traceability Table
- Source Traceability Table
- Dependency Traceability Table
- Subsystem Traceability Table
- Interface Traceability Table

34. Define Quality Function Deployment [QFD].

Quality Function Deployment [QFD]:

- Technique translates the needs of the customer into technical requirements
- "Concentrates on maximizing customer satisfaction from the software engineering process"

35. What are the Benefits of Analysis Pattern?

Benefits of Analysis Pattern:

- Speed up development of Analysis model
- Transformation of Analysis into the Design model

36. What is System Modeling?

System Modeling:-

- Important Element in System Engineering Process
- Define Process in each view to be constructed
- Represent Behavior of the Process
- Explicitly define exogenous and endogenous inputs

37. Define CRC Modeling.

CRC Modeling:-

- Class Responsibility Collaborator Modeling
- Collection of Standard Index Card.Divided into 3 sections
    1. Name of class at Top
    2. List of class Responsibilities at Left
    3. Collaborators at Right
- Classes that Cover the Information to complete its responsibilities

38. List out the Factors of Data Modeling.

Factors of Data Modeling:

- Data Objects
- Data Attributes
- Relationship
- Cardinality and Modality

39. Define Swim Lane Diagram.

Swim Lane Diagram:

- Variation of activity diagram
- Allows Modular to represent the flow of activities
- The actor responsible for the activity

40. What is the Selection Characteristic for Classes?

Selection Characteristic for Classes:

- Retained Information
- Needed Services
- Multiple Attribute
- Common Attribute
- Common operations
- Essential Requirements

41. Define Steps in Behavioral Model.

Steps in Behavioral Model :

- Evaluate all Use Cases
- Identify Events
- Create Sequence for each use Cases
- Build a State Diagram
- Review Model for Accuracy and Consistency

42. Define the terms in Software Designing.

(*a*) Abstraction

(*b*) Modularity

(*a*) **Abstraction:**

1. **Highest Level:** Solution is stated in a broad term using the language of the problem environment

2. **Lower Level:** More detailed description of the solution is provided

(*b*) **Modularity:**

- Software is divided into separately named and addressable components, called Modules that are integrated to satisfy problem requirements

43. How Architecture Design can be represented?

- Architectural Design can be represented by one or more different models. They are
  1. Structural Models
  2. Framework Models
  3. Dynamic Models
  4. Process Models

43. What is the Advantage of Information Hiding?

Advantage of Information Hiding :

- During testing and maintenance phase if changes require that is done in a particular module without affecting another module

44. What types of Classes does the designer create?

- User interface Classes
- Business Domain Classes
- Process Classes
- Persistent Classes
- System Classes

45. What is Coupling?

Coupling:-

- A quantitative measure of the degree to which classes are connected to one another
- Keep coupling as low as possible

46. What is Cohesion?

Cohesion:

- Indication of relative functional strength of a module
- A natural extension of Information Hiding
- Performs a single task, requiring little integration with other components

47. Define Refactoring.

Refactoring:

- Changing software system in a way that does not alter the external behavior of the code

48. What are the Five Types of Design classes?

Five Types of Design classes :

- User Interface Classes
- Business domain Classes
- Process Classes
- Persistent Classes
- System Classes

49. What are the Different types of Design Model? Explain.

Different types of Design Model:

- **Process Dimension:**

  Indicate the evolution of Design model as design tasks executed as part of the software   process

- **Abstraction Dimension:**

  Represent the level of detail as each element of the analysis model is transformed into design equivalent

50. List out the Different elements of Design Model.

Different Elements of Design Model :

- Data Design Elements
- Architectural Design Elements
- Interface Design Elements
- Component Level Design Elements
- Deployment Level Design Elements

51. What are the Types of Interface Design Elements?

Types of Interface Design Elements:
- User Interfaces
- External Interfaces
- Internal Interfaces

52. What Types of Design Patterns are available for the software Engineer?

Types of Design Patterns :
- Architectural patterns
- Design Patterns
- Idioms

53. Define Framework.

Framework:
- Code Skeleton that can be fleshed out with specific classes or functionality
- Designed to address specifies problem at hand

54. What is the Objective of Architectural Design?

The objective of Architectural Design:
- Model overall software structure by representing component interfaces, dependencies and relationships and interactions

55. What are the important roles of Conventional component within the Software Architecture?

- Control Component: that coordinates invocation of all other problem domain
- Problem Domain Component: that implement Complete or Partial function required by the customer
- Infrastructure Component: that responsible for functions that support processing required in the problem domain

56. What are the Basic Design principles of Class-Based Components?

Basic Design principles of Class-Based Components:

- Open-Closed Principle[OCP]
- Liskov Substitution Principle[LSP]
- Dependency Inversion Principle[DIP]
- Interface Segregation Principle[ISP]
- Release Reuse Equivalency Principle[REP]
- Common Closure Principle[CCP]
- Common Reuse Principle[CRP]

57. What should we consider when we name components?

- Components
- Interface
- Dependencies and Inheritance

58. What are the Different Types of Cohesion?

Different Types of Cohesion:

- Functional
- Layer
- Communicational
- Sequential
- Procedural
- Temporal
- Utility

59. What are the Different Types of Coupling?

Different Types of Coupling:

- Content Coupling
- Common Coupling
- Control Coupling
- Stamp Coupling
- Data Coupling
- Routine Call Coupling
- Type Use Coupling
- Inclusion or Import Coupling
- External Coupling

60. What is Program Design Language [PDL]?

Program Design Language [PDL]:

- Also called Structured English or Pseudocode
- Pidgin Language in that it uses the vocabulary of one language and the overall syntax of another

61. What are the Basic Principles of Software Testing?

Basic Principles of Software Testing:

- Traceable to Customer Requirements
- Planned long before Testing begins
- Pareto Principles applied to Software testing
- Begin small and progress towards testing
- Exhaustive testing is not possible
- Conducted by independent third party

62. List out the Characteristics of Testability of Software.

Characteristics of Testability of Software:

- Operability
- Observability
- Controllability
- Decomposability
- Simplicity
- Stability
- Understandability

63. List out various Methods for finding Cyclomatic Complexity.

- Number of Regions
- Cyclomatic Complexity V(G), for Flow Graph
  $V(G) = E - N + 2$
- Cyclomatic Complexity V(G)
  $V(G) = P + 1$

64. Define Smoke Testing.

Smoke Testing:

- Integration testing
- Commonly used when software products are being developed

65. What are the Attributes of Good Test?

Attributes of Good Test:

- High probability of finding errors
- Not Redundant
- "Best of Breed"
- Neither too simple nor too complex

65. Define White Box Testing.

White Box Testing:

- Also called Glass Box Testing
- Test case design uses Control Structure of Procedural Design to derive test cases

66. Define Basic Path Testing.

Basic Path Testing:

- White Box Testing
- Enable test case designer to derive a logical complexity measure of a procedural design
- Use this measure as a Guide for defining a basis set of execution paths

67. Define the terms:

- *a.* Graph Matrices
- *b.* Connection Matrices

Graph Matrices:-

- To develop software tool the data structure used is Graph Matrix
- Square Matrix
- Size equals the number of nodes on the Flowgraph

Connection Matrices:-

- If Link Weight =1 => Connection Exists
- If Link Weight =1 => Connection Does not Exists

68. What is Behavioral Testing?

Behavioral Testing:

- Also Known as Black Box Testing
- Focuses on the Functional Requirement of software

- Enables Software engineer to derive a set of input the condition that fully exercises all functional requirements of a software

69. What are the Benefits of conducting Smoke Testing?

Benefits of conducting Smoke Testing:

- Integration Risk is Minimized
- Quality of end-product is improved
- Error diagnosis and Correction are simplified
- Progress is easy to assess

70. What errors are commonly found during Unit Testing?

- Misunderstood or incorrect arithmetic precedence
- Mixed Mode Operations
- Incorrect Initializations
- Precision Accuracy
- Incorrect Symbolic representation of the expression

71. What problems may be encountered when Top-Down Integration is chosen?

- Delay is tested until stubs replace with actual modules
- Develop stubs that perform limited functions that simulate the actual module
- Integrate the software from the bottom of the hierarchy upward

72. What are the Steps in Bottom-Up Integration?

Steps in Bottom-Up Integration:

- Low-level components are combined into clusters perform specific software subfunction
- The driver is written to coordinate test case input and output
- Cluster is tested
- Drivers are removed and clusters are combined moving inward in program structure

73. What is Regression Testing?

Regression Testing:

- Re-execution of some subset of tests that have already been conducted
- To ensure changes have not propagated unintended side effects

74. What are the Characteristics of "Critical Module"?

Characteristics of "Critical Module":

- Addresses several software requirements
- Has High Level Of Control
- Complex or error prone
- Has Definite Performance Requirements

75. What are the Properties of Connection Matrices?

Properties of Connection Matrices:

- Probability that link will execute
- Processing time expended during traversal of the link
- Memory required during traversal of the link
- Resource required during traversal of the link

76. What is Flow Graph Notation?

Flow Graph Notation:-

- Simple notation for representing Control Flow
- Draw only when the Logical Structure of component is complex

77. Define Cyclomatic Complexity.

Cyclomatic Complexity:-

- Software Metric
- A quantitative measure of Logical Complexity
- Number of Independent Paths in the basis set of program

78. What is Equivalence Partition?

Equivalence Partitions:-

- Derives an input domain of a program into classes of data from which test cases are derived
- Set Of Objects have linked by relationships as Symmetric, Transitive and Reflexive an equivalence class is present

79. List out the possible errors of Black Box Testing.

Errors of Black Box Testing:

- Incorrect or Missing Functions
- Interface Errors
- Errors in Data Structures or external databases

- Behavioral or Performance errors
- Initialization or Termination errors

80. Define Data Objects.

Data Objects :

- Represent Composite Information
- The external entity, thin, occurrence or event, role, organizational unit, place or structure
- Encapsulates Data only

81. What are the Components of the Cost of Quality?

Components of the Cost of Quality:

- Quality Costs
- Prevention Costs
- Appraisal Costs

82. What is Software Quality Control?

Software Quality Control:

- Involves a series of inspections, reviews, and tests
- Used throughout the software process to ensure each work product meets requirements placed upon it

83. What is Software Quality Assurance?

Software Quality Assurance:

- Set of auditing and reporting functions
- Assess the effectiveness and completeness of quality control activities

84. What is the Objective of Formal Technical Reviews?

The objective of Formal Technical Reviews:

- Uncover errors in function, logic, and implementation for the representation of software
- Software represented according to a predefined standard
- Verify software under review meets requirements
- Achieve software developed in Uniform Manner
- Make projects more manageable

85. What Steps are required to perform Statistical SQA?

- Information about software defects is collected and categorized
- An attempt is made to trace each defect
- Using the Pareto principle, isolate 20%
- Once vital causes are identified, correct problems that cause defects

86. Define the SQA Plan.

SQA Plan:

- Provides a roadmap for instituting SQA
- The plan serves as a template for SQA activities that instituted for each software project

87. What are the Baseline criteria in SCM?

- Help to control Change
- Specification or product that has been formally
- Reviewed and agreed upon serves as the basis for future development
- That can be changed only through formal change control procedures

88. Define Status Reporting.

- Also called Configuration Status Reporting
- Is an SCM task that answers
  1. What Happened?
  2. Who did it?
  3. When did it happen?
  4. What else will be affected?

89. What is the Origin of changes that are requested for software?

Origin Of Change:-

- New Business or Market Condition
- New Customer Needs
- Reorganization or business growth/downsizing
- Budgetary or Scheduling constraints

90. List out the Elements of SCM.

Elements of SCM:-

- Component Elements
- Process Elements

- Construction Elements
- Human Elements

91. What are the Features supported by SCM?

Features supported by SCM:

- Versioning
- Dependency tracking and Change Management
- Requirements tracking
- Configuration Management
- Audit trails

92. What are the Objectives of the SCM Process?

Objectives of SCM Process:

- Identify all items, collectively define software configuration
- Manage changes to one or more these items
- Facilitate the construction of different version of an application
- Ensure that the software quality is maintained

93. What are the issues to be considered for developing tactics for WebApp Configuration Management?

- Context
- People
- Scalability

94. Define CASE Tools.

CASE Tools:

- Computer Aided Software Engineering
- It is a System software
- Provide Automated support for software process activities
- Includes program used to support software process activities
- Such as Requirement Analysis, System Modeling, Debugging and Testing

95. How do we define Software Quality?

Software Quality:

- Conformance to explicitly stated functional and performance requirements, explicitly documented development standards
- Implicit characteristics, expected for professionally developed software

96. Define the terms:

a. Quality of Design

b. Quality of Conformance

Quality of Design:

- Characteristics, designer specify for an item Quality of Conformance:
- Degree to which design specifications are followed during manufacturing

97. What is the Type of CASE Tools?

Types of CASE Tools:-

- Upper CASE Tools
- Lower CASE Tools

98. Define Software Reliability.

Software Reliability:

> Probability of failure-free operation of the computer program in a specified environment for a specified time

99. How the Registration process of ISO 9000 certification is done?

The registration process of ISO 9000 certification has the following stages

1. application
2. Pre-assessment
3. Document Review and Adequacy of audit
4. Compliance Audit
5. Registration
6. Continued Surveillance

100. What are the Factors of Software Quality?

Factors of Software Quality:

- Portability
- Usability
- Reusability
- Correctness
- Maintainability

Short Questions with Answers

1. **Define software engineering**

   The establishment and use of sound engineering principles in order to obtain economically software that is reliable and works efficiently on real machines.

2. **Differentiate software engineering methods, tools, and procedures.**

   Methods: Broad array of tasks like project planning, cost estimation, etc..

   Tools: Automated or semi-automated support for methods.

   Procedures: Holds the methods and tools together. It enables the timely development of computer software.

3. **Write the disadvantages of classic life cycle model.**

   Disadvantages of the classic life cycle model :

   (i)   Real projects rarely follow the sequential flow. Iteration always occurs and creates problem.

   (ii) Difficult for the customer to state all requirements

   (iii) A working version of the program is not available. So the customer must have patience.

4. **What do you mean by task set in spiral Model?**

   Each of the regions in the spiral model is populated by a set of work tasks called a task set that are adapted to the characteristics of the project to be undertaken.

5. **What is the main objective of Win-Win Spiral Model?**

   The customer and the developer enter into the process of negotiation where the customer may be asked to balance functionality, performance and other product against cost and time to market.

6. **Which of the software engineering paradigms would be most effective? Why?**

   Incremental / Spiral model will be most effective.

   Reasons:

   (i)   It combines the linear sequential model with iterative nature of prototyping

   (ii) Focuses on delivery of the product at each increment

   (iii) Can be planned to manage technical risks.

7. Who is called as the Stakeholder?

A stakeholder is anyone in the organization who has a direct business interest in the system or product to be built.

8. Write the objective of project planning?

It is to provide a framework that enables the manager to make reasonable estimates of resources, cost, and schedule.

9. What is Boot Strapping?

A sequence of instructions whose execution causes additional instructions to be loaded and executed until the complete program is in storage.

10. Write a short note on 4GT.

Fourth Generation Technique. 4GT encompasses a broad array of software tools. Each tool enables the software developer to specify some characteristics of software at a higher level.

11. What is FP? How it is used for project estimation?

Function Point. It is used as the estimation variable to size each element of the software. It requires considerably less detailed. Estimated indirectly by estimating the number of inputs, outputs, data files, external interfaces.

12. What is LOC? How it is used for project estimation?

LOC: Lines of Code. It is used as an estimation variable to size each element of the software. It requires a considerable level of detail.

13. Write the formula to calculate the effort in person-months used in Dynamic multivariable Model?

Software Equation: $E = [LOC * B0.333/P]3 * (1/t4)$, where E is an effort in person-months, t is projected duration, B is a special skills factor, P is productivity parameter.

14. What is called object points?

It is an indirect software measure that is computed using counts of the number of screens, reports, and components.

15. What are the four different Degrees of Rigor?

Four different degrees of Rigor is

Casual

Structured

Strict

Quick reaction

16. Write about Democratic Teams in software development. (Egoless Team)

It is an egoless team. All team members participate in all decisions. Group leadership rotates from member to member based on tasks to be performed.

17. What are the two project scheduling methods?

PERT- Program Evaluation and Review Techniques

CPM- Critical Path Method

18. What is called support risk?

The degree of uncertainty that the resultant software will be easy to correct, adapt and enhance.

19. What is RMMM?

Risk Mitigation, Monitoring and Management Plan. It is also called Risk Aversion.

20. What are the four impacts of the project risk?

Catastrophic, Critical, Marginal, Negligible.

21. List the tools or methods available for rapid prototyping.

Rapid prototyping (Speed)

(i)   4GT

(ii) Reusable software components

(iii) Formal specification and prototyping environments.

22. What is the need for modularity?

Need for modularity: Easier to solve a complex problem. Can achieve reusability. Best effort and complexity reduce.

23. What are the five criteria that are used in modularity?

Modular Decomposability

Modular composability

Modular understandability

Modular continuity

Modular protection

24. What is Software Architecture?

The overall structure of the software and the ways in which that software provides conceptual integrity for the system.

25. What are the models used for Architectural design?

Structural models

Framework models

Dynamic models

Process models

Functional models

26. What is cohesion?

It is a measure of the relative functional strength of a module. (Binding)

27. What is Coupling?

The measure of the relative interdependence among modules.

(Measure of interconnection among modules in a software structure.)

28. List the coupling factors.

Interface complexity between modules

Reference to the module

Data pass across the interface.

29. Define Stamp coupling.

When a portion of the data structure is passed via the module interface, then it called stamp coupling.

30. Define common coupling.

When a number of modules reference a global data area, then the coupling is called common coupling.

31. Define temporal cohesion.

When a module contains tasks that are related by the fact that all must be executed with the same span of time, then it termed as temporal cohesion.

32. Write short notes on structure charts.

These are used in architectural design to document hierarchical structure, parameters, and interconnections in a system. No Decision box. The chart can be augmented with the module by module specifications of I/P and O/P parameters as well as I/P and O/P attributes.

33. What do you mean by factoring?

It is also called vertical partitioning. It follows a Top-Down strategy. We can say that there are some top-level modules and low-level modules.

Top level modules - Control functions, actual processing works

Low-level modules -Workers. Performing all input computation and output tasks.

34. What is Aesthetics?

Aesthetics: It is a science of art and beauty. These are fundamental to software design, whether in art or technology.

Simplicity, Elegance(refinement), clarity of purpose.

35. What do you mean by common coupling?

Common coupling: When a number of modules reference a global data area, then the coupling is called common coupling.

36. Write about Real-Time Systems.

It provides a specified amount of computation within fixed time intervals. RTS sense and control external devices, respond to external events and share processing time between tasks.

37. Define Distributed system.

It consists of a collection of nearly autonomous processors that communicate to achieve a coherent computing system.

38. Compare Data Flow Oriented Design with data structure oriented design

Data flow oriented design: Used to represent a system or software at any level of abstraction.

Data Structure-oriented design: It is used for representing information hierarchy using the three constructs for sequence, selection, and repetition.

39. Define Architectural Design and Data Design.

Architectural Design: To develop a modular program structure and represent the relationships between modules.

Data Design: To select the logical representations of data objects, data storage and the concepts of information hiding and data abstraction.

40. What are the contents of HIPO diagrams?

A visual table of contents, set of overview diagrams, set of detail diagrams.

41. What are the aspects of software reuse?

Software development with reuse

Software development for reuse

Generator based reuse

Application system reuse

42. Define Configuration Status Reporting.

What happened? Who did it?

When did it happen? What else will be affected?

It is also called status accounting.

43. What is the need for baseline?

Need for Baseline:

(i) Basis for further development

(ii) Uses formal change control procedure for change

(iii) Helps to control change

44. Define SCM.

It is an umbrella activity that is applied throughout the software process. It has a set of tracking and control activities that begin when a software engineering project begins and terminates only when the software project is taken out of operation.

45. List the SCM Activities.

(i) Identify a change

(ii) Control change

(iii) Ensure that change is being properly implemented

(iv) Report changes to others who may have an interest

46. What is meant by software reusability?

A software component should be designed and implemented so that it can be reused in many different programs.

47. What is CASE?

CASE: Computer Aided Software Engineering

CASE provides the engineer with the ability to automate manual activities and to improve engineering insight.

48. Write the distinction between SCM and software support.

SCM: It has a set of tracking and control activities that begin when a software engineering project begins and terminates only when the software project is taken out of operation.

Software support: It has a set of software engineering activities that occur after the software has been delivered to the customer and put into operation.

49. What is the difference between basic objects and aggregate objects used in software configuration?

Basic Objects: It represents a unit of text. e.g. Section of requirement specification, Source listing for a component

Aggregate objects: Collection of basic objects. And other aggregate objects. e.g. Full design specification

50. What is configuration Audit?

Has the change specified in ECO been made?

Has formal technical review been conducted?

Software Engineering procedures for noting the change, recording it, reporting it been followed?

SCI is updated?

Essay Type Questions (in Brief)

51. Explain the Linear Sequential Model and prototyping model in detail

Linear Sequential Model: Explanation, Diagram, Advantages, Disadvantages

Prototyping model: Explanation, Diagram, Advantages, Disadvantages

52. Explain the Spiral model and win-win spiral model in detail.

Spiral Model - Six Task Regions:

Customer Communication, Planning, Risk Analysis, Engineering, Construction and Release, Customer Evaluation. Diagram, Details of four circles

Win-Win spiral model-

The customer and the developer enter into the process of negotiation, where the customer may be asked to balance functionality, performance, and other product against cost and time to market. Activities, diagram, explanation

53. Explain incremental model in detail.

Explanation of increments in the stages of Analysis, Design, Code, Test.

54. Discuss fourth generation techniques.

4GT: It encompasses a broad array of software tools. Each tool enables the software developer to specify some characteristics of software at a higher level.

Explanations of: 4GT Tools, 4GT Paradigm, Current state of 4GT approaches.

55. **Explain the Activities of Project Planning**

   Software scope with an example (Conveyor Line Sorting System)

   Resources

   Hardware/ Software Tools

56. **Explain the cost estimation procedure using the COCOMO Model.**

   It is algorithmic cost model. (One of the Empirical estimation model)

   COCOMO Model: 10 steps

   3 different sizing options. Explanation.

57. **Explain the following:**

   (i)   Delphi Cost Estimation

   (ii) Putnam Estimation model

   (iii) Decomposition approach:

   (*i*)   **Delphi cost estimation** - Procedures to calculate

   (*ii*) **Putnam estimation model** (Dynamic multivariable model).
          Explanation of the software equation

   (*iii*) **Decomposition approach** - Write an algorithm

58. **Explain the organizational structure of software development.**

   Explanations of Project structure, Programming team structure, Management by objectives.

59. **Explain the process of 'Risk Analysis and Management.'**

   Risk Identification

   Risk Estimation

   Risk Assessment

   Risk Management and Monitoring

   Risk Refinement

60. **Explain the following**

   (*i*) **Software requirement specification.**

   (*ii*) **Specification review**

   (i) **Software Requirement Specification:**

      Description

      Functional Description

      Behavioral Description

Validation criteria

Bibliography and appendix

Preliminary user's manual

(ii) Specification Review: Explanation

61. **Explain the types of coupling and cohesion.**

    Coupling: Measure of the relative interdependence among modules.

    Types: Data coupling, Stamp coupling, control coupling, External coupling, Common coupling, Content coupling

    Cohesion: It is a measure of the relative functional strength of a module.

    Types: Coincidentally cohesive, Logically cohesive, Temporal cohesion, procedural cohesion, communicational cohesion, High cohesion, sequential cohesion.

62. **Explain the various software design concepts**

    Explanations of Abstraction, Refinement, Modularity, Software Architecture, Control hierarchy, Structural partitioning, Data structure, Software procedure, Information hiding, Verification, Aesthetics.

63. **Explain Software Design Documentation in detail.**

    Design Documentation: (Explanation of the following items and sub-items) Scope, Reference Documents, Design Description, Modules, File Structure and global data, Requirements Cross Reference, Test provisions, Packaging, Special Notes, and Appendices

64. **Discuss the design procedure for Real-time and distributed system software.**

    Real Time and distributed system design:

    Real-Time systems: It must provide specified amounts of computation within fixed time intervals. (Explanation)

    Distributed system: It consists of a collection of nearly autonomous processors that communicate to achieve a coherent computing system. (Explanation)

65. **Explain Jackson system development with an example.**

    Steps are: Entity Action step, Entity Structure step, Initial modeling step, Function step, System Timing step, Implementation step

    Example: University with two campuses.

66. **Explain Software Design Notations**

Explanations of Data Flow diagram, Structure charts, HIPO diagrams, procedure template, pseudo code, structured flow chart, Structured English, Decision Tables.

67. **Explain Data Flow Oriented design in detail.**

The objective of this design is to provide a systematic approach for the derivation of program structure.

Design and information flow

Design process considerations (At least one of the following with an example)

Transform flow and analysis

Transaction flow and analysis

68. **Explain programming standards in detail**

Explanation of all standards.

69. **What is software reuse? Explain the various aspects of software reuse.**

A software component should be designed and implemented so that it can be reused in many different programs.

Explanation of Aspects:

Software development with reuse

Software development for reuse

Generator based reuse

Application system reuse

70. **Describe the various software configuration management tasks in detail.**

Brief explanations of SCM Definition, Activities, Process, Baselines, Software Configuration Items, Identification of objects, Version control, Change control

Configuration Audit, Status reporting

71. **Write notes on Version Control and Change control**

Version control: Description

Representations: (Evolution graph, Object Pool)

Change control: Description

Process of change control

72. **What are CASE tools and their usage in Software Engineering? Discuss each tool in brief.**

Business process Engineering tools, Process modeling and management tools, Project planning tools, Risk Analysis tools, Project management tools, Requirements tracing tools, Documentation tools, System software tools, Quality Assurance tools, Database management tools, Software configuration, Management tools, Analysis and design tools, PRO/SIM tools, Interface design and development tools, Prototyping tools, Programming tools, Web development tools, Integration and testing tools, Static Analysis tools, Dynamic analysis tools, Test management tools, Client/Server testing tools, Re-Engineering tools,

73. Explain Integrated CASE Environment in detail.

Explanations of Integrated CASE Environment, Benefits, Integration Architecture

74. Explain CASE repository in detail

Definition, Functions, Features and content, DBMS features Special features of CASE, Repository features.

75. Explain Building blocks for CASE

CASE Tools, Integrated framework, Portability services, Operating system, Hardware platform, Environment Architecture

Model Test Papers

Question Paper 1

Full Marks – **70**   *Time* – **3 Hours**

Question No.1 is compulsory and any five from the rest.

1. **Answer the following questions:**   **2 X 10**

    (*a*) Define software engineering. What is the difference between just writing software and software engineering?

    (*b*) How cohesions and coupling are related?

    (*c*) What makes software design different from coding?

    (*d*) What do you mean by the term functional independence in the context of software design?

    (*e*) Explain the difference between black box testing and white box testing.

    (*f*) What are the two most important aims of software inspection? What are the three basic input documents to any inspection?

    (*g*) Is lines-of-code (LOC) a useful productivity measure?

    (*h*) What is SPMP document?

(i) What are the main steps that must be taken to ensure there is a high degree of reusability in a software system?

(j) What is the new COCOMO-II formula for calculating project effort?

2. (a) What is the principal aim of software engineering discipline? What do you mean by the term software reverse engineering? Why is it required? (5)

(b) Do you design software when you "write" a program? What is a good software design? (5)

3. (a) Explain how to select the best risk reduction technique when there are many ways of reducing risk. (5)

(b) When a software project has got seriously behind schedule it is not usually appropriate to add more staff. Explain why this is so and suggest what effective actions might be taken to best recover from the situation? Justify the actions you would take. (5)

4. (a) Create a use case diagram for the following description:

A professor uses an office for preparing classes and carrying out research. Both activities include studying the relevant literature. The office is also used for meeting students. (5)

(b) How do we construct a black box testing plan? Who should do the testing? (5)

5. (a) What is a user interface portion of a software product? What are the characteristics of a good user interface? (5)

(b) Define, compare, and contrast KLOC and FP metrics. What are pros and cons of each? (5)

6. (a) Develop an activity diagram showing the following activities and their synchronization. Use concurrent activities where it is possible.

Problem description: To develop a software system, the first step is to develop the system architecture. Base on the system architecture a system design can be developed and then implemented. The architecture can also be used for defining test cases. In addition, it can be used as a basis for the user manual. When all things are available, the system can be delivered to the customer. Then it will be installed and beta tested. (5)

(b) What is the purpose of Capacity Maturity Model? Given a particular experiment and findings, access the reliability of the findings. (5)

7. (a) What are the Lehman's law for software evaluation? What are the different problems associated with software maintenance? (5)

(*b*) What is the relationship between cyclometric complexity and program comprehensibility? Can you justify why such an apparent relationship exists?

8.   (a) How do we assess the quality of software design?   (2.5)

(b) What is the role of interfaces in a class-based component level design?
    (2.5)

(c) Explain what is the main goal of a high level of architectural design and how it differs from the detailed design phase?   (2.5)

(d) Define and differentiate between the Waterfall model and the Spiral model?   (2.5)

Question Paper 2

Full Marks – 70   *Time – 3 Hours*

Question No.1 is compulsory and any five from the rest.

1. **Answer the following questions:**   2 X 10

(a) Distinguish between a program and a software product?

(b) What are the important activities that are carried out during the feasibility study phase of the classical Waterfall model?

(c) Which are the two current metrics used for project size estimation? Which one is better than the other and why?

(d) List the five desirable characteristics of a good Software Requirement Specification (SRS) document.

(e) What is the meaning of the terms 'Coupling' in the context of software design? What problems are likely to arise if two modules have high coupling?

(f) What do you understand by the term 'UML' and 'Use Case' in the context of the object-oriented design of software?

(g) What are the differences between a Graphical User Interface (GUI) and a Text-Based User Interface?

(h) What is the difference between coding standards and coding guidelines? List at least two coding standards.

(i) What are the three levels of testing of any software product?

(j) What is software reverse engineering?

2. (a) Distinguish between control flow based design, data structure oriented design, data flow oriented design, and object-oriented design of software products?   (5)

(b) Give a brief explanation with schematic diagram the prototyping model of software development.   (5)

3. (a) Give a brief comparison of the different life cycle models. Explain in brief the classical Waterfall model.   (5)

(b) Which life cycle model you would follow for developing extremely large software that would provide, monitor and control cellular communication among its subscribers using a set of revolving satellites. Justify your answer.   (5)

4. (*a*) What is the SRS document? Who are the typical users of the SRS document? (5)

   (*b*) Give a broad structure of a good SRS document. Specify some characteristics of a good SRS document and some characteristics of a bad SRS document?

5. (*a*) Briefly highlight the difference between 'Code inspection' and 'Code Walk-through'. Compare the relative merits of code inspection and code walk-through. What is the difference between verification and validation of a software product? (5)

   (*b*) Distinguish between Unit testing, Integration testing, and System testing. Explain how unit testing is done with Driver and Stub modules. (5)

6. (*a*) What is Black Box testing? Explain the equivalence class partitioning and Boundary value analysis approaches with examples to designing of Black Box test cases. (5)

   (*b*) Explain various strategies for White Box testing. What do you understand by the statement "Strategy A is stronger testing than strategy B"? (5)

7. (*a*) Write short notes on: (5)
   (*i*) SEI Capability Maturity Model (CMM).
   (*ii*) ISO 9000 Certification.

   (*b*) State Lehman's first and second law in connection with software evolution. Explain with a schematic diagram the process of 'software reverse engineering'. (5)

8. (*a*) Specify different software maintenance process models and explain any one of the models with schematic diagrams. How would you select an appropriate maintenance model for a maintenance project at hand? (5)

   (*b*) What are the different COCOMO models used for estimating cost and effort for a software project? Which model is better? Explain in brief the Basic COCOMO model. (5)

Question Paper 3

Full Marks – 70   *Time – 3 Hours*

Question No.1 is compulsory and any five from the rest.

1. **Answer the following questions:**   **(2 X 10)**

    (a) Which phases in the Waterfall life cycle model consumes the maximum effort for developing a typical software product?

    (b) Which parameter (s) is/are used in COCOMO estimation model?

    (c) Who is responsible for developing the SRS document?

    (d) What is the difference between revision and version?

    (e) What is object persistence? How a persistent object can be realized?

    (f) Is the UML (Unified Modeling Language) is strictly a language? Justify your answer.

    (g) What is Rapid Application Development (RAD)?

    (h) What do you mean by smoke testing?

    (i) What is the pattern in object-oriented analysis and design?

    (j) What do you mean by Key Process Areas (KPAs) in the context of SEI CMM?

2. (a) Draw a schematic diagram to represent the iterative waterfall model of software development.   (6)

    (b) On your diagram represent the deliverables produced at the end of each phase.   (4)

3. (a) What are the different categories of software development projects according to the COCOMO model?   (5)

    (b) What are the relative advantages of using either the LOC or the function point metric to measure the size of a software product?   (5)

4. The system analysis group working on a system design project estimated the schedule of activities as given below:

Activity	Notation	Must Follow	Expected Time (Days)
Draw DFD	A	None	9
Draw decision tree	B	A	12
Revise tree	C	B	3

Write up report	D	C, H	7
Organize data dictionary	E	A	11
Do output prototype	F	None	8
Revise design	G	F	14
Design database	H	E, G	5

    (*a*) Draw PERT diagram based on the above-mentioned data. (6)

    (*b*) List all paths and identify the critical path. (4)

5. (*a*) What do mean by the term cohesion and coupling in the context of software design? (6)

    (*b*) Why high coupling and low cohesion in a design are preferable? (4)

6. Explain with appropriate examples the following: (4+3+3)

    (*i*) DFD

    (*ii*) Structure chart

    (*iii*) Data dictionary

7. (*a*) What do you mean by the following views a system? (2 X 5)

    (*i*) User's view

    (*ii*) Structural view

    (*iii*) Behavioral view

    (*iv*) Implementation view

    (*v*) Environmental view

8. (*a*) Schematically draw the architecture of a CASE environment and explain how the different tools are integrated. (5)

    (*b*) What do you mean by the term "Software Reengineering"? Why it is required? (5)

Question Paper 4

Full Marks – 70   *Time – 3 Hours*

Question No.1 is compulsory and any five from the rest.

1. **Answer the following questions:**   **(2 X 10)**

   (*a*) What is the principal aim of software engineering? Draw the pyramid diagram for OOSE Architecture.

   (*b*) What are the three different kinds of testing associated with system testing?

   (*c*) What are the prominent qualities in system design with the OO method?

   (*d*) What do you mean by software process?

   (*e*) What is the role of the data dictionary in the CASE environment?

   (*f*) Differentiate between object-oriented analysis and object-oriented design.

   (*g*) Define the term cohesion in the context of the object-oriented design of the system.

   (*h*) What are the advantages of encapsulation?

   (*i*) What is the difference between a coding standard and coding guideline?

   (*j*) What is meant by a code walk-through?

2. (*a*) Why should a requirement analyst avoid making any design decisions during requirements analysis? Must a good programmer also be a good requirement analyst?   (5)

   (*b*) Discuss the major advantages of object-oriented design methodologies over the data flow oriented design methodologies.   (5)

3. (*a*) What is meant by the structural complexity of a program? Define metrics for measuring the structural complexity of a program. How this is different from the computational complexity of a program? (5)

   (*b*) Draw a data flow diagram for the inventory of a large medicine store.   (5)

4. (*a*) Why is it important to properly document a software product? What are the different ways of documenting a software product?   (5)

(*b*) What is stress testing? Why is stress testing applicable to only certain types of system? (5)

5. (*a*) What is regression testing? Why regression testing is necessary? How is regression testing performed? (5)

(*b*) Discuss the relative merits of ISO 9001 certification and SEI CMM based quality assessment? (5)

6. (*a*) What are the different types of views that can be modeled using UML? What are the different UML diagrams which can be used to capture each of the views? (5)

(*b*) What do you mean by repeatable software development? Organizations assessed at which level of SEI CMM maturity achieves repeatable software environment? (5)

7. (*a*) Discuss how the reliability changes over the lifetime of a software product? (5)

(*b*) How cohesion and couplings are related? Give an example where cohesion increases and coupling decreases. (5)

8. (*a*) Define and differentiate between software engineering and software reengineering. (2.5)

(*b*) If a module has logical cohesion, what kind of coupling is module likely to have with others? (2.5)

(*c*) Define the metrics to measure the software reliability. (2.5)

(*d*) Define and differentiate between CASE roll and CASE environment. (2.5)

Question Paper 5

Full Marks – 70   *Time – 3 Hours*

Question No.1 is compulsory and any five from the rest.

1. **Answer the following questions:**   **(2 X 10)**

    (*a*) Discuss the major advantages of OOD methodology over the data flow oriented design methodologies.

    (*b*) Explain why the spiral life cycle model is considered to be a metamodel.

    (*c*) Define Risk leverage.

    (*d*) Enumerate two different types of coupling that exist between two modules.

    (*e*) Distinguish between a DFD and a flow-chart.

    (*f*) What are the advantages of UML class diagrams?

    (*g*) What is meant by a code walkthrough?

    (*h*) How can you determine the number of latent defects in a software product during the testing phase?

    (*i*) What are the main advantages of using CASE tools?

    (*j*) What is an application generator?

2. (*a*) What are the symptoms of the present software crisis? What factors have contributed to the making of the present software crisis? What are the possible solutions to the present software crisis?   (5)

    (*b*) What do you understand by the visibility of design and code? How does increased visibility help in systematic software development? (5)

3. (*a*) What do you understand by the term 'phase containment of errors'? Why is phase containment of errors so important? How can phase containment of errors be achieved?   (5)

    (*b*) Explain with suitable examples the type of product developments for which the evolutionary life cycle model is more suitable and the type of problems for which the spiral model is more suitable.   (5)

4. (*a*) What do you mean by the term cohesion and coupling in the context of software design? How are these concepts useful arriving at a good design of a system?   (6)

    (*b*) Compare the relative advantages of the object-oriented and function-oriented approaches to software design.   (4)

5. (a) What are the different system views that can be modeled using UML? What are the different UML diagrams which can be used to capture each of the views? Do you need to develop all the views of a system using all the modeling diagrams supported by UML? Justify your answer. (7)

   (b) What causes increased productivity when the object-oriented paradigm is adopted? (3)

6. (a) Differentiate between black-box testing and white-box testing with suitable examples. (4)

   (b) What is meant by the structural complexity of a problem? Define a metric for measuring the structural complexity of a program. How is structural complexity of a program different from its computational complexity? (6)

7. (a) What do you understand by Key Process Areas (KPAs) in the context of SEI CMM? Would there be any problem if an organization tries to implement the high-level KPAs before achieving a lower level of KPAs? Justify your answer using a suitable example. (6)

   (b) What is a legacy software product? Explain the problems one would encounter while maintaining a legacy product (4)

8. (a) What do you mean by the term software reverse engineering? Why is it required? Explain the different activities undertaken during reverse engineering. (5)

   (b) What do you understand by the term faceted classification in the context of software reuse? How does faceted classification simplify the component search in a component store? (5)

Question Paper 6

Full Marks – 70   *Time – 3 Hours*

Question No.1 is compulsory and any five from the rest.

1. **Answer the following questions:**   **(2 X 10)**

   (a) What do you mean by a software process?

   (b) What do you mean by the term phase containment error?

   (c) Which are the 7 standard software quality characteristics?

   (d) Define CASE tools and CASE environment.

   (e) What is stress testing?

   (f) What is the use of a Use Case diagram in software design?

   (g) What do you mean by the term software reverse engineering?

   (h) Define and differentiate between corrective and perfective maintenance.

   (i) What is the new COCOMO-II formula for calculating project effort?

   (j) What do you understand by a layered software design?

2. (a) What is a prototype? Under what circumstance is it beneficial to construct a   prototype?   (5)

   (b) Who are the different users of SRS document? What are their expectations from the SRS document?   (5)

3. (a) Discuss how the effort spent in the different phases of the iterative Water Fall model is spread over time?   (5)

4. (a) Explain coupling and cohesion in the context of software design. Describe the type of coupling and cohesion.   (5)

   (b) How can management organization and the systematic application of methods increase the chance that a development project will succeed?
                                                                      (5)

5. (a)   What are the features of good software design? Can quality be measured?   (5)

   (b)   Explain the various steps in the cost estimation procedure using COCOMO.   (5)

6. (a)   Development methods involve building models to describe the system being investigated. What are the three kinds of the model developed during object-oriented analysis and design?   (5)

(b) Discuss the relative merits of ISO 9001 certification and SEI CMM based quality assessment. (5)

7. (a) Differentiate between alpha and beta testing. (2.5)

   (b) Differentiate between software validation and verification. (2.5)

   (c) Differentiate between CASE environment and CASE tools. (2.5)

   (d) Differentiate between object oriented and function-oriented design. (2.5)

8. "A system is required to maintain an inventory of the contents of a warehouse. Items are delivered for storage at any time during the day and must be allocated space. An identification label must be attached to each item before storage and some items need to be stored in a refrigerated unit. An item can be stored for any period of time but some items have an expiry date by which they must be removed from the warehouse. When items are removed, they need to be labeled, packaged for delivery and put on the correct delivery truck. The truck driver should be given a list of delivery addresses for the items. The system should be able to generate reports showing the current contents of the warehouse and the last day's deliveries and collections."

   (a) Taking an object-oriented point of view, draw up a list of potential classes, attributes, and external entities using the specification above as a guide. (5)

   (b) Starting with the classes you have identified in part (a), generate a class diagram for the warehouse software system. Make sure each class is labeled with any key attributes or operations.

Lightning Source UK Ltd.
Milton Keynes UK
UKHW031823281021
393006UK00008B/1772